D1570181

DYING
for
GOLD

DYING

for

GOLD

THE TRUE STORY of the
GIANT MINE MURDERS

LEE SELLECK and
FRANCIS THOMPSON

HarperCollins*PublishersLtd*

First edition

Map detail work, text design and composition: Susan Thomas
Base art for maps by Multi Mind Productions, Vancouver, B.C.

Canadian Cataloguing in Publication Data

Selleck, Lee, 1955–
Dying for gold : the true story of the giant mine murders

Includes index.
ISBN 0-00-255754-1

1. Giant Mine Strike, Yellowknife, N.W.T., 1992.   2. Strikes and lockouts -
Gold mining - Northwest Territories - Yellowknife.   3. Warren, Roger - Trials,
litigation, etc.   I. Thompson, Francis, 1967–   II. Title.

HD5329.M732 1992   Y45 1997   331.892'8223422'097193
C97-930258-7

97 98 99 ❖ HC 10 9 8 7 6 5 4 3 2

Printed and bound in the United States

For Phil Kirkland, who has dedicated most of his life
to good, honest labour relations;
for our families who supported us; and for
Richard Gougeon and Kay Kriegel, friends whose spirits live on

CONTENTS

Within some thousandths of a second after the initiation of the explosive there occurs in a charged hole a series of events which, in drama and violence, have few equivalents in civil technology. The chemical energy of the explosive is liberated and the compact explosive becomes transformed into a glowing gas with an enormous pressure which, in a densely packed hole, can amount to and exceed 100,000 atmospheres. The amount of energy developed per unit of time is, even in a tiny hole drilled with a hand-held machine, of the order of magnitude of 25,000 MW [megawatts], that is to say it exceeds the power of most of the world's largest power stations. That is not due to the fact that the amount of energy latent in the explosive is extremely large but to the rapidity of the reaction. What is especially characteristic of the explosive as a tool in rock blasting is its ability to provide concentrated power in a limited part of the rock.

—U. Langefors and B. Kihlstrom
The Modern Technique of Rock Blasting

It's one of my philosophies that people have to be responsible for their actions ... I don't think anyone in this room can understand what it's like to have employees killing each other.

—Peggy Witte, president of Royal Oak Mines
November 8, 1993

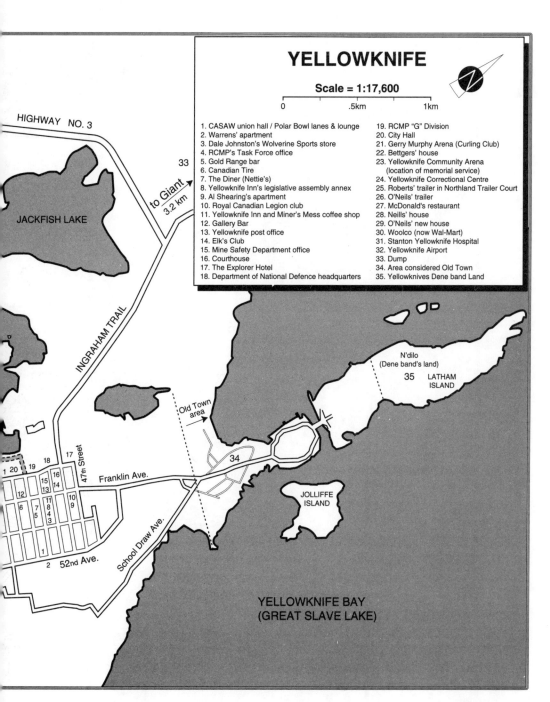

YELLOWKNIFE

Scale = 1:17,600

0   .5km   1km

1. CASAW union hall / Polar Bowl lanes & lounge
2. Warrens' apartment
3. Dale Johnston's Wolverine Sports store
4. RCMP's Task Force office
5. Gold Range bar
6. Canadian Tire
7. The Diner (Nettie's)
8. Yellowknife Inn's legislative assembly annex
9. Al Shearing's apartment
10. Royal Canadian Legion club
11. Yellowknife Inn and Miner's Mess coffee shop
12. Gallery Bar
13. Yellowknife post office
14. Elk's Club
15. Mine Safety Department office
16. Courthouse
17. The Explorer Hotel
18. Department of National Defence headquarters
19. RCMP "G" Division
20. City Hall
21. Gerry Murphy Arena (Curling Club)
22. Bettgers' house
23. Yellowknife Community Arena (location of memorial service)
24. Yellowknife Correctional Centre
25. Roberts' trailer in Northland Trailer Court
26. O'Neils' trailer
27. McDonald's restaurant
28. Neills' house
29. O'Neils' new house
30. Woolco (now Wal-Mart)
31. Stanton Yellowknife Hospital
32. Yellowknife Airport
33. Dump
34. Area considered Old Town
35. Yellowknives Dene band Land

HIGHWAY NO. 3

to Giant 3.2 km

33

JACKFISH LAKE

INGRAHAM TRAIL

N'dilo
(Dene band's land)

35   LATHAM ISLAND

Old Town area

34

47th Street

17

18
1 20 19
15 16
13 14
12
6 7 8 10
5 4 9
3

Franklin Ave.

School Draw Ave.

1

2   52nd Ave.

JOLLIFFE ISLAND

YELLOWKNIFE BAY
(GREAT SLAVE LAKE)

MAP A

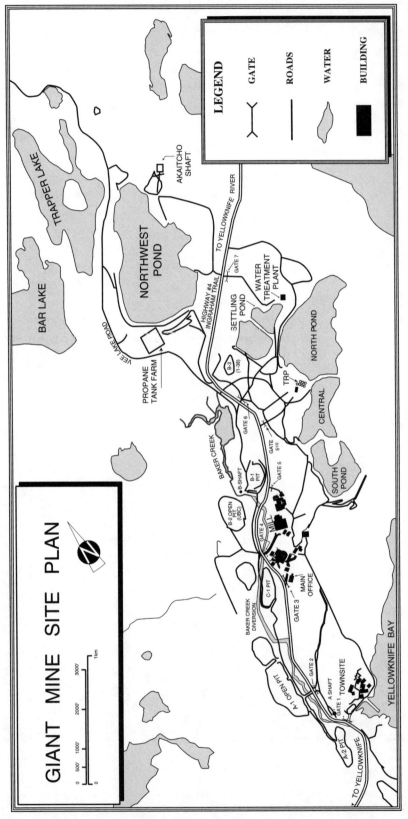

GIANT MINE SITE PLAN

LEGEND

GATE

ROADS

WATER

BUILDING

MAP B

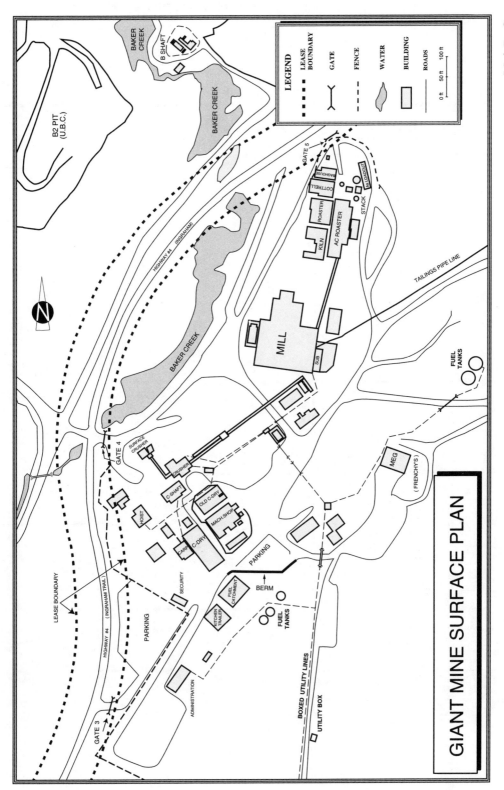

MAP C

GIANT MINE SURFACE PLAN

LEGEND

- **·········** LEASE BOUNDARY
- ⅄ GATE
- ‒ ‒ ‒ FENCE
- WATER
- ▢ BUILDING
- ROADS

0 ft   50 ft   100 ft

B2 PIT (U.B.C.)

BAKER CREEK

B SHAFT

BAKER CREEK

BAKER CREEK

HIGHWAY #4 (INGRAHAM)

GATE 5

COTTRELL

BAGHOUSE

BULLDOZER

ROASTER

KILN

AC ROASTER

STACK

MILL

SUB

TAILINGS PIPE LINE

SURFACE CRUSHER

CRUSHER

C-SHAFT

HOIST

OLD C-DRY

MACH.SHOP

CARP C-DRY

GATE 4

MEG

(FRENCHY'S)

FUEL TANKS

SECURITY

FUEL CATCHMENT

BERM

KITCHEN TRAILER

PARKING

PARKING

FUEL TANKS

ADMINISTRATION

BOXED UTILITY LINES

UTILITY BOX

LEASE BOUNDARY

HIGHWAY #4 (INGRAHAM TRAIL)

GATE 3

GIANT MINE CROSS SECTION

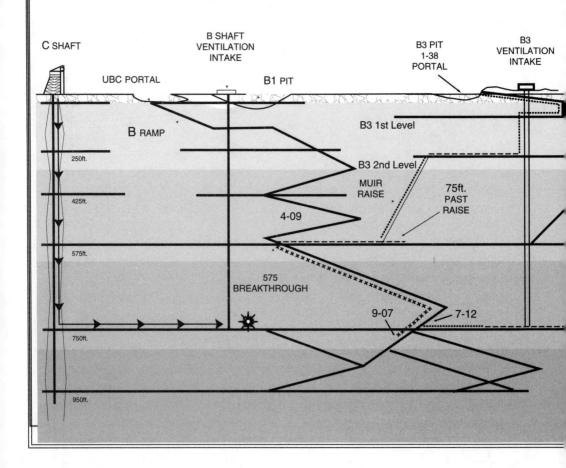

C SHAFT

UBC PORTAL

B SHAFT
VENTILATION
INTAKE

B1 PIT

B3 PIT
1-38
PORTAL

B3
VENTILATION
INTAKE

B RAMP

B3 1st Level

250ft.

B3 2nd Level

425ft.

MUIR
RAISE

75ft.
PAST
RAISE

4-09

575ft.

575
BREAKTHROUGH

9-07

7-12

750ft.

950ft.

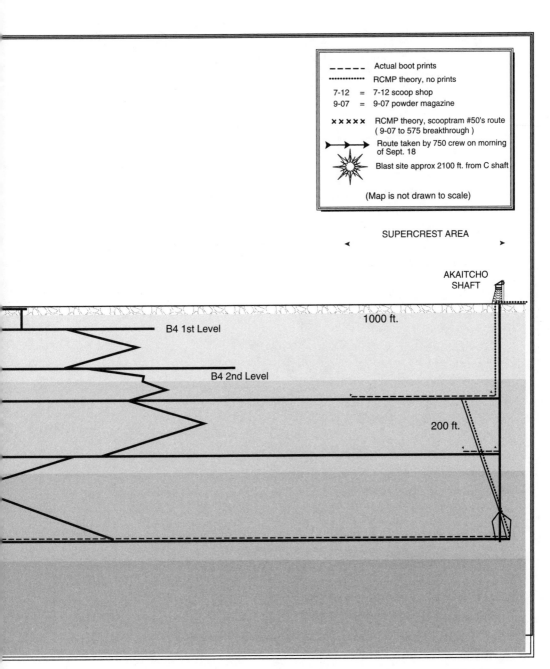

Actual boot prints
.... RCMP theory, no prints
7-12 = 7-12 scoop shop
9-07 = 9-07 powder magazine

× × × × × RCMP theory, scooptram #50's route
(9-07 to 575 breakthrough)

Route taken by 750 crew on morning
of Sept. 18

Blast site approx 2100 ft. from C shaft

(Map is not drawn to scale)

◄ SUPERCREST AREA ►

AKAITCHO
SHAFT

1000 ft.

B4 1st Level

B4 2nd Level

200 ft.

MAP D

Composite drawings made by Pamela MacQuarrie-Higden with the RCMP of two men she saw in the early morning of September 18, 1992—the day of the blast—on Giant mine property.

ACKNOWLEDGMENTS

The authors thank Bill and Verla Selleck for their tireless help in editing the manuscript. It shows on every page. We are also grateful for a grant obtained through the Explorations Program of the Canada Council.

PREFACE

You are standing at the doors of Giant's headframe, a structure looming about 200 feet above you, and the cool breath of the underground is in your face. The air is damp and fresh in a muddy sort of way. You step into the cage to descend—in a steel elevator on a steel cable that is your lifeline into the darkness because you do not want to have to climb back out. Down you go, your ears feeling the pressure. The metal around you is wet, rusty, and banged up by a hundred-thousand cargoes. The pant legs of your coveralls are tucked into your high, heavy, steel-shanked boots. Around your waist is a belt, weighted by an emergency breathing device and a metal-cased battery. From the battery a black rubber cable runs to a small lamp that clips onto your hard hat or chest pocket. That light is yours to shine as you will, focus where you will, once you step into the mud and muck in the drifts of Giant mine.

You are in a different world now. Nothing is quite the same. The sounds of surface life are gone, replaced by the gurgle of water, the loud hiss of muck filling skip buckets, the rumble of rock descending chutes, the labouring clamor of diesel engines in tight spaces, the pounding roar of pneumatic drills spinning into stone. You are a stranger here, and, without the man next to you, you are lost.

This book presents the untold story of one of the nastiest industrial battles in Canadian history—a story thus far silenced by the neat, tidy face all accounts to date have put on the messy and complicated events that led to families being torn asunder and a small northern city being caught in the pincers of a disaster. The conflict could have been like any other strike or lockout had it not been for the mine owner's attempt to break the union and reliance on the wholesale use of strikebreakers. Royal Oak Mines Inc. challenged the Canadian labour movement by trying to supplant industry's traditional code of conduct toward labour with more belligerent tactics borrowed from the United States. The risks that attend such actions are a matter of historical record. Resisting the corporate juggernaut was a small union with stubborn and/or inexperienced leaders. Early on, they fell into a classic trap, making mistakes that played into the hands of the company. Some members resorted to foolhardy and criminal acts. Eventually, the union thwarted precedents in Canadian labour law that could only have led to future strife.

The rift created by this industrial dispute was deepened by a federal government with close ties to the mining industry, police who, in our view, aided the company, and the tragic death of nine men in an underground explosion. It was impossible to predict their grim fate, but violence or death was predictable.

It's a story we worked on for five years, from the first signs of trouble at the gold mine. At first we were reporters for *The Press Independent* and *yellowknifer*, two local newspapers; then we became full-time authors.

We, too, were strangers to the world of mining. We were allowed just one trip underground at Giant by Royal Oak Mines Inc., so we are thankful for two visits to Con, a mine across town. And we immersed ourselves in research. We taped about 300 in-depth interviews with union members, company managers, strikebreakers, police officers, politicians, and academics. Some conversations lasted six or seven hours, and we are deeply grateful to all the people who gave their time so generously.

People were so willing to talk, despite the intense suspicion toward journalists that developed during the 1992–93 strike/lockout, because there is unfinished business in this dispute. The truth of what happened has never come out, and parts of it probably never will. People will take some tales to their graves.

The murder investigation was one of the most intense in Canadian history. There have been dozens of criminal trials, two Canada Labour Relations Board hearings, and an RCMP Public Complaints Commission investigation into the police's handling of certain incidents. But none has provided a full answer as to *why* the dispute turned out as it did, why nine men were killed and thousands of other lives were turned inside out.

In pursuit of an explanation, we often felt like a commission of inquiry without the legal clout. We filed about fifty access-to-information requests, including some in the United States. Politicians, civil servants, and union leaders generously gave us personal notes and other papers to show us what happened behind closed doors. Librarians and academics offered valuable reading tips, and even private lessons in labour law and history. The resulting files—tens of thousands of pages—filled our shelves, then our office space, and later spilled over into living rooms and bedrooms.

In most cases, we have identified the sources of information presented here. However, some sources cannot be revealed, and others are not significant. The cast of characters is large, and we tried (though you may not believe it) to limit them. For every person whose name you read, there are dozens more to whom we are indebted for sharing their knowledge and feelings. In recounting a few events, we relied on only one witness, but that is stated, unless we were eye-witnesses. There were events at which one or both of us were present, but so much went on that many other sources of information were tapped for the accounts you read here. When people are quoted directly, either we were present or quotes were corroborated by video- or audiotape, documents, or others present. If thorough verification was not possible, either because the number of witnesses was limited or because their accounts varied too widely, we've used quotes within quotes to make the source clear.

One of the toughest decisions we made was how to deal with our own roles in the events. We were subpoenaed as witnesses in court and labour board cases; one of us had film seized by the police for use in a trial. Some of our private communications with other participants in events were bugged by the RCMP, as police officers confirmed to us. One of us was tailed on occasion by the RCMP during the murder investigation. Like many of the participants, we did not trust the privacy of our own homes, cars, or phones.

These problems obviously influenced the way we worked and what we could do. Various parties exerted a lot of pressure on us from time to time, both intentionally and inadvertently. Occasionally we were the only people to whom all the parties were talking, and we felt the weight of that responsibility.

On the eve of putting our work before you, we feel that weight again. We've had some sleepless nights thinking about the people who gave us so much, whose input is not apparent on the surface. We can only hope that the spirit of their experience slips out from between the lines. *Dying for Gold* is our best effort at mining for truth. We felt compelled to tell this story for—in no set order—ourselves, the community of Yellowknife, and everyone who endured—and those who did not—the Giant mine dispute. We hope our work helps in some way to avert another tragedy like this.

Lee Selleck and Francis Thompson, March 1997

DYING
for
GOLD

CHAPTER ONE

BOOMTOWN BLUES

Life blood—it can ooze slowly onto the parched desert, trickle from the eyes of a man swiftly blinded, or disappear in an explosion so sudden that skin and bone are atomized. Death is part of life, like a trade, life for death. So is commerce: Make and break. Wheel and deal. Live by your principles. No pain, no gain. Bust a gut. The bottom line is everything—but not always what it seems.

Opportunity first brought Margaret K. "Peggy" Witte to Yellowknife in the mid-1980s. Canada's Northwest Territories appealed to her. The vast land around Great Slave Lake appears harsh and rocky to many visitors, but Witte was no tourist. She knew there was gold in the ancient Precambrian rock, as valuable as water that could transform desert into an oasis. Her parents, Kenneth and Gloria Kent, had done just that in arid Nevada, leading the state legislature to proclaim that her family's business, founded in 1892, was synonymous with Churchill County. The Kents, hardworking pioneers, had dominated commerce in Fallon, Nevada, extending credit to those who deserved it. The family sold groceries and farm implements, milled alfalfa, ran a garage, ranched cattle, and grew renowned "Heart of Gold" melons on the fringe of the Forty Mile Desert, which had claimed the life of many a traveler, some of them would-be miners during the California gold rush of 1849.

Fallon has grown like a wild weed along Highway 50, "the loneliest road in America," running parallel to the historic Pony Express Trail. Grocery stores and garages house slot machines, and Maine Street hosts gambling casinos. The US Navy's most advanced air force training base, the TOPGUN pilots' school, is in Fallon. The Kent ranch is prime land for development, in a state known for free-wheeling business, mining, and rugged individualism.

The Northwest Territories, by comparison, seemed tame in all but climate, which is as cold as Nevada's is hot. The cold posed some challenges to a metallurgist who wanted to start a gold mine, but Peggy Witte does not shrink from challenges. Where there is challenge, there is opportunity, and that philosophy accompanied Witte as she made the rounds of Yellowknife's stubby office towers, clustered at the end of a long, lonely road, trying to raise government money for her new company.

Yellowknife is known as "Sombak'e," meaning "Money Town," to the original inhabitants, the Yellowknives Dene. The capital of the Northwest Territories is bathed in summer sunlight into the subarctic night, but folded in daytime darkness in winter, and so cold that tough materials snap under moderate pressure. Peggy Witte would choose to live in Vancouver, British Columbia, where the climate is temperate and junior mining companies spring up like weeds. Rusted mining equipment and a wagon wheel would grace the front yard of her ranch-style house, with its indoor swimming pool and panoramic view of the Strait of Georgia. Witte's fortune was entwined with Yellowknife's, although she would never share community life like the Kents do in Fallon. Nonetheless, it would have been absurd then to think that Witte would preside over a mine in which nine men would die during an industrial dispute, or that a longtime local miner and sportsman, Roger Warren, would be convicted of murder for a crime he probably did not commit.

Derek Roberts stepped out the kitchen door into the trailer's porch. He put his lunch pail on the clothes dryer, slipped into his boots, and turned to give his wife, June, a quick kiss.

"See ya," he said. It was 6:30 A.M., and it was already broad daylight. Spring was coming and the snow wouldn't last much longer. "Yessss!" June cheered to herself. "I'll never go through another winter in this place, I swear it." June Roberts had said this at the start of each of the previous five springs, even though, since she was from Happy Valley/Goose Bay, Labrador, cold and rugged country were in her family's blood; her grandmother was Inuit.

June and Derek's old trailer was one of many packed along a narrow crescent, a few rows from Frame Lake. The lakefront lots were nicer. There were some bugs in the summer, but light breezes usually kept them away. They had a view of the water and the reddish rock on the other shore. But the Roberts's vista was a picket fence, a parked snowmobile, and a street lined with cars and trucks.

"Derek won't be home until 4:00 P.M. at the earliest," June thought, adding, with a smile, "if he can keep his skinny little butt out of the hardware store. But you fell for that butt practically at first sight, many moons ago." June wanted a break from Yellowknife, and wondered if Derek had booked their vacation with his shift boss yet. Everyone wants to take off in the spring or summer, and things were hectic at Giant mine this year. Judging from what Derek said, the bosses were running around, kissing ass, as if the new owner and her little Napoleon manager were gods. But Derek had said that Royal Oak isn't a rich company, so June resigned herself to hearing more of the same gossip until some money was milked from the mine and the new owners settled down like the others had. Until then, June doubted that Derek would find time to fix up the kitchen and the bathroom, and make a play area outside for the kids, as he'd promised to do this summer.

Waiting for the children to get up, June poured boiling water into a teapot and went to dress. When she plunked herself on the sofa with her mug of tea, her small body barely filled a corner. She put her knees up and pulled a comforter over them, looking out the front window at mounds of dirty snow, piled high where shovelers had left it.

The Robertses lived in Northland trailer court, which was almost a miners' colony. June knew only a few of their neighbours, but recognized the miners by their gear and the hours they worked. There were also construction workers, and prospectors, like Walt next door. June liked him, his shaggy beard, the whimsical art he was famous for—colourful, caricature-filled paintings of Yellowknife's landmarks, including the Gold Range bar downtown and the Canadian Broadcasting Corporation's stone office fortress with mammoth mosquitoes buzzing over it. June and Derek kept an eye on Walt's place when he was out staking claims on the tundra. It was easy to do—if they opened the side windows, they could converse from trailer to trailer.

Crystal came into the living room, ready for school. "Help Brittany get dressed while I get some breakfast," June said. Morning tasks were almost mechanical now. In the month since Sabrina's premature birth in January 1991, there had hardly been time to think. Her birth had been difficult, and the doctor advised June not to have any more children. With three now, she'd given up on returning to secretarial work with the government of the Northwest Territories. Day care would cost $1,500 a month. June thought she might be able to make some money by opening a mini day care of her own.

Jane O'Neil sat in an easy chair in the living room of their house trailer, reading a novel while Katie, who was just a year and a half old, napped. Their trailer was tucked in by a big rock at the end of a cul-de-sac, a stone's throw from Frame Lake. The O'Neils had put new siding on the addition, and torn down interior walls to open up some space. They painted, put in new floors, and renovated the kitchen. New insulation and a woodstove kept winter's chill where it belonged. Their picture window faced down the street—a vista less crowded than the

Roberts's, but with too much traffic to suit Jane. Neighbourhood kids raced up and down the street, having fun. Jane wondered if they were sometimes up to no good.

A walk through beautiful spruce and birch along the lake led to a sandy park, where there was a tennis court and a playground, by the old curling rink downtown. "Too bad," Jane thought. "We'll be moved before Katie is really old enough to play there." But Jane knew they'd make money on the sale of the trailer, and looked forward to a new house, probably out in Frame Lake South. That would be good for Katie too.

It was Saturday; Jane's husband, Jim, had walked a couple of blocks to see Derek Roberts and give him a hand fixing his truck. They had worked near each other at Giant mine for years, though most of their contact was by phone. Jim was a cage tender, traveling with the mine's elevator, moving men, gear, and supplies up and down the main C-shaft, loading and unloading along the way. Derek was a hoistman, controlling the motors that raised tons of gold ore to the surface in "skips" on thick wire cables, strung up the steel headframe that is Giant's main landmark.

When Jim came home, he slipped off his shoes and went to the fridge to guzzle milk from the carton. He was slim and fit. "Hey, Derek and June might like to buy the place," he said. "When we're ready to sell it, June wants us to let them know." It was common for houses, trucks, snowmobiles, boats, or campers to be sold or traded among friends or acquaintances at Giant, or, for that matter, in Yellowknife as a whole.

Jane had been born and raised in Yellowknife. Her dad used to work at Con mine, across town from Giant. A petite, trim brunette, she was too intelligent, critical, and unconsciously feminist to appeal to most men, attractive though she was. But these were qualities Jim O'Neil admired. They met in 1980 on his first day in town. He was preparing to open the city's swimming pool, where Jane was a part-time lifeguard. "I was doing tile work—I had a little apron on and I was mixing up the mortar," Jim says. "She looked down at the pool and saw this guy and said, 'I wonder what it would be like to be married to him.'"

Jane soon learned that Jim was from Ontario and loved Harley Davidsons. He cofounded the Northern Breed Motorcycle Club in Yellowknife, renowned for its parties in a funky Old Town clubhouse, where he often tended bar. Planes were another of his obsessions. He had a commercial pilot's license, and loved to fly over the vast northern bush, landing on obscure lakes to fish and explore. A wall of the den in the trailer featured a huge flight map of the Northwest Territories from the Arctic Ocean south to the 60th parallel. A small charter company hired Jim to fly part-time. Dozens of old mining camps dotted the land around Yellowknife, and he loved to hear old-timers' accounts of wild characters and stock market scams.

Rock does not remember miners. They invade it with their pneumatic drills, then they load their drill holes with a stable mixture of fuel oil and fertilizer, and some stick powder, to which they tie a blasting cap with detonator cord. Then they wire the cap to a dormant electrical circuit. The stage set, the miners leave, their cap lamps piercing the thick, humid darkness that is unique to the womb of the earth. A central blast triggers explosions which cut another 6 or 8 feet from each man's rock face. Thousands of tons of rock are blasted each day in Yellowknife's two mines, Giant and Con, defying the force of gravity to fill in what has been taken out.

This has been Yellowknife's underground rhythm, day in and night out, for five decades. Just a hundred years ago, the Yellowknives Dene lived to a different rhythm—that of a hospitable spot on Great Slave Lake, near caribou migration routes, bountiful fishing waters, firewood, and moose habitat. Their lives changed forever sixty years ago, when white men's shacks mushroomed near the water's edge and Depression-driven gold seekers—rough-and-tumble miners, prospectors, and fishermen—roamed the subarctic. In 1935, two prospectors staked claims on the land that would become Giant mine—guided, Dene elders say, by a local woman. The Dene have managed to preserve their claim to a settlement on the north end of town.

As the 1990s began, old men hunched over long wooden tables at the Miner's Mess café, sipping weak brew from chipped mugs, and sighed as they recalled the good old days in the 1940s, when Yellowknife was a bunch of frozen shacks "on the back of beyond," when Canada's misfits and adventurers arrived in bush planes, and hoped for the miracle of a big strike. Nostalgia for the gold rush days has existed since Yellowknife became the capital of the Northwest Territories in 1967 and civil servants began pouring in from Ottawa. Their migration turned Yellowknife into a transportation hub. The town's population grew from about 1,000 in 1940 to more than 15,000 by 1991, more than a third of the increase having been recorded since 1980.

What is new in the 1990s is that even the government crowd misses the friendly little boomtown of the past. Recessions had come and gone "down south," but in Yellowknife the boom continued until about 1990. In the coffee-nooks and boardrooms of office towers, government employees reminisce about the days when the pace was slower and their futures were brighter—before cutbacks in the federal and territorial governments, and paranoia over the prospect of self-government by aboriginal peoples.

It is a town caught in contradictions. People cheered the arrival of chain stores and fast-food stands that sprang up in Frame Lake South, but complained about rush-hour traffic on Franklin Avenue. Others saw a decline in nightlife and downtown shopping as a sign that an era was coming to an end. Heritage buffs saw tourism as a growth industry, but they were losing the battle to save the historic, semilegal shanties on the lakeshore, now inhabited by Métis, fishermen, former hippies, and young people earning low incomes. Ten years earlier, there were few hotels and fewer tourism promoters; now there are Japanese visitors hoping to see the Northern Lights and ride in dogsleds.

With the exception of the Dene and Métis, people who worked at the two big gold mines have the most to be nostalgic about. They once owned the town. Soldiers returning from Europe in 1946 to work in the mines established the Royal Canadian Legion and made it a centre of community life. They scrounged or stole lumber from the mines to build Yellowknife's first private houses. They dreamed up schemes to attract women to this "godforsaken" bit of the subarctic, where snow blankets the ground for half the year.

"The lives of the workers were tightly tied to the mine," says Bruce Bannister, a hoist operator at Giant mine who arrived in 1964. "The Giant Mine Recreation Association was a going concern. We had picnics, we had parties, we had dances, we had night-shift curling, for heaven's sake. We went curling at three o'clock in the morning, and it was fun. We had fishing contests. There are still old trophies kicking around the Giant office from those days. And there was no fear nor favour to either staff [management] or hourly [union employees]. If you happened to be on staff and you won a trophy, fine, you won a trophy."

Bannister came to Giant as a surveyor fresh out of the army. He grew up in mining camps across Northern Ontario, so Yellowknife's cold and isolation didn't bother him. He soon married the daughter of a longtime Giant metallurgist. To make more money, Bannister asked to go underground as a miner, eligible for big production bonuses if he could break enough rock. Such promotions were easy to get then. Mine operators were desperate for workers, because so many men left for jobs down south after spending a winter in Yellowknife.

The money was good, but Bannister soon learned that mining is a risky trade. "I was working underground on night shift, and I was very nearly squashed by an enormous fucking chunk of loose [rock]. And I said, that's it, my wife doesn't need to be a widow after one year of marriage."

Bannister transferred to the hoist room, on surface, running the cage as it went up and down the shaft. Almost anywhere else in Canada—and just a few years later in Yellowknife—the transfer would not have happened. Hoistmen earn the highest wage in a mine (though often without a miner's bonus), and are trusted, senior men. Except during shift changes, hoistmen aren't much in demand, but someone has to be there in case of an emergency. Like firefighters waiting for alarms to ring, they played cards so much they could read the hands at a half-second's glance. And the hoistmen would read, day in, day out.

With a young family, a wide circle of friends, his gun club, and later a house they built at Prelude Lake in Yellowknife's cottage country, Bannister came to love the North. He grew a beard and a bit of a paunch. His smile and easy laugh made him a good Santa Claus at Christmas parties.

Bannister became a union activist in 1980. He wasn't the president, but he was heavily involved in bargaining and, when talks collapsed, in the strike that followed. It was the first big strike in Yellowknife's history, despite a long tradition of union activism. Even before pouring the first gold at Giant mine in 1948, most workers at Giant and Con joined the International Union of Mine, Mill and Smelter Workers. Mine–Mill was the proud heir to fifty years of tough, sometimes bloody battles over working conditions and union recognition at mines across western North America.

In 1944, at the height of the Second World War, the federal government adopted the system of labour law passed in the United States in 1935. It forced employers to bargain with certified unions. The new rules, and six years of fighting for democracy in Europe, made workers eager to join unions.

Mine–Mill had a radical image, and was hounded out of "mainstream" labour in both Canada and the United States after refusing to expel Communist activists. But the bitter southern struggles between social democrats and Communists never divided Yellowknife's union local. The town was too isolated; the men learned to rely on themselves for contract negotiations, grievance hearings, and health and safety meetings.

Mine–Mill became the main source of local politicians, from aldermen to mayors and, later, a member of Parliament. The town's first hotel was built by a former labour radical. In the 1940s and 1950s, union activists produced local radio programs and organized community groups such as the Elks.

Yellowknife's mines made big money, so owners didn't really fight Mine–Mill; Giant's profit margin was 50 percent in the early 1960s. Companies had to pay high wages to lure workers north, so if having a union helped bring in men, so much the better. There was no need for strikes.

In southern Canada, however, Mine–Mill was on its last legs by the mid-1960s. For twenty years the United Steelworkers of America had been raiding Mine–Mill locals, and its exhausted leaders accepted a takeover by Steel. Without a vote, Steel was certified at Giant and Con in 1968. But Steel never really took hold at Giant. The men had managed their own affairs for too long to accept the new union's authoritarian methods and centralized structure. Steel's envoys would negotiate a contract with mine management in a few hours. In late 1974, the local executive revolted over a decision made in Pittsburgh to raise union dues.

Steel was replaced by the Canadian Association of Smelter and Allied Workers (CASAW). It was a fledgling Western union with most of its members at the Alcan smelter in Kitimat, BC. CASAW was founded in 1972, and relied heavily on a sister union, CAIMAW (Canadian Association of Industrial, Mechanical and Allied Workers). Both were part of a movement to chase United States-based unions out of Canada. They held that international unions controlling the Canadian Labour Congress were undemocratic, dedicated to serving the interests of union bureaucrats, and willing to sacrifice union jobs in Canada to save those in the United States. As always, only a minority in Yellowknife paid any heed to union politics; they just wanted local control in their struggles with Falconbridge, the corporate operator and dominant shareholder of Giant mine.

By this time, Giant's days as an inexhaustible cash cow were over. The best ore, rock containing visible gold, was gone. Old workings were remined for low-grade ore, and the mine was deepened. Occasional jumps in gold prices kept Giant profitable, but the company had curtailed major investments. Meanwhile, high inflation in the 1970s forced workers to push for big raises to keep pace. It all came to a head in 1980, when gold prices skyrocketed to $850 an ounce, driven by the revolution in Iran and the Soviet army's march into Afghanistan. Falconbridge claimed it was just a blip. CASAW's president pointed out that Giant's wages had fallen well below those at other northern Canadian mines. A brief wildcat strike in April was followed by a legal walkout in July.

Union members, even those who crossed their own picket line in 1992, have fond memories of the 1980 strike. Management greatly underestimated their determination. Work stopped for four months which would have been the most profitable in the life of the mine, since gold prices later plummeted. Falconbridge eventually gave in, raising wages more than 50 percent. The strike itself was mostly fun. The men stood at the mine gate, shouting insults at passing supervisors. But after they finished work for the day, some shift bosses would come to the picket line and talk, maybe even drink a beer. There was some vandalism, but there usually is in mine strikes. In the throes of the 1992–93 dispute, Bruce Bannister would try to cheer up fellow CASAW members with the Case of the Missing Contact Lenses. At one of the mine gates in the summer of 1980, picketers stopped a company truck. A striker was on his hands and knees, inspecting the gravel.

"Please don't move," Bannister told the driver. "He's lost one of his contact lenses."

Bannister and his fellow pickets kept the driver entertained for at least fifteen minutes while the search continued. Meanwhile, someone's wife sneaked around the truck and spooned sugar into the gas tank. The striker, who had excellent vision, finally got up off the ground. "I found it!" He beamed. Pickets and driver wished one another a good day, and the truck drove off—for a few hundred yards.

The 1980 strike changed Yellowknife from a place to make a quick buck to a place to settle and raise a family. Tramp miners, single men who drifted from mine to mine, blowing their money on booze and sex almost as fast as they earned it, gradually disappeared. Until 1980, they had made up most of Giant's workforce. There was always at least one full-time recruiter to lure men north from across Canada. Veterans like Bannister were regularly breaking in new hires. When the strike started, the company shut down the bunkhouses where most of the single men lived. But when Giant reopened, the bunkhouses stayed closed. As a result, mine workers would increasingly be older, married men whose wives worked for the expanding NWT government or downtown businesses. After the strike, Falconbridge sold its downtown houses; Yellowknife was no longer a company town.

The mine still turned a profit, but gradually became run-down. Buildings on surface were sturdy but poorly maintained asbestos-sided constructions in the style of Second World War army bases. Equipment in the mill, where thousands of tons of rock were pulverized and treated with chemicals to extract a few ounces of gold, hadn't been adequately upgraded since the 1950s. The mine's huge stockpile of arsenic trioxide, a toxic by-product of Giant's ore, was a major environmental problem no one knew how to solve. The situation underground was no better. Some diesel equipment supplemented the old and inefficient electric trains used to transport ore. But to get diesel vehicles underground, they had to be dismantled, lowered down the shaft in pieces, and reassembled. The ventilation system was inadequate to flush diesel fumes from the mine, thus creating a health problem.

When gold prices fell in 1981–82, after the strike, Falconbridge almost closed Giant. Local managers insisted that, with some modernization, the mine could turn a profit, and they were right. A ramp was cut into the mine so vehicles could drive in and out. Mining methods were improved. Later the company replaced C-dry (the locker-room and shower area) and added offices above it. In good years, there was money for new mining equipment.

Few jobs age a man as quickly as mining. As he drops down the shaft in the cage at the start of each shift, water and mud either leak or pour over him, depending on the season. Then there's the long trip to his stope, his work area. On some levels, he squeezes into a man-car, which has to be jacked back onto narrow-gauge tracks when it derails. Or he gets in a diesel-powered vehicle with big wheels and bounces along the drift (tunnel). In good years, Giant kept a man grading roadways full-time, trying to reduce back injuries caused by repeated, kidney-jarring punishment. The din of diesel engines is thunderous. A miner's gear is heavy, and he sloshes through water and mud that hide potholes in the floor.

At the stope, his first job is to dislodge loose rock from the back—the ceiling—with a scaling bar. If it takes too long, he won't finish drilling and loading his round with explosives, costing him a day's production bonus. But if he scales too little, a rock will injure or kill him someday. He checks to see if all the shots went off in the last blast. Did the scooptram operator, shoveling out rock with a special front-end loader, do a good job? He marks old blast holes with paint so he doesn't drill the same spot again, then washes off any explosive residue from the rock-face. After that he drills his pattern—the set of holes for the next round of explosives. This requires hours of drilling with pneumatic tools that take their toll on his body. His hearing goes; his back and knees are punished by the weight and constant vibration; nerves are damaged, usually in his hands, which lose feeling and turn white from lack of circulation. Water flows through the drills into the holes and puddles at his feet. The threat of an accident is always present, an accident that's almost inevitable. All mine workers have hair-raising stories about close brushes with death.

Miners find various ways to live with the threat of dying. Some suppress thoughts of danger with alcohol and drugs, becoming risks to themselves and others. Some become fatalists: if God wants me to die today, it doesn't matter where it happens. Others become perfectionists. They study rock like some people study car engines. They learn to slant drill holes at exactly the right angle. They put in just the right amount of explosives to break the rock without disturbing the whole stope. They tell themselves that rock kills foolish miners, not the professionals. Perfectionists are respected. They are usually the best producers, so they receive the largest production bonuses. Their pay can be more than a mine manager's. Young, ambitious miners develop friendships with the best veterans, hoping to work with them and learn their methods.

By the mid-1980s, Giant's top miner was probably Roger Warren. In his 40s, he had more than twenty years of mining experience. He suffered from whitehand, but he could earn $90,000 a year if he worked overtime. Playing hockey and fastball helped him keep in shape. Warren could be abrasive with coworkers. "Roger Warren didn't have time for very many people," says a fellow miner. "He had to find a quality that he liked in you." Warren formed close bonds with a few men—hard workers, interested in sports or mechanical tinkering, and informed enough to discuss the state of the world. While he was mining in Manitoba in the mid-1970s, he took an ambitious young miner under his wing and taught him the trade. Keith Murray and Warren mined together for years, and shared a passion for hockey. They moved to Yellowknife to work at Giant in 1978. Murray retained a deep respect for Warren, even when they found they were on opposite sides of the picket line in 1992.

Warren's faith in his own invulnerability was badly shaken in April 1987, when a blast went off in a work area nearby. The two workers involved, Vince Corcoran and Dan Mino, were trying to clear up a bad blast. Some of the shots from the previous round hadn't gone off and the rock hadn't broken well. As they tried to pry away some rubble with a pick, looking for the unfired shot, the detonator went off. Alerted by the blast, Warren and a shift boss ran to the scene, then called for help. Corcoran was dead. Warren tried to comfort Mino, a former mining partner, cleaning his bloodied face and assuring him he would probably see again. He never did, but a first-rate rescue team led by mechanic Al Shearing got Mino safely to surface. Warren spoke little of the accident, but he couldn't stop thinking about it. He quit his job at Giant and left town, giving up a decade of job seniority and pension contributions. He soon returned, to work at Con mine, across town. But he didn't like Con: it was much deeper and hotter than Giant, to which he returned a few months later.

Corcoran's death was the first at Giant in more than ten years—a very good record, especially in the Northwest Territories, where government enforcement of mine-safety laws was lax. The lack of deaths was in part attributable to very solid ground conditions, which reduce the frequency of cave-ins and falling rock. Back sprains and twisted knees were another matter. Giant reported more accidents than any other NWT mine through the 1980s.

Managers suspected that some accidents were a devious way for workers to get a few days off. But workers who called in sick or missed shifts, usually because they were hungover, were a more serious problem. The union cooperated in setting up a treatment program for heavy drinkers; after a while CASAW even pointed problem drinkers to the program. "It's the North," says one former personnel manager. "You're isolated, long winters. A lot of people come here to get away from problems, thinking, we'll start another life ... That doesn't happen; they come with you." Counseling, treatment, and education were undertaken to solve safety and attendance problems, but also because managers cared about the men who were their neighbours and friends. Steve McAlpine, a senior manager through the 1980s, played hockey with Roger Warren and many other miners. Finding money for such "soft" items as counseling became more difficult after 1986, when Falconbridge sold its stake in Giant and it was sucked into a maelstrom of speculation and stock-market shenanigans. Control wound up with a group of Australians who repeatedly changed their Canadian managers.

I sold fur coats in the middle of the summer, in the middle of the desert.

—Peggy Witte, August 1994

I'd just hate to meet her on a used-car lot. God knows what I'd end up buying.

—Royal Oak director Ross Burns, about Peggy Witte, August 1994

The Australians went bankrupt in early 1990, for reasons unrelated to their mines in Canada. Creditors rebuffed an offer from some senior managers to buy Giant, and their talents were soon lost to other firms. Almost no one else wanted to buy timeworn gold mines like Giant or Pamour mine in Timmins, Ontario. Gold prices were lower than they'd been for a decade, with no rises on the horizon. The only nibble came from Royal Oak, a tiny company with no mines. Finally, in November 1990, the creditors sold their majority stake in the two mines to Royal Oak for the absurdly low price of $35.6 million, most of it borrowed.

Royal Oak was a unique company. First, a kinetic woman was at the helm. Peggy Witte knew just what to say to obtain financing from banks and stock markets. She made all the important decisions, which were to be dutifully carried out. As Witte later said in a speech, "Managers have to have the logo of the company stamped on their forehead."

Many mining-industry insiders were not impressed with Witte at first. She did not project the image of a powerful chief executive. At 36, she was plump and appeared somewhat self-conscious in the limelight of media attention. It's no wonder that Witte was perceived as an upstart. She was born in November 1953 to a prosperous Nevada rancher and a schoolteacher who instilled a strong perfectionist streak in her children. Peggy and her brother sold corn at a roadside stand and played in a musical combo dubbed "The Deadbeats," earning money to attend the University of Nevada, where she enrolled in 1971. She switched from music to chemistry, eventually earning a master's degree in metallurgy. Soon after her marriage to Bill Witte in 1976, Peggy went to work at a copper mill in Tucson, Arizona. It was an unpleasant experience, from the little she has said publicly. She came across as "a know-it-all with a university degree," and her crew locked her in an elevator for six hours, she later told *Chatelaine* magazine.

Bill and Peggy Witte moved to Canada when she accepted a research position near Toronto, bringing the spirit of Nevada with her. She sought, not water, but gold, and a niche in the Canadian mining industry. Two years later, she resigned and founded Witteck Development to advise mining companies on mill efficiency and metallurgy. Her clients included a new gold mine at Hope Brook, Newfoundland; she had a mentor at Teck Corporation, a Vancouver-based mining powerhouse. Witteck was a success, thanks to Witte's uncanny skill at selling her ideas.

Dispensing advice did not satisfy Witte's yearning to run a mine or for "the glamour of publicly traded companies." Many Canadian mining firms had excellent assets but were very conservatively managed, so there was room for a scrappy innovator like Witte. Her first attempt was to develop Colomac, a massive open-pit gold mine about 250 kilometres north of Yellowknife. The ore was very low-grade, so huge tonnages of rock had to be processed, using methods unproven in the subarctic. With little money of her own, she engineered a $90-million loan from the Bank of America. Promising jobs for unemployed youth in small aboriginal communities, she won the support of local Dene leaders. Witte's luck finally ran out in 1989. She was unable to raise enough money, and her partners forced her out of Colomac mine.

Witte was bitter, but she emerged with $2 million and a passion to build a major mining company. She spent $1 million on Royal Oak, a shell company with few assets, trading on the Toronto Stock Exchange. Her new recipe was to buy mines with high operating costs when the price of gold is low, slash costs, survive until the price of gold rises, rake in profits and shareholder praise, and then buy something bigger. At last, with $100,000 in Royal Oak's coffers, Witte cut a deal for control of the Giant and Pamour mines, on the strength of bank loans, and with Teck Corporation—with its excellent connections to the ruling Progressive Conservative government—as an investment partner and source of board members. The deal "took balls—a lot of them," says Royal Oak's former treasurer.

Witte's next move was equally dramatic. She fired virtually all the mines' headquarters staff in Toronto and moved the office to a modest two-story building in Vancouver. Royal Oak would do without the layers of management and office staff most other mining companies had, she boasted. The shock wave soon hit Yellowknife, where many of the local managers were long-term residents who had risen through the ranks. Witte immediately announced the closure of Giant's new tailings-retreatment plant, where the previous owner had had marginal success extracting gold from old mining waste. Twenty-eight jobs were eliminated. Managers who didn't fit the lean-and-mean mould were dismissed. Others were told they had a few months to change their style or they, too, would be fired.

Royal Oak's approach to firings was ruthless. One married couple, Colin and Gerry Hudson, worked in the human resources department. Colin had worked at Giant for ten years. Three weeks into Royal Oak's reign, with no prior warning, he was told on a Friday afternoon to clear out his desk by the end of the day. On Monday, his wife, Gerry, had to explain Giant's filing system to her husband's replacement, an industrial relations graduate in her late 20s with one year's work experience. Colin Hudson sued for wrongful dismissal, and won the case two years later.

The swift purge in Yellowknife inspired many staffers to send out résumés, hoping to quit before they were fired. Those who feared the recession, or wanted to stay in Yellowknife, kept quiet and worked longer hours. Hourly workers, better protected by CASAW against firing, complained that Giant was losing the supervisors with the most experience and best rapport with their men. Some replacements were young, inexperienced, abrasive, and ambitious.

Giant's new boss was recruited in a state where antiunion sentiment runs as deep among the elite as in Witte's native Nevada. Mike Werner arrived in January 1991 from a copper mine in Superior, Arizona. A Mormon with a fierce work ethic, Werner had earned his doctoral degree by his mid-30s. At the same time, he worked full-time and he and his wife produced a large family. Werner's short stature made him the butt of workers' jokes. They considered him a little spark plug with something to prove. Werner, like Witte, expected an almost military level of obedience and devotion from workers. He put in long hours, sparing no time for socializing outside his family. He couldn't understand or tolerate employees for whom Giant was just a job.

Werner believed that costs had to be cut quickly for Royal Oak to survive. In 1990, Royal Oak's average cost to produce an ounce of gold was $395 US; the spot price on the world market was about $350 US. Besides the need for profit to please shareholders, the company had loans to repay. High-grading, or mining the best ore and leaving the lower-grade rock in the ground, was a poor option. Instead, Werner introduced a complex system to stabilize the grade, which made the mill more efficient. Waste of supplies and equipment was reduced. But the biggest single source of savings, Werner believed, lay in rooting out incompetence and laziness.

In Werner's first week at Giant, three scooptrams caught fire. Supervisors' explanations irked Werner. Not only was there no program to stop grease from accumulating on the scoops, but the mine didn't even have a proper machine to wash them. So Werner continued the purge of managers. At a mining conference later that year, he boasted that only two of the pre–Royal Oak managers "survived the transition with the new management." Werner's hard-nosed style upset many people, but there was also grudging admiration for his single-minded push for efficiency. And the new managers he hired from down south were grateful for their promotions.

The crunch came when Werner turned his attention to the related problems of accidents and absenteeism. Of the 234 CASAW members at Giant, an average of forty were absent each day—including those who had sustained major injuries and would likely spend the rest of their lives on workers' compensation. Others had recurring knee or back problems, broken bones, or muscle sprains. A few hard partyers regularly had the flu on Mondays or Fridays. Some didn't bother to tell their shift boss—usually called a shifter—they weren't coming to work, or showed up late. Werner lectured workers about "time thieves" stealing wages for work not done. He applied the same moralistic approach to accidents. If a worker had a mishap because he broke a safety rule, he should be disciplined. Men who were accident-prone should be fired.

That was where the trouble really began with the workers at Giant. They risked their lives daily and slowly ruined their health. The payoff had always been that no one hassled them. The shifter might check on his crew twice a shift, and ask if they needed supplies. Now, Royal Oak threatened the men with dismissal to improve safety. At the same time, many complained that the company undermined safety by pushing so hard for more production.

Soon after Werner came to Yellowknife, a miner almost died in a careless accident. It confirmed Werner's belief that the mine was lax on safety. The victim was Ben Weir, who had thirty years of mining experience. Weir is a cautious, thoughtful family man, respectful of his bosses. This time, he crawled under a rock ledge without checking thoroughly whether it would hold. It didn't. The 3- to 4-ton ledge slipped down a few inches, pinning Weir. It ripped open his bladder, but could have snapped his spine. In terrible pain, he worried he'd never walk again while he waited an hour in the gloom for someone to find him. By coincidence, Werner was one of the first men on the scene after Weir was discovered. On his heels was mechanic Al Shearing's mine-rescue team.

Shearing says he arrived just in time to stop Werner from making a big mistake. Werner planned to lift the rock off Weir by slinging a chain around it and hooking the chain to the bucket of a scooptram. Shearing worried that, if the rock broke as it was lifted, it would crash down on Weir and kill him.

"You get the fuck out of here!" Shearing shouted at Werner—not yet realizing, he says, that this was the new mine manager. Shearing and his crew slipped timber in between Weir and the rock and slowly jacked it up. One man chattered to Weir to keep his mind off the pain. Weir was free and on a stretcher in about half an hour. He was rushed to a helicopter and flown to Edmonton. Weir spent two months in the hospital and recovered almost fully, though nerves in his leg were damaged.

Werner maintains that he controlled the entire rescue operation. Although Shearing and his team arrived, "we didn't need mine rescue to get this done. Mine rescue's trained to fight underground fires."

Shearing's complaint that Werner had stuck his nose into something he knew little about was spread far and wide. Shearing, a wiry, forty-three-year-old Newfoundlander, had trained for mine rescue for years. Few men have more pluck. He took great pride in being the fastest and the safest mine-rescue man around, and put his heart into the regular mine-rescue competitions between NWT mines. All teams consisted of workers and supervisors, and Shearing allowed no one to boss him around at a rescue scene where he was the captain.

Shearing had the same attitude toward his daily work. He was an effective underground mechanic who found ingenious ways to repair equipment. He poked fun at shifters if he thought they were incompetent or monitored him too closely. The sauciness of men like Shearing infuriated Werner.

That spring, Werner and the workforce both proved their mettle. Heavy snowfall and a quick thaw threatened the mine's future. So much water cascaded from various levels into C-shaft that it was almost impossible to take down men or equipment. The water poured down to 2,143 feet underground and filled all the side passages up into the 2,000-foot level. With their jobs on the line and the regulations limiting working hours suspended, workers put in marathon shifts. Some went two or three days without sleep. Shearing and a beefy coworker, Tim Bettger, pulled on scuba-diving suits and swam the length of a frigid underground holding pond to shut off a crucial valve.

On the surface, water had backed up in the ditch beside the public highway through Giant's property and was flowing into the mine. The only hope was to rip up the road and put in a new culvert. "You better get permission," workers advised Werner. "We don't have to," Werner is said to have replied. "This is our mine and we'll do whatever we want."

A burly driller who had just put in a twelve-hour shift was assigned to dump rock in strategic locations with a truck. Mark Eveson, alternatively known as Rambo and Dark Cloud, had truck-driving experience and didn't think Werner's route was practical. So Eveson did it his own way. After three or four loads, Eveson relates, "Werner's standing right in the middle of the road.

"'I told you ...' he says.

"And I said, 'Mike, I really don't care. I'm already into sixteen hours now. I'm here working just as hard as you to save this fuckin' mine, and I know better than you, I've been doing this. So why don't you just fuck off.' And he backed down and went away."

Eveson was bitter when his bonus was only $900 for working twelve- to sixteen-hour shifts, thirty-nine days straight during the flood period. In mining, people who can't be supervised easily because they work in isolation receive incentive bonuses of up to several thousand dollars a month if they are successful miners. But for helping with flood control, some workers got less than Eveson; they were given a ticket for a meal at one of Yellowknife's better restaurants.

"I don't think they got any bonus at all for it," Werner says, noting that they were paid the overtime rate. "If they let the mine flood, they don't have a job, so I'm not sure what they're complaining about."

Peggy Witte also found her way into Eveson's bad books. In July, she came to Yellowknife to fly Royal Oak's colours in an impressive media campaign. The day before she was to tour the property, Werner came to see Eveson. "'The boss is coming tomorrow and we're going to bring her out here,' [Werner said to me]. I said, 'That's good—so Miss Piggy's coming to town, eh. Oooops. That slipped out. No malice intended.'

"'Yeah, I know,' [Werner] said, 'but I'll tell you, and you should pass this on to everybody: Whenever she hears herself referred to as Miss Piggy, she turns bright red and sweat literally pops off her forehead and she grinds her teeth. You guys really shouldn't call her that.'

"So I sort of laughed, I said, 'All right! OK.' Sometime the next day, sure enough, and this was the first time I ever saw her. She was in a brand-new, clean pair of coveralls and a white hat ... And I got the impression I was supposed to shake her hand. My hands are all greasy and dirty, I was filthy!" Eveson says he wiped his hand on his coveralls and tendered it. "She looked at me and spun around, and just walked away. Like I was just garbage [or] part of the drill, eh."

"INDUSTRIAL DICTATORSHIP"

Underground is like a reverse hierarchy. The miners are the gods. Everybody else is subservient to them, even the supervisors. You don't just become a good miner overnight. It takes years.

—former miner Bob Robertson, March 22, 1995

Peggy Witte prides herself on knowing the technical operations of "her" mines in minute detail. You can't keep costs down unless you keep track of your subordinates, she says. So, when Mike Werner wanted to buy equipment—such as a new drill costing a few thousand dollars—he had to call headquarters for Witte's permission.

Werner applied the same vigilant supervision to his subordinates. He prided himself on having worked as a miner, though many miners doubted that he's spent much time at the profession. Most bit their tongue when Werner came around, hoping he'd grow out of it. Some turned up their drills to drown him out; bolder men tried to scare him off.

There's nothing novel about friction between young managers and workers, but at Giant it quickly got out of hand. Even before Werner arrived, CASAW's local leaders were complaining about Royal Oak's methods. It started with little cost-cutting measures, such as the last-minute cancellation of the workers' traditional family Christmas party and elimination of anniversary gifts to employees with many years of service.

There was also the issue of the grievance backlog. While the owners were in bankruptcy, CASAW and a caretaker manager had postponed their discussion until a new owner took over. Now union leaders wanted the grievances dealt with quickly. Royal Oak's managers didn't want to talk about issues they considered to be ancient history. Many of the supervisors involved were being fired anyway. As a gesture of goodwill, why not just drop all the old grievances? they asked at a meeting with union leaders.

"As a gesture of goodwill, why don't you just *grant* all the old grievances!" CASAW local president Bill Schram exploded. It was CASAW's duty to act on members' grievances, not scrap them to please the company.

Royal Oak further infuriated Schram and other activists by claiming that workers were filing grievances to scam money from the company. The biggest rip-off concerned overtime, the new owners argued. Under the contract, shifters had to offer men overtime according to seniority. Because some workers never accepted, shifters often quit asking. An overlooked worker could then file a grievance and be paid for a weekend shift he had not worked. The union countered that a contract is a contract; if grievances aren't filed, shifters will simply give the lucrative overtime to their favourites.

This was the atmosphere when Werner introduced a new discipline system about a month after his arrival. From then on, workers' offenses would be tabulated. Four "steps" in one category, or seven in total, and a worker was automatically fired. Multiple steps could be given, depending on the severity of an incident. "Insubordination" served as a catchall category, and was often used if a worker resisted discipline over something else. Such systems are quite common, though none had ever been used consistently at Giant.

Werner called special meetings of each shift to explain the system. There would be no leniency or exceptions: arrive five minutes late for your shift and you would be sent home. Looking back, Werner says he has only one regret about that part of the policy: "If you were a worker that had been there for twenty years and never missed a day, and you really did have a problem getting to work, then we would step you just like everyone else. The problem is, in a unionized organization, you can't show favourites. You don't have the right to take that guy's record under consideration."

A majority of the men received at least one disciplinary step in the first year, including workers who hadn't been disciplined in decades. When the steps seemed too outrageous, workers would chant "Strike! Strike! Strike!" at their supervisors.

A typical case is that of mechanic Gerry Drover, who volunteered to come in two hours early during the winter to start the heavy machinery. (When it's minus 35 degrees Celsius, as it often is in Yellowknife, starting a motor can be a problem.) That meant arriving in the dark at 5:30 A.M. "I did this for three months, seven days a week," Drover says. One day he overslept, and called his shifter's answering machine at 5:50 to say he'd be late. When he got to work, he was sent home for the day without pay, and was not even allowed to work his normal shift.

By the fall of 1991, some workers had enough steps to lose their jobs. In the next seven months, eight were fired—probably as many as in the previous five years. Rumours circulated that the company had blacklists of union activists and older, less productive workers. One company list of workers "who seem to have frequent accidents" was taken by a union member, photocopied, and posted around the property.

The practice of giving steps to workers who had accidents was opposed by Giant's safety superintendent, but Werner implemented it anyway. Werner was careful to say he was punishing the men for violating safety rules, not for hurting themselves, but the difference was often hard to distinguish. CASAW activists said Royal Oak's real aim was to improve the mine's dismal safety record by discouraging workers from reporting minor accidents. A better record would eventually lead to a cut in workers' compensation premiums. Werner's retort was that any worker who was found not to have reported an accident would get a step.

Werner seems to have believed that most workers approved of the step system. "You'd go underground and talk to the miners, when the disciplinary policies were put in place. Most of them understood what was going on. I would say the majority supported it. They knew that the mine was in trouble and a lot of them didn't like working around people that weren't competent."

No one can accuse union leaders of keeping their opinions to themselves.

"They're trying to bring in an industrial dictatorship!" CASAW president Bill Schram often insisted. Once, he allegedly shouted at senior company managers that they were a "bunch of fucking Americans" who should be deported, a statement he denies having made. Schram and the rest of the executive got union members to file grievances against every disciplinary step, hoping that an arbitrator would eventually throw out the whole system. The clogged grievance system thus ground to a halt. CASAW and Royal Oak argued over arbitration dates. Labour-management meetings became shouting matches.

Some of the new managers were disturbed by CASAW's criticism. Probably the worst off was Kim Cornwell, who had replaced Colin Hudson in the human resources department. She handled the paperwork for the new step system, which was a bureaucratic nightmare, and attended every meeting with the union executives. "I sensed an awful lot of bitterness from some of those people. I thought, 'What happened to you in your life that you are so bitter?'" Cornwell says. "It was so negative, it devastated me." She used to go home at night wondering, "Am I that terrible a person?"

Werner, on the other hand, says he laughed at CASAW's "self-destructive" conduct, especially when Schram accused him of trying to break the union. "It's like they wanted you to go and screw with the union ... They were fighting battles that were silly if you wanted to keep solidarity and strengthen your union." He thought they would have been more effective if they'd chosen a few grievances to push to arbitration.

Arguments about safety intensified in July 1991, when Royal Oak geologist Toni Borschneck came from Vancouver to see Giant firsthand. On her first trip underground, she was taken to a stope on the 1,200-foot level. The joint union–management health and safety committee came through at the same time on a safety tour. Suddenly, a 150-pound rock crashed from the ceiling onto her head and dealt a glancing blow to a bystander. Uncomfortably aware that more rock could fall, men rushed to Borschneck's rescue. She was bleeding from the mouth and nose, but still breathing. They gave her mouth-to-mouth resuscitation and cardiac massage, then got her on a stretcher, up to surface, and into an ambulance. Borschneck, just 32, died on the way to the hospital, while the man who'd given her his breath trembled in a corner of the headframe.

The death shook Werner too. All his sermons about checking for loose rock hadn't prevented this. A year later, Werner and Royal Oak were in court, charged with violations of the Mine Safety Act. The ceiling was far too high to dislodge any loose rock with a scaling bar; wire mesh should have been installed to catch falling rock. In spite of this, Werner and Royal Oak were acquitted, on the basis that due diligence had been exercised.

The accident sparked more debate with CASAW about safety. The union accused Royal Oak of talking tough but neglecting precautions that cost money or slowed production. CASAW local vice president Harry Seeton brought the issue to a head two weeks later by invoking his right under the Mine Safety Act to refuse unsafe work. He said there was a bulge near the bottom of the skip shaft, used to haul ore to the surface, that could burst. Anyone working below it could be buried, Seeton insisted.

A Nova Scotian with fifteen years at Giant and a union man to the core, Seeton was detested by management, who accused him of being lazy and a troublemaker. He is always intense, whether in anger or laughter. Seeton was chairman of CASAW's grievance committee, so he'd participated in many of the nastiest arguments with Royal Oak, during which he would take off his glasses and rub his head as his frustration mounted. Seeton took his complaint about the skip shaft directly to the government's mine inspectors. (He had the right to do so, but normal practice was to talk to managers or the mine's health and safety committee first.) Werner was furious. He felt miserable over Borschneck's death and was fiercely protective of his image with the government.

Personal animosity likely played a large part in Werner's contempt for the union's leaders. For him, there were two kinds of workers at Giant. The majority were hard working, real men who understood the need for tight management. A minority were troublemakers and misfits; to Werner, most of the union leaders were in this latter category.

CASAW president Bill Schram worked in the mill and knew little about the underground. He took history books and odd magazines to work, and played Dungeons and Dragons. He walks and talks stiffly, overcoming his shyness only when he loses his temper or gets to know a person well. He hadn't been elected to the presidency; he was vice president when the elected president resigned, about the time Royal Oak arrived, and moved up. Schram was well versed in labour history, but had little negotiating experience.

Secretary-Treasurer Bob Kosta looked like a refugee from the counter-culture 1960s, with his shaggy black beard and frizzy hair. He had a huge and eclectic music collection, and cycled around town with his daughter in a child seat— which real miners just don't do, at least in Werner's experience. And he worked with Seeton, maintaining the shaft.

Then there was Steve Petersen, cochairman of the health and safety committee, a tall, big-framed man who'd worked as a dryman (janitor) since a mysterious illness several years earlier left him barely able to walk. Petersen recovered partially, and insisted he'd been poisoned by chemicals used in the mine's refining process, but it was almost impossible to prove. He was articulate, quick-witted, and disdainful of Werner. "So, Mikey, do you have to stand on a chair to reach your phone?" he taunted Werner. Petersen knew mine-safety regulations by heart, pounced on violations, and complained loudly when the company failed to make promised changes.

A few weeks after the flare-up with Seeton, Royal Oak laid him off, along with Kosta and Petersen, citing financial reasons. Kosta and Seeton had enough seniority to "bump" back into other jobs, but it was more difficult for Petersen. Royal Oak said he wasn't physically able to work in most areas, and men in other, less physically demanding jobs had more seniority.

CASAW publicly accused the company of plotting to destroy the union, and said the three layoffs were part of it. Front-page news in *yellowknifer,* the larger of two local newspapers, it was one of the first public indications of trouble at Giant.

Schram and CASAW's executives were worried. The mine's three-year contract would expire soon, and they were sure Royal Oak was planning for a lengthy lockout or strike. In the union hall, men speculated that Werner was a professional union buster who had CASAW in his sights. Schram said that the step system wasn't designed as much to save Royal Oak money as to empty the union's treasury. Arbitration is expensive, and though the cost is split fifty–fifty, the company had the deeper pockets. Also, Royal Oak took a much harder line in grievance hearings than previous owners had, forcing the union to choose between referring most complaints to an outside arbitrator or dropping them altogether. But, when a union member was fired, CASAW's only option was to fight. Schram had to beg CASAW's national office in British Columbia for money to keep his local afloat.

In November 1991, Schram convinced the membership to double union dues to help pay for arbitrations. It took a second vote, a special referendum, but Schram says that 92 percent of members voted for the increase. "It was pretty fantastic. And it should have warned the company what was happening."

Royal Oak needed no warning. Werner had his chief engineer, Gerry Wolfe, planning for a strike of "indefinite" length to start April 1, 1992. Reviewing the financial data and assuming that all unionized staff would go out, Wolfe calculated that Giant could run "at breakeven during a strike for an indefinite period" by reassigning nonunion staff and managers to essential jobs. If manpower proved to be in short supply, he offered several sources, including staff from Royal Oak's mine in Timmins. He predicted a critical shortage of mechanics and tradesmen, but made only two oblique references to strikebreakers in his

November 28 draft report. As well, he noted that four people would be needed for security, since "some people can be expected to attempt sabotage, especially if the strike is long and bitter. There is historical evidence of attempted sabotage and violence here in the past." Damage was anticipated to buses carrying staff through the picket line. The plan was probably impractical over time—and it was definitely drafted without Werner's or Peggy Witte's assessment.

Union leaders knew that such plans existed. Obviously, Royal Oak was planning for a fight, but probably wouldn't hire "scabs," a drastic measure that all but wipes out a union's economic power. Union busting has been illegal in Canada since 1944, and Royal Oak has always vigorously denied it wanted to destroy CASAW. If the union had accepted the discipline system, CASAW wouldn't have been in such deep financial trouble, managers say. Royal Oak got along with the Steelworkers' local at Pamour, the company's other mine, as Witte, Werner, and other managers pointed out regularly. However, such rhetoric only heightened CASAW's suspicion. Those who'd been union activists for a few years had heard many dark stories about Steel. It had allegedly worked hand in glove with Inco to destroy the old Mine–Mill union in Sudbury in the 1950s and 1960s. And Steel had used every legal trick in the book, and maybe some illegal ones, to block independent Canadian unions in British Columbia.

In Yellowknife, Steel showed no sign of trying to recruit discontented CASAW members, although the local was still coveted, according to a former president of Con mine's Steelworkers' local. A couple of years later, a Steelworkers official in Timmins said that his union was approached by Royal Oak around this time. He says a senior Royal Oak manager supplied a list of the company's Yellowknife employees to a Steel activist in Timmins. The manager wanted Steel to send someone to Yellowknife to quietly recruit workers for an anti-CASAW campaign. The activist is said to have given the list to Steel headquarters in Toronto. Nothing came of it—at least publicly. According to the RCMP files, a list was also given to management at Con.

ROLLING THE DICE TILL YOU GET TO SEVEN

Men darted after hockey pucks and women played broomball in Yellowknife's arena. In early 1992, political gossip at Centre Square Mall or the co-op store centred on the new premier, Nellie Cournoyea, an Inuvialuit from the Arctic coast. She had a reputation for getting the job done in every forum she'd entered, from land claims to the legislature, to halting bar brawls, and she was upbeat about the Northwest Territories' economic prospects. People who were really in the know whispered about diamonds. Some geologists said that the NWT could become the new South Africa. Mining outfitters geared up for a spring rush of prospectors looking for a big strike on the tundra north of Yellowknife. Maybe the recession was just a blip, here in the eternally booming North.

Even at Giant, where the collective agreement would expire on March 31, things seemed calm. Pessimists had worked as much overtime as possible for months, saving money in case of a strike. Others now followed their lead. Giant's productivity for the next three months hit a record high.

CASAW's core of activists came to every meeting, but most members attended only during contract negotiations. Many of the least involved worried that union hard liners might push everyone into a strike nobody really wanted. So, when it came time to volunteer for the union's steering committee for the bargaining strategy, a group of moderates signed up. Following tradition, the steering committee asked union members what they wanted in the next contract. Not much, the men replied; times were tough and they'd accept a wage freeze. Since many men were getting on in years, any extra money should go to indexing pensions. The twenty-four-member steering committee chose a six-man bargaining team. From Royal Oak's viewpoint, they were fresh faces and not radicals, except CASAW president Bill Schram. Bruce Bannister, the hoistman who was one of CASAW's elder statesmen, was elected spokesman for the bargaining committee. He hadn't held a union post in about ten years, but he was stirred to return to politics by bad blood between Werner and the CASAW executive. Bannister had no love for Royal Oak, but shared Werner's belief that some of CASAW's leaders were too confrontational. "The lunatics were in charge of the bloody asylum," he says now with uncharacteristic bluntness.

Mike Gross, Royal Oak's vice president of operations, headed the company's team. He had avoided most squabbles with CASAW, and was probably Royal Oak's most moderate executive. But Gross had a shopping list of changes to make to the contract when negotiations began in late January. As usual, Royal Oak was in a hurry, and hoped to undo about twenty years' worth of union gains on everything from who chose safety equipment to how overtime was allocated.

In numerous long meetings, Bannister and his team argued the company back to the status quo on most issues. On the rest, the union committee agreed to a few ambiguous changes, and some concessions that seemed minor. Six weeks into the talks, Royal Oak abruptly asked the federal government for a conciliator under provisions of the Canada Labour Code, which covers all industries in the Northwest Territories, unlike in the provinces. Royal Oak was showing its impatience; conciliation is required by law before a strike or lockout.

"We were making progress," Bannister says. "[Then] we were informed that the company had applied for conciliation, without warning. We were very angry."

The conciliator got negotiations moving again in early April. Royal Oak and the union even agreed to have a grievance mediator from Labour Canada help them deal with the backlog. The mood at the table was tense but businesslike, but they still hadn't talked about monetary issues.

Bannister put out several bulletins to inform the rank and file about the talks. Among those who paid close attention and began to worry was Dale Johnston, a former national president of CASAW and for a long time local president (before Bill Schram's day). He is a crafty negotiator who had earned grudging respect from Giant's previous management. He had been a charismatic leader, and was generally trusted. But few people enjoy his full trust, because he has a nose for conspiracies and a weakness for backroom intrigue. Johnston seemed to be out of the picture at Giant by 1992, but he was officially on extended leave. His efforts were concentrated on his small store, Wolverine Sports.

Johnston had strengthened CASAW's contract over the years and didn't want hard-won clauses lost by Bannister, whom he mistrusted. So Johnston asked CASAW national president Ross Slezak to help keep Bannister from giving away the farm. Slezak is a salty, friendly fellow, almost a caricature of a union leader. Having watched Royal Oak's behaviour carefully and perceptively, well served by twenty years of union activism, he arrived in Yellowknife for the start of serious bargaining on monetary issues.

The talks began on Good Friday, April 17. Later, no one could quite agree who got crucified. Royal Oak wanted a 6 percent wage cut; CASAW halfheartedly demanded a raise of 6 percent, expecting to break even. After making a series of concessions on contract language, Bannister hoped to get indexed pensions—he needed a gain in a key area so members would support the deal. To cover the cost, Bannister's committee agreed to let the company drop free bus service between the town and the mine, a benefit no longer widely used.

Debate was in full swing between Bannister and Royal Oak vice president Mike Gross when in walked John Smrke, the company's director of human resources, fresh off the plane. Union sources say Smrke told everyone that he'd just listen and get up to speed. Then Gross revealed that indexed pensions would cost about $160,000 a year, a figure CASAW had sought for months—this was less than the $250,000 cost of the bus. Smrke called a caucus of the company's team. After lunch, Smrke became Royal Oak's spokesman, and said that he wouldn't have provided some of the information that the union had received. To CASAW's team, it was clear that Gross had been replaced for being too conciliatory. Gross refuses to say what happened, but within a few weeks he left the company, and Smrke became Witte's right-hand man at Royal Oak.

Smrke's new offer was a four-year contract with wage increases tied to the price of gold. Wages would be frozen unless gold markets improved for an extended period, then the workers would get a share of the profit. And if gold dropped in price later, wages would go back to the previous level. The union team decided to think about it.

This was Slezak's last chance to bawl out the local's bargaining team for the concessions they had already made and were considering. Instead, he asked the union committee if they were comfortable with what they were doing and if the membership was well informed. The consensus was that they could gain little or nothing more from Royal Oak without a strike—the last thing Slezak wanted. He'd seen enough of Royal Oak to know that a work stoppage would be long and nasty. CASAW's national finances were already shaky. CASAW Local 1, Slezak's home local, did not plan to sacrifice its healthy strike fund to anyone else's fight.

The next day, Easter Saturday, CASAW's team agreed to the wage freeze and the gold clause. Bannister persuaded the company that, if the price of gold went up, the contract could be renegotiated after three years, but otherwise it would be a four-year deal. The union team agreed to a few more minor concessions after some haggling, and the two sides had a tentative agreement. Smrke exacted a promise that the entire bargaining committee would recommend the tentative agreement to CASAW's membership; Bannister said it would be hard to sell. The two sides shook hands and told each other that relations would be better from then on. Royal Oak's committee, which had never expected to get a deal with CASAW, went off and had a party.

Bannister and his team didn't feel like celebrating. They'd swallowed more than twenty concessions and received little in return. By the conciliator's estimate, they had agreed to only $400,000 of the $1.6 million in concessions Royal Oak had demanded. But CASAW had never before made concessions. Indeed, it had made substantial gains in wages or language in every contract since its first one in 1976.

Tempers flared when the bargaining team reported to the union's membership on Easter Monday. Contract talks were CASAW's one chance to show Royal Oak that the workers wouldn't be bullied. (In Canada it's only when the collective agreement has expired that a union may strike.) Yet the union bargaining team had seemingly folded, in a way that looked suspicious to many of the men. On Thursday, the possibility of an agreement seemed remote; monetary issues still hadn't been discussed. Four days later, union negotiators were recommending a tentative agreement rife with concessions. One shop steward was so upset that he accused Bannister, wrongly, of taking a bribe from the company. Dale Johnston and others were furious with Ross Slezak, whom they saw as encouraging workers to act like sheep instead of as stalwarts determined to give Bannister the backbone he seemed to lack.

Bannister and his team made another crucial mistake. Short of time to type up the tentative agreement, they distributed a company-prepared list of changes to the existing contract. The list was bewildering to anyone who hadn't memorized all the clauses in the old contract. It took several hours of review to figure out what had or hadn't been conceded to Royal Oak. To skeptical union members, it was more evidence that someone was trying to pull a fast one.

"Nothing personal, nothing against the bargaining committee, but this is a piece of shit!" local vice president Harry Seeton reportedly exclaimed at a membership meeting. Bannister has bitter memories of the experience, but Seeton wasn't the only one to react. Union activists who weren't on Bannister's team held hurried meetings, finding more loopholes in the tentative deal that benefited Royal Oak. There was, for example, a new rule on overtime. Previously, all weekend work earned higher, overtime rates. Under the new deal, an employee was not eligible for overtime in any week without having worked forty regular hours that week. This meant that someone could be sick or laid off for two days during the week and have to work for normal pay on the weekend. It was angrily pointed out that the new rules would allow the mine to run seven days a week, paying almost no overtime. This scenario was plausible. In documents to shareholders, Royal Oak had talked about implementing a seven-day schedule, and later did so. In theory, this schedule was intended to lower equipment costs, since fewer men would work at any one time.

The tentative agreement, if ratified, would also terminate or reduce various benefits. The cuts might have been easier to accept a year earlier, when Royal Oak's financial future looked precarious. However, pleas of poverty were harder to believe when the company had just reported a $4-million profit for the last quarter of 1991 and had bought the Hope Brook gold mine in Newfoundland with Royal Oak shares. Company officials insisted that Giant mine was barely breaking even, but many CASAW members, aware that Pamour mine in Timmins was losing money, suspected the company of fudging figures.

For reasons that have not been well explained, the company also asked for, and received, new contract language on safety inspections. Until then, the mine's health and safety committee was to inspect every work area once a month. Because miners are widely dispersed at Giant, this inspection round could take a week. In the tentative agreement, the committee was to be "responsible for ... seeing that there are two days devoted to inspections underground and one day devoted to inspections on surface per month." Bannister interpreted this to mean that there would be a *minimum* of three days' inspection. Critics said the company would cut corners on safety and leave work areas uninspected—they said the clause stipulated a *maximum*.

Royal Oak wanted a quick vote by CASAW on the tentative agreement, rightly believing that delay would give opponents time to organize. But an overwhelming majority of union members wanted more time to look at the deal, so the vote was set for April 28, more than a week later. The agreement was in deep trouble. Opponents put out a flyer against it. Talk both on and off the property was running toward a "no" vote, even among men who would later cross their own picket line. The last meetings before the vote turned into pep rallies for the "no" side. Only a few workers argued in favour of the tentative agreement.

Meanwhile, Royal Oak's senior executives were in Geneva promoting company stock to European investors. On the eve of the vote, Witte wrote to the workers about ratifying the tentative agreement. "These difficult times in the gold mining industry are unfortunately taking the [*sic*] toll on many gold mining companies, and a large number of mining employees are already jobless. I am hopeful that you will consider the importance of your decision today so that the Yellowknife Division will be in a position to continue to operate," Witte wrote. "The Company cannot afford to alter the package ... and as a result, the Company is not prepared to return to the bargaining table."

Witte's thinly veiled threat to shut down the mine angered most CASAW members, even some who had planned to vote for the tentative agreement. The letter was so effective at turning opinion further against the deal that Bannister believed Royal Oak's intention was to provoke a strike. When votes were tallied the next evening, 83 percent opposed ratification.

Local president Bill Schram's credibility was fading. He'd signed a deal that had been roundly rejected. Now he told the media that the vote wasn't a decision to strike; rather, it was a veto of concessions, and CASAW wanted to resume bargaining immediately. The two sides met, but the company offered no way for Schram and Bannister to save face. Royal Oak would consider only a union proposal incurring costs no higher than those of the defeated agreement. CASAW's hard liners were also prevailing. The only concession from the old contract that the union would make now was to trade bus service for indexed pensions, renouncing three months of negotiations. The talks were stalled.

Royal Oak then spread word that strikebreakers would be hired if CASAW didn't back down. Behind the scenes, bids had been sought as early as February for such things as catering and housing. Southern contractors snooped around the mine and prepared cost estimates to provide crews. Shift bosses lectured their men that Witte was deadly serious about scabbing the mine. Some warned union members that if they went on strike they would never return to work at Giant. The men found that an incredible intimidation tactic, tantamount to a declaration of war. It seemed unlikely that the whole workforce could be replaced. Nobody at Giant had lived through a mine strike in which strike-breakers had been used. Nobody had successfully scabbed a Canadian mine since 1957.

The 1957 dispute had occurred in Quebec, where labour legislation still lagged behind the rest of Canada's. That dispute, technically an illegal strike by Steelworkers' members at Noranda's copper mine in Murdochville, lasted six months and produced major political fallout. Strikers and their supporters had pitched battles with security guards and strikebreakers. In mid strike, three union men injured themselves in an explosion evidently intended to sabotage the mine. One later died, and the Steelworkers suggested he was an *agent provocateur,* a company spy sent to discredit the union.

Outside Quebec, the last mining dispute involving strikebreakers took place in 1941–42, when gold companies in Kirkland Lake, Ontario, decided to crush Mine–Mill—the same union that signed up Giant six years later. But that was long ago, when unions had little legal recourse in countering management's belief that its absolute control of the workplace was the right and natural order.

In short, many CASAW members saw little risk in calling Royal Oak's bluff. Still, some men had no stomach for a strike. Mining jobs were scarce. Wages in Yellowknife were among the best in Canada. Workers who hadn't followed union affairs and got on well with their shifters were mystified by union activists who agitated for a strike. Keep your head down, do as you're told, work hard, and Giant was still a good living. Was it worth risking that for contract language? To keep free airfares, a perk dating back to the days when Yellowknife had no road link with the outside world? To punish Mike Werner for insulting union leaders? But only a few strike opponents spoke up at union meetings, and some didn't bother attending.

There was Joe Pandev, a Yugoslav immigrant, an old-timer at Giant, a Knights of Columbus stalwart. His longtime mining partner, Martin Kolenko, had once been president of the union local (in Steel's day) but was now a supervisor. They planned to retire in a year and move to British Columbia together. And CASAW wanted Pandev to go on strike for abstract principles? There was Craig Richardson from Thunder Bay, a high-strung loner who disliked the unions he'd had at other mines. In one meeting, he accused union leaders of lying about the contract and Royal Oak. Even if the tentative agreement wasn't great, he argued, they'd be crazy to go on strike during a recession with the mining industry in a slump. Vice President Harry Seeton stepped in to stop the boos from drowning out Richardson's remarks. Richardson says his speech stirred up the hard liners, who whipped the crowd back into a prostrike frenzy. Gojko Samardzija, a talkative Serbian old-timer better known as George the Trackman, says he argued that it was better to take some concessions than have people lose their homes during a strike. "Fall into company trap," he says. "Company want strike worse than you do."

Some strike opponents say now that they were too intimidated to speak up at CASAW meetings. At one, a hot-blooded miner who showed up in a motorcycle helmet brandished a steel pipe and announced that the first scab to come past him on the picket line was "going to get this." This story quickly spread around town, altered and exaggerated to the point that many people thought the strike vote had practically been extorted. By the time the story reached the mayor, for example, it was about a bunch of union radicals who had walked into a meeting and commanded members to vote for a strike if they wanted to get out of the room alive.

In fact, there was a secret-ballot vote, held separately from any union meeting. On May 11, 72 percent of the local's 234 members voted to walk out— unless one believes widespread rumours that the ballot boxes were stuffed or the counting was rigged. Given the number of CASAW members who later crossed the picket line but admit to having voted for a strike, vote tampering is unlikely. The rumours seem to have originated from discrepancies between the strike vote and an informal head count by the mine's shifters, who went around asking men how they intended to vote. This, like Witte's letter, fanned the fires of discontent with Royal Oak.

The strike vote taken, the worrying began that Royal Oak wasn't bluffing. Families estimated how long their savings would last, which bills could safely be left unpaid, which relatives could help out in a pinch. Some veteran, high-bonus miners had money in the bank or substantial stockholdings, but they were a minority. Many workers had cut their spending and saved what they could in case of a strike or lockout. Other families, many of them young, lived from month to month, just keeping up with high prices and their children's needs. June and Derek Roberts were typical of those up to their ears in bills. His job as a hoistman didn't come with a big production bonus. While the men cursed "Piggy" Witte and prayed for a miracle, June worried about the relationship between the union and the town. She'd gone to the grocery store and realized that she didn't know most of the people she saw. How would they react if there was a strike? What did they really know about mining? June had worked in government and knew that, although civil servants were unionized, they didn't necessarily sympathize with miners. Roberts started to think about what she could do to wake people up to events at Giant.

News of the Westray mine explosion on May 9 hit hard in Yellowknife. Twenty-six men died in the Nova Scotia colliery, and news reports alleged safety violations by Curragh Resources, headed by Giant's former chief executive, Clifford Frame. To the CASAW men who wondered if they should back down and agree to Royal Oak's terms, it was a cruel reminder of how jealously they needed to guard their safety on the job. CASAW made a donation to the families in Nova Scotia.

On May 15, federal Labour Minister Marcel Danis officially released Royal Oak and CASAW to take industrial action—a lockout or strike—as of May 23.

Meanwhile, Mike Werner had returned from Newfoundland, where he had prepared to reopen Royal Oak's new mine. On Saturday, May 16, someone alerted the fire department to a bomb in the company guest house where Werner and his family were staying. No bomb was found. The next day, Royal Oak's press release implied that CASAW was responsible. "There was speculation the bomb threats were linked to the contract deadline," the release read. Witte called it "cruel and cowardly." Union members speculated that the bomb threat was a hoax perpetrated by the company to discredit CASAW. Either way, the incident raised tensions in town, and the Royal Canadian Mounted Police were investigating it.

Despite the bomb scare, Werner tried to get a last-minute proposal from the union, at the same time he was preparing for a massive influx of replacement workers and setting up for a long siege. It appears that Werner and his second in command, Terry Byberg, were freelancing; they had no mandate from Witte to negotiate. All they could do was ask CASAW again for a proposal costing no more than the tentative agreement. Werner called Bruce Bannister and Harry Seeton to his office and asked what it would take to get an agreement. According to Seeton, Werner offered an extra day of safety inspections per month, if that would help. Seeton replied that, if the company wanted to talk, they should return to the bargaining table.

The RCMP were planning for more trouble. Superintendent Brian Watt warned Alberta's K Division on May 18 that a riot squad might be required in Yellowknife. "As it is the mine's intention to remain operating throughout a strike, the potential for violence is significant," Watt wrote. He asked the Department of National Defence (DND) to fly in the riot squad, if needed. DND's and K Division's plans were ready by May 21.

Alarm bells were finally ringing at the NWT government, which had no jurisdiction over labour relations. Justice Minister Dennis Patterson, a likeable and seasoned politician, was responsible for mine safety but knew little about labour issues. He supported antiscab legislation, not that it was a hot issue in his Iqaluit riding, 2,250 kilometres east. On May 21, Patterson was visited by Jim Evoy, president of the NWT Federation of Labour, and former CASAW president Dale Johnston. Patterson had tussled with both men before and respected them; they served on the Workers' Compensation Board, Patterson's responsibility. Evoy was blunt, but canny. He and Johnston had no official standing with CASAW, but likely had the union's pulse.

"I'm here because I'm worried," Evoy told Patterson. "If this thing goes ahead, I just got this feeling there's going to be people killed. I'm afraid of this thing."

Johnston stressed how important it was for the RCMP to handle the dispute sensitively, especially if Royal Oak scabbed the mine. He asked Patterson to bring in Sergeant Lynn Kraeling, the RCMP's only trained labour-liaison man in Canada. "I was glad to advance that [to the RCMP]," Patterson says. But he was struck by Johnston's description of Giant's environmental hazards. The tailings pond was full of toxic chemicals; the mill's roaster had outdated arsenic filters that required servicing by experienced workers. Patterson envisioned Yellowknife's water supply poisoned by a huge chemical spill, or an explosion at the propane tank farm.

The same day, Patterson met with Mike Werner, hoping to broker a last-minute deal between the two sides. Werner was contemptuous of the union and in no mood to compromise. "Having seen him on the heels of Dale Johnston, who was quiet but terrifying, I realized that this was going to be a horrible confrontation," Patterson says.

He did not trust Ottawa to do anything about it, and neither did his colleague, Mike Ballantyne, who was Speaker of the NWT legislature, the member representing Giant's riding, and a former Justice minister. Ballantyne had been a CASAW executive when he worked at Giant in the 1970s. Later, he was elected mayor, and then to the legislature, joining the Progressive Conservative party along the way. Ballantyne kept in touch with mining friends inside and outside the union, and what he heard scared him. He begged Bill Schram on May 21 to think twice about getting embroiled in a huge labour dispute.

Schram pleaded with the NWT government to pass antiscab legislation, banning the use of replacement workers during a strike or lockout, a matter within federal jurisdiction. "He didn't want to deal with the fact that we couldn't magically fix that problem. And he didn't want to listen," says Ballantyne.

CASAW had given notice of its intent to strike as soon as it was legally possible, on May 23. Even Bannister agreed that there was no choice, no other way to get Royal Oak to bargain again.

It was just above freezing when the day shift got to Giant on Friday morning, May 22. Most men were told to get their gear and leave. Royal Oak officials said they were afraid union members might sabotage equipment. As mechanic and mine-rescue captain Al Shearing prepared to leave, he was summoned to

Werner's office. Shearing deduced that Werner probably wanted to promote him to supervisor so he could cross the picket line. The company would need mechanics who knew the equipment, and a mine-rescue team. Shearing brought Seeton along as a shop steward. When they showed up, Werner told Seeton to leave. This wasn't a disciplinary meeting, so Shearing had no right to a steward. Shearing got up to leave too. Werner told Shearing he'd be fired for insubordination if he didn't stay; he left anyway. According to Shearing, Werner shouted down the corridor, "You're fired! You're fired! You're fired!"

Werner denies that he wanted to offer Shearing a staff job. He says Shearing had boasted to a secretary about vandalizing Giant property, and was going to warn against doing so.

News of Shearing's encounter spread quickly. The workers, not yet legally entitled to strike, protested outside Giant's gates. The federal conciliator told Werner a firing like that was the last thing anyone needed on the verge of a work stoppage.

But company envoys were already going to workers' houses with invitations to cross the picket line and work individually under the terms of the tentative agreement. A copy of it was provided. "You may notice small variations in your pay as the Company will not be deducting union dues," the letter slyly noted. Royal Oak was trying to unilaterally impose new terms of employment, and would send Schram an official lockout notice on May 23. A labour lawyer in Vancouver advised that Shearing's firing and the illegal lockout on May 22 were unfair labour practices, and that complaints should be filed with the Canada Labour Relations Board. In his opinion, Royal Oak could not legally refuse to deduct union dues. But CASAW was woefully unprepared to do battle at this level. Money was so tight that no action was taken.

Werner's phone practically bounced off his desk on May 22. Ballantyne was one of the callers. "Look, if you don't use replacement workers, I predict this strike will be over in three weeks or a month," Ballantyne told him. "[In this] economic climate, if you guys just play ball the normal way, you can settle this thing ... You bring in replacement workers, you're going to cause major problems."

It was too late. Strikebreakers were already on the property. The first nine contract workers from Procon Miners included two mechanics, four miners, and a hoistman. A security force from Ontario had also arrived.

The last, false glimmer of hope was a professional review of Giant's books by a prominent firm, which Royal Oak had allowed after some cajoling. The two sides disagree on why it took so long, but on May 22, hours before the strike deadline, CASAW national president Ross Slezak received the report, which warranted study. He hoped the old contract could be extended for a few days while the union examined the report. He called Bill Schram.

"Well, Ross, fuck the audit! We're going on strike and I got the press waiting for me." Slezak says that Schram then hung up. Slezak phoned back, chewed Schram out, and convinced him to ask Werner if the contract could be extended until Monday. Union executives supported the effort; the federal conciliator implored Werner to agree, in vain.

Werner's reply was that Witte would consider an extension only if union leaders agreed to another vote on the tentative agreement. The idea of revoting to satisfy Witte—"rolling the dice till you get to seven," as one union member put it—was unacceptable. The men who milled around the mine gate and assembled picket crews in the union hall downtown would be out for another eighteen months.

CHAPTER TWO

DRIVING THE WEDGE

I knew as soon as [Royal Oak] came in, what they wanted to accomplish. A rock fell down the shaft, it broke my shoulder blade. Fucking bone sticking out; I barely got up to surface. They were trying to say it happened uptown. Maybe because I worked in the shaft with Seeton and them for too long.

—skip tender Terry Coe, July 14, 1993

That sunny Friday afternoon, May 22, security guards hustled the second shift of workers from the mine as if they were bums crashing an elegant party. Guards with Cambrian Security of Sudbury, Ontario, barked orders at men who'd been at Giant for decades.

"Get the hell off the property. NOW!" the security chief shouted at one group. "Not now, RIGHT NOW!"

It was no use telling twenty-one security men, many of them looking fresh out of high school, that Royal Oak could not legally lock out the union before midnight. They had their orders.

CASAW's men were almost happy that the gloves were finally off. Royal Oak had killed any chance of a last-minute settlement. There was little debate about picketing tactics, because the men agreed that the mine should not be allowed to operate during the labour dispute. The only way to maintain real economic leverage was to seal off the mine—to stop strikebreakers and supplies from going in, and gold from coming out. Few men seemed worried that this was illegal and would cause friction with the police.

The mine's geography made it a challenging battleground (see map B). A public highway north from Yellowknife slaloms through the property, giving clear views of open pits, the mill, the smokestack, and headframes over vertical shafts that lead underground. The road passes the old recreation hall and bunkhouses, long since closed. Just behind them is the quaint little town site where Giant's managers live in houses overlooking Yellowknife Bay and where some men now on strike were raised as children.

To isolate the mine, CASAW had to watch at least eleven entrances to the property, which required pickets at seven or eight locations. For the moment, union men scrambled to set up effective picket lines. They'd already elected picket captains, and men had signed up for shifts on the line. But picket crews still needed to communicate with the union hall, 5 kilometres away. Since CB radios were useless in the hilly terrain, they had rented professional radio gear. In the tobacco smoke and commotion at the hall, men slapped together picket signs. Hundreds of people would drive by every day, going back and forth to lake-country cottages, picnic spots, and the community of Dettah.

Security was a nightmare for the company. The highway made it impossible to keep out intruders, especially those who knew their way around. In most areas, there wasn't even a fence. "Should the miners decide to destroy the mine," RCMP superintendent Brian Watt reported to Ottawa, "no specific number of tactical personnel will be able to protect the property."

By early evening, Giant's picket line was bustling. Bonfires and alcohol gave people warmth. Picket captains tried in vain to keep liquor off the line. It was the beginning of the dispute—the traditional time for rowdiness—and the first blush of spring added to the spirit. At this time of year, the night never really darkened beyond a bluish dusk. Most of the union's members were there, suddenly free, cruising along the road in pickup trucks, chatting with people they vaguely knew from other parts of the operation. Some of their families came too, showing support and making new acquaintances. Dozens of workers from Yellowknife's other mine, Con, helped their friends and had a bit of a party. There was a hard edge to much of the joking, the brotherly trading of insults mine workers seem to love. Some men wondered if they hadn't made the mistake of their lives by voting for a strike. But that feeling was mixed with relief, for now, from the grind of work. The men believed their cause was just, and that the town was sure to support them against an American absentee owner like Peggy Witte.

Excited reporters swarmed the picket line that night, sensing a big story, but unsure what it was. Union leaders were holed up downtown, getting organized, so journalists nabbed picketers almost at random. "How do I tell my daughter— it's her birthday on Monday and she's had her eye on a mountain bike—how do I tell her I can't afford it because some scab is taking my job?" asked an outraged welder. "Those scabs are going to have to go over me!" Journalists tried to get a crash course on two years of Giant's history, but each picketer seemed to have a different reason for being on strike. Baffled by the men's varying complaints about Royal Oak and the rejected tentative agreement, most reporters focused on the crowd's potential for violence and vandalism.

Some strikers did their best to meet reporters' expectations. Gordie Kendall, a hard-drinking, middle-aged miner, teed off sometime after midnight. With remarkable precision, he drove golf balls through the windows of Giant's main office. The guards were made to earn their keep in other ways as well, when strikers crept onto the property and surprised them. The guards were spread out all over the property, one to a pickup truck. Some were jolted by pranksters banging on their doors, while others had CASAW stickers plastered to their vehicles.

Night belonged to the picketers, but the next morning, May 23, Royal Oak demonstrated that it would own the day. Mine manager Mike Werner's top priority was to get the courts and the RCMP on the company's side. When the witching hour was over and picketers were thinking about breakfast, Werner loaded supervisors onto a rented school bus and sent it to Giant's main gate. The aim wasn't to get staffers home to sleep; CASAW had already agreed to let them walk through the line and take taxis to town. Werner admits that he wanted the strikers to block the bus and give him ammunition for a court injunction against picketing. Exhausted, and in some cases hungover, the men rose to the bait. "There are scabs on that bus!" several shouted. Gordie Kendall, still liquored up from the night before, threw himself in front of the bus and dared the driver to run him over.

Preventing someone from crossing a picket line is illegal. Kendall's stunt was all Royal Oak's lawyers needed to apply for a court order to limit picketing. Such "ex parte" injunctions are quickly obtained and temporary. The union generally has some time to impose discipline on picketers before having to appear in court. But in the Northwest Territories, judges and lawyers had little experience with labour disputes and had no local laws to complement the Canada Labour Code. With a local lawyer who was a novice on labour law, CASAW was at a disadvantage in fighting Royal Oak's tactics. The court order was issued on Sunday, the second day of the strike/lockout. The limit was set at just five picketers per gate; only CASAW members were allowed on the line, which theoretically barred spouses, sympathizers, and even reporters from being there; and Gate 4, the "muck crossing," was to be kept clear because ore trucks regularly cross the highway there, going from the open pits to the mill.

The court hadn't ordered enforcement of its injunction, however. Royal Oak could sue if picketers broke the rules, but it could not have them arrested. Police said they wouldn't be the mine's security force, patrolling the property and looking for trouble. They would only take and investigate complaints.

Royal Oak held a press conference on Saturday afternoon to push for tougher policing. Grim from lack of sleep, Werner painted a dark picture of lawlessness, of union thugs threatening "the lives and personal belongings of anyone doing business with the Giant mine or crossing the picket line." He pointed to broken windows in the mine's main office building, and spoke of golf balls and ball bearings whizzing by managers' heads in the night.

Werner presented the decision to hire strikebreakers as a last-ditch effort to avoid closure of the mine. It cost $500,000 a month to do maintenance and pump water out to prevent flooding, he said, and Royal Oak could not afford that if the mine did not generate revenue. "The president of the company is absolutely paranoid because I'm not producing gold today."

Known to be a very religious man, Werner said that he'd sworn to Harry Seeton on the Bible that there had never been any discussion on the Giant mine property of busting CASAW. The company was doing its best to avoid confrontations, he claimed. But, within hours, a helicopter made its first of many flights from Yellowknife's airport to Giant. The company would ferry in strikebreakers and supplies over the picketers' heads, if that's what it took.

Anger ate into the men as they thought about the money Royal Oak was spending on the chopper. How could Witte plead poverty? And what good was a picket line that couldn't stop helicopters? "That was the worst," says mechanic Terry Legge, a passionate union member from Labrador. "If I didn't have family, b'y, I'd be in jail today. I would have took that fucking chopper down myself. There was times that the only thing that stopped me is that I knew that there was staff on it, people that I cared about, and I didn't want to see them get hurt."

Early the next morning, a striker left a terse message with the president of the helicopter company: ground that chopper or lose it. It was the first of several warnings. Rumour has it that Royal Oak president Peggy Witte argued with her managers about whether to take the threats seriously. Witte won, and the helicopter kept flying, without the requested use of the RCMP/National Defence hangar as a secure loading point for strikebreakers.

In case the court order, public relations barrage, and helicopter weren't enough, Royal Oak made a sneak attack on CASAW's unity. The company had claimed for weeks that a minority of hard liners had stampeded the union rank and file into a strike. Now Werner and his second in command, Terry Byberg, set out to prove it by cultivating CASAW's moderates.

Strike opponents and supporters were still friends. People from both sides met on Saturday night, May 23, to celebrate a coworker's marriage. Videos from the reception show men who would soon be ready to fight each other joking nervously about who would be the first to "go scab."

One young miner and strike opponent, Chris Neill, went from the reception to the picket line. In a particularly rambunctious mood, Neill threw rocks at the guards and painted "Mikey [Werner] Sucks!" on the side of a big tank. Neill was like that. He tried to be friendly with everyone, to be one of the boys. He was a volunteer firefighter, and his easy manner made him popular at the fire hall. Some of the older men at Giant thought Neill was too cocky about his mining abilities, but liked him nonetheless.

The strike/lockout didn't fit into Neill's plans at all. His wife, Tracey, a secretary at the federal Department of Justice, didn't approve, especially when it came to vandalism and picket-line shenanigans. They'd been married only a year and a half and had a mortgage on a big new home in Frame Lake South. "Chris and Tracey were social butterflies," a friend says. Neill had always been eager to please his supervisors and work extra hours. So he was feeling sheepish about his outbreak of rowdiness when he bumped into manager Terry Byberg on the picket line a few hours later. They talked about the dispute, in a friendly way. Byberg had a more relaxed manner with the men than Werner did. He told Neill that contract negotiations weren't as blocked as the union executive let on, and that the company was willing to make changes in contract language. Neill may not have known, but Werner and Byberg had cast similar lines elsewhere.

Neill rushed to the union hall at about 6:30 A.M. with the news that Royal Oak was ready to talk, or at least Byberg was. Neill's friend Jim O'Neil, who had manned the radio and phones all night, was equally excited. But union executives said that if Witte wanted to talk, she knew how to contact the bargaining committee. Anything else was either freelancing by Byberg, or a tactic to split the union. They told O'Neil that Royal Oak was spreading rumours about the state of bargaining. That logic rang hollow to O'Neil, who had a simmering personal feud with CASAW vice president Harry Seeton. For their part, Seeton and some other leaders had already pegged O'Neil as a troublemaker who talked too much.

That evening, Neill and O'Neil decided to go it alone. After a series of phone calls, they had a two-hour conference call with Mike Werner and Terry Byberg. Neill and O'Neil had no mandate from the union, and Werner emphasized that he wasn't speaking for Royal Oak. But the four men went over a series of bargaining issues, with copies of the rejected tentative agreement in front of them. Werner listed some minor changes in contract language that he thought Peggy Witte might accept. There could be an extra day for safety inspections, for example.

"We feel we resolved the majority of language issues," O'Neil said the next day. Neill claimed that, if it wasn't for hard liners in the union executive, "we could be back to work tomorrow." Buoyed by their "breakthrough" and armed with detailed notes, Neill and O'Neil tried to find a union executive to talk to, but they were avoiding the union hall, and even their own homes, to escape being served with injunction papers. Bargaining committee chairman Bruce Bannister refused to meet with Neill and O'Neil, so they conferred with a disgruntled committee member instead.

The next morning, Neill and O'Neil took their campaign to the media. On the air at the town's most popular radio station, they accused union executives of lying about Royal Oak's position, and blamed union hard liners for the dispute. Then they sped to the CBC's headquarters. Neill was talking with a reporter when his portable radio scanner crackled with picketers' talk:

"What should we do?" one asked, according to a listener.

"Kill 'em, I guess," another replied casually.

A miner who heard the scanner exchange remembers it differently. "I heard one person say, 'Well, I'm going home to get my gun,' and another person say, 'I'm going uptown to look for him.' The two guys that said it never left the picket line. They knew Chris had a scanner."

Neill and O'Neil interpreted the message as a death threat, so CBC staff rushed them into a room that had a steel door. The two men called the police and Royal Oak's lawyer. Others (including O'Neil's wife, Jane) dismissed the radio comment as a figure of speech. Neill thought he recognized at least one of the voices. The RCMP took the complaint but never arrested anyone. However, the incident reinforced the impression in town that the strikers were hooligans. "From then on, we sat at home with loaded rifles," O'Neil says. "Day and night we waited for the guys to come. They never came, but I couldn't handle it anymore." At the RCMP's suggestion, he left town. He propelled his truck down the dusty highway south, a lonely road through a seemingly endless stand of spruce. "I've got a loaded rifle," he remembers. "I got tears in my eyes. I got to leave my town, my family, and my life because of what was happening at the mine."

Jane O'Neil stayed behind, since it was impractical to leave her government job. Jim felt ashamed that he had left his family alone, even though he'd done it on the RCMP's advice. At High Level, Alberta, he reported to the police station and bought a tiny trailer to live in. He was lonely and didn't find work. One day, he called a friend at Giant for the latest news. She was a nurse and had just stitched up an injured rottweiler, one of the guard dogs brought in by the security force. As she spoke, "she stayed back from a window because she could get hit by glass. There was a lot of rock throwing at the main gate. She said a prayer for me," O'Neil recalls. "And then I just said, 'Fuck it, I got to head back. I can't leave my family up there if that's what's going on.'" He returned to Yellowknife early in June.

RUMOURS OF WAR

Peggy is terrified ... Peggy Witte feels negotiations are over.

—Mayor Pat McMahon, May 26, 1992

They didn't need that riot squad. The riot squad blew this thing way out of proportion. While everyone's getting mad, no one is thinking of a settlement.

—Chris Neill, July 7, 1992

Two critical things happened while Neill and O'Neil were negotiating with Royal Oak.

First, the union women organized, quickly and effectively. They revived CLASS, the CASAW Ladies' Association Support System, founded during the 1980 strike. It was about the only morale booster for the strikers that first weekend. CLASS's first demonstration, on Sunday, May 24, was inspired by housewife June Roberts. She'd been unable to sleep much the previous night, so she jotted down her ideas. In the morning, she stirred the wives into action at CLASS's first meeting. They went home, made protest signs, and then met at a local Shell station, because the Shell bulk plant was rumoured to be supplying fuel to the mine. Next, they trooped to the Woolco store, then protested helicopter flights at the airport. About sixty women and children then marched on the mine, defying the newly imposed court injunction against sympathy picketing.

The march surprised the women themselves. Only hours earlier, few of them knew more than one or two of the other wives. Now they strode side by side with dozens of women, forming the quick, intense friendships of soldiers in battle. A radio reporter wandered up to June Roberts to get a quote on the demonstration. "It's a really nice, sunny day," he said. "Wouldn't you ladies rather be at home working in your garden?" It wasn't the question to ask Roberts, who would spend the next year living and breathing union politics.

The other major event of May 24 was the NWT government's support of a decision to summon more police. Panic had seized local politicians. At the centre of it all was Justice Minister Dennis Patterson, briefed by Superintendent Brian Watt, head of the local RCMP force and a veteran of the armed standoff between police and the Mohawk people of Oka, Quebec, two years earlier. Watt said that the twenty-four local officers could not handle serious trouble on the picket line, that police were staying neutral and trying to preserve calm. But he also had alarming intelligence reports about strikers' plans, Patterson says. Watt spoke of "caches of high-powered rifles" to shoot down helicopters, and "arms and dynamite ... They were quite sure that they were planning to use them. [The RCMP] were confident about their information, from various sources, which included someone in the force who had a friend who worked in the mine or was in the mill or was a striker." It appeared that the RCMP already had informants.

Watt's entreaty for more police came as Werner, Byberg, and Peggy Witte lobbied politicians to deter "union lawlessness." At 2:45 A.M. on Sunday, May 24, Byberg had called Patterson and chewed him out about police inaction. "Can it wait till morning?" Patterson asked. He says the reply was "They would be on our ass—where is the fucking law in this country?"[1] Royal Oak soon made similar complaints to a Justice Department lawyer, who informed Watt. He instructed the lawyer to tell Royal Oak that "we are taking action, but [we are] not prepared to confront the union until sufficient resources [are] available ... If we step in, there will be violence." At the same time, Watt stated in an internal memo that the RCMP would be "as nonconfrontational as possible," but, "as the mine is adamant about continuing to operate and to confront the union at any opportunity, we are likely going to be forced into a large-scale arrest and confrontation with 250 local union workers."

That afternoon, Patterson asked the RCMP in Ottawa to send emergency reinforcements for the Giant dispute. Although the NWT government would be expected to pay for the extra officers, the RCMP were not accountable to the territorial Justice minister. Under the territorial policing contract, the RCMP have full authority to decide what they need and what action to take. While Patterson was roundly criticized by the union, the RCMP told the media that calling in a riot squad was Superintendent Watt's decision, and Watt's notes show that was his plan if the injunction was not obeyed. Later, Patterson's deputy minister said the decision was made by the attorney general of Canada.

Watt's ploy was reminiscent of the time when the Northwest Territories was governed by the RCMP rather than by an elected body. The police's apparent treatment of the union as a criminal conspiracy or front for terrorists rated with the court's injunction against picketing as one of the most important decisions of the entire labour dispute—after Royal Oak's to use strikebreakers.

The incident that triggered Patterson's call for additional police, according to senior government officials, was a picket-line scuffle involving Mike Magrum, the president of the NWT Chamber of Mines. He is a likeable fellow who counts a cabinet minister in the NWT legislature among his longtime friends. But Magrum's dislike for CASAW dated to the 1980 strike, and he seemed to revel in provoking the strikers. He scooted his pickup truck around pickets at the main gate on Sunday, onto mine property. When Magrum tried to drive out a few hours later, the strikers blocked him. It was lunchtime, so Magrum ordered chicken from a take-out restaurant and walked across the line to get it when it was delivered to the main gate. As he sat in his truck, munching his food, strikers screamed "Scab!" through his window. When reporters asked, Magrum said he had business to do at the mine, and he was legally entitled to come and go as he pleased.

Jim Evoy, the tough-talking president of the NWT Federation of Labour, showed up on the picket line about then. CASAW wasn't a member of the federation, but Evoy supported the union. He was furious with Magrum.

"You fat cocksucker!" Evoy hissed. Magrum, never a fan of Evoy's, drawled, "Well, if it isn't the eloquent and outspoken president of the Federation of Labour."

Later that afternoon, Magrum tried again to leave Giant, this time backed up by security trucks. As he advanced into the crowd, three picketers fell in front of his pickup, having been hit. The union called ambulances; the three were soon released from the hospital. Meanwhile, a picketer sprayed oil on Magrum's windshield. Another smacked him through his open side window. Magrum retreated, abandoned his pickup, and left by helicopter. Assault charges were later filed against three picketers and the wife of one of them. In a press release, Evoy accused Magrum of deliberately trying to provoke violence on the line.

The Magrum incident caused fewer injuries than many a bar fight at the Gold Range, but it convinced Patterson that violence could erupt and extra police were needed. "I thought that people would be killed otherwise," he says.

Royal Oak enlisted Ottawa's help in obtaining assistance from the RCMP. A complaint was registered with Solicitor General Doug Lewis early on May 25. Superintendent Watt summoned the riot squad at 2:45 P.M.

On the morning of May 26, a military Hercules aircraft squatted on the runway of Edmonton's municipal airport. It was loaded to the gunwales with clothing, combat boots, riot helmets and shields, billy clubs, M-16 automatic rifles, smaller semiautomatic rifles, and two megaphones, waiting for an RCMP "tactical team," or riot squad, and its companion "emergency response team" (ERT) to arrive. About seventy men streamed in from various detachments in central Alberta.

The operations commander was Inspector Dennis Massey, forty-three, a lanky career officer and natural glad-hander. He was a firearms expert whose burning interest in guns was manifested in an amazing personal collection. It was a passion he shared with numerous CASAW members, but few, if any, could boast an arsenal like Massey's. He had moved to Red Deer in 1990 after a fourteen-year stint in British Columbia, where some officers considered him flamboyant and egotistical. In thirteen years with the drug squad, he did multikilo drug deals as an undercover man, and his international assignments included investigating a Colombian cocaine cartel. He spent nine months masquerading as a heroine addict in Regina, sporting a goatee and hair to his waist, but now his thatch was thin, with an unruly shock atop his round face. He'd handled security for visiting dignitaries, from Rajiv Gandhi to Dolly Parton. He was also trained in disarming explosives and had received many commendations. The CASAW men didn't know all this, but soon nicknamed him John Wayne.

Massey had met the officer in charge of the emergency response team while they were stationed at Oka with about 100 other officers from Alberta and British Columbia. The ten-man ERT included a communications man, snipers, and an assault team, experienced in hostage takings, barricadings, airplane hijackings, and emergency security for large sporting events. They had not been trained for, or deployed during a labour dispute, except for the assault-team leader, who had patrolled an Alberta oil-sands property with a shotgun.

Superintendent Brian Watt briefed Massey on arrival. Besides commanding the ERT and tactical troop, "I don't believe I was given any role—I ended up with it by default," Massey says. Within hours, he was the RCMP's main man on the picket line.

The arrival of the RCMP's elite force caught CASAW by surprise. "This isn't a war," President Bill Schram complained to reporters. But few people in town realized that a paramilitary force was amassed at the National Defence hangar at Yellowknife airport, watching intelligence videos of the mine shot from Royal Oak's helicopter.

Royal Oak took the RCMP's arrival as a license to test the picket line again. Mine manager Mike Werner had failed to get a transport truck through the line on Monday, even though he'd waded into a crowd of angry picketers. The next day, May 26, he had company lawyers contact the NWT government to ask for the RCMP's help to move a truck onto the mine property. The government's reply is unknown, but the police refused. Werner then tried a ruse. He used his supervisors, loaded on a school bus and eager to go home for a break, as a diversion. The bus advanced slowly toward the main gate. Picketers hurried to block it, redoubling their insults every time the bus driver inched forward. But it looked like the bus would be allowed to pass. Then a tractor trailer barreled around the corner, between a line of cars and people along the edge of the narrow road. The truck raced onto Giant property through Gate 4 before anybody realized what was going on.

"Scabs!" howled the large crowd at the main gate. Forcing the bus back, a striker hit the windshield with a two-by-four. Filmed by a CBC camera crew, the image became one of the most widely shown "Kodak moments" of the dispute. A group of picketers hurried to Gate 4, the muck crossing.

The attack on the bus probably wasn't started by a CASAW member. A former miner and Steelworkers' president from Con mine, Bob Robertson, then a service officer with the Union of Northern Workers, claims that he was responsible. "I had six beers in my belt. I was feeling no pain and I said, 'OK, you guys, you want to see some leadership—this is how Steelworkers strike.' I went up to the bus, and started ripping off these Plexiglas shields. It was just like the spark that hit the powder keg ... I was being provocative, and I was doing it deliberately." This incident and others reinforced CASAW executives' fears that no one could be trusted. The line became blurred between support and foolish, perhaps intentional, meddling.

Meanwhile, about 200 metres down the highway, a striker's brother jumped in his pickup and followed the tractor trailer onto the property. In the ensuing confusion, he rammed a security truck, injuring Cambrian's head of security, Bill Tolmie. The pickup's driver tried to run away, hobbling badly from a leg injury. By one account, he was actually run over by a security truck.

Then a vehicle backfired and everyone wondered if it was a gunshot. Whoever called for Tolmie's ambulance mentioned this, although most people had already identified the source. The crowd, probably fifty-strong, streamed into the company parking lot, up to the inner fence. "No sticks!" someone yelled. "Just peacefully! No sticks!" Inspector Dennis Massey was at the inner gate to stop them. A few people threw rocks at the Giant office. Others demanded to inspect the tractor trailer, suspecting scabs had been smuggled in.

Massey was one of only a few police officers on the scene. He was nose to nose with shouting picketers, but stayed calm. He decided to let two or three picketers check the trailer, but Royal Oak refused to let him on the property. So he snapped the lock on the gate with bolt cutters and opened it a crack. Several men slipped in, with reporters on their heels. The trailer doors were flung open, revealing a load of mattresses for supervisors and strikebreakers confined to the Giant property. It was also learned that the truck belonged to Mike Magrum, who rode in the passenger seat.

One or two strikers got into C-dry, the mine's locker room area, and sprayed it with chemical fire extinguishers. But Massey, remarkably cool, talked everyone into leaving since no strikebreakers had been found.

Then the CLASS women arrived, many near tears, demanding to know who had been shot, whose husband was dead. "Dead?" everyone asked.

"We heard it on the radio," the women cried. "Somebody's been shot out at Giant."

The call for an ambulance and report of the backfire had been heard by the fire department, and someone had given the message to a popular private radio station. The news director, about to read a newscast, ran the story: "There are unconfirmed reports that a man has been shot at Giant mine." Women attending a CLASS meeting heard the item and rushed to the mine, only to be frustrated by a roadblock set up by the RCMP to prevent traffic heading toward Giant. There were scuffles as anxious and angry wives tried to get through. One was thrown to the ground by a policeman and later taken to hospital in an ambulance, crying, bruised, and probably suffering from shock. After a few minutes, the police let the women through.

Massey's apparent calm was deceiving; he was angry. "That truck almost ran over and injured people. It was a setup, we were set up," he fumed later, claiming that he knew Mike Werner was responsible. Mike Magrum and the man who drove the tractor trailer later had a heated encounter with Massey, who suggested they might end up with a bullet through their windshield if they ever repeated the stunt.

The tractor-trailer incident was the end of the evening for most people at the mine's gates. However, for those inside, it was just the beginning. Picketers didn't know that security chief Bill Tolmie's injury was the last straw for Cambrian Security. The guards told Mike Werner they were quitting, effective immediately. A guard had been assaulted the previous day, ball bearings and rocks had been fired at them, and their boss was in the hospital. Royal Oak wanted them to carry guns, Cambrian claimed later. Cambrian's men didn't want to get killed, so Royal Oak had no security force. But the guards had a problem—they couldn't get off the property.

Until then, most people inside the picket line weren't really frightened. There were tense moments, and picketers did their best (and were effective, using a megaphone and an air horn) to keep everyone awake at night. But supervisors felt disbelief and frustration more than fear. They'd known these workers for years, shared beers and personal problems with them. And the union men had always told them they wouldn't bother supervisors, just strikebreakers and union members who "scabbed." Yet when the supervisors got on the bus to go home, picketers wouldn't let them pass. Shifters were sometimes allowed to walk through the line to get taxis, but not always, since picketers wanted to keep the helicopter crowded. Most staffers had to wait days for a helicopter ride, sleeping in the town site or the office building, in violation of fire regulations.

When Cambrian quit, Werner says he was tempted to follow suit. He ordered everyone into C-dry. They barred the doors, armed themselves with clubs, and hoped for the best. "That night we were anticipating being overrun; we were going to beat the crap out of anybody that came in. Frankly, we anticipated they'd burn the whole property down and we were looking at the insurance," Werner says.

A few fires had been set, most of them harmless brush fires. The previous night, two strikers had torched a shed in an isolated area. This night they set fire to two buildings. One was quickly extinguished, but the other was in a shed next to the arsenic plant and no one was sure of the consequences if it spread. The fire department turned out in force, including two CASAW members, Chris Neill and Steve Moss, both of whom were volunteer firefighters. News of the fires spread panic among managers' spouses and off-duty employees who lived in the town site. Some thought that Giant's mill was burning, and that the rowdy picketers might be dangerous. "I stayed up till five o'clock in the morning," says Kim Cornwell, the manager of human resources, "in bed with my clothes on, shaking, with a flashlight in my hand and wondering if someone was going to come through the door and do damage to me or my house. I've never been that afraid in my life."

Werner and Byberg drove over to close one of the gates after the fire trucks left. An angry picketer smashed a large rock through their truck window. They were frightened but unhurt. Amazingly, none of the strikers discovered that Cambrian had quit, and calm returned by sunrise.

Calm did not prevail behind the scenes. While Royal Oak told the NWT government that there would be no negotiations with CASAW, Peggy Witte urged Yellowknife's mayor, Pat McMahon, to declare a state of emergency. In a May 27 meeting with NWT cabinet ministers, McMahon prodded Superintendent Watt to get the police to Giant, predicting the situation would blow up. "What will provoke the RCMP to act?" she asked. McMahon discussed invoking the riot act with Watt, which would have put the RCMP in a position to take drastic action. In his notes about the conversation, Watt wrote: "only solution, tanks running miners out of [the] mine," which may have been Witte's advice. Tanks had been brought in at an infamous Arizona strike against copper giant Phelps Dodge in 1983.

The evening of havoc at Giant and Cambrian's defection finally got the town's attention. Angry picketers weren't uncommon on TV, but blocking roads, setting fires, rumours of gunshots—that was outrageous. As in most small towns, rumour was as important as news. A notorious one concerned the children of managers who lived at the mine's town site. They took a bus to school in town every day. Picketers checked the bus for strikebreakers as it came and went from Giant. Not surprisingly, some children were scared by scruffy-looking men boarding the bus. Several mothers complained to aldermen or reporters. Royal Oak had rented another yellow school bus for supervisors and, CASAW men suspected, strikebreakers. This was the bus they shouted at and attacked with sticks. But the term "school bus" stuck in people's minds, and soon rumour had it that union thugs were terrifying schoolchildren and attacking their bus.

Another strange story circulated about this time, especially among civil servants. People claimed to have seen some union men spending money on big-ticket items like motorboats. It was perhaps simply an expression of resentment that some miners earned more than they did. Some saw the strike as a sign of arrogance.

Not that the town was wildly anti-CASAW. Other mine workers supported them. Most other residents adopted a "pox on both your houses" attitude, annoyed about the inconveniences the dispute caused. They wanted the government to stop the nonsense.

The NWT government responded quickly. A review of the city's economy showed that, if the mine closed, "the viability of Yellowknife" was at stake, a cabinet official said. Without so much as a phone call to federal officials—even to Labour Canada—acting premier John Pollard (Nellie Cournoyea was hunting near Tuktoyaktuk) made a three point public proposal to the two sides:

1. The Giant town site—the staff housing—would be declared a neutral area and patrolled by RCMP.

2. Royal Oak would remove all replacement workers.

3. A new mediator would be appointed and bargaining resumed.

It was a naive proposal, asking Royal Oak to give up its biggest bargaining chip—strikebreakers—in return for an end to harassment of managers' children that had been exaggerated by the rumour mill.

CASAW accepted, but suspected the NWT government of using the plan to buy peace on the picket line so that imported policemen and Royal Oak security could get their bearings. The government's envoy to the union, Yellowknife North MLA Mike Ballantyne, was not well trusted, even as a former CASAW executive, because he was also known to be very friendly with deputies in the Justice Department and high-level RCMP officers. He argued with unionists for hours, urging them to give the government a chance to work for a backroom solution to the dispute. Or, he warned, "if you blow it on the line, we're out— we'll visit you all in jail."

Peggy Witte flatly rejected Pollard's plan and demanded to know why the RCMP wasn't enforcing the court's restrictions on picketing. "They are certainly not here to be a security force for the mine," Pollard retorted. The important thing is to get bargaining back on track, he said.

There would be no negotiation with the union, Witte said, whether there's a new mediator or not, unless CASAW sent her a proposal that was endorsed by its membership and cost no more than the rejected tentative agreement.

Pollard hinted the government might use the Mine Safety Act to shut Giant down. Government mine inspectors were recommending closure at the time. They had little confidence that the mine could be run safely in these conditions with inexperienced workers and overworked managers. "Given the inability of Royal Oak to maintain security of the mine site, the next act of vandalism could result in fatalities," three safety officials warned their deputy minister on May 27.

"So you're willing to close us down for infractions against the Mine Safety Act, but you're not willing to request the RCMP to enforce the injunction?" Witte responded. Then she threatened a lawsuit.

The Pollard plan was dead. Witte could afford to snub Pollard. His government had no jurisdiction over labour relations, and the company was radically altering the balance of power at the mine by moving in more strikebreakers and security from Pinkerton's of Canada.

Royal Oak's choice of security firms was intriguing. Cambrian's claim to fame in mining was its handling of the 1990 strike by the Steelworkers at Dome mine in Timmins, Ontario. That strike lasted nearly six months, ending in almost total victory for Placer Dome. The Dome strike featured an alleged bombing plot and an arson attack, but Cambrian had kept control. Royal Oak managers had studied the Dome dispute and seemed to think Giant's would take a similar course.

The choice of Pinkerton's (over a firm associated with the Outlaws motorcycle gang in Ontario, according to a police source) was also significant. Pinkerton's Detective Agency had achieved fame as the most notorious professional union buster of the nineteenth and early twentieth centuries. Those who were familiar with labour history, and several strikers were, knew Pinkerton's primarily from the Molly Maguires episode of the 1870s, when Pinkerton's crushed unionism in Pennsylvania coal mines, and nineteen Irish-American union activists were hanged on what some historians insist were trumped-up charges. Pinkerton's claimed to have unearthed a secret terrorist organization of Irish immigrants called the Molly Maguires, said to be behind a series of coal-mine strikes. Labour supporters and Irish groups countered that the Molly Maguires were an invention of Pinkerton's, designed to play on then-widespread prejudices against the Irish.

Officially, Pinkerton's got out of muscular union busting before the industry was banned in the United States in the 1930s. It has about 5,000 employees in Canada and 50,000 worldwide, doing business totaling about $750 million US a year. CASAW had little information and assumed they were dealing with union busters. The presence of Americans among the Pinkerton's men did not ease CASAW's fears.

When Royal Oak hired Pinkerton's, assisting with the deal was William Sheridan, a partner in the prominent Toronto law firm Lang Michener and a corporate director of both Royal Oak and Pinkerton's. The decision to replace

Cambrian was made before the firm officially withdrew, Mike Werner asserts. The Pinkerton's advance team was briefed by Royal Oak management on May 26 at an Edmonton hotel teeming with strikebreakers signed up to work at Giant.

PINK AND BLUE

> *Yellowknife was the perfect setting for this dispute ... All of us are pawns in an awful big and deadly game.*
>
> —Jim O'Neil, February 4, 1994

> *It is anticipated that through close hands-on contact* [sic] *this matter can be resolved with the minimal amount of resources being expended to gain the maximum possible impact.*
>
> —Inspectors Dennis Massey and George Shillaker,
> "Conclusion" of Project Tundra, May 27, 1992

A helicopter zipped from Yellowknife's airport through thick fog to Giant mine on the morning of May 27, its blades stirring up brown dust as it came to earth. A Pinkerton's boss stepped away from the chopper with a determined hunch. "The first six guys were over 6 foot tall and over 200 pounds," Mike Werner recalls. "[There] had been all kinds of violence thrown our way and, nothing given in return ... And here's some people that were professionally capable of taking prisoners. We were going to make citizens' arrests. Yeah, that was a bright day."

Chris Morton, head of labour disputes and investigations at Pinkerton's Toronto office, assessed what security was needed "to effectively do the strike." He says he reported directly to the head office in Montreal. His partner, Major Ralph Sinke, was imported from the company's world headquarters in Los Angeles. With his bald head and bulging muscles, Sinke is hard to miss. He'd joined the US Marine Corps in 1966, was awarded five Purple Hearts during the Vietnam War, and became an adviser to the Vietnamese Army in 1968, receiving the Viet Cross of Gallantry, and, later, two presidential citations. Sinke glories in his military past and his days as a professional football player. He also writes poetry, styled after Robert Service and Rudyard Kipling.

Pinkerton's brought a paramilitary approach to patrolling the property, using video cameras, motion detectors, and infrared binoculars at night. They had a kennel full of German shepherds and rottweilers. "We have special teams" for labour disputes, explains Paul St. Amour, CEO of Pinkerton's of Canada. "They are either ex-police officers or have some training. There are many skills required—mostly being able to keep a cool head and handle discipline."

CASAW men soon complained that the Pinkerton's guards provoked incidents on the picket line by throwing rocks and shouting insults, and that they followed strikers around town. The union regularly complained to the RCMP about the guards, but charges were rarely laid. The RCMP understood the problem. Superintendent Watt would soon report to Ottawa that "[Witte] is intent on provoking the union," and he implored Royal Oak "not to take any action which will provoke the union and limit the chance for a successful settlement" of the labour dispute. Cambrian Security also warned the RCMP that the Pinkerton's men would stir up trouble.

As the Pinkerton's team arrived, the head of the RCMP reinforcements, Dennis Massey, wrote an operational plan titled "Project Tundra" for round-the-clock policing of the labour dispute—and preparing for a major clash at the mine. A command post was set up at RCMP headquarters. A communications van equipped with scanners monitored picketers' radio frequencies; Massey said later that the Pinkerton's radios were also monitored. Records were kept, intelligence reports were produced, and Massey was briefed daily, at least. Nine "voice privacy" radios were used for critical RCMP communications. Massey devoted himself to Project Tundra, working sixteen to twenty hours a day for twenty-four days, and driving 4,000 kilometres within the environs of Yellowknife.

The RCMP continued to tell the public that policing of the dispute was strictly neutral. Yet, at public hearings in February 1995, Massey stated that Pinkerton's "had direct access to the communication post we had set up ... [They] knew what our capability was. They were given intelligence for what was going on, and the potential for threat against them."

In Stage V of Project Tundra, Massey described the use of the riot squad and emergency response team. Four vehicles would block the highway north and south of Giant mine. "Four ERT snipers [on the hills across from the main mine gate will] provide high ground support," he wrote. "All radio transmissions of the strikers involved will be jammed to prevent support personnel being advised to proceed to the strike area."

With Massey in charge, the RCMP acted as security for Royal Oak, though emphatic public denials continued. On the afternoon of May 28, the day after the first Pinkerton's men arrived, "the ERT provided escort/security for [a] busload of replacement workers who were being dropped off throughout Yellowknife—they were being followed and harassed by strikers," according to a police report.

Watt laid all the cards on the table for his superiors in Ottawa on May 29. "It is quite evident the Company seems intent on breaking the Union ... These actions only incite the Union, as they are adamant they will not turn their jobs over to anyone else. They have openly stated that the Mine will be destroyed if they lose their jobs," he wrote in an encrypted fax message.

Records obtained under the Access to Information Act did not include a reply to Watt's fax, but the next morning at 3:50 A.M., armed ERT officers took off for a rendezvous about 300 kilometres southwest of Yellowknife. The RCMP plane landed on the public highway so the ERT could escort a busload of replacement workers to a gravel pit near Yellowknife. Police then "provided security while replacement workers were shuttled to [the] mine site via helicopter," RCMP documents say.

Dennis Patterson, the territorial justice minister who endorsed Watt's order for extra police, says he was not told that the RCMP escorted strikebreakers. The reporting mechanisms set up in Project Tundra covered the riot troop, but not the ERT, thus enabling the latter to be deployed secretly.

Inspector Massey wasn't content with shuttling strikebreakers and planning to suppress riots. He also tried his hand at mediation. Dressed in his dark ERT uniform, a 9mm pistol in his holster, he went to the union hall with another officer. It was a rare quiet hour in the hall. Massey stopped about halfway between the door and a desk where Secretary-Treasurer Bob Kosta was learning the union's first computerized accounting system. One can only guess what Massey thought of Kosta, whose dark, tight curls and thick beard lent him a revolutionary look. Kosta thought he must have slipped into a movie as he peered up at Massey, who had his hands on his hips.

"What will it take to settle this strike?" Massey asked.

"This," interjected a striker, walking toward Massey and waving a green pocket version of the expired contract.

Kosta explained a few issues, emphasizing that the union wasn't looking for a wage increase. "But you can't settle this," he told Massey. "You're not the mediator."

Nonetheless, the RCMP began to report the two sides' bargaining positions to territorial cabinet ministers, informing them that the company was conciliatory to the union, except for twenty or thirty people. "No one who has been out there ranting and raving and doing damage will ever work at Giant again," reported Superintendent Watt. The politicians told him, "If you can find out what it takes, then go for it." In the panic that had gripped government, the ministers seemed to have forgotten all about Labour Canada. CASAW was beleaguered and disorganized, but street sense told them that the RCMP was in charge, along with Peggy Witte.

Mine manager Mike Werner was showing signs of strain by Saturday, May 30—or maybe he was especially cocky, since the ranks of strikebreakers had grown by thirty-seven men overnight and the Pinkerton's force was up to about forty-five men. Werner got into a rock fight with picketers that morning and was spotted by a reporter. Massey said later that Werner came close to being arrested. Werner refuses to talk about the incident, but Royal Oak quickly dispatched him to its mine in Newfoundland. Terry Byberg took over as mine manager in Yellowknife. Between Werner, Massey and his troops, the Pinkerton's team, the helicopter, all the strikebreakers who had arrived at Giant that week, the Pollard plan, the media, and picket duty, CASAW's rank and file had little chance to think about bargaining. CASAW national president Ross Slezak flew in from British Columbia to persuade them to make concessions to Royal Oak. He got a nasty shock when his talk of compromise was met with scorn at a union meeting held at the local cinema on Saturday, May 30. The men were alternately furious with Peggy Witte and the "scabs" and desperate over the union's inability to control the situation.

At the end of the meeting, former union president Dale Johnston stood up to ask for volunteers. According to witnesses, he wanted single men "willing to wear helmets and carry baseball bats." Nobody explained what Johnston was up to, and Slezak didn't want to know. Slezak says he chewed out the executive for letting Johnston, who didn't hold elected office, play such a big role in the dispute. The executive, still angry at Slezak for his role in the tentative agreement, told him to keep out of local affairs. Slezak was barely able to get permission to visit Witte in Vancouver, and it was to be granted only if he told Royal Oak that CASAW wouldn't negotiate until the strikebreakers were removed—a foolish precondition.

The police probably heard almost immediately about Johnston's strange request, which could only have reinforced their belief that picketers were dangerous. That belief almost got someone killed two days later, on June 1. The picket captain for the afternoon shift was Blaine Lisoway, a diamond driller from Saskatchewan who had moved frequently as a contract miner before taking a permanent job at Giant a year earlier. It was overcast, the temperature was falling, and it looked like rain. Picket schedules were still rather loose, so Lisoway hung around after his shift to make sure each gate was manned.

It promised to be a miserable night, and unusually dark; after a busy weekend, the turnout was thin. James Mager, a hot-blooded, wiry trammer—a man who loaded and ran underground ore trains—showed up with a bottle of rum. Sometime before midnight, he and Lisoway checked into a small tent at Gate 5, nearest the mill, to warm up with a toddy or two and escape sporadic drizzle and rain.

Some Pinkerton's men, clad in dark blue coveralls, ambled over to Gate 5 and talked in the shadows of the mill, flying the flag in front of the CASAW "boys." Meanwhile, security manager Chris Morton rode around in a pickup truck with a senior Royal Oak official. They stopped near the mill stack (see map C).

Mager emerged from the tent at Gate 5. Someone split wood and stoked the bonfire. Mager looked over the pile of muck, waste rock, that spanned the fence between the picket line and the property, and saw Pinkerton's guards lurking in the shadows. "Why the hell don't you go home?" he bellowed. "Why are you here protecting these scabs and letting her pull this shit off?" Getting no response, he strolled to the woodpile, picked up an axe, and clambered over the muck pile onto the property. Both Pinkerton's guards and union witnesses say Mager was drunk; he insists he wasn't.

Lisoway watched uneasily as his comrade approached a guard who was accompanied by a dog. Lisoway shouted at the Pinkerton's men through the rain to let Mager talk himself out. It almost happened, but Pinkerton's boss Chris Morton decided to talk to Mager. "For every step I move toward this guy, take a step back," Morton ordered his guards. Ignoring his order, they advanced behind him. In front of Morton and Mager, a group of strikers stood on the rock pile; a few were on the property. "Get back!" Morton commanded his men. "Go over by the shed. Don't let anybody come up behind us." Two dog handlers went that way with their animals.

Lisoway got the shock of his life when he saw them "sneaking up around the building, to try to get in behind [Mager] ... So I walk off the picket line with a pickax handle. The next thing I know three guys come running around the corner, shooting and screaming, and one sticks a gun in my face."

Morton says he was equally surprised. "My first thought was, it must be my staff," he said later. "My concern was, what were they doing?" But the three armed men were policemen from the ERT, and one was Inspector Dennis Massey. Wearing combat pants and dark jackets, they were hard to distinguish from the guards. They'd come because the Pinkerton's guards had reported that four men with axes were on a rampage, destroying property in the mill area. Massey says he happened to be driving by with another officer when the complaint was made, but logs from the RCMP's command centre state that calls came from both the mine "and our members," and Massey told Watt that the "ERT team had been requested to respond."

The RCMP were met with a barrage of rocks from the picketers. "One whistled by my head," says Constable Amrik Virk. In a split second, he saw twenty or more shadowy figures, some armed with sticks or clubs. "I saw the glint of the ax [in Mager's hands]," he said.

The officers say they shouted "POLICE!," but most people, including Morton, say they didn't hear it. Virk and another constable, David Joyes, fired seven quick shots from their semiautomatic pistols. The strikers turned and fled to the muck pile.

"Drop the fucking ax before we both get shot!" Morton hissed to Mager, who obeyed.

Constable Virk had his gun aimed at Lisoway's face and was squeezing the trigger. "Stay back or I will shoot you!" Virk says that Lisoway stepped back, screaming, "'Go ahead and shoot me!' It was rage, an incredible amount of rage in that face. He kept his eyes on me."

Lisoway says that Virk then panned his weapon across a group of picketers nearby. Seeing his chance, Lisoway thumped Virk below his gun arm with the ax handle and scampered back to the muck pile. "I thought he was going to shoot me." But Virk insists that he was hit from behind. He says he slumped, then turned his gun on Lisoway, who was ready to strike again. But Lisoway backed off as commanded. Wherever the blow came from, Virk was in excruciating pain.

Someone yelled, "It's the cops, let's get the fuck out of here!" Morton says.

Meanwhile, Massey and Joyes had each forced a striker to the ground. Joyes had pounced on James McAvoy, who "calmed right down" when told that Joyes was RCMP. According to Joyes, he'll never forget what McAvoy said, interpreting it to mean that the strikers had planned the melee: "My wife told me not to come to this thing tonight, because I can't run and I can't fight."

Lisoway slipped into the crowd of strikers at the muck pile, with Virk right behind, panning his pistol. "His eyes were bulged out" and the veins of his neck stuck out, Lisoway says.

"Back off! Back off, back off!" Virk screamed, his finger on the trigger of his gun. People backed off. Then the ERT's sharpshooters arrived, carrying M-16s and semiautomatic rifles. Strikers and their supporters drifted away.

Lisoway, charged with assault with a weapon, was found not guilty in December 1993 after pleading self-defence.[2] Almost none of the story became public at the time; reporters did not know that the ERT had been deployed, only that warning shots had been fired. The RCMP's press release reinforced the impression that the union was out of control. The union interpreted the incident as proof that the RCMP and the Pinkerton's were working hand in glove, or that guards were armed and masquerading as police. The rising number of police and security guards heightened tensions on the picket line and made confrontation likely, perhaps inevitable. Pinkerton's manager, Chris Morton, observed that "we had no physical confrontations" during the previous week because only a handful of guards had arrived.

The RCMP seem not to regret their handling of the incident. Massey says he, too, believes it was a setup, but by union members.

Though no one had been killed, everyone was convinced that the other side was armed and dangerous. Superintendent Watt informed Ottawa that "the local union executive has no effective control over a substantial number of their workers, several of which are involved in sabotage and arson." Later that day, the RCMP received an anonymous, emotional call from a woman who said that, at a private meeting between Con and Giant workers on June 1, it had been decided that Giant mine would be blown up if unionized workers didn't get their jobs back. A similar, calmer call had been made at 1:45 A.M., Watt heard in a meeting with the mayor and cabinet officials. The threats were investigated, and Royal Oak was warned.

MUSCLES, NOT EARS

I had a chance to spend a couple of hours with our replacement workers ... [They] gathered around me and thanked Royal Oak for the opportunity to have a job. All these replacement workers are working for less money than CASAW Local 4 members received in their old contract. I saw a group of people which included eighty of our staff members, a catering crew, a helicopter pilot, a security force, and a group of replacement miners and mill workers working together, shoulder to shoulder, to keep the tired, old Giant mine a mainstay of the Yellowknife community.

—Peggy Witte, to *yellowknifer*, circa June 8, 1992

Despite the confusion and panic that gripped Yellowknife, a few people remembered that this was a labour dispute that should be resolved by negotiation. Under tremendous pressure to do something, CASAW local president Bill Schram wrote to federal Labour Minister Marcel Danis, asking for a mediator. Territorial ministers phoned Danis with pleas for quick action.

Danis appointed Bill Lewis, an experienced federal mediator from British Columbia and the conciliator during the negotiations that produced the tentative agreement of April 18. He had tried to get the parties to bargain in the weeks before the strike/lockout. Lewis called a meeting in Yellowknife for June 6. He was annoyed and shocked by the dramatic, rapid escalation of the dispute, and baffled by the call for RCMP reinforcements. And he didn't appreciate NWT ministers' clumsy efforts to broker a deal between Royal Oak and CASAW. "People were making desperate attempts to resolve this thing," Lewis says. "It was distracting the parties."

When Lewis arrived at the Yellowknife airport, he was dismayed that the RCMP offered him an armed escort. "I don't need that," he told the officers. "I've been in this business for twenty years, and I've never needed a police escort to or from a dispute." Royal Oak's people accepted RCMP protection, Lewis says.

The mediation session was held at the Yellowknife Inn, the town's oldest hotel. On the ground floor was the busy, smoky Miner's Mess, where photographs of the old days helped make the homey but spacious coffee shop the town's traditional gossip centre. (It was torn down soon after.) The Legislative Assembly was housed in rented space in the newer part of the building.

Lewis started the meeting by sending out Pinkerton's Ralph Sinke and Chris Morton, who flanked Peggy Witte and Vice President John Smrke. Witte said her life had been threatened, and she wanted bodyguards. Lewis was adamant that outsiders had no place in negotiations.

Both sides tried to set preconditions for any discussion of a new contract. Royal Oak demanded that CASAW agree to cover the company's strike costs to date—for security, strikebreakers, and lost production. This would require $1.5 million in concessions beyond those in the tentative agreement of April 18. Witte proposed that union workers could work without pay on Saturdays until strike costs were paid off. Royal Oak also wanted the union to allow dismissal of "troublemakers"—presumably picketers who had committed acts of vandalism or sabotage. CASAW's preconditions were that Royal Oak had to agree that strikebreakers would be removed, that mechanic Al Shearing's firing would be rescinded, and that no legal proceedings would arise from the strike. Lewis said that, if anyone insisted on preconditions, he'd pack up and go home. He persuaded Royal Oak to at least listen to the union's proposal.

Local vice president Harry Seeton opened with a passionate half-hour talk on the union's frustrations with local management and the need for better labour relations. Then CASAW national president Ross Slezak unveiled the details of CASAW's position. Slezak had implored the Yellowknife leadership to soften its demands, with little success. The local still wanted a return to almost all terms of the old collective agreement, effectively taking back all concessions made by the bargaining team from January to April. But, Slezak told the company, the union would temporarily suspend some benefits until the price of gold went up, and perhaps sacrifice some holiday pay to help the company out. CASAW's position was "entirely negotiable," he stressed.

Talks adjourned for lunch. Witte later testified that she and Smrke calculated the cost of the union's proposal during the break. She was indignant when she returned to the bargaining table, and asked the union team if they knew how much their proposal would cost. Then Royal Oak retabled its preconditions, and insisted that CASAW accept the principle of paying the company's strike costs before discussion could resume.

"I terminated the talks at that point," Lewis said much later. He didn't give details, but it appears he warned Royal Oak that they were flirting with a bad-faith bargaining charge. Under the Canada Labour Code, unions and companies are legally obliged to bargain in good faith. When a party files a complaint, the Canada Labour Relations Board has broad corrective powers to use on guilty parties. But Lewis's stern warning had no effect. The talks ended almost before they began. CASAW's bargaining team went away confused and angry. They couldn't imagine workers donating their wages to pay for strikebreakers who were stealing their jobs.

The show was not over, however. Royal Oak's media consultant led reporters up a back stairwell to a hotel room. Everyone entered and the door was locked and guarded. Major Sinke, looking like a rugged Kojak with a neatly trimmed mustache, ordered reporters to sit, and not stand without permission. A senior territorial official later commented that Sinke had "muscles on his ears."

The room was small, the blinds were drawn. Witte, Smrke, and Terry Byberg were lined up behind a table, under a harsh light. It resembled a press conference held by some guerrilla group to announce the kidnapping of a celebrity. Witte apologized profusely for the cloak-and-dagger atmosphere. "In the last twenty-four hours my life has been threatened," she stated, but admitted that the incident had not been reported to the police.

The union proposal amounted to a 10 percent annual raise, more than $1 million yearly in extra costs, Witte claimed. "We were totally shocked ... The company [and] the city of Yellowknife ... have been lulled into the false impression the union's problems were health and safety when the problems are monetary in nature." (Witte's incorrect statement about a 10 percent raise made a big impression in Yellowknife and was repeated by national media for months. The union didn't make a public statement about the meetings until two days later, by which time the damage to its public image had been done.)

Witte denied that strikebreakers had been hired in an effort to break the union, but agreed the practice could have that effect. She insisted there were no plans to run the mine permanently with outside workers. The company would take back about 200 of the 234 strikers, Witte said—but not those involved in "violence" against the company.

While she had the floor, Witte criticized the people of Yellowknife, the territorial politicians, the RCMP, and "everybody against us." Without more cooperation from local authorities, she said, Royal Oak might shut down Giant mine.

The authorities were annoyed too. NWT premier Nellie Cournoyea had helped Witte with her earlier attempt to develop Colomac mine. In a private meeting, Cournoyea demanded that Witte try to break the logjam in talks with CASAW. Witte replied that the NWT government should support her, and told the premier to "grow some balls." Nevertheless, Cournoyea's officials understood that Witte promised to stay in Yellowknife and make a counterproposal to the union within forty-eight hours. She would reconsider accepting the terms of the tentative agreement and let them know. Instead, Witte left town, after being driven to the airport by Inspector Massey, on orders from Superintendent Watt. Cournoyea reportedly felt betrayed. An official described their meeting as "outlandish," adding that "the company knows exactly what it's doing [but] the union doesn't seem to have any strategy." Mediator Bill Lewis had told the government that the union was in total disarray and could not reach a consensus position.

Territorial officials were so concerned about the collapse of mediation that they hired a Toronto labour-relations expert, John Sanderson, to provide an opinion on the dispute. He offered little hope that it would be resolved peacefully or quickly. Sanderson also mentioned the possibility of a bad-faith bargaining charge against Royal Oak for imposing preconditions, withdrawing them, and reimposing them.

Ironically, CASAW seemed to be the only party that didn't consider the option of a bad-faith bargaining complaint, probably because a lawyer had been hired to deal only with criminal charges, not with labour matters.

Cabinet sent Justice Minister Dennis Patterson and MLA Mike Ballantyne to Ottawa to plead for help in ending the Giant dispute. Members of the NWT legislature do not run as members of political parties, but Patterson and Ballantyne were well-connected Tories. On June 10, they made a personal and carefully rehearsed pitch to federal Labour Minister Marcel Danis, believing that this might be their last chance to prevent deaths.

Danis, a lawyer, is a political science professor and a self-described Red Tory. Perpetually tanned from trips to Florida, he comes from a rich, longtime Conservative family, and became Deputy Speaker of the House of Commons after heading the party's provincial wing. Like some of his Quebec colleagues, Danis is a firm believer in antiscab legislation—which put him in a strange position as Labour minister in a very probusiness government. But the 1977 antiscab law in Quebec was effective, and had reduced picket-line violence. So, when Danis was asked to intervene at Giant, he was sympathetic but pointed out he could not get a quick ban on strikebreakers from Prime Minister Brian Mulroney's cabinet. Mulroney himself understood the issues; he had been a prominent magagement-side labour lawyer in Quebec, and had served as president of the Iron Ore Company of Canada.

"Somebody could get killed," Ballantyne said early in the two-hour meeting. "Neither side has either the will or the skills to put this deal together ... In the public interest, something very unusual has to happen." Witte thumbed her nose at us when she reneged on her promise to make a counterproposal, Patterson added.

With no hope of an antiscab law, Patterson and Ballantyne asked Danis to appoint an industrial inquiry commission (IIC), a semijudicial body that could subpoena witnesses and eventually make recommendations for a settlement. But Danis pointed out that an IIC wouldn't solve the dispute quickly, since it couldn't impose a contract.

Patterson and Ballantyne then unveiled their last option, a special federal law to impose binding arbitration that would put the union men back to work. Danis countered that the federal government had never legislated an end to a private-sector dispute unless some national interest was at stake. He suggested that perhaps responsibility for labour matters in the Northwest Territories could be swiftly transferred to the territorial government, allowing it to do the dirty work. Patterson and Ballantyne knew that would take months, and there was a danger that Yellowknife, thousands of kilometres from emergency services, might become a battleground between big business and big labour over antiscab legislation. Such laws were being planned in Ontario and British Columbia, and both sides were looking for ammunition.

Danis asked them to get the NWT Legislative Assembly to vote on an official request for back-to-work legislation. He would think about it very seriously, he said. Patterson and Ballantyne were optimistic that Danis would act. A few days later, the legislature unanimously passed a motion supporting back-to-work legislation. Danis decided to call a meeting of the federal cabinet's ad hoc committee on labour to discuss the Giant dispute. Before they could meet, all hell broke loose.

FISHING TRIPS AND ROAST PIG

We will continue to explore ways to bring our Yellowknife workers back to work ... under terms that both the company and the actual workforce can agree to ... We would like to see our hourly workers represented by a union—or a bargaining unit.

—Peggy Witte, June 6, 1992

Union busters are not welcome in our country. Scab labour is a despicable corporate tactic of using the unemployed against working people. Royal Oak Mines may have thought they were simply taking on a small local in the Northwest Territories. They were wrong. They were taking on all *of organized labour.*

—Bob White, president of the Canadian Labour Congress,
July 8, 1992

Royal Oak didn't stop talking to strike opponents within CASAW, though consultation was never as public as Jim O'Neil's and Chris Neill's conference call with company managers on May 24. Before the mediation session of June 6, Royal Oak had evidence that CASAW was disintegrating. NWT government officials also knew about the dissension.

Chris Neill had slipped onto Giant property by helicopter. He stayed one day, and later told a fellow striker that he'd helped Royal Oak set up a mine-rescue team. Another friend says Neill was mining, but was terrified of leaving his wife, Tracey, alone while Giant's gates were blockaded. When Chris flew out, she picked him up outside of town, hiding him in the trunk of her car so no one would know he had crossed the picket line.

O'Neil, for his part, sought legal options to unseat CASAW's leadership. According to later sworn testimony, O'Neil called mine manager Terry Byberg and asked him "if he knew any good labour lawyers." Byberg forwarded the request to Peggy Witte, who got a list of five possible labour lawyers from the board member Royal Oak shared with Pinkerton's of Canada. O'Neil chose Israel Chafetz, a Vancouver lawyer with a promanagement reputation. O'Neil says Chafetz told him about the Canada Labour Code's rules on the "raiding season," that CASAW's legal right to represent the workers couldn't be challenged until six months into the strike/lockout.

Meanwhile, other strike opponents within the union met to discuss strategy; O'Neil went to at least one of their meetings. There were about ten regulars, all of whom worked underground and were used to big production bonuses. The group was divided on how to end the strike/lockout. Some wanted to push for a re-vote on the April 18 tentative agreement, as Witte had requested earlier. Others preferred to break with the union altogether and cross the picket line in a group of thirty to forty men, hoping for safety in numbers. Keith Murray, a first-rate miner who had been promoted to shift boss shortly before the dispute started, was the malcontents' go-between with manager Terry Byberg in discussions of the terms under which they would work.

The lean and laconic Murray was in the centre of a complicated web of relationships. Two of his good friends, miner Roger Warren and mechanic Terry

Legge, were die-hard CASAW loyalists who no longer talked to him. His sister was married to Max Dillman, who had opposed the strike but refused to cross the picket line. Murray's common-law wife used to be married to Burke Driscoll, another union man the strike opponents hoped to recruit. Murray was also a volunteer firefighter, working side by side with Chris Neill and several CASAW loyalists.

The strike opponents discreetly started a petition for a re-vote on the tentative agreement. Two men visited the homes of others who might oppose the strike, hoping to gather a few dozen names before the union executive learned about it. But it is hard to keep a secret in Yellowknife. Max Dillman saw some union dissidents meeting at a private home. Then he got a phone call from a striker working down south, who said he'd heard from Chris Neill that the dispute was over and the men were going to work. Dillman alerted the union executive, who called an emergency membership meeting for June 12.

Some petition organizers were afraid they might be lynched if they went to the meeting. One member, Craig Richardson, insisted that they should go and be candid. The way to resolve the dispute with Royal Oak was to reclaim the union from the "radicals," not to undermine CASAW in secret, Richardson said.

The union held the meeting in the Elk's Hall. The RCMP did surveillance from a government building across the street. The meeting was packed and emotional. The union executive demanded to know who was circulating the petition. Craig Richardson explained his involvement. Three or four others supported him, but he says most of his group did not stand up to be counted, and even destroyed the signatures they had collected. There were shouts and taunts.

"I started moving toward the front, because I thought I was going to have to defend [Richardson]," says union loyalist Mark Eveson. "But it never came to that ... A lot of people said, 'You got to give the guy credit, at least he's got the balls to stand up and say what he felt.'"

But Richardson was the exception, and the antistrike group laid low for the next two months.

Strike opponents were not the only ones meeting in secret. Militant CASAW loyalists also engaged in clandestine activities. It started with simple sabotage, carried out by small groups of men. They selected targets that would stop production without forcing permanent closure of the mine. One favourite was the tailings lines, which carried waste from Giant's mill to a holding pond across the road, and from there through treatment systems to Yellowknife Bay (see map C). One striker specialized in drilling holes in the lines and cutting power to water pumps. "You could let them do whatever they wanted or you can annoy them," he recalls. "If we had been passive, she'd [Witte] have run the operation a lot more efficiently. Who knows what would happen, would we ever be back to work?"

Electrical lines were another target. Some CASAW members reviewed the mine's power sources with sympathetic workers at the power company, then aimed at the weakest points. They used axes, chainsaws, and even arson to bring down poles, not always successfully. By far the best way to knock out the power was to "go fishing." The saboteur using this technique attached a length of metal wire to the end of a spool of fishing line, cast it over a power line, then reeled it in until the metal wire shorted two of the cables. There was usually a tremendous flash. Then, if the shorting wire had fallen off the power cables, the saboteur put it back on, so that, if the power company got the electricity flowing again without checking all the lines, there would be another short.

Outages shut down the mine's ventilation system, and cut the air pressure miners need to operate their tools, effectively halting all work. Strikebreakers usually waited underground until power was restored, but sometimes they had to climb ladders up from the deep. It was a grueling trip if they were far underground. The narrow wooden ladders, slick with moisture and grime, are set on a steep angle from landing to landing in the shaft's man-way.

Anywhere from six to several dozen of CASAW's 234 members were involved in sabotage. It was hard to determine how many, because men exaggerated their exploits or told tall tales. For many picketers, knocking out the power was a badge of honour.

Many people in Yellowknife were horrified by this "terrorism," which often cut power to the town as well. "Knocking the power out, as far as public opinion, hurt us," says diamond driller Mark Eveson, who resented hearing complaints about missing popular TV shows: "I'm losing my fuckin' life here. So I'm supposed to care about *Oprah*?"

CASAW's leaders regularly condemned terrorism and violence, but some rank-and-file members felt the union had to fight fire with fire. Royal Oak was breaking the rules by trying to destroy their union, and the police and the courts seemed willing to help the company, they reasoned. Strikers alleged that they were ignored when they filed complaints about Royal Oak or Pinkerton's personnel.

Despair and anger, mainly, motivated the vandalism. There was, however, another element that a few strikers admit: it was fun. A small minority enjoyed the excitement; being commandos and thumbing their noses at the Pinkerton's men relieved boredom and frustration, and countered the feeling of being helpless victims.

A dark blue pickup sped south on the same road Jim O'Neil had taken a few days earlier—but this time the driver was Jim Evoy, the president of the NWT Federation of Labour, going to the annual convention of the Canadian Labour Congress (CLC) in the first days of June. Drumming up support for CASAW was his top priority. The union was not an affiliate, but images of women marching around town with their baby strollers while their husbands paced at Giant's gates galvanized Evoy's determination to help.

His timing was good. In Yellowknife, Royal Oak and CASAW would meet with mediator Bill Lewis in a few days, and the CLC's support might help pressure Peggy Witte to bargain. In British Columbia and Ontario, the New Democratic governments were pledging to ban the use of strikebreakers. Outgoing CLC president Shirley Carr and her future successor, Bob White, promised Evoy they would help, and the convention passed one of its rare emergency resolutions in support of CASAW. The CLC would also lobby Labour Minister Marcel Danis and Prime Minister Brian Mulroney.

Evoy was starting to cheer up—until he met CASAW's envoy to the convention. It was Gordie Kendall, the miner who had laid down in front of a company bus on the first day of the dispute. Forty-six years old, silver-haired, and boisterous, Kendall had been around. He had hired on as a miner in January 1990, just months before Royal Oak took over, and claimed he and company vice president John Smrke were "very close" when they had both worked for Falconbridge in Sudbury. He has a ruddy complexion and the yellow fingers of a chain-smoker, and "shoots the shit" like a pro. He says he was also a good shot with a rifle, having been a sniper in the army in the mid-1960s. Later, "I used to rob banks for a living," he says. "The one I did time for was the biggest bank job in Manitoba history." It was a theft of $1.8 million, in 1978.[3] He claims to have friends in the Mafia in Montreal, and to have been a Steelworkers organizer at a Timmins, Ontario, mine "where a lot of guys were fired for joining a union."

Kendall came to Vancouver with a letter from Local 4's president, Bill Schram."This will introduce our brother Gordon Kendall, and he will be embarking on, or performing special projects and you are asked to provide any assistance he may request," it said.

Evoy was shocked. He thought Kendall was either a company plant to subvert the union, or just a haywire old miner who enjoyed trouble for its own sake. Yet Kendall had sweet-talked Schram into letting him represent the union in Vancouver, though few CASAW members knew that until later.

Kendall says that his special project was to work his connections—among them the president of the Steelworkers' local at Royal Oak's mine in Timmins.

The local was negotiating to renew a contract due to expire on June 30. "I told 'em, you got to scrap those negotiations," Kendall says. "I told 'em, if you don't, there's going to be a lot of dead bodies lying around."

Sources say that Kendall also did "preliminary work" for a professional hit on Peggy Witte. The price to carry it out was $5,000. Many months later, Kendall would tell the RCMP that the price was $50,000. Kendall said he would do it himself for that money because he was pretty broke.

According to sources in Yellowknife, about a month later an official of a southern union told "a couple" of CASAW members he had been approached about a plan to assassinate Witte. "The union did not want nothing to do with it," says a man familiar with Kendall's activity. "The national and the executive did not want to get involved in something like that ... [To Kendall], killing her seemed like a simple solution to a complex problem," but no money was collected for the job.

There was $2,000 raised for a "rocket launcher," Kendall says. "I was going to knock out the helicopter and the [hoist]." Kendall insists he was not a plant, spy, or *agent provocateur*.

Kendall's stay in Vancouver also featured a march from the CLC convention to Royal Oak headquarters. The march, with 275 participants, was organized by the Steelworkers and also sponsored by Kendall. It was a typical protest until somebody called out, "Office tour!" About 100 demonstrators stomped into the company's ramshackle office building. Peggy Witte gathered her staff in an office and locked the door. The crowd overturned some furniture and flooded the bathrooms.

"That building was shaking," says Jim Evoy. "Stuff started coming out the fucking windows—pots, plants." After a few minutes the demonstrators left, but a group of hulking Steelworkers had some loot—a framed picture of Giant mine, which they carted triumphantly into the convention hall. There were no arrests. Later some unionists theorized that Kendall had organized the office tour to get CASAW and the Steelworkers bad press coverage, though there's no evidence it was his idea. Kendall says it was started by "a beautiful little girl from Sudbury."

Despite Kendall's antics, Evoy's mission of recruiting support for CASAW from mainstream labour was accomplished. The Canadian Labour Congress was on side, led by the Steelworkers and the Canadian Auto Workers.

Even within the RCMP, there were doubts about the strategy of using paramilitary force and riot-control techniques to police a labour dispute. Evoy discovered this firsthand at the CLC convention when he was approached by Sergeant Lynn Kraeling. Kraeling is the RCMP's only full-time labour-liaison officer—stationed in British Columbia, where there's a history of tense disputes. CASAW had lobbied NWT politicians to have Kraeling sent to Yellowknife before the Giant dispute even started. They'd heard good things about him from BC unionists. Kraeling knows labour history and realizes that it has taught trade unionists to distrust men in uniform. So he wears plain clothes on picket lines, never packs a firearm, and doesn't drive a squad car. He builds trust with unions and companies. His low-key approach has defused many tense picket-line situations.

Evoy hoped Kraeling could work some magic in Yellowknife, and he seemed eager to come north. "We've got to work together. I'll see you in Yellowknife, Jim," Evoy recalls him saying. Evoy was already impressed, despite his own distrust of police. Kraeling knew how to walk into "the jaws" of the labour movement and he was direct. "I know he's going to try to use me," Evoy says. "But we want peace, and it's not headed for peace, it's headed for fucking disaster. So I got a responsibility to deal with this guy."

But Kraeling never came. The idea was vetoed by either the RCMP or higher powers in Ottawa. "I was never told why," Kraeling says. "I have my own thoughts. It could've been a political decision."

Meanwhile, news of events in the Canadian Auto Workers' (CAW) strike at the Clearwater lobster-processing plant in the Cape Breton fishing community of Arichat met with cheers in front of the TV set in CASAW's hall. That strike had started a week before the one in Yellowknife. Clearwater brought in strikebreakers after ten days. The workers attempted to storm the plant five days later, but were thrown out by security guards and the RCMP. Then, on June 11, the Cape Breton strikers brought in several hundred supporters from Sydney and other nearby towns. The crowd brushed past guards and the RCMP, and into the plant; the company had to evacuate strikebreakers by helicopter. The next day, the Nova Scotia government appointed an industrial inquiry commission.

Television images of the victorious Arichat crowd and the hasty evacuation electrified the men in Yellowknife, many of whom were from the Atlantic Provinces. They noted with interest that the police had stepped aside. However, Arichat struck a chord in Yellowknife primarily because many unionists had considered doing something similar at Giant. The idea had probably been brewing since the May 30 meeting at which former president Dale Johnston allegedly asked for volunteers to put on helmets and carry baseball bats. Some men held clandestine meetings at various locations outside of town. They were too suspicious of RCMP surveillance to discuss the idea on the phone or in the union hall. Perhaps forty staunch union members and supporters were invited; probably fewer than twenty came. Johnston himself stayed aloof. These "secret" meetings probably did not lead to a definite plan of action. Not all the men who attended trusted one another, correctly assuming that the RCMP and Royal Oak had informants in the union. There was, however, general agreement that a group of men would storm the fence, barricade themselves in the mill or C-dry, and refuse to leave until Peggy Witte agreed to withdraw the strikebreakers and start negotiating. There was talk of arranging for sympathizers from Yellowknife's other gold mine, Con, to create a diversion by demonstrating or attacking security guards at another gate. It appears that no date was set for the big raid, but word got around.

On June 7, the union called a membership meeting at the main gate, in defiance of the court order limiting the number of picketers. When CASAW president Bill Schram explained what had happened in the mediation session the previous day, frustration erupted among the 125 people there, including many wives. Managers inside the gates feared the crowd might tear down the fence.

"What the hell's our next step?" yelled Bob Hopson, one of CASAW's dissidents. "What about a little rollback? I'd say a dollar an hour."

Miner Roger Warren jumped in. "Somebody that would put scabs on a fucking mine property and you're going to give 'em a dollar an hour?"

"What are you going to do?" Hopson returned. "You're going to give 'em a fucking no-union deal at all, that's what's going to happen!"

"Go in and get those guys out of there, there'd be no more problems, they'd be negotiating," Warren said, pointing beyond the fence.

From the back of the crowd, driller Conrad Lisoway's voice boomed over the rest: "Somebody have to fucking die before we get rid of these fucking scabs?"

"Yeah they do. I thought about it ...," someone said.

"They do—and you better soon get it done," Warren said. The exchange was captured by television cameras.

As tempers flared, CASAW's local lawyer advised Schram and the executive to leave the picket line, to the dismay of national president Ross Slezak. Soon afterward, a small group rambled onto the parking lot, where they threw rocks at Pinkerton's men, shouted, and rattled the chain-link fence in view of Witte, whom they could see. Slezak says he persuaded the police to let the crowd blow off some steam, and things soon calmed down.

But behind the scenes, all parties were gearing up for a major clash. Superintendent Watt informed Ottawa that two bomb threats had been made against Giant on June 9. Police dogs were used to sweep the site, and the RCMP's information was that "strikers now have the capability of destroying the headframe and mill." Pinkerton's own riot group, dubbed the "Sierra team," held regular practices with shields and sticks, sometimes in view of the pickets. On June 10, the same day that Patterson and Ballantyne met with Marcel Danis in Ottawa, Watt was told by Pinkerton's of Canada in Montreal that "they have an informant who says that the union has hired The Rebels motorcycle club to fly up, with explosives, and blow up the mine. They will follow up with their informants and keep us advised." Documents obtained from the RCMP do not reveal the extent of their investigation of this alleged threat, or the reliability of the information. With chapters in Edmonton, Calgary, Moose Jaw, and Saskatchewan, The Rebels are reportedly a hang-around club linked to the Vancouver Hells Angels. The Montreal chapter is Canada's most notorious, but Hells Angels have been convicted in various countries of murder; illegal sales of drugs, weapons, and explosives; and other crimes.

On the picket line, there were daily, minor hassles between strikers and Pinkerton's men, and strikers and police, who observed that patrols by the ERT "cause the picketers to become agitated." The mood was tense, and Inspector Massey was busy day and night. Police escorted company vehicles and personnel through the picket line. The RCMP reinforcements were replaced by a new crew of southern officers, flown in on a chartered Boeing 737. Massey stayed on, telling Watt that RCMP labour specialist Lynn Kraeling wasn't needed, and claiming that rapport with union members had developed so well, it would be foolish to replace him.

The union men didn't agree. On June 13, they caught Massey on videotape, running after a picketer's pickup truck, swinging his billy club, and shouting "You cocksuckers!" at them.

That afternoon at a local beach, the Steelworkers held a "Pig Roast" for CASAW members, their families, and strike supporters. Kids played in the sand, women chatted in the warm sun, and men drank beer while a whole pig sizzled and browned on a spit over the fire. When the meat was done, everyone lined up for slices of pork. "That got the tensions running," says Evoy. Word got around there would be a big meeting at Giant's main gate the next day.

The pig roast was no secret. After the feast, says Pinkerton's boss Chris Morton, men in pickups cruised past the mine, shouting to the guards that they'd see them tomorrow, and "the next time, we're going to take the property." Pinkerton's relayed the message to the RCMP, who had also been tipped off by informants, perhaps as much as four days earlier. According to former Con miner Bob Robertson—the man who had provoked an attack on a company bus in late May—"I would phone periodically, if something was going down that I felt was illegal, or was going to get the guys in trouble." He told the RCMP to expect trouble on June 14.

Everyone was ready to rumble.

CHAPTER THREE

THE GREATER

FORCE

The company is in the process of trying to get an order to facilitate the police to operate.

—Superintendent Brian Watt, June 8, 1992

I didn't think they were going in and break windows; I thought they were going in just for the scabs. I think [union members] have been pretty patient. It has been a two-way street, the violence.

—picketer Rick Titterton, June 14, 1992[1]

When the sun took its short, obligatory dip below the horizon at about 2:30 A.M., it was plain that June 14 would be a glorious day. It was the hottest of the entire summer. The mercury rose above 29 degrees Celsius, too hot for mosquitoes and too early for blackflies. Picketers lounged in lawn chairs, about three per gate. Many wore shorts and had their shirts off, soaking up the rays. Several wives came to visit; tape players and radios blared.

After lunch, Inspector Dennis Massey patrolled in short sleeves, stopping at the gates to talk. Along the way, he got the impression that a gathering at the picket line planned for later would not be a normal union meeting. A similar report came from the RCMP's command post at about 5:00 P.M. Nothing was amiss at Gate 3 half an hour later, but after 6:00 P.M. the number of picketers grew. Massey radioed the riot troop in the National Defence hangar at the airport, then sped over to brief them. Some men were still eating. "We may not have time, go now," Massey urged. He wanted the emergency response team (ERT) in place north of the mine, and the tactical troop in their bus on a side road to the south.

A carnival atmosphere prevailed at the main gate by 6:30. A stereo system blasted upbeat tunes, and people milled about, talking and joking, including many women and a few children. A couple of police watched from a Suburban van, and a few more officers were on the property. Traffic was heavy, much of it the usual weekend flow to the lakes. Members of the ERT slipped by unnoticed, stopping just beyond the Yellowknife River. Soon after, roadblocks went up at both ends of the mine, thwarting by minutes the arrival of about forty union supporters—most of whom were probably Steelworkers. Many of these men had hockey gear and were prepared for a brawl with guards or police. They may have been the group that was supposed to create a diversion at a smaller gate, or they may have expected to join the crowd at the main gate.

Pinkerton's twelve-member "Sierra" riot team was ready too. Strikebreakers waited in C-dry, armed with axes and pick handles. A 35-ton haul truck and a pickup were parked inside the security gate, between it and the kitchen trailer. Guard Karl Tettenborn sat in the cab of a dump truck parallel to the fence, using powerful binoculars to scan the crowd to look for people he knew. He had been there most of the day, jotting down names and descriptions. The son of a Royal Oak staffer, Tettenborn had been hired by Pinkerton's two days earlier. He'd lived all his twenty-two years in the Giant town site and knew many union members.

With the RCMP and Pinkerton's guards in position, Royal Oak's famous yellow bus chugged up to the main gate at 6:50 P.M. It could have exited at the muck crossing, where picketing was forbidden. Instead, it was sent to the main gate, where people were gathering, and where getting the bus out "was always an adventure," according to Pinkerton's boss Chris Morton. But within minutes, the picket-line coordinator had cleared the way.

The crowd had swelled to about 150 people. Picketers Frank Maille and Dave Madsen walked across the company parking lot to the inner gate. They had a few words with two Pinkerton's men just inside the fence, Morton and Major Ralph Sinke. Three more union men wandered up, and stood around talking. According to several picketers, Maille came back to the crowd and launched into a tirade. "Are we mice or are we men?" one man remembers him saying. Maille was told to relax, that there weren't enough men on hand to do anything. Then some men carried a picnic table to the inner gate, apparently intending it to serve as a speaking platform, as it had a week earlier outside the main gate. Inspector Dennis Massey walked with the union crowd, unlocked the pedestrian gate, and joined Major Sinke on the other side. Three guards stood nearby with dogs. The "Sierra" team was about 15 yards inside the gate, in plain view of the picketers. Some had helmets and riot shields, and most had billy sticks.

Insults and rocks flew almost immediately; each side claims the other started it. The Pinkerton's men fended off rocks with their shields, some returned fire. "Let them come in!" Massey hollered to the Pinkerton's team, according to witnesses from both sides. (Massey denies having said this.)

There was a lull in the rock throwing, and someone snipped a wire on the fence. Then about twenty men rocked it back and forth until it lay flat on the ground.

"Now!" someone yelled.

"Back off, boys!" Massey shouted before lobbing a stun grenade toward the breach. About the same time, striker Shane Riggs broke through the line of three trucks, only to meet Pinkerton's chief Chris Morton. They both stopped, but Riggs was standing over the grenade. It exploded with a flash and a deafening boom, giving his bare leg an ugly burn.[2]

The three Pinkerton's dog handlers retreated hastily as the "Sierra" team and Tettenborn took cover behind their row of plastic shields. Rocks shattered the windows of the kitchen and dining room, where some mine workers and guards were eating. A striker arrived, "smashing everything in sight," according to a witness.

Perhaps forty or fifty strikers swarmed onto the property, including former CASAW president Dale Johnston, who pointed out Pinkerton's men holding video cameras on top of the administration building. Rocks were thrown at them, and several strikers ran in that direction. Others reached a refrigerator trailer and yanked on wires and hoses.

The "Sierra" team scattered under a barrage of rocks. Some went toward a shallow catchment pond that was surrounded by a berm. Someone ran at Major Sinke and threw a large rock that knocked off his hard hat. Sinke says the assailant screamed, "Die, motherfucker!" He accused striker Jim Fournier of the attack, and said another CASAW man, Garth Beck, ordered Fournier to "kill that bald-headed motherfucker." (Both were later charged and, much later, found not guilty.) A free-for-all ensued. Beck, who was wearing gloves, threw back tear-gas cannisters and concussion grenades fired by police.

To the strikers who had talked of storming the mine, this was a "premature ejaculation." They didn't have enough men, and they knew the police riot squad was coming. But it was too late to pull back, so several rushed to help their friends. Meanwhile, James Mager and Kelly Rhodes got an excited call on the radio while they manned the picket line at Gate 1. They jumped in Mager's van, arriving seconds later at Gate 3. Mager grabbed a lime-green balaclava he kept in the van with his hunting gear, picked up a stick, and ran through the breach in the fence.

The heaviest action was by the catchment pond, behind Massey's tear gas and smoke, and away from most of the video cameras and neutral witnesses. Accounts of what happened there vary widely. It appears that guard Eric Melançon, despite his riot shield, helmet, and billy stick, couldn't fend off attacks by strikers, who bludgeoned him at least three times before he went down. Melançon was then kicked in the ribs before he managed to retreat into the pond.

Dennis Massey, now wearing a gas mask, saw this beating and aimed his gun. "I thought he was going to die," he says. "But I couldn't get a shot. If I could've identified a target, positively, I would have shot him." Instead he fired two warning shots.

Then Melançon looked up to see striker Jim Fournier standing over him. Fournier, who had not seen the earlier attack, berated the guard as a coward who'd failed to defend his friends. Melançon says Fournier raised a big rock over his head and cried, "You're going to die!"—a statement Fournier denies.

Massey aimed his gun again and shouted, "Drop the rock!" and fired two more warning shots, according to Major Sinke and Chris Morton. Fournier hesitated, Sinke says. "It went through my mind, 'Massey is going to shoot him.' As, in my mind, he should've."

Fournier says he didn't see Massey or hear the gunshots, but did throw the rock toward Melançon, splashing him. Melançon says the rock hit him in the side. Then he got out of the water and fell to the ground, unconscious.

Other Pinkerton's men, including Sinke, had taken refuge on a big pile of gravel. During the melee, they bombarded any invaders they could with rocks. After getting hit himself, temper got the better of Tettenborn, the fresh recruit, all 230 pounds of him. He thundered down the slope toward a wiry man in a green balaclava, not recognizing striker James Mager. But Mager knew Tettenborn, who used to come around to see Mager's daughter. They charged at each other, and may have traded blows.

"Let's get him!" shouted Pinkerton's guard Hank Dorn, before a winner emerged. Guards tackled Mager, grabbing him around the neck. He struggled, and swung a billy stick before he was clubbed from behind. Four strikers, including Roger Warren, saw Mager's plight, but Massey intervened before they could help. Some strikers were carrying sticks. Shop steward Edmund Savage demanded Mager's release. Massey drew his gun, leveled it at Savage's head, then panned to the others.

(J. HOLMAN / THE PRESS INDEPENDENT)

A view of downtown Yellowknife from an office tower on Franklin Avenue.

(L. SELLECK / THE PRESS INDEPENDENT)

Giant mine from the air, July 1992. The long building to the right of the C-shaft
headframe is C-dry, the locker room area. Strikebreakers slept in an open,
barracks-like room upstairs early in the strike/lockout.

(L. SELLECK)

Veteran miner Art St. Amand drilling a round of holes. Drill steel protrudes from the wall. Each hole will be packed with explosives.

An open man-car on its narrow-gauge rails on the 1100 level. The photo was taken with a high-powered flash. It's easy to imagine the effect of one's puny cap lamp on the mine's darkness. When it's turned off, blackness is absolute.

Terry Wells protests his firing in January 1992 at Giant's main gate.
His case went to arbitration in 1994. He got his job back.

Giant mine manager Mike Werner in his office in the administration building in May 1992.

Mine manager Mike Werner, mine superintendent Terry Byberg, human resources manager Kim Cornwell, and chief financial officer Chris Serin at Royal Oak's press conference on Sunday, May 24, 1992.

Women of CLASS march past Gate 3 and into Giant mine's parking lot to berate guards and strikebreakers on May 24. In the centre is Shirley Mager, whose husband James would serve jail time over clashes on June 14.

(C. LOCKERBIE / NNSL)

(Left) Mike Werner wades into the picket line at Gate 1 on May 25, to be met by Sam Pawluk, Conrad Lisoway and Tim Brown. In sunglasses and white shirt, to Werner's left, is Bob Robertson.

(L. SELLECK / THE PRESS INDEPENDENT)

(Right) Miner Lew Whalen exchanges words with RCMP inspector Dennis Massey at Gate 3. It was May 26, Massey's first day facing the picketers.

(L. SELLECK, THE PRESS INDEPENDENT)

(Left) CASAW picket captain Terry Regimbald at Gate 3, the main gate, on May 26, 1992.

More than 150 demonstrators chanted "scabs go home" in a march in downtown Yellowknife on May 28, 1992.

CASAW president Bill Schram *(l.)* and vice-president Harry Seeton on the picket line in June 1992. Schram resigned in August and Seeton inherited the job. Behind them, on the "Know Your Scab" poster, is NWT Chamber of Mines president Mike Magrum.

(L. SELLECK / THE PRESS INDEPENDENT)

Police used tear gas and stun grenades on June 14, 1992 when about 50 union members pulled down a fence and streamed onto mine property. After the mêlée, picketers and police confronted each other in an uneasy standoff at Gate 3.
Tim Bettger *(c.)* and Al Shearing were there.

(L. SELLECK / THE PRESS INDEPENDENT)

Tear gas and concussion grenades are set off in the parking lot at Giant mine's main gate near the end of the June 14 skirmish.

This police officer and his dog had little support as the June 14 skirmish came to an end, but the strikers who had gone inside the fence were already retreating.

Miner Gordie Kendall with a picket sign in July 1992. Kendall was suspected of being an agent provocateur by the union; he was questioned by the RCMP. His second polygraph examination took place two weeks before Roger Warren confessed to the crime.

"It was pointed directly at my heart," says Garth Beck, a soft-spoken but muscular welder. "Don't shoot, Dennis, don't shoot that gun," Beck says he told Massey. The strikers backed off. Now Massey turned his gun on the Pinkerton's guards, ordering them to release Mager.

"No way in hell," Sinke told his men. "Don't let him go." The stalemate was broken when a police officer took custody of Mager, who was still trying to get away.

"The riot cops are coming!" The cry sounded from the main gate, down the parking lot and onto the property. The picketers' air horn blasted nonstop. From their dull green military bus, the RCMP tactical team marched in a rectangular formation from the road to the main gate, knocking down a pregnant woman. She left for the hospital in a taxi, blood trickling down her neck. "Two of them hit her under the chin with their shields," a cab driver said. The RCMP later alleged that the woman had thrown rocks at them.

The police phalanx, helmeted and anonymous, inexplicably swept north across the parking lot to the fence, and then south along it to the security gate (see map C). They banged their shields in unison with their clubs. The ERT, toting M-16s or other weapons, had also arrived with two German shepherds tugging hard on their leashes. One dog handler met a hail of rocks in the parking lot and had to retreat. His dog was hit after it nipped a union member.

When the riot troop got back to the main gate, most of the demonstrators were already there. A long line formed on the highway, jeering strikers facing masked police. The police were sweltering in their gear, some of it stamped "US Army." Behind the row carrying shields, several ERT officers roved with their automatic pistols drawn, ready to fire. The line was flanked by snipers with M-16s. A dog handler brought his nervous animal to one end of the line, near mechanic Yvan Brien. Unprovoked, an officer broke from the ranks and put a choke hold on Brien with a stick. He was dragged behind the police line and surrounded, but was soon released.

June Roberts's husband, Derek, videotaped the standoff with the RCMP. "They were all in full battle gear. They've got all their training ... We were standing there in shorts. They were swinging the clubs and pushing and shoving ... They thought we were nuts—you know, their bang clang, one step forward, bang their thing, and then take another step. They thought they'd get us running." The crowd didn't drift away until about 8:00 P.M. Four people were hospitalized, and seven others were injured.

Little of the story became public at the time; even the gunshots got scant attention. The lone reporter on the scene couldn't see all the action, and RCMP press releases were terse, reporting only that "a small amount of tear gas was used."

Many union men believed that they'd been lured into a trap. Some blamed a picketer at the inner gate, who they suspected of being a company or police plant. He was not seen beyond the fence, and wasn't charged. Others blamed the police, particularly Massey, who they felt wanted the riot.

The territorial and federal governments had been arguing about who should pay for the extra police. A decision on bringing in the next group of reinforcements had to be made the very day of the melee. A new squad came the next morning, temporarily ending the debate.

It has never been explained why Massey told the Pinkerton's guards to let the crowd pour through the hole in the perimeter fence. He denies having said it, although both union and Pinkerton's men insist that he did. Tettenborn, the new guard, said the idea was to have any clash with picketers in the open, rather than between the trucks just inside the fence.

Massey probably hoped to arrest most of the crowd, which was almost hemmed in by the Pinkerton's men, the ERT, the riot team, and the fence. The picketers were saved by RCMP mistakes. "There was a foul-up in the directions given to the riot troop, and they did not arrive as quickly as they should have ... Everything would have worked out properly if it had not been for [that]," ERT sergeant Al Macintyre wrote in an internal RCMP report.

HIGHER POWERS

These thirty-eight men are never going to be allowed on the property again. The strike will go on forever. I am pissed off the company fired these guys. The company should have tried to get rid of these guys through the disciplinary system.

—Chris Neill, July 6, 1992

The June 14 melee occurred while federal Labour Minister Marcel Danis was still considering whether or not to introduce back-to-work legislation. Three days later, on June 17, Peggy Witte, opposed to the legislation, went to Ottawa to lobby Danis. Witte and her vice president, John Smrke, met with Danis, and as usual she was very convincing. She told Danis that, if there was a problem at Giant, it wasn't the company: Royal Oak had unions at its two other mines, and got along well with them. The problem in Yellowknife was a small, radical minority in CASAW, she insisted. Danis says Witte also told him about rumours that the union's votes on the April 18 tentative agreement and the strike itself were improper, and that a fair vote would end the dispute.

The minister asked Witte if the company would resume negotiations with CASAW. "She said she was going to go back to the bargaining table," Danis says. "I thought when the meeting was over that we'd made a positive step." Danis's senior advisers were skeptical. "They were telling me that she was being very well briefed about what she could and could not do," Danis says. "And she was always saying the minimally acceptable thing." Royal Oak obviously had legal advice on its duty under the Canada Labour Code to bargain in good faith, but remarks to other government officials were less cautious. Superintendent Watt learned on June 16 that, before Royal Oak would take back twenty to thirty strikers it planned to fire, Giant mine would be shut down and the government of Canada would "wear the consequences." Terminations of strikers had become the central issue of the labour dispute, before they had even been fired.

Danis reviewed the Giant dispute with members of the ad hoc cabinet committee on labour on June 18. The main order of business was the NWT government's request for a special law to send all the unionized employees back to work. The committee was chaired by Senator Lowell Murray, a longtime friend of Prime Minister Brian Mulroney's. Other ministers probably included Justice Minister Kim Campbell, Solicitor General Doug Lewis (the RCMP's boss), and House Leader Harvie André. Danis won't disclose details of the meeting, but there are strong signs that he believed a forced settlement was the only way to avert a disaster at Giant. But the counter-argument prevailed: The public interest was not involved because the mine did not provide an essential service; if the government set a precedent by legislating an end to a work stoppage that was becoming too violent, any union losing a dispute would have an incentive to be violent on the picket line. Danis was left with only the hope that the two sides might soon come to their senses.

That afternoon, during Question Period in the House of Commons, Danis was testy when pressed to intervene in the Giant dispute. "It would be helpful if people try to stay out of this dispute ... I have been told by the parties that is hurting the situation instead of providing for a settlement."

NWT Justice Minister Dennis Patterson and his colleagues in Yellowknife took Danis' remark as a personal affront. "He had led us on and not delivered anything, and then we got this patronizing comment in the House of Commons," Patterson says. Territorial politicians assumed that Danis had stabbed them in the back, unaware that it was a federal cabinet committee's decision.

Despite resistance by the RCMP, Patterson wrote to Danis and Solicitor General Doug Lewis, demanding that the RCMP reinforcements be removed unless Ottawa paid for them. The NWT government wanted nothing more to do with the Giant dispute.

Royal Oak won a crucial legal battle, thanks to the June 14 skirmish. Four days after the clash, Justice Mark de Weerdt authorized the RCMP to arrest violators of the court's May 24 order limiting picketing. Royal Oak no longer had to sue the union for blocking traffic; the company could simply ask the police to haul away offending picketers.

The RCMP's approach to enforcing the court's restrictions had not been clear up to that time. Even after June 14, the Crown argued in court against allowing police to make arrests, saying it would strain police resources. But behind the scenes, federal officials appeared to take a different tack. More than a week before the riot, Royal Oak representatives met senior officials from the RCMP and the federal Department of Justice to discuss policing. CASAW was not told about the meeting. "The company is in the process of trying to get an order to facilitate the police to operate," Superintendent Brian Watt informed territorial politicians.

The RCMP promptly began picking up strikers and charging them for offenses allegedly committed during the melee of June 14. Chris Neill, who was still on strike, and another union member who had crossed the picket line helped police identify fellow union members on Pinkerton's videotapes. Twenty-four men were charged, most with damage under $1,000 or possession of a dangerous weapon—a stick, baseball bat, ax handle, or rock. James Mager, who allegedly beat Eric Melançon over the head, was charged with mischief and six counts of assault with a weapon. Jim Fournier, accused of throwing a large rock at Melançon, faced several charges, which were later boosted to attempted murder.

Strikers accused of injunction violations now had to sign a pledge to stay away from the picket line, or they would be jailed. Many of the alleged rioters were among the most faithful picketers, so CASAW faced a potential shortage of men to hold the line. Strikers began to complain that police were using any excuse to lay charges, to strip the picket line. At least two people were charged who weren't at Giant on June 14. One was CASAW's secretary-treasurer, Bob Kosta, supposedly identified by an effeminate throwing motion. Another had been stuck at the police barricade past Yellowknife River, with his wife.

Royal Oak started firing strikers on June 23, as Witte and other managers had threatened to do weeks earlier. In the next ten days, identical letters of dismissal were sent to thirty-eight of CASAW's 234 members, of whom about 100 were active picketers. (Many strikers left Yellowknife for temporary work, or to escape the city's high cost of living. Superintendent Watt reported to Ottawa that, after school ended on June 29, "some miners are expected to pull up stakes and leave town." That weekend, he personally briefed Commissioner Norman Inkster and the deputy solicitor general.) Many people in town assumed that the company's crackdown was the result of the June 14 riot. But even before that, human resources manager Kim Cornwell had gone to Vancouver with personnel files and picket-line videotapes to decide whom to fire. She did not work on this in Yellowknife because the company believed that CASAW had somehow bugged offices at the mine.

The mass firings fueled the unionists' belief that Royal Oak had a secret agenda. Witte's objective was more than contract concessions; she probably wanted to ensure that, if the workers ever returned to their jobs, it would be without CASAW activists. There was a precedent for this sort of purge—the 1990 strike at Dome mine in Timmins, Ontario. After a six-month work stoppage, the company won the right to ignore the seniority list and take back only half the unionized workforce, "coincidentally" excluding most activists in the Steelworkers' local.[3]

Royal Oak had researched several acrimonious disputes, including the devastating Phelps Dodge copper strike in Arizona in the 1980s, which, states lawyer and journalist Jonathan Rosenblum, "helped to perfect a new logic in labour relations: If you can't live with a union, then kill it, legally, with permanent replacements." Witte may have even had a copy of the strikebreaking manual included in a book entitled *Operating During Strikes,* partially funded by Phelps Dodge. But the Dome dispute in Ontario was of particular interest. It happened under the noses of managers John Smrke and Kim Cornwell, both of whom worked in Timmins at the time. Royal Oak had studied the Dome strike, blow by blow, before Giant's began, and Cornwell's study of "poststrike job security of strikers and replacement workers" in the United States versus comparable outcomes in Canada had already been published by Queen's University in 1990. (Ironically, she saw more fairness in Canada's system.)

If Royal Oak hoped to purge troublemakers through mass firings, the tactic backfired. The impersonal way in which the men were dismissed, often on the basis of a doubtful identification of figures on blurry videotape, made martyrs of them. They now depended entirely on the union to get their jobs back, which encouraged them to become activists if they weren't already. The terminations became the main issue of the labour dispute—and they would be a big card to play in all attempts to end it.

THE MOLLY MAGUIRES COME TO YELLOWKNIFE

Gordie Kendall was starting to attract attention among union members. Many mistrusted him because he talked too much and told wild stories, but one idea that he claimed as his own looked promising. A few men could sneak into the mine, disable some equipment, and leave evidence that they had been underground. This would show strikebreakers that they were vulnerable, that the mine's security system was ineffective, and that it would be wise to quit their jobs if they valued their health.

Mine-rescue expert Al Shearing worked on practical details of the plan, which he says was originally to spend four weeks living underground. Two friends who worked at Con mine cobbled together some lamps from discarded parts. Shearing, fellow mechanic Tim Bettger, and miner Art St. Amand figured out the best route for slipping in and out of the mine without getting caught. They chose the Akaitcho shaft, a little-used entry 2.5 kilometres from Giant mine's main gate. This meant a long descent, on old ladders in the man-way next to the shaft, to the mine's 750-foot level, and a trek along the drift. Since nobody worked in that area, there was little risk of detection and they could take their time. Kendall, who wasn't in very good physical condition, wouldn't come along, and had failed, Shearing says, to get food for an extended stay.

Another striker, Luc Normandin, dropped the three men off near Yellowknife River at about 11:30 P.M. on June 28; it wasn't yet dark. Their gear included miners' lamps and belts, hard hats, boots, bolt cutters, and a camera. Outside the building over the Akaitcho shaft, an oil drum sat conveniently beneath a broken window. The man way leading underground was covered by only a sheet of plywood, which they pulled off its nails. Beneath that was a hinged steel grate. It was midnight.

Descending in the dark, they kept a distance between themselves to be clear of falling debris. At the end of each ladder was a landing, but the first level was 425 feet down (see map D). From there down, spring runoff was heavy, Tim Bettger says; "basically, the ladder is in the middle of a waterfall. You're soaked, you can't avoid it." There was a short jog from one man way to the next on the 575 level, then down to 750, where they stopped. St. Amand would later testify that he forgot to retrieve a homemade billy club he'd left on a hanger supporting air and water pipes, but Shearing claims the club was his.

Then they set a steady pace along the drift, single file, between the narrow-gauge rails for ore trains. They felt at home in the cocoon of darkness. Water, trickling in the ditch beside the tracks, sounded a bit like the murmur of miners ahead. St. Amand knew that area best, but the route to the 7-12 scooptram shop was simple.[4] Bettger and Shearing had both worked there before. They arrived about 2:00 A.M.; opened the back door of the large, garagelike shop; and saw some strikebreakers working late. So the trio scouted around before going into the shop, where they had time only to spray paint graffiti such as "Scabs go home." A scooptram was baptized "Scabmoble [*sic*]" in large letters.

According to shifter Keith Murray, another message was "The Molly Maguires were here." It was sly irony; the original Molly Maguires had been discovered—or invented—by Pinkerton's in the nineteenth century, during a campaign to crush a miners' union in Pennsylvania. Their reputation, which included terrorism with explosives, was now used by CASAW members to spook strikebreakers, a century and half a continent away.

Bettger photographed the graffiti before they began the knee-cracking ascent. Much later, all three men said they went back out Akaitcho, but Roger Warren says he heard from St. Amand in a bar one night that they had left by a different route, up the B-3 ventilation raise, where they kicked out a board at the top to get out of the mine.

On their way out, explosions echoed loudly through the mine, shaking the rock around them. It was the central blast, the simultaneous firing of explosives at each active workface in the mine. Shearing, Bettger, and St. Amand weren't worried; they were far from any work area. It was about 6:30 A.M. when they arrived at Gate 7, where they got a ride into town.

The next morning, Keith Murray and two supervisors were the first company men in the 7-12 shop. They summoned the Pinkerton's guards to investigate and take pictures. Murray says he was puzzled by one of the spray paintings: "Fuck off, Stubble-Jumper!" Miners have a long tradition of giving each other nick-names, and that was one of his—but it dated back to the days when he was a supervisor in Giant's small open-pit operation, so only the men then on his crew and a few other old-timers would be likely to know it. Murray tried to figure out who it was.

Murray was already worried about mine security. The Pinkerton's guards were aggressive, but didn't seem to realize how vulnerable the mine was to tres-passers, with its dozens of entrances. Mine foreman Noel O'Sullivan, the head supervisor underground, also complained bitterly about it. He and Murray began testing the Pinkerton's men, to see if intruders could get into the mine undetect-ed. The results were not reassuring.

The graffiti expedition quickly became public. Film from the caper was given to Gordie Kendall, who put it, along with a cryptic note, on the desk of CASAW president Bill Schram. Kendall later said that he was also given some caps and stick powder stolen from underground magazines. Much later, Kendall told the RCMP he had disposed of the explosives in the river.

Kendall treated the photos of the graffiti like a trophy, passing them around. He had them in the courthouse for one of the many proceedings against CASAW members. Some men wondered if Kendall was trying to get the union into trouble. Officially, he'd been fired, but was he being paid by the company to lure members into illegal activities? Suspicion spread rapidly in the union hall. Kendall soon quit coming in, turning up only occasionally at the bar next door.

Royal Oak made no official complaint about the graffiti expedition until months later, according to police. Keith Murray claims Pinkerton's called in the RCMP as soon as the spray painting was found. Royal Oak also had some prior warning about the raid. By June 26, Giant had heard about "a surprise party for the scabs" that would involve explosives. The same day, the RCMP passed on "intelligence ... that strikers have been underground at least twice on covert missions." Police instituted a file-management system for major crimes on June 27. Royal Oak's reported vigilance, and the almost daily, covert presence of the RCMP's emergency response team at Giant, had failed to prevent the break-in of June 29.

The next day, June 30, CASAW tipped off territorial Mine Safety inspectors that some machinery at Giant was unsafe. A mechanic who wasn't involved in the raid had drawn up a list of long-standing problems with underground equipment, which the union passed on to Mine Safety. Inspectors checked and ordered Royal Oak to make repairs. They knew that someone had broken into the mine, but did not order the company to seal any of the numerous accesses to the underground. Inspectors merely advised Royal Oak to review its security measures.

Equipment inspections were only the beginning of Royal Oak's summer-long feud with government agencies. The decision to house strikebreakers on mine property was another major issue. There was no place to accommodate that many men legally, and the NWT fire marshal regularly tried to catch the company in the act. Twice inspectors arrived before strikebreakers had a chance to roll up their sleeping bags and clear their makeshift quarters.

There were battles about zoning too. CASAW and Royal Oak alternately trooped to city hall to argue about whether the company should be allowed to house strikebreakers at Giant. The RCMP obliged Royal Oak by helping to move bunkhouse trailers onto the property at about 3:00 A.M. on July 13. Police had known for weeks that this was to be a permanent camp to house Giant's new workforce. That day, Superintendent Watt was told by mediator Bill Lewis that CASAW would probably be broken, though some union workers would return to Giant (presumably, he also provided this opinion to his superiors within the Department of Labour). Intelligence from a union meeting led Watt to conclude that CASAW had "very little support at this stage." But CASAW finally won the seesaw zoning fight in early September.

On July 23, Mine Safety officials charged the company and former mine manager Mike Werner with failing to secure the area where geologist Toni Borschneck was killed by falling rock. It was exactly a year since the accident, and it was the last day the government could legally file charges. Royal Oak's managers grumbled that the charges were purely political, a way to lean on Peggy Witte for her tough bargaining. The charges played into the hands of the union, which had been accusing Royal Oak of ignoring safety. But, in fact, Mine Safety had been on the offensive since the recent arrival of Dave Turner, the division's new head, who was determined to crack down on what he saw as lax safety practices in some NWT mines.

SUPERVISORS SHAFTED

I would never not pay someone the money that they were rightly owed. I would never steal or use anybody to get what I wanted. I have high moral and ethical standards.

—Peggy Witte, October 3, 1992

Cramped quarters and poor living conditions didn't hurt morale behind the picket line as much as strikers hoped. The strikebreakers were accustomed to isolated camps where there is nothing to do but work. Most of them came to Yellowknife for six weeks, worked and slept, then flew home for two weeks off before their next tour of duty. Their worst discomfort was knowing they were strikebreakers in a heavily unionized industry. Many stayed just long enough to qualify for unemployment insurance. "If I could have got a job anyplace else, I wouldn't have come here," said a strikebreaker from Ontario. He was particularly reluctant because he had worked in Yellowknife before. "I didn't want to cross the picket line, because of friends and family. I had [a relative] standing out there with the ladies at CLASS." He didn't go into town all summer. Strikebreakers often asked supervisors and CASAW's line-crossers to buy cigarettes and other supplies in town. Strikebreakers moving around mine property tired of constant abuse from picketers. But the pressure from union men venting their frustration also helped ease the usual conflicts between crews and supervisors. Strikers were their common enemy.

Supervisors' morale fell in early July when Royal Oak refused to pay for overtime worked in June. A lot of money was involved. Terry Burkholder, who supervised the mill mechanics, filed for $5,000 in overtime. Like other shifters, he'd worked long hours to keep the mill functioning and he was marooned at Giant whenever picketers blocked traffic. Burkholder's check for June included his overtime pay, but a later printout of his bank account showed it was $5,000 short. Burkholder's boss told him that Witte was outraged when she saw Giant's overtime bill. He says he learned that Witte had the bank stop payment of the overtime portions of the checks until Royal Oak's accountants had reviewed the issue. That took about a month, and in the end many supervisors were paid for only a fraction of their overtime. Royal Oak suggested that some shifters tried to profit from the labour dispute.

Peggy Witte and John Smrke flew in for a staff meeting. Mike Caron, a supervisor who quit over the issue, says Witte took personal responsibility for cutting overtime pay. She said the company would pay only for time actually worked, not for the many hours shifters spent waiting for a helicopter to ferry them across the picket line. Caron was furious. "I stood up and walked out, because I just couldn't sit there and listen to the crap anymore. It was inconceivable to me that a company would do something like that to her staff when she needs them the most. What the hell is she going to do when times are good?"

THE FIRST BLAST

Union politics were also in turmoil. CASAW Local 4 was desperate for full-time organizing help, but the national executive insisted it had no money for that. President Bill Schram was showing signs of strain. Former president Dale Johnston was recruited as strike coordinator, but had a business to run and couldn't keep up with the load.

The Steelworkers volunteered their staff lawyers in early June. Although CASAW desperately needed legal help, some of its leaders refused Steel's offer, suspecting it was part of a plan to take over their union. The decision was not popular with all Local 4's members. "It was like we were going down and somebody was throwing us a life jacket," Mark Eveson says. "And we were saying, 'Oh no, I don't want that brand of life jacket, throw me a different brand.'"

CASAW turned instead to the Canadian Auto Workers. By a quirk of history, the CAW was already paying much of the roughly $150 per week each Giant picketer earned in strike pay. Many years earlier, CASAW Local 4 had made a mutual-defense pact with the BC mining locals of the old Canadian Association of Industrial, Mechanical and Allied Workers (CAIMAW). That meant each local would raise union dues to provide strike pay to locals on strike. When the CAW absorbed CAIMAW, one condition of the merger was to continue the pact with CASAW.

The CAW sent organizer Harold David to Yellowknife on July 21, a CAIMAW veteran who'd known some of CASAW's men for years. David has an amazing collection of books on labour history, a signed photograph of American singer and political activist Paul Robeson, and some experience with tough labour disputes. Officially, David was also embroiled in one. After four years of legal battles, he was still locked out of his longtime job at a mill owned by Western Canada Steel.

A few hours after Harold David arrived in Yellowknife, someone blew a hole in a TV satellite dish at Giant mine. The saboteurs hiked to the satellite dish, up the hill from the town site, at about 1:30 A.M. They loosened bolts anchoring the dish and attached a few sticks of powder, to which they hooked up some tape fuse. Rumours that some miners had smuggled explosives and detonators from their workplaces were not unfounded.

According to the police, the fuse at the satellite dish was long enough to give the saboteurs 6.5 minutes before the powder blew. Security guards and picketers heard the blast. Nobody was hurt and the damage was minimal; the dish did not come off its moorings.

The Pinkerton's guards didn't even find out what had been damaged until late the next morning. By that time, strikers Al Shearing and Tim Bettger were on the road to British Columbia. Talk soon spread on the picket line that they were responsible for the satellite-dish caper; the RCMP heard the story too. Information and rumour spread quickly. Generally, people at Giant joked that the strikers were so incompetent they couldn't even blow up a satellite dish. Still, if someone could wander onto mine property undetected and blow up something small, they could also do serious damage. The blast was probably meant to scare Peggy Witte into making concessions—a serious miscalculation.

Mediator Bill Lewis had convened a session in Yellowknife for the next day, the first mediation round in six weeks. Harold David barely had time to assemble a proposal. CASAW's main demand was that Royal Oak rescind all the firings. Satellite blast or no, Witte insisted that the terminations were final. The parties never met face-to-face before Lewis had to adjourn the meeting.

Later, Witte would publicly imply that there was a link between Harold David's arrival and the attack on the satellite dish. The company pegged him as a dangerous radical, but David was popular with many rank-and-file union members. He steeped them in labour history, fostering the feeling that they were fighting for a grand cause. At a membership meeting a couple of days later, he gave a pep talk said to have lasted two hours. "You aren't fighting alone, all of Canadian labour is behind you, he stressed. This is a historic dispute, an attempt to introduce US-style union busting into Canadian mining, something we haven't seen for decades. We will back you, and you will eventually win," he said.

David was impressed with many of the union members' wives, particularly CLASS president June Roberts. He told some of the women that, while the men were on the picket line, only they could ensure the strike's success. He gave Roberts a book called *Holding the Line* that extolled women's fortitude and organizing ability in the Phelps Dodge copper strike, one of Witte's own examples of union busting. He urged CLASS women to think big in their planning; he'd help if he could.

For now, the wives had other worries. Many families were negotiating with their banks, unable to meet mortgage payments. Some borrowed money from relatives and friends. High payments on homes meant less money for food and clothing. David told them to stop making mortgage payments. He negotiated with local bankers to delay foreclosures. He promised that union members would make up the missed payments when the dispute was resolved.

David spent a lot of time chatting with the strikers. When former local president Dale Johnston mentioned casually that one of the older members had a history of heart trouble, David asked, "Do we have life insurance for the guys on the picket line?" No, Johnston replied. Nobody in Yellowknife had even thought about the fact that, when the men hit the picket line, Royal Oak stopped paying their insurance premiums. David said it was standard practice for unions to pay the premiums during labour disputes. He obtained information on the company life insurance plan and promised to deal with it when he got back to Vancouver. He left early on July 25. At home, he had a message to call Yellowknife. Striker Ken Cawley, CASAW's national vice president, and another union leader had been killed in a car accident the night before. They were attending CASAW's national convention in British Columbia.

Cawley was married, with four children. His wife, Linda, was his childhood sweetheart. They'd grown up together in Sarnia, Ontario, and moved around the country from one mining town to another, until they settled in Yellowknife. Ken was a hockey enthusiast, putting in long hours as a volunteer referee and unofficial coach to his teenage sons. Cawley was also one of CASAW's many volunteer firefighters. He had kept a fairly low public profile during the labour dispute, and was generally considered a union moderate. Jim O'Neil, for example, found Cawley reasonable and approachable.

Royal Oak had fired Cawley a month earlier. The company claimed he had assaulted a company supplier on May 24. His widow insists the alleged assault was a case of mistaken identity. This was important because automobile insurance would cover the loss of future earnings only if Cawley was employed at the time of his death. Linda Cawley was surprised when she received a sympathy note from Peggy Witte, with an invitation to let her know if there was anything she could do. Cawley and CLASS president June Roberts drafted a reply, asking Royal Oak to declare the firing a mistake. This would cost the company nothing but could mean her family's security. The company refused, and the legal battle dragged on for years.

Little was accomplished at CASAW's annual convention after the deaths. Al Shearing and other Yellowknife delegates arranged to send Cawley's body back to Yellowknife. Shearing and Tim Bettger went on to Vancouver while the rest drove home.

The police would soon make a major issue of Shearing and Bettger's trip to Vancouver. Shearing says the main reason for it was to pick up the son of his common-law wife. But Shearing and Bettger also did some shopping. Among the things they bought were a hunting knife, a weight for diving, and running shoes. Bettger bought six quartz movements for clocks. According to Shearing, Bettger planned to make clocks for relatives as gifts. The fact that most of their purchases were charged on Bettger's Visa card later allowed the police to trace them.

Bettger and Shearing checked out Royal Oak's head office, and plastered a CASAW poster on the company's door. They thought they were being tailed by the RCMP. An incident on the beach reinforced their suspicion. "We're sitting at a picnic table, having a hamburger and a hot dog," Shearing says, chuckling at the memory of Bettger's account. "And these three guys stuck out like sore thumbs. They're not people that's supposed to be on the beach. And I says to Tim, 'Watch this.' So all of a sudden I disappeared, because these three guys are not looking at me. I went to the washroom. And Tim was looking at these guys. And they went hysterical, because they didn't know where I went."

Shearing came back to the picnic table, and Bettger took his turn going to the bathroom, to see if he'd be followed. "This one comes running into the washroom," Shearing says. "And this guy pretends he's not doing anything, goes over and washes his hands. And then Tim, he's not even pissing, he's just standing there ... This guy must've washed his hands for ten minutes."

Shearing and Bettger had one errand they definitely didn't want the police to know about. According to Shearing, fellow striker Gordie Kendall had asked Bettger, just before the trip south, to take a sealed envelope to someone in Vancouver. Kendall arranged for Bettger to deliver the envelope to a man they were to meet in a shopping mall, Shearing says.

RCMP documents reveal that, in 1993, Bettger had told another union member about giving Kendall a "written rendition" of the route he and Shearing had used to slip into the mine via the Akaitcho shaft. "It was just a regular white letter envelope, and I know exactly what it contained," Bettger said in an interview. "It wasn't an artistic map. By following the directions, a person entering through Akaitcho would've very quickly found themselves on 750 ... in the exact neighbourhood of [the] 7-12 shop." Bettger refuses to describe Kendall's mysterious associate, but Shearing says the man's jacket had once sported insignia shaped like those used by the Hells Angels motorcycle club. They suspect the man was either a member, or a plant who wanted them to think so.

Shearing and Bettger returned to Yellowknife by bus, stopping briefly in Edmonton on August 1, doing some more shopping on Bettger's credit card.

CROSSING THE LINE

You're driving by all your coworkers, led by these radical leaders. We hoped maybe them seeing us go in might be some sort of salvation, they might see the light.

—Jim O'Neil, February 1993

Scabs are fucking scabs and they can't justify what they did.

—Jim Evoy, president of the NWT Federation of Labour,
January 1994

Only a dozen CASAW men had crossed the picket line by late July, most of them early in the dispute. But company managers phoned union members, or talked to them in town or on the picket line, applying pressure to cross. Miner Roger Warren says he was approached by mine manager Terry Byberg and Major Ralph Sinke a couple of days before the riot. Sinke allegedly maligned CASAW's leaders with his own account of the June 6 mediation session. "These guys you got representing you are no fucking good," Warren recalls him saying.

Royal Oak's recruiting paid off. According to a procompany source, as many as seventy of the union's 234 members had told Royal Oak by mid-July that they wanted to return to work but were afraid of fellow strikers. Several asked for special protection, or for money to relocate their wives and families. By early August, some CASAW men began to think the union was doomed. The number of men on the picket line dwindled. Several dozen union stalwarts were banned from the line while they awaited trials; others disapproved of picket-line antics. Many men, unable to live on picket pay, found work in southern Canada, or in prospecting camps or hunting lodges.

A group of strike opponents, including Chris Neill, organized a back-to-work movement. Neill and another CASAW member, Dave Vodnoski, were particularly active in phoning other union dissidents, saying there would be safety in numbers if they all crossed the picket line together. One man went back to work on July 26 to test the waters. Nothing happened to him, so, on August 4, Neill, Vodnoski, and O'Neil crossed with five others.

That night, "SCAB" was painted on three line-crossers' homes or cars, including O'Neil's new house. Most Giant-related vandalism had been confined to mine property; now it was in town. The next night, someone painted "CASAW SUCKS" on a striker's truck.

Previous defections were hushed up by the workers involved and Royal Oak, but, this time, Neill and O'Neil talked to reporters. The day before he went in, Neill said that strike opponents were tired of being intimidated; "I think we'll see these guys intimidating the union now." He said fifty to sixty men would return to work in the next few weeks, in addition to the twenty-five to thirty already inside the line. (In fact there were fifteen at most.) This could deprive CASAW of its "striking rights," Neill said—meaning the union could be decertified or a majority of union members could vote to accept Royal Oak's terms.

Jim O'Neil says his decision was guided by his conscience, not by money. He believed CASAW was corrupt, had abandoned its democratic principles, and was sponsoring violence. He did not go to union meetings, but admits that crossing the picket line was the hardest thing he ever did. No wonder; O'Neil's family has a history of union activism. His uncle is national secretary-treasurer of the Canadian Auto Workers. Before working at Giant, O'Neil was a local officer of an airline union that merged with the CAW. He had promoted a CASAW–CAW merger several times. Other CASAW members had dismissed him as a Jimmy-come-lately who'd done nothing for the local but wanted to change everything.

Strikers had another interpretation of O'Neil's decision to cross. They pointed to the new house he and his wife, Jane, moved into on August 1. Jane had a well-paid government job, but the mortgage payments were high. However, the O'Neils had made a deal to buy the house after the tentative agreement was reached in April. But now, if Jim was going to organize a rival to CASAW, a topic he had discussed with a lawyer in early June, he didn't want to be personally liable for the costs. The house was registered in Jane's name on September

14; Jim says all their assets were transferred to her. "All I've got is socks and underwear," he quipped later.

Jim's crossing the picket line was a turning point in the couple's lives. In May, while Jim fretted, Jane believed that "strikes don't last long, we can handle it." When Jim was away flying small-plane charters from Cambridge Bay, Jane felt free of the stress of the labour dispute. "I never got hassled. I felt comfortable, pushing my stroller through Northland," past strikers' homes. "It was only when Jim came back that it [got] heavy again." After Jim crossed, she was glad they had moved to the suburbs. "If we were still in Northland, I would've felt vulnerable," Jane says. "Before, a lot of the guys thought he did some things wrong, but he still wasn't a scab."

Jim felt the pressure too. Once, on July 17, he and Chris Neill and another friend flew to Fishing Lake for a break. Chris was interested in flying, and this common interest strengthened their friendship. When Jim was offered a pilot's job in Cambridge Bay for the fall fish haul, Neill talked him out of it by saying the battle at Giant was coming to an end. "Personally, I thought the strike was pretty much over after the riot," O'Neil says. "I phoned to see if I still had a job out there," and talked to Terry Byberg.

Management told line-crossers to come to work through Gate 4, where picketing was forbidden. Standing at gates that were rarely used, picketers felt useless, and angry at scabs who avoided facing their former coworkers. A roadside sign labelled Neill as a "coward scab." By this time, only about seventy-five regular picketers remained to man five gates, twenty-four hours a day. More than 100 strikers had left town, at least temporarily, and there was talk of women helping to hold the line.

CASAW's leaders weren't surprised by the back-to-work movement. "It's good to keep the scabs all in one place," declared former president Dale Johnston. The line-crossers were known strike opponents, and had tried to cut special deals with the company ever since the dispute started, he said.

One of the men who crossed the picket line on August 4 was a surprise. Shane Riggs, nicknamed Spanky, a happy-go-lucky scooptram operator, had been an active picketer. He shared a trailer with his sister, Lynda, and her boyfriend, a municipal bylaw officer. Riggs had many friends at both local mines, and had been charged with possession of a dangerous weapon at the June 14 skirmish. The Pinkerton's video allegedly showed him throwing rocks. When Riggs appeared at the mine with Neill and O'Neil, Royal Oak sent him home. But Neill helped get Riggs's charges dropped. "I'm footing his lawyer bill ... He spent two solid days with the RCMP," Neill said.

Despite the publicity, the back-to-work movement wasn't as successful as Royal Oak had hoped. Only thirty-eight CASAW members had crossed the picket line by September 1, Terry Byberg said later. When school started, "we expected an influx of people. It was quite apparent that we were not going to get a lot more coming back in. We went out to hire a permanent workforce by the 10th or 13th [of September]." It was an attempt to alter drastically the landscape of Canadian labour relations. Unlike their US counterparts, Canadian labour boards had never permitted permanent replacement workers.

There were nevertheless some major losses for CASAW. A picket captain, Verne Fullowka, crossed the line. "The guys" knew he was in financial trouble. They tried to talk him out of it; Roger Warren says he offered to lend Fullowka money. A rumour soon circulated that Fullowka had kept a diary of other strikers' illegal activities.

O'Neil says he understood Fullowka's dilemma. "I was asked to go see him. I went over with Chris [Neill]. There was Verne, and some other people in the kitchen. I had a drink of whiskey ... He was torn. I could see it in his face. I didn't say anything about crossing the picket line. I just said, 'It's a tough call—it's your call.' I didn't know this guy very well, eh. But I did know he was a picket captain and that his wife was pressuring him."

Another serious defection was boilerman Jim Gauthier, a member of the union bargaining committee that signed the April 18 tentative agreement. His crossing was considered treasonous, and caused doubts among many CASAW members about his performance as a member of their bargaining team. Bruce Bannister, the head of the bargaining team and a close friend of Gauthier's, tried to talk him out of crossing. "I explained that it would just make things tougher for the rest of us if he's in there helping them run the operation," Bannister says bitterly. "He said that he was under severe pressure at home. He was going to lose his marriage and all kinds of other shit if he didn't."

"Inside" was another world, one miner says. "It was like a new mine." Royal Oak segregated contractors and its own employees. The two groups didn't earn the same wages or benefits, but they did the same work. The workforce was going full tilt, putting in more hours than was legally allowed. Royal Oak's managers were obsessed with production. Line-crossers toiled on weekends; contractors worked six weeks straight. The company would not admit it, but its bottom line was taking a beating.

The remaining strikers were not cowed by the back-to-work movement. The RCMP noted renewed activity on both sides of the picket line, and in town in late August. CASAW "is hostile to the local police," noted Sergeant Bill Code, the RCMP's liaison officer. The union was no longer accepting his rationale for the RCMP's conduct. Code advised bringing in Sergeant Lynn Kraeling, the

RCMP's labour specialist in British Columbia, as CASAW had been asking since May. "All members are swamped with minor complaints from both sides. If Kraeling can talk to [them], it may result in a reduction of nuisance files. He could benefit us," Code informed Superintendent Watt. The idea was rejected. "This member can do no more than what we are doing," Watt responded. Tension on the picket line continued to escalate.

Al Shearing says he kept a vigil on a "nice little hill" where for months he'd watched Pinkerton's guards on their rounds, and police who tried to drive secretly onto the property at Gate 7. He sprinkled pepper as security against dogs. "If anybody snuck in behind me, I'd know it, because [as] soon as the dogs pick [it] up, they start to sneeze. And they can't run." Guards even walked their dogs through the gates, right up to the picketers. "Some [guards] like to get a fight going," a company staffer said at the time.

Fewer union men made night raids on the property, but those who did knew how to avoid traps. Bragging and questioning about people's exploits grew less common. "People just didn't discuss stuff they saw," says miner Roger Warren. "It was sort of like, see no evil, hear no evil ... Nobody wanted to be looked on as a rat."

The power company had isolated Giant from the rest of Yellowknife, so knocking out Giant's electricity could now be done with impunity. The most spectacular outage occurred on August 20, when saboteurs felled four power poles in a rugged gully. Giant was cut off for twenty-one hours.

Much more serious were a series of underground break-ins. The RCMP's intelligence was that at least two had taken place by June 26, before the graffiti caper on June 29. Additional break-ins on July 23 and during the first week of August produced more graffiti and sabotaged equipment. They were not reported at the time, according to both the RCMP and the chief mine inspector, Dave Turner. He said that, if he had known, he would have told Royal Oak to beef up its security.

Security cost money, however—about $607,000 in August, according to company figures—and Royal Oak was frugal. Pinkerton's manager Chris Morton says he and Byberg argued about the bills for security, while "Peggy Witte was screaming" on the phone for the force to be downsized. Within days of the underground break-in on June 29, the RCMP were informed that twenty-two security men would leave and not be replaced. But reductions to security personnel, expertise, and equipment had begun even earlier, to Pinkerton's alarm. In a letter to Witte dated August 7, Pinkerton's CEO Paul St. Amour cited concerns for "personal safety" and warned Royal Oak that it might be vulnerable to lawsuits over incidents resulting from a breach of security. He noted that "Royal Oak has assumed all liability during the labour dispute coverage for a reduction of your hourly rates ... Based on the the results of our recent security audit and ongoing situational analysis, there is every indication our risks and exposure will increase ... Troublemakers might gain access to the most vital points of Royal Oak Mines and paralyze operations. The potential for loss is inestimable." St. Amour also advised Royal Oak to bolster its video and electronic security.

It was possible that, even if Royal Oak had beefed up security, intrusions might have continued and mine inspectors might have declared Giant unsafe and closed it. On both sides of the picket line suspicious graffiti was attributed to rivalry between local line-crossers and strikebreakers from the south, or to practical jokes between men on different shifts.

The break-ins raise unsettling questions. How much did the RCMP know about the graffiti runs? How much blame do they bear for doing nothing about them? Had informants already told police what was going on? One of them, Steelworker Bob Robertson, says he learned later that the RCMP knew not only about the break-ins and stolen explosives, but also about Al Shearing's part in these activities. He claims that police and Royal Oak laid a trap to catch intruders red-handed. "That's why security was so lax—it was done on purpose." Robertson had kept a low profile since his arrest for attacking Royal Oak's bus on May 26. His arrest was an embarrassment to the Union of Northern Workers, where he worked, and he had promised to stay out of trouble. That wasn't easy for Robertson. "I like to explore and try new things, and take chances and play life to the extreme," he says. At thirty-six, he'd packed a lot of living into a short time. He'd raced cars as a hobby, mined for two years at Giant, worked at Chrysler, and returned to Yellowknife to mine at Con. He'd been a crusader for mine safety. Taller than average, with a broad, open face and a ready laugh, he makes friends easily. He's smart and glib, which had helped vault him into the presidency of the Steelworkers' local at Con in the 1980s. "I could bring the guys to a strike-feverish pitch just by one speech," he says, snapping his fingers.

On the other hand, Robertson was dubbed "Ashes Brain" because of his heavy use of pot, hash, and other drugs. "I would be buzzed from the first thing in the morning to the last thing at night," he admits. "I've done acid underground, the whole bit." In 1988, he was fired from his mining job at Con for safety violations.

When it became clear in 1995 that Robertson had been an informant, stories surfaced that he'd been busted for drugs in 1992; that the police had obtained his services in return for not charging him; that Robertson's arrest on the picket line on May 26 could have been a ploy to boost his credibility with union hard liners. This theory is given some credence by the fact that the RCMP tried to recruit half a dozen CASAW members as informants during the summer of 1992. Robertson scoffs at such speculation. He says he learned about various illegal schemes at Giant from friends talking in bars. As he was a mine-safety advocate, the information troubled his conscience to the point that he occasionally called in anonymous warnings to police—like the tip-off on June 14, before the melee. The implication of forays into the mine and vandalism with explosives particularly upset him, Robertson says. In the first few days of August, he says, he asked the advice of Austin Marshall, a local lawyer, on whether or not he should report what he knew to the RCMP. "I'll never forget what he told me. He says, 'Bob, you could be implicating yourself.'" Robertson says he didn't tell police anything until much later. It's clear that he did see Marshall, who won't discuss the matter.

SHADOW DIPLOMACY

The back-to-work movement probably contributed to an internal shake-up in CASAW. The first to go was lawyer Richard Peach, a gun-club acquaintance of local president Bill Schram. By early August, the union executive realized that CASAW owed Peach about $106,000. Schram was criticized because he had not kept track of Peach's hours. Despite his hard work, Peach was unpopular because he'd advised men who were charged with offenses to simply accept being banned from the picket line. The real issue, however, was Schram's leadership. There were complaints that he could not handle the stress of the job. His exit was graceful. Schram announced his candidacy for CASAW national vice president, the position held by Ken Cawley before his fatal car accident. He resigned as president of Local 4, passing on the job to Vice President Harry Seeton. It was widely assumed that Schram's decision was voluntary, but sources say there was a behind-the-scenes meeting at which he was told to bow out. To Schram's surprise, he lost the election for national vice-president to Fred Couch, a yarn-spinning, hard-drinking Scotsman who had ferried supplies to the picket line and whose converted school bus served as shelter at Gate 3. Schram took defeat well, becoming a stalwart on the picket line, often putting in double shifts.

CASAW replaced Peach with a Vancouver law firm, McGrady, Askew & Fiorillo. They specialize in labour law and had often worked with the old CAIMAW union. The firm's youngest partner, Gina Fiorillo, had cut her teeth on the Western Canada Steel dispute that cost Harold David his job. Fiorillo burst onto the scene in Yellowknife in mid-August. She quickly made the Giant dispute her personal crusade; she became the local's lawyer, adviser, and part-time therapist.

Harry Seeton, the new president, soon relied heavily on her advice and friendship, and spent long hours with her on the phone when she wasn't in Yellowknife. Fiorillo is small and sturdy, with a dark, Mediterranean complexion. She seems turbopowered by nicotine and coffee, and looks as if her natural habitats are smoky union halls and late-night cafés where patrons discuss philosophy. Many of the miners, after three disastrous months on the picket line, developed an almost religious belief that Fiorillo and her law partner, Leo McGrady, could save their union. Fiorillo was their hero. "In the middle of going around the clock preparing for court cases there'd be a knock on the door, and a plate covered over [was] left," she says. "And that would be a caribou dinner, hot, with gravy. Just so amazing, so kindhearted."

Fiorillo's first task was to prepare an unfair labour practice complaint against Royal Oak, asking the Canada Labour Relations Board (CLRB) to declare illegal the company's mass firing of strikers. The union had only ninety days from the first firing, on June 23, to file a complaint. The other urgent problem was that CASAW had no one to represent its members in court. The NWT bar finally permitted Fiorillo to handle civil cases like contempt-of-court proceedings strikers faced when they were accused of breaking the picketing injunction. Local lawyer Austin Marshall agreed to take the criminal cases. After a hectic week in Yellowknife collecting evidence, Fiorillo returned to Vancouver to write the union's complaint to the CLRB.

Fiorillo's presence also inspired CASAW's women's group. CLASS was about to begin its most important initiative of the entire labour dispute. President June Roberts had thought of a way to raise money to pull CASAW families through the seemingly inevitable financial disasters ahead. She proposed that local strike supporters and southern trade unionists "adopt a family" for the duration of the dispute. Contributors would be told about the families they adopted, and sent news bulletins. She timidly pitched the idea at a multiunion committee meeting in early August, but no launch date was set.

After mediation failed on July 23, both federal and territorial politicians tried unconventional ways of settling the Giant dispute. Federal Labour Minister Marcel Danis says he believed that Peggy Witte was the main obstacle to a settlement, so he quizzed his cabinet colleagues about contacts in the mining industry who might induce Royal Oak to soften its position. According to Danis, Indian and Northern Affairs Minister Tom Siddon had the best contacts. Siddon had worked in the industry and was a friend of the Keevil family, whose mining empire included Teck Corporation, with a minority stake in Royal Oak.

Siddon denies the entire episode. "I was not asked to facilitate anything that would amount to any interference by the federal government," he says. "In my recollection."

"Siddon talked to them," confirms former NWT Justice Minister Dennis Patterson, who had also urged Siddon to approach the Keevils. "They didn't want to be involved."

The NWT government was also looking for a backroom miracle. Yellowknife bureaucrats had no faith in federal mediator Bill Lewis, and felt that personality clashes at the bargaining table were hurting the chances of success. So the territorial government enlisted the help of John Parker, a former commissioner of the NWT—the equivalent of lieutenant governor of a province. Parker knew the North, had experience with difficult negotiations, and was a mining engineer with good contacts in the industry.

A government official also met with Jim Evoy, the president of the NWT Federation of Labour. Evoy had no official power over CASAW, but was respected. For all his tough rhetoric, the bureaucrats knew Evoy was reasonable and more likely to get a deal cut with Royal Oak than CASAW's official leaders were.

Parker phoned Witte in mid-August. He didn't tell her the NWT government had enlisted him, just that he was personally concerned about the Giant dispute. Things weren't going well, he told her. "She agreed," Parker says, "but her position was that Royal Oak needed a concessionary contract to exist," and she wouldn't budge on the thirty-eight firings. "There was a problem with ... what the mine saw as their good workers [versus] those who were now leading the strike."

Parker and Evoy met secretly in a Yellowknife hotel room on September 2, along with the assistant deputy minister of justice. Evoy predicted that CASAW and the Canadian Auto Workers would merge. This would address Witte's complaints about CASAW being a small, radical union, but the merger could take a year. The firings were the biggest stumbling block. CASAW still demanded amnesty for all strikers, Evoy said. He and Parker agreed to involve John Sanderson, the NWT government's main labour-relations consultant. They seemed to think he might replace mediator Bill Lewis, or at least prompt Royal Oak to negotiate. When Parker called Witte on September 8, she was not enthusiastic about accepting Sanderson's intercession. "She told me that there were forty to fifty workers that had now returned to the operation," Parker says. Witte assumed that CASAW's members would soon cross the picket line and vote to disband the union. "She was aware ... of a move toward decertification." She clearly felt that she was winning the dispute and could wait until the union collapsed, Parker says. "It was fairly clear that Bay Street and the money markets were pretty much behind Royal Oak's actions."

Royal Oak had just raised $12 million through the sale of share warrants, and the stock price had moved up smartly. "Capitalists hate seeing these high-paid, noneducated mine workers," says one Vancouver stockbroker. "They *love it* when a hard-nosed manager gets up on her podium and says, 'Get a life, guys.'" Royal Oak stock was nevertheless pressured by short-sellers betting it would tumble. The company was even labeled "Royal Joke Mines" on the front page of the *Financial Times* on August 24, but Witte was tough enough to ride out such ridicule.

Parker called Sanderson on September 15, and he in turn called Witte, who was on vacation in Hawaii. But Parker's initiative was soon drowned in a tidal wave of events.

The remaining option to advance a settlement was an industrial inquiry commission, or IIC—as the NWT government had suggested to Marcel Danis on June 10. Commissioners could at least force Royal Oak and CASAW to talk. Several union leaders thought Witte would make such unreasonable demands at an IIC that she could then be found guilty by the Canada Labour Relations Board for bargaining in bad faith. CASAW officially requested an IIC on August 22. The idea quickly gathered support. NDP Labour critic Joy Langan endorsed it almost immediately. She had kept in touch with CASAW all summer and pushed the issue with the Department of Labour. Within a couple of weeks, the federal Liberals publicly joined the chorus for an IIC, and questioned "unduly harsh police intervention" in the dispute, and had already announced support for a law banning the use of replacement workers. (The party has since reversed its position.) Langan believed Marcel Danis was about to act.

THE SECOND BLAST

They're blasting at night without permits. We don't mind Pinkerton's and dogs, but it's getting too dangerous.

—mechanic Terry Legge, September 2, 1992

CASAW was slowly maneuvering into a better legal and political position, but many men still worried that they would never get their jobs back, that Witte would run Giant forever with strikebreakers.

Power outages had caused only temporary inconvenience for Royal Oak. So

Shearing, Bettger, Terry Legge, and Conrad Lisoway decided in late August to attack the ventilation system, one of Giant's vulnerable points. The entire mine depended on pressurized air to clear out dust from blasts and fumes from diesel engines, and to power miners' tools. Disabling the ventilation plant on surface would have shut Giant down, probably for months. The four men decided to warn Royal Oak by first blowing up the heater that warmed the air going underground. This wouldn't stop operations, but, with winter coming, the company would have to scramble to replace the heating system. "The intent of setting this explosive was to draw attention to the mine site and to get the company and the union to sit down and talk," Shearing says.

According to RCMP documents, the saboteurs met on August 31 to develop a plan. Bettger had made a timer from one of the clock movements he had bought in Vancouver a month earlier. The timer was hooked up to an electric blasting cap that would ignite sticks of powder. Batteries would power the timer and trigger the explosion. The four men slipped easily onto Giant property. Lisoway and Legge kept a lookout while Shearing and Bettger planted the time bomb. They waited and waited for the explosion, but nothing happened. Bettger suspected that the battery's voltage was too low and planned to fix it the next night. Legge said he chickened out of the second mission, suddenly afraid that a security guard on patrol might wander by and get hurt. The other three made the repairs.

The blast went off just after midnight on September 2. The heating plant was destroyed. No one was injured, but men working at the mine were shocked and scared. The heater was propane-fired; what if the nearby propane tank had exploded and the ventilation fans had kept turning? "That is the main ventilation shaft," said an underground supervisor. "A serious fire, a serious explosion, a serious inrush of poisonous gas could cause major havoc. Probably not injuries, probably fatalities." Many workers were angry with the security guards. "How did these guys get in here?" asked shifter Keith Murray. "We're paying this Pinkerton's outfit big bucks and guys come in and put a bomb in the vent plant ... I thought of it as a warning of things to come."

A CASAW spokesman, probably Harry Seeton, told Sergeant Bill Code that he feared a confrontation was brewing out of the continual hassles with Pinkerton's on the picket line. Royal Oak's contact told Code that a confrontation was inevitable unless circumstances changed. The RCMP soon sent an ERT into the bush near Giant to find good locations for full-time surveillance, led by their media-liaison officer, Dave Grundy.

Chief mine inspector Dave Turner was alarmed. But the NWT government now claims to have no mine inspectors' reports pertaining to the explosions of July 22 or September 1, and no reports at all for the period between August 4 and September 28.

There was surprisingly little public outcry about the latest explosion, despite its ominous nature. An editorial in *yellowknifer* lamely called on Royal Oak and CASAW to negotiate "a Canadian compromise" before events escalated further. Townspeople did not realize that the armies had dug in, and nothing short of drastic action would alter the battle lines. "It seemed like this was all just normal behaviour ... to look for license plates, grope around in the dark, go down to the mine site and burn something," line-crosser Craig Richardson said later.

Royal Oak was aggressively hiring its own workforce to replace Procon's contract workers, cutting the wage scale at the same time. A deadline was set to prod union members who lacked faith in CASAW to cross the picket line: those who crossed after September 14 would be paid up to $5 an hour less than previously. Only a few men crossed. "They love it every time someone goes back," Chris Neill said on August 31. "We've gone back to work with lots of protection." The company helped put in surveillance cameras, extra lights, and motion sensors at his house, and "is paying my electrical bill ... Jim's [O'Neil's] place looks like Fort Knox," he added—and the company was paying for damage to vehicles related to the dispute. (The O'Neils deny that Pinkerton's or Royal Oak paid for any of their security measures.) Neill had faith in the Pinkerton's guards. "They're antagonizing them [strikers]," he said. "Now, the Pinkerton's can show their power. They're showing their power right now." Besides Major Sinke, another sixty-two-year-old Pinkerton's man had been an intelligence officer in Vietnam, Neill claimed. "They've got guys in town. They've got guys hanging out with the union guys"—supporting unionists' suspicions about plants and *agents provocateurs*.

Union families felt ostracized, that they were being driven out of town and the community condoned it. "I was like a lot of other people," remembers June Roberts. "You get pissed off, you wish the fucking place would burn to the ground. [We were] so sick of it dragging on. [There was] harassment and constant abuse. Not only for yourself, but for people around you."

Time and vandalism at Giant had eroded support for CASAW, even among members of other unions, particularly the public-sector Union of Northern Workers. Corrections officer Dave Talbot had often visited the picket line and had joined demonstrations. "I knew Al Shearing for close to twenty years, and spoke to him quite a lot out there. He discussed things with me at the picket line that eventually led me, because I was a peace officer, to feel that I shouldn't go out anymore," Talbot says.

Police officers were weary of people's taunts and of petty crimes they couldn't solve. They had more complaints, real and bogus, than they could handle, about thrown rocks, spotlights aimed at drivers on the road, intruders on mine property, threats made on the picket line by both Pinkerton's guards and strikers, vehicles driven without lights at night, drivers with improper licenses, and so on. Pinkerton's men and strikers had chance encounters in the dark, sometimes when men went into the bush to relieve themselves. Both sides had spies in the bushes, listening, watching, and playing tricks. Officers reacted by issuing arbitrary orders to picketers, such as not to wear camouflage clothing and not to walk between picket gates. "One side provokes the other every day," intoned Corporal Grundy.

In early September, the women of CLASS got a taste of nighttime confrontation. They began walking the highway from gate to gate, defying the RCMP and court restrictions on picketing. Most union men were uneasy about the women's marching at night, but the women had fun. The practice drove the Pinkerton's guards crazy. Picketers had acquired one of Pinkerton's two-way radios, and used it to send guards off chasing phantoms. CLASS president June Roberts recalls an encounter on September 11, when she and about sixteen other women walked the length of the property. At one point, a guard walked along near them, with a fierce-looking dog on a leash. "When we got to the crusher gate, he was close to the road, and some of the women were scared to go past," Roberts says. "I didn't put it past him that he'd sic the dog on us. So I radioed in: 'Got an asshole here with a dog!'" Some CASAW men rushed over; the guard jumped into the ditch, cursing and swearing at the women. "The dog was just going mental. Then he got it all calmed down, and I started going, 'meeow, meeow.' All the girls started doing it, and the dog was going bonkers and this guy's just hanging on; the dog almost got us."

Things were more serious the next night. Pinkerton's had started patrolling the highway in the maroon sedan normally used by Royal Oak executives. As the car went by some picketers, someone smashed a large rock into the driver's side of the windshield. Hours later, a rock shattered the windshield of a sports car driven by Shawn Johnston, son of former CASAW president Dale Johnston. He and his two passengers, all high-school students, were taken to the hospital. He believed that the rock was thrown by a guard on a hill. The RCMP made no arrests in either incident and said little to the media. The mine had become a "banana republic," as some people called it, where normal rules no longer applied.

Sometimes there were battles in town. On September 11, Al Shearing and Tim Bettger drove to a convenience store to investigate a report that two Pinkerton's guards were staked out there. Bettger got out of his truck to ask the guards what they were doing; the guards decided to leave. Shearing then threw what he describes as a 3-foot broom handle after the truck, hitting it. Shearing was arrested two days later, charged with assault with a weapon, and jailed in maximum security. To many union members, it was a bit like arresting the

Lone Ranger, though Shearing's nickname on the line was "The Weasel." In recent weeks, he'd had several run-ins with the police, but he remained as calm, cheerful, and resourceful as ever.

From the first days of the dispute, Shearing had led scavenging expeditions to the city dump, hunting for Royal Oak's garbage. Shearing could find buried treasure when everyone else failed. When Royal Oak began shredding documents, he sorted the strands and reassembled them with tape. Inspired, teams of volunteers, many of them from CLASS, spent long nights in the union hall and at home picking through hundreds of bags of sometimes soggy paper. The payoff was phenomenal. Eventually, union executives would be privy to production data, memos between staff, accident reports, and employees' time sheets. CASAW also learned they had their own leaks—papers from the union hall turned up in Royal Oak's trash.

On September 16, CASAW national vice president Fred Couch, sporting prison stripes and handcuffs, was escorted by miner Dan Noel at the head of a column of about 100 marchers protesting the RCMP's handling of the strike. Guarding his charge, Noel wore a visored helmet and carried a police riot shield recovered from the dump, and a homemade billy club. Marchers included many women, CASAW members, and Steelworkers, toting signs that declared Yellowknife a police state. Police watched from upstairs windows in their headquarters and heard the chants to free Al Shearing. It was rush hour when the demonstrators marched down the main street to the jail, causing panic inside. CASAW's new president, Harry Seeton, was finally allowed to see Shearing, who had not been permitted visitors. The guards were edgy when the crowd arrived, Shearing recalls. "Harry wanted to see if I had bruises on me. They didn't know if the cops would beat me up." Within minutes, Seeton was back outside the jail's fence. "He's OK. He told me to tell you he's going to stay in there as long as he has to," Seeton reported, as if Shearing had a choice. The protesters were satisfied that they had made their point.

The next day, September 17, union lawyer Gina Fiorillo filed CASAW's unfair labour practice complaint with the Canada Labour Relations Board in Vancouver. It focused on the thirty-eight fired workers, but there was pointed rhetoric about Peggy Witte and Royal Oak. "While the Company has a legal right to utilize scabs, it knowingly provoked a violent and confrontational labour dispute when it chose to continue operations at the mine by hiring scabs in an effort to break the Union," Fiorillo wrote.

Fiorillo then flew to Yellowknife. She went directly to the courthouse, where Shearing was being released on bail. Then she rushed to the union hall to toil over a hot photocopier with Tim Bettger for a few hours, making copies of the CLRB complaint. The men snapped them up.

Shearing and his wife, Kara, meanwhile, were helping a friend move out of his apartment. After his truck was loaded, Kara and Al walked to the Polar Bowl pub next door to the union hall, he says, at about 9:00 or 9:30 P.M. Shearing says he and Kara left the bar just after 11:00 P.M., walking with Joe Ranger, a young fellow fired from Giant before the strike/lockout began. Others present remember events differently. One man recalls Kara leaving at least an hour earlier. But according to Blaine Lisoway, "we were in the Polar Bowl, me, Wayne Campbell, Al Shearing, Tim Bettger, Joe Ranger, Fred Couch, right till it closed [at 2:00 A.M.]. And we were slobbering drunk." From there, Lisoway says, they went partying at the Campbells'.

Before the bar closed, people wandered back and forth to the union hall, where it was business as usual. Around 10:30, Roger and Helen Warren came in for coffee, as they often did. Roger's car wasn't running well and he wanted a ride to the picket line with someone on night shift. About midnight, Warren and miner Max Dillman drove to Gate 6, the farthest from town. Things seemed quiet. Temperatures could dip below freezing at night now, so the fire pit was kept stoked when people were outside. There was a grate on the fire for cooking or warming a pot of coffee. Some picketers flung wood into the back of a truck to stock another gate. Warren and a few others chatted by the fire. Inside the tent trailer Brian Drover was a fuzzy form in a friendly glow. Tom Krahn drove up a short time later, ready for his nightly hike from gate to gate. He was a good, young miner with a promising future. Lean and fit, Krahn took what jobs he could besides manning the line. Without fanfare, he resisted bullying by police but stayed out of trouble. Roger Warren liked him; perhaps he reminded Warren of his own youth. And like Warren so many years before, Krahn had two little daughters, the youngest one as pretty as golden pretty could be. The two men talked for a few minutes before Krahn set off toward Gate 1.

Inside the mine, Milan Tuma ran a scooptram on the 750 level, clearing muck from headings that miners drilled on day shift. A fifteen-year veteran of Giant and a union loyalist in the 1980 strike, Tuma had crossed the line only a few days earlier, just before Royal Oak changed the pay scale. About forty-five minutes before quitting time, Tuma lost the forward gears in his scooptram. Coasting and backing up, he coaxed the machine back to the 7-12 scoop shop, where he left it with a mechanic. A spare scoop, number 50, was operational. It was smaller, noisy, and slow, but it would do to finish up. When Tuma was done, he parked in the 7-12 shop, the bucket facing the door, ready to go (see map D).

Soon, the rest of the crew shuffled into the shop and boarded the waiting man-car. Tuma drove the small, battery-powered train back to the C-shaft station, as he usually did, lighting the track ahead with his cap lamp. When they got to the surface around 3:00 A.M., a bit late, Tuma thought the mine was empty, but it wasn't. Two Procon strikebreakers worked late that night. Tuma drove out the main gate just about the time the central blast went off at 3:16 A.M. It gently rocked the earth below the town, filling the mine with dust, fumes, and smoke. It cleared quickly from well-ventilated areas, but lingered for a few hours elsewhere.

That night, for the first time, shifters Denis Morin and Gord Edwards acted on a long-standing offer to work overtime. With production levels off sharply since May, the mine manager was anxious for "extra muck." Shifters don't make bonuses like miners, but, with the union gone, supervisors could do "hourly" work. Morin and Edwards had planned to work on the 750 level, but changed their minds at the last minute. At 4:00 A.M., they took the C-shaft cage down to the 1500 level, where they commandeered two scooptrams. Down the ramp they went to 1650, where they "mucked out" for about three hours. A skip tender was on duty too, loading muck onto the skip hoist that hauled it to surface for the mill. On their way up, Edwards and Morin stopped at several levels. They saw no signs of trouble, or visitors.

Striker Brian Drover was puzzled by Pinkerton's curiosity that night as he watched a guard park a truck above Gate 6, where it sat with its headlights off. Guards appeared every half hour, but nothing seemed to be going on. Then, in the early hours of the morning, the guards drove down to the 1-38 portal, in the open pit where a ramp exited from underground. Here, scooptrams and the shifters' beefed-up Toyota trucks could be driven in and out of the mine. Drover saw the guards shine their lights down by the portal entrance, as if they were looking for something. That was unusual; they never went down there, he thought. A man in a truck also stopped there and then took off, spinning its wheels and kicking up rocks. Drover didn't think much of it at the time, it was just the "Pinkies" playing games. That's why he didn't sleep on the picket line like some men did.

There were tints of dawn at the edge of the blue-black sky by 6:00 A.M., but it was still dark. It was cool, maybe freezing. When Drover left the tent trailer for some fresh air, he saw a figure walking down the road toward the gate. He couldn't tell who it was, but a few minutes later, Roger Warren returned.

"The Pinkerton's have been pretty busy," Drover commented.

"Do them guys ever drive around here with the parking lights on?" Warren asked.

"Yeah they do," replied Drover, a regular at Gate 6.

Brian Broda climbed into his pickup to do his rounds. It was part of a mill shifter's routine, and Broda was almost on automatic pilot, since he'd been at Giant for eighteen years. He drove along the big black tailings line, looking for leaks, then by the 1-38 portal and over to the water-treatment plant. Everything was normal, so he drove to Gate 7, turning left on the highway, toward the main gate. Coming down the hill, he was surprised to see a man walking, wearing a brown and green camouflage outfit, including the cap. He slowed down, trying to get a good look, but the man put his hand up to shield his face. Broda saw only light hair and fair skin. It was probably just a picketer playing games, but, at 6:05 A.M., Broda reported the sighting to security.

Pamela MacQuarrie-Higden didn't sleep well on the night of September 17, but she had to go to work anyway. She was a nurse at the Con mine. Getting there was an ordeal, because her Toyota truck looked just like the new ones at Giant and she had to pass the picket line. Nevertheless, she supported the strikers, so each day when she went by she kept a lookout for suspicious activities, making notes in her journal. Just five days earlier she'd seen two men in camouflage gear, on mine property near A-shaft. The taller of the two had noticed her as she stopped to watch them with her binoculars.

When MacQuarrie-Higden drove down the hill toward Gate 6 on the morning of September 18, she noticed heavy smoke coming from Giant's stack. That usually meant a lot of arsenic was being released. She fished for her journal, but couldn't come up with it. Then she saw them. Two men in camouflage gear, standing beside the pipeline not far from Gate 6. "One was tall, and the other was shorter," she remembers. Both men wore caps, and the shorter one wore glasses. She thought they were the same men she'd seen five days earlier. She couldn't know then that this chance observation would cause the police to interrogate her repeatedly. Eventually, an RCMP hypnotist would probe the depths of her memory.

CHAPTER FOUR

CATACLYSM

A little work, a little sleep, a little love and it is all over.

—Mary Rinehart (1876–1950)

It's hard to reconcile union charges of unsafe operations with these figures.
Our lost-time accident frequency is only a quarter of what it was before the
strike began.

—Brian Hagan, Royal Oak's safety superintendent
September 17, 1992

A sprinkle of snow glinted in the sun as dawn broke at 7:12 A.M on Friday, September 18. It was the year's first snow, and it wouldn't last. The day was sunny but cool, peaking just below the 5 degrees Celsius it was in the mine.

Miner Tom Krahn had returned to Gate 6, where he again saw Roger Warren. They drove back to Gate 3 to watch the "scab" workforce arrive. "I was almost seen on the property," about 100 yards into 1-38, Warren said. It didn't pay to be nosy, so Krahn didn't ask for details. He parked at the main gate.

Chris Neill, Shane Riggs, Verne Fullowka, and the other line-crossers streamed past the picketers, on their way to C-dry, giving and taking the one-fingered salute. Neill felt good giving the picketers some of their own medicine. He wasn't intimidated, he wasn't taking any more shit, and he was even working weekends. He'd talked to some of the other men about throwing their union cards out the window as they went through the line. "We still want to have a union on the property. I don't think it'll be CASAW," he'd said a few days earlier. He felt that CASAW was doomed.

At about 8:00 A.M., a Titan motor used to pull ore trains was found out of place on the 750 level. Most of the crews were underground by 8:15, when the shift started, but shifter Don Moroz had called a safety meeting in C-dry for the thirteen men he was sending to the 7-12 area, on the 750 level. They watched a video on scaling practices, Moroz says—the art of bringing down loose rock with a metal bar. When it ended, mine manager Terry Byberg came in to say a few words. Then the men took their gear from suspended buckets where it had dried, donned their overalls and black protective boots, and grabbed their helmets and lamps. Mine foreman Noel O'Sullivan, still a fiery Irishman after thirty years in Yellowknife, miner Fritz Ramm, and a shifter were descending too. They stood close together on the 10- by 4-foot metal floor of the cage. The black rock slipped quickly by. Ramm and O'Sullivan got off on the 575 level, twelve others got off at the station on 750, and then the cage went down to 1500.

The miners, already late, were impatient. As usual, the night shift had left the Mancha motor and a covered man-car, the "silver bullet," ready at the station. Eight men entered the car through the narrow front door, carrying their thermoses and a few tools, and sat facing each other, their knees touching. Sometimes they left the door open and a man in the front would light the rails ahead with his cap lamp. Chris Neill liked to do that. Some men had their lamp beams aimed at the floor. Arnold Russell, a replacement worker, drove the Mancha, and the little train clunked and swayed down the drift at about 4 kilometres an hour until it disappeared in the darkness. Two trammers, Serge Duguay and Henry Puzon, and trackman Gojko "George" Samardzija, intended to walk in behind the train. But, first, they stopped for coffee in the small lunchroom off the machine shop by the station.

At 8:35 A.M., "we heard an explosion, very strong. We look at each other. Surprised. Walls shake," says Samardzija. They couldn't tell where the blast was, so he phoned his shifter, Don Moroz, who was still in C-dry. There was a lot of static on the line, but he heard Samardzija say something about a blast going off.

"Stay put, George, I'll come down," Moroz replied. On a large gauge, he noticed the air pressure had fallen dramatically. "I wasn't overly concerned [yet]," he said later. So he went to the warehouse to pick up something, then drove down B-ramp in his jeep. On his way, he saw a scooptram parked on 575 at the breakthrough doors where the ramp met the track drift.

Shifter Keith Murray came in from another work area and met Samardzija and Duguay in the station at about 8:40. "George said he'd heard a blast,"

Murray says. "I said, 'It was probably just my crew blasting a miss-hole. I'll check and see.'"

"No, it can't be," Duguay said. "The concussion was too big for just a miss-hole"—a drill hole packed with about 4 pounds of explosive that fails to fire in the central blast.

"You guys get your train together and go tramming," Murray said.

"So I went and seen my crew, and they hadn't blasted," Murray recalls. "When I come back, I brought one guy with me to the station because I had a powder shipment coming down that morning. I saw George again and he was really upset about this blast. And I said, 'Well, my guys didn't blast.'" The powder for Murray's crew was brought down on the cage, just after 9:00 A.M.

By this time, Duguay and Samardzija were sure this was no miss-hole going off. Don Moroz hadn't arrived, so they took a motor down the track toward the 7-12 scoop shop. They traveled about 2,000 feet before smoke filled the drift. The Mancha motor was dead on the tracks ahead. From the noise and the fog, they knew that the water and air lines were ruptured. Duguay was too scared to advance, so they went back to the station at C-shaft, where he phoned the mechanics in the 7-12 scoop shop. They hadn't seen the miners. "I think somebody blasted the man-carrier," Duguay said. Then he phoned Keith Murray.

"Oh, somebody probably just went down and blasted the [motor]. Don't go past [it]," Murray said. "Don't let anybody past you until I get there." About 9:45 A.M., he told the mine superintendent to phone the RCMP (who were not notified until 10:15) and the mine inspector, and descended to 750 with cage tender Jim O'Neil to check the damage. As they walked along the drift, they saw a light moving toward them faster than a man usually walks. It was Serge Duguay, who must have ignored Murray's order. He was out of breath and practically raving; he looked sick. "They're all dead!" he cried. "They're all dead!"

Noel O'Sullivan was on the 575 level when he heard the blast. He checked his watch, but says he disregarded the explosion. He gave miner Fritz Ramm some instructions, and then, walking briskly with long strides, he went north and through the 7-28 crosscut into the 7-12 scoop shop. The miners' equipment was still there. A scooptram was running. The air chart, a record of air pressure, was at zero. Looking around, he encountered shifter Don Moroz.

"The boys didn't leave very good word where they left the number 50 scooptram last night," Moroz said. "It's at the 575 breakthrough."

"The boys don't always," O'Sullivan replied. "Maybe it's the supervisors to blame. It's not far to get, anyhow."

Nobody was in the lunchroom. Moroz picked up the phone, but the line was dead. A truck rumbled up the ramp from 9-24. In it were the two Procon mechanics who had left the 7-12 shop after Duguay's phone call. Moroz told them to go get the scoop on 575 if it wasn't broken down.

"Things don't seem to be right this morning. Is there anything you can tell me?" O'Sullivan asked them.

"I heard on the phone there was a man-car blasted," one man said.

Moroz peered down the 750 main line. It was smoky and he couldn't see the man-car. "I'm going to walk out," he said.

"I'll come with you," said O'Sullivan. Off they went, O'Sullivan tall and lean, and Moroz, short and sturdy. They walked about 1,200 feet. Thick smoke and fog reflected their lights. The air lines roared. "That's the problem," thought Moroz. "The air line's broken. The guys can't get past this." He and O'Sullivan entered an area where the drift was widened by shallow slashes, cut on each side. "Visibility was almost zero," O'Sullivan recalls. "I could make out the chassis, the steelworks of the man-car. It was across the drift." He sent Moroz to shut off the air and water.

O'Sullivan advanced alone into the blast area at 9:55 A.M. "At first I thought somebody had pulled a prank as a warning threat," that somebody had loaded a car with mannequins. "I realized I was standing on part of a body. My mind told me, 'It is not a fake, it is the real thing.'" The lone man alive in a holocaust, O'Sullivan cried out, asking if anyone needed help, screaming against the howl of the broken pipes. "I didn't think anyone would need help. Nevertheless, I called out again," he says.

It was a relief to see lights coming from the direction of C-shaft. O'Sullivan waved his own lamp, detached from his helmet, signaling the men to stop. As he walked toward them, a hush fell—Moroz had shut off the air and water, which had blasted and spewed from a 6-inch, high-pressure air line, a 4-inch air line, and a 2-inch water line. The newcomers—Keith Murray, Jim O'Neil, Henry Puzon, and George Samardzija—looked for survivors. The nearest man was Arnold Russell. O'Neil checked his pulse. "He wasn't beat up too bad," Murray remembers. At first they thought he was alive, but it was wishful thinking. They lifted Russell from the ditch and placed him between the tracks. From Russell's pocket, O'Sullivan took a five-point safety card. Then the men checked the other bodies, vainly hoping to find life. They were able to make out seven bodies. Dismembered remains and bits of clothing were strewn on a stack of rails in the slash on the right of the drift, adjacent to the man-car. Human tissue and splinters of wood were embedded in the ceiling above the track. It was a scene so horribly surreal that it resembled a wax museum, O'Neil said later, shell-shocked by memories of bloodless, twisted limbs in the mud.

Little more could be done. O'Neil, Moroz, and Puzon guarded the site until the police came. Murray and O'Sullivan ascended to the surface at 10:20 A.M. O'Sullivan told Byberg and vice president John Smrke that he figured two bags of Amex powder (50 kilos) had exploded. Then he spoke to an RCMP officer who happened to be present. "There is no explosives stored in that part of the mine," he explained. "It's a travel way for men and ore haulage. I think it was a deliberate set incident, timed to go off either by a tape fuse or [by] something on the track when the man-car would go over it."

After Royal Oak's workforce arrived, the night-shift picketers went home. Roger Warren rode to town in Leo Lachowski's jeep, bouncing over the frost-heaved pavement. When Warren got back to his apartment at about 8:00 A.M, his daughter Ann was getting ready for work. Of Helen and Roger Warren's two daughters, Ann looks most like her father. She is fair-haired, with a broad, disarming smile. Like her dad, she is athletic. The two of them spent endless hours practicing softball and, like him, she played all-out. Roger loves her with all his heart. Ann was running late and asked her dad for a ride. He dropped her off, then stopped at The Diner. Inside the door, Warren paused for a second, wiped his feet, and glanced around the room. He was tired from his walk the night before, and sat down at a table by himself. Lost in his own thoughts, he ate a Denver sandwich.

Across the room, a short, fidgety man had seen Warren enter. Robert Carroll had worked on a project with Warren in Manitoba, but they didn't really meet until they both wound up in Yellowknife. They had coffee together now and then in the Miner's Mess café, but this morning Warren wasn't in the mood to talk to him. To Warren, Carroll was the kind of guy who latched on, insecure, a diamond driller who always worked for contractors. "He's one of those guys who thinks he'll strike it rich," Warren says.

Warren wanted some time alone to mull things over. He had already been charged for picking up a stick in the June 14 riot, and he had been fired for it. He was almost fifty and had driven more drift than most miners could even dream about. It looked like his fate would be in the hands of arbitrators if this strike ever ended. And now, Pinkerton's, or whoever was running around in the 1-38 pit the previous night—whatever they were doing, they'd probably seen him and he'd be in a lot more trouble.

Warren paid his bill and drove out to see the guys on the picket line. He had cruised past all the gates, planning to turn around at the Yellowknife River bridge, when two company pickups sped up the mine road toward the tailings pond and the Akaitcho headframe. "They were going really fast. I was wondering what could possibly be wrong up there," he says.

Terry Byberg answered his phone at 9:30 A.M. On the other end was Nick Luzny, lead hand for the heavy-equipment crew on surface. He wanted Byberg to come to the garbage dump near the Akaitcho headframe.

"Do you need me right away?"

"Yes," Luzny said. He said little else because his transmission could be picked up on scanners, but evidently a haul truck had overturned.

Ten minutes later, Byberg was driving north on the Ingraham Trail. As he passed the 1-38 pit, he saw Roger Warren's car come toward him and stop by Vee Lake Road, near Gate 6. In his rearview mirror, Byberg saw Warren walk to the front of his car. Byberg ordered the Pinkerton's guards to check on Warren, but he was gone by the time they got there.

The first call that Mine Safety inspectors got that morning was about the haul truck. A junior inspector went to investigate and was at Giant when he heard about the underground blast. The nine-bells emergency signal had not been sounded in C-shaft, as outlined in Giant's written safety procedure.

At 10:07 A.M., the Yellowknife Fire Department became the first outside agency to be notified of an explosion. Two ambulances were dispatched, and moments later another call warned that there might be multiple deaths. The hospital was put on alert at 10:20, and Dr. Ross Wheeler was sent to Giant.

Minutes later, stench gas was released in the mine—the signal to evacuate the underground. Some men had not felt the blast, although it shook the whole mine and rippled through the earth, registering on earthquake-detection equipment at the Geological Survey of Canada station east of the airport. News of an accident rippled through town too. People in the union hall knew there had been a disaster from radio messages on the scanner mentioning "mass casualties" and requesting that all doctors in town be available.

Al Shearing promptly started organizing his mine-rescue team. "You can't go out to the line," lawyer Gina Fiorillo reminded him.

"Fuck the injunction. Go to court and get it lifted," Shearing told her. A couple of hours later, Fiorillo and Austin Marshall tried to amend the injunction, but the court refused. "The Crown's position was that it wasn't necessary, according to their information," Fiorillo recalls.

Meanwhile, CASAW president Harry Seeton had phoned Giant and said that a mine-rescue team was getting ready. Minutes later, he and Shearing arrived at the main gate. Shearing hid in Fred Couch's bus. When the team was ready to don the draegers (mine-rescue gear including breathing apparatus), national vice president Fred Couch phoned Giant, informing them that the men were waiting if they were needed—fulfilling a public pledge made when the dispute began.

In the union hall, the phone rang off the hook. Speculation mounted. Peggy Witte was discussed without being named. "Let's see her say it's not a safety issue," grumbled Conrad Lisoway.

"We said that from the very beginning, somebody's going to get killed," Couch said.

"Even the RCMP said that," replied miner Brian Wells. "It had to happen. They're putting guys underground that don't even know what's going on there."

"If there's somebody dead, she should be taken to court and charged with murder," Lisoway said.

"That might happen," Couch agreed. "I know one thing. She's not going to be the head of Royal Oak anymore. They'll toss her out, just like an old fuckin' shoe, man."

On the picket line, the RCMP were in no mood to accept rescuers from CASAW's ranks. An officer tersely read the injunction to them. "Until you're needed, only five per gate," he warned. The men were disgusted. Most didn't leave. Sergeant Bill Code, the one policeman picketers still respected, came and thanked the men. He told them that mine-rescue teams had gone down, but "right now, it's not a matter of rescue." It was just after 11:00 A.M.

As Shearing's team got ready, another team descended to 750 in the C-shaft cage. The column set off walking, led by Noel O'Sullivan. His bosses, vice president John Smrke and Byberg, were accompanied by mine inspector Lloyd Gould, physician Ross Wheeler, a policeman, and a coroner. It was Wheeler's first trip underground. He is a friendly and sensitive man who respects miners' ability to work in damp darkness every day. It is a harsh world, and, as one of Yellowknife's longest-serving doctors, he knows only too well the risks of injury and death that miners face. As he walked, he steeled himself for the grim work ahead. He felt encapsulated by the rock, knowing already that this great hole was a tomb.

"We got there and stared in stunned silence," Wheeler later told the *Edmonton Journal*. The bodies were such a mess that he could not count them. From the team's uncertainty grew the irrational hope that two men might still be alive somewhere in the mine—a hope that later obsessed one of the widows, Doreen Hourie. Wheeler officially confirmed that there were no survivors at the scene, and the team left, silenced by horror and shock.

Mine workers who came up from the depths and got the news were enraged; they knew that this could have happened to them. They hung their tags on the board used by supervisors to keep track of who is underground. When the evacuation was complete, nine tags were missing.

Wives and family of men who worked at Giant were frantic with worry when they heard the earliest reports. As is usual with mine disasters, the company didn't allow the men to phone out and say they were safe, for fear of tying up phone lines and spreading alarming rumours. Calling Giant from outside was next to impossible. Some wives did not learn that their husbands were alive until the men came home that afternoon.

Jane O'Neil and Michelle Ramm, the daughter of miner Fritz Ramm, who worked together, rushed to Giant. "It was kind of freaky because they were directing everybody to their administrative buildings, and somehow we wound up in C-dry," O'Neil says. "There was people everywhere, 'cause all the guys were there. Within less than a minute, she found her dad and I found Jim. Which was really ... it was a good, good thing."

Downstairs in the administration building, Doreen Vodnoski, the wife of miner Dave Vodnoski, waited longer than most for news. A tall, forceful, striking-looking woman, she had been with Dave for three and a half years and the two had married only three months earlier. They had two sons, but "were forever laughing and bugging each other like they were dating," says Doreen's sister. When the crowd had thinned out, the RCMP finally came with news. "You know, there's a 99 percent chance that your husband's been killed," Jane O'Neil recalls them telling Vodnoski. Doreen's legs buckled and she sank to the floor as police led her out the door. Alone, another anxious woman began to cry; nobody had located her husband. Hearing her sobs, O'Neil went to C-dry and found him.

By 1:35 P.M., some men were allowed to leave the mine. A few came to the main gate on foot, braving a throng of reporters. "They put a bomb on the track where the man-carrier was taking 'em in to work," one said angrily—killed eight or nine guys. Some were already pointing fingers at the union. "You murdering assholes," line-crosser Nick Luzny shouted to the picketers at Gate 1.

Delivering body bags was Constable Myles Mascotto's first duty at Giant that day. Then, in the afternoon, he went with two Royal Oak staffers to check all entrances to the mine. Mascotto says they checked four before getting to the Akaitcho shaft at 2:35 P.M. Here he found a Pinkerton's man on guard, unlike the previous locations. Beneath a shaft-house window sat a rusty 45-gallon drum, which hadn't been moved since the June 29 graffiti raid underground. There was a partial footprint on top of it. About two hours later a police officer took pictures and found more prints in the dirt of the building's floor. They appeared to lead toward the access underground, which was closed. Police searched for more tracks around the building, and reportedly found none. But on September 22, two senior officers found signs that "individuals have traveled from [the] headframe to Vee Lake Road."

Behind the scenes, the RCMP moved quickly. According to police documents, striker Marvin Ferriss heard about the blast sometime in the morning of September 18 in Chetwynd, British Columbia, where he'd gone for a family gathering. He got the news from an in-law, RCMP constable A.W. Martin, who asked him to become a police informant. Ferriss seemed like a nice guy, skinny and a little ragged-looking, with a thin, tawny beard. A miner with a reputation for cutting corners on safety, he was a motorcycle and snowmobile enthusiast, with all the leather trimmings. He also had a taste for marijuana and had trafficked "fairly reasonable quantities," as he later testified in court. At the start of the strike, mechanic Tim Bettger says, Ferriss was broke and everyone knew it. Early on, he'd proven adept at quietly collecting intelligence on the company.

Line-crosser Craig Richardson—one of the few CASAW members to speak publicly against going on strike in the first place—left Giant in a blind fury. Picketers say he made death threats on his way out. Richardson claims the picketers clapped and cheered, presumably at news that men had been killed underground.

Richardson and another line-crosser intended to get drunk. They drove to the liquor store and bought beer. Then they stopped at CASAW's hall, only a block away. Richardson threw a full beer bottle through a plate-glass window. Inside, two startled women were showered with glass and had to be treated at the hospital.

Richardson was a gun enthusiast, and rumour soon spread that he had bought ammunition and was planning a shooting spree. The union wanted Richardson arrested immediately. The RCMP, occupied with the blast investigation, arrived at the union hall to take statements from witnesses about an hour after the beer-bottle incident. Richardson wasn't picked up, but the police called him the next day; he admitted he'd thrown the bottle. A month later, Richardson was fined $288 in court for the incident. To the judge's annoyance, the Crown prosecutor failed to mention, until after sentencing, that two people had been hurt.

Lawyer Gina Fiorillo was quicker than most to assess the situation. As people streamed into the union hall, she urged them to write down everything they could recall about where they'd been, whom they'd seen, and what they'd done before the blast. In the office near the back of the hall, she helped some people with the task.

People were surprised when miner Gordie Kendall showed up at the union hall after an absence of several weeks. Tim Bettger, who was involved with Kendall in the June 29 graffiti run, says he told him to get ready for a visit from the RCMP. "You better have an alibi," he told Kendall.

"I don't need an alibi. I'm on drugs and I can't remember. I wasn't here," Bettger says Kendall replied. Bettger was surprised by Kendall's appearance and manner. "He looked as if he'd been working under a car for a couple hours. And he was very, very harried and nervous."

According to Bettger and Shearing, Kendall gave them a grocery bag and told Bettger to get rid of its contents. Bettger won't say what was in it; Shearing claims there was a tape fuse and a blasting cap, which miners use to set off blasts. Bettger says he gave the bag to another man for disposal. In a statement to police three weeks later, Kendall mentioned the conversation, but made no reference to a bag containing explosives. It's not surprising that after the deaths in the mine, anyone possessing explosives would want to get rid of them.

At 2:30 P.M., the RCMP announced that they were "treating this matter as a criminal investigation." Police spokesmen carefully noted that they didn't know what had caused the blast and that it could have been an accident. But privately police had been talking for hours about a trip wire having been used. Shortly after 1:00 P.M., Superintendent Brian Watt told NWT cabinet ministers that a murder investigation had begun, and he had summoned the RCMP's postblast team from Ottawa.

The names of the nine blast victims were disclosed at 4:00 P.M. in another dry press release from the RCMP. Six were local union members who had crossed the picket line: Verne Fullowka, Norm Hourie, Chris Neill, Joe Pandev, Shane "Spanky" Riggs, and Dave Vodnoski. Three Procon miners were also dead: Malcolm Sawler and Robert Rowsell, from Ontario, and Arnold Russell, from New Brunswick. Friends and relatives in Yellowknife were steeled for the shock; the entire town had practically shut down while people waited for the names. It was another matter for those down south. Malcolm Sawler's wife, Bonnie, got her first indication that evening that something might be wrong.

"I had talked to Malcolm on the Wednesday night [September 16]," Sawler recalls. "He usually called about every second day, so I was expecting a phone call on that Friday night ... I had come home from work and went out with friends to take my dog for a run. When I came home, a friend called me from Newfoundland and said, 'Did you hear about what happened in Yellowknife?'" But the friend hadn't heard any names. Sawler turned on CBC-TV. A neighbour called the RCMP in Yellowknife for her; the police said her husband was on the list of the missing, but that didn't mean he was dead. So Sawler stayed glued to her TV set. "His name came up on the TV and the phone rang at the same time," she says. "It was the RCMP, calling to confirm."

Malcolm Sawler had gone to Yellowknife on August 1 for a six-week stint with Procon. He was due back in Thunder Bay on September 22. Bonnie was left with a four-year-old son and her memories.

With the first suggestion that the blast was deliberate, CASAW clammed up. Men and their wives gathered in the union hall. Silence fell like a curtain when news reports came on. Harold David, who had returned to Yellowknife as strike coordinator a few weeks earlier, had spent much of the day on the phone with southern unionists, pleading for help and support. David had heard accounts that suggested an accident, despite what the company and the RCMP said. A union member who'd crossed the line had sent a load of explosives down in the cage to the 750 level after the men had gone down, but before he'd heard about the blast. David jumped on this news. If the crew had taken some explosives with them on the man-car, in violation of mine-safety rules, they could have blown themselves up. Local 4's vice president, Rick Cassidy, had talked to the truck driver who had delivered the explosives to the mine. The police wouldn't say anything about the explosives delivery to 750, and company vice president John Smrke denied it altogether. This, and slow reporting of the incident, made it look as if the company was hiding something.

Many people interpreted the union's silence as an admission of guilt, or at least a signal that CASAW's leadership knew that strikers were responsible for the explosion. In the absence of facts, rumours mushroomed: CASAW had hired a hit man from down south to kill some scabs. Or the police already knew who had set the bomb, but wouldn't arrest him because they wanted to nab the instigators. Or picketers had warned shift bosses and miners not to go to work that day, if they valued their lives. Or strikers had cheered in the bar when the names of the blast victims were announced.

There was a confrontation at the union hall in late afternoon. Rick Boyd, a former staffer who'd turned strikebreaker when his contract ran out, opened the hall door and shouted "Murderers!" at the crowd of strikers. He was hustled out. Harold David realized that bar fights were inevitable. He says he called bar owners, asking them to close immediately. They didn't.

Another target of anti-CASAW feeling was the union's so-called Road of Shame along the highway to Giant. A few months earlier, strikers put up signs naming line-crossers, hoping to embarrass them. The line-crossers hated these signs, which they passed every day. So when they remembered on September 18 that some of the blast victims' names were on the signs, they plucked them all from the gravel by the side of the road and dumped them on Giant's property. The next day, union lawyer Gina Fiorillo recovered them and had them reinstalled, minus the names of blast victims.

The union broke its silence at 8:30 P.M. with a short statement that did nothing to calm the town. The union offered its "deepest sympathies and moral support to the families of the replacement workers." But at Harold David's insistence, an accident theory was included. "Replacement workers have reported to the CASAW Office that mine workers were being transported *with* a load of explosives ... It is a cardinal rule that you never transport explosives along with workers, no matter how much time or money it might save." Figures were given on the amount of explosives supposedly transported with the victims: fifty bags of Amex, ten boxes of stick powder, and two boxes of pressure-activated B-line detonator. The hypothesis was that some B-line might have dangled beneath a wheel of the man-car and been set off by the pressure, triggering a larger explosion.

The idea that the entire shipment of explosives might have gone underground with the 750 crew was absurd, unless they had a flatcar to haul it; no flatcar was found at the blast scene. There would never have been enough room in the man-car for fifty bags of Amex, and that much Amex igniting in one place would have shaken buildings on surface. Though the accident theory was flawed, Harold David was right in that miners do sometimes violate safety rules and take explosives with them on man-cars.

That night, people gathered in the union hall, a haven from pointing fingers. Some brought their children; others sent them to stay with relatives or friends, fearing that the hall was a target. The Pinkerton's guards cruised past, June Roberts said. "A lot of people are scared," she explained at the time. The guards "know where we live."

Out on the picket line, strikers were uneasy. Some didn't go to the line, feeling vulnerable and fearing for the safety of their families in town. Several reported that a police officer visited them that afternoon and warned, "If Tim [Bettger] is on the line tonight, get him off. Because people in [the mine] are coming out for him." Some picket crews asked for reinforcements from the union hall. More men responded, including some who weren't allowed near the mine because of the picketing injunction. They hunkered in tents and trailers and Fred Couch's bus, playing cards and drinking through the night. Roger Warren spent the night at Gate 6 with four other CASAW men, discussing the blast. Like many other strikers, Warren knew there were miners' lamps kept at Gate 5 and that some fuses were stashed under a slab of rock, so he went to look for them. "There was nothing there—totally bare," he says. The union soon decided to picket only Gates 1 and 3, reluctantly weakening the line. Royal Oak filled the abandoned lanes with rock.

The real action that night was in the bars. Crazy with grief and anger, some strikebreakers went out to get drunk. Strikers were worried, and furious that many townspeople blamed them for the blast. Their supporters from Con mine were in a foul mood too. Fist fights broke out in the Gold Range, the town's toughest bar. Police cleared the place out. Brawls followed at two bars nearby. They also closed, at the RCMP's request.

At the mine site, two workers were taken to the hospital after being hit by a drunk driver.

REVERBERATIONS

Nine men have lost their lives to keep the Giant mine open.

—Peggy Witte, September 20, 1992

News of the blast found Peggy Witte vacationing in Hawaii. She boarded a plane for Yellowknife, not knowing how many miners had been killed. She arrived at 3:00 A.M. on Saturday and promptly took charge.

The blast put Royal Oak in an awkward financial situation. The recently acquired Hope Brook mine had been producing gold since July, so the company now had three mines instead of two, but Giant had been the top producer before the labour dispute. And Royal Oak's chief claim to fame with the business press came from Witte's toughness in the Giant mine dispute. Now it looked possible that the mine might close, as Westray had in Nova Scotia. Hope Brook's former owner, BP Canada, canceled plans to sell its 5.5 million shares of Royal Oak stock, acquired in exchange for the mine.

Soon after her arrival, Witte approached the mine inspector who had spent most of September 18 at the gruesome blast scene. Around 11:00 A.M. on September 19, fourteen hours after the blast, she asked when she could reopen Giant. The inspector told her to call Dave Turner, the head of Mine Safety. Witte went instead to the top of the NWT government, demanding to reopen the mine and threatening court action if mine inspectors kept it closed.

"I was absolutely appalled that she asked to open the bloody thing the next day," Turner says. "I'm pretty sure she was covered by insurance for that." After some heated discussion, Witte agreed to meet him the next day to work out a schedule for reopening the mine.

Witte also had to decide what to do with the workers, many of whom still lived at the mine site. She called a meeting the same morning. More than 200 men squeezed into an upstairs room in Giant's old office building. Witte was vague as to whether or not the mine would reopen. She offered strikebreakers a choice of leaving immediately, either for a holiday or permanently, or staying to help with maintenance and securing some of the mine's many entrances. It was already obvious that Mine Safety would not allow Giant to reopen unless the company could prevent intruders from getting underground. None of the workers seemed to feel Giant should be closed. "After everything that you went through and all the hours that you put in, working there and taking all the bullshit ... [shutting down] was a defeat," says a shift boss.

Many southern strikebreakers accepted Witte's offer and left town on a special charter in the early-morning hours of September 19. But others felt that leaving meant that they were yielding to intimidation, and decided to stay—including several strikebreakers who arrived the day of the blast. Every union member who had crossed the line stayed on. All summer they'd endured abuse from the strikers, and many had wondered if crossing the line was the right thing to do. Now they were united in wanting to break CASAW, believing that strikers were responsible for the murders.

A team of RCMP postblast experts descended to the 750 level that afternoon. They approached the blast scene as if it was an archaeological dig, sifting through each square yard before advancing farther along the drift. They set up a system to catalog what they found. They would collect thousands of exhibits, test for explosive residues, and analyze their data using computerized models, reporters were told.

Royal Oak staffers guarded the blast scene around the clock. "Those first few days were horrible," one shifter recalls. "We worked twelve-hour shifts. Boy, that's one of the roughest jobs I've ever had. It was a mess."

Other RCMP officers set up shop on the surface to interview all security and mine employees, beginning with those on the 750 level.

The company called a news conference in the afternoon of September 19, in time for the TV news in central Canada. Reporters had arrived from across the country. "I'm led to believe the investigation will be a very lengthy one," vice president John Smrke began. His mission was damage control. "I read some reports that the mine is shut down indefinitely, and I'd like to assure [you] that's not the case," Smrke said; "Giant could be up and running again in a week." He attacked CASAW's accident theory. Yes, he now admitted, explosives were delivered the previous day—but they went down the shaft half an hour *after* the blast, before anyone on surface realized that something was seriously amiss underground. He took the television cameras and journalists outside to look at a man-car in which eight stocky workers were seated. There was no room for fifty bags of Amex, and this was true even if the man-car wasn't the same as the one on 750.

Reporters' questions came fast and furious. Why did it take more than an hour and a half to notify authorities about the blast? Smrke said that blasts were normal occurrences underground (though not usually at the start of a shift). Nobody realized anything was wrong until the air pressure started to drop, which affected ventilation and shut down pneumatic tools, he said. Then mine workers had to determine where the problem was, discover the blast scene, and walk far enough out to be able to call someone on the surface for help.

The media wanted details. How safe was the mine from intruders? Was there enough security? Were strikebreakers working safely? Someone finally asked about the families of the blast victims. "We met with all the families yesterday," Smrke said. "Our benefits administrator will arrive tonight and meet with each of the families." Smrke's assurances annoyed at least one of the victims' families. "No one from the mine has contacted my family," one woman said on September 20. "No flowers, no kiss-my-ass, no condolences, nothing ... They're very, very insensitive and heartless." Others said they were treated well.

When most strikebreakers left town in the first hours of September 19, it seemed impossible to strikers that the police could have done thorough interviews so quickly. Had they even bothered to check the strikebreakers' identification? Or did the RCMP assume that the bomber was a union loyalist?

Union leaders met in the NWT Federation of Labour office on the morning of September 20 to mull over such questions and develop a strategy. CASAW had never before had such a team of southern advisers, including Gina Fiorillo's senior law partner, Leo McGrady; the secretary-treasurer of the Confederation of Canadian Unions, John Lang; and Harold David. Three veteran miners, including Roger Warren, joined them to avoid further public relations disasters ensuing from a lack of technical knowledge. Outrageous statements were made, Warren says. "I tried to tell them, 'We better get some more information ... I didn't know [Royal Oak was] hauling powder down the track ... I tried to keep 'em sensible," but most of the southern advisers "haven't got a clue about underground."

The first priority was to hold a press conference to finally give a full response to the blast. The group decided to call for a public inquiry, with input from Mine Safety. CASAW still hoped the federal government would set up an industrial inquiry commission to help end the strike/lockout. CASAW had prepared a thick press package, including extracts from the Mine Safety and Public Inquiries acts and the report of an inquiry into a death at another NWT mine seven years earlier.

When the time came for the press conference, many reporters had waited all weekend to talk to someone from the union; most southern reporters had never met anyone from CASAW. Many strikers stayed to watch the national media in action. The union hall was packed. Jim Evoy, president of the NWT Federation of Labour, began by emphasizing the union's "shock and sorrow" about the lives lost. But, he added, the union could not understand why the RCMP were investigating the explosion without help from Mine Safety inspectors. That and other unanswered questions justified a public inquiry, Evoy said. Strike coordinator Harold David had more questions he wanted made public. How could the explosion have been thought to be a normal blast when it was many times more powerful than any usually done at that time of day? Why did Royal Oak vice president John Smrke go to the scene of the blast before government inspectors, when people had been killed and the scene was not to be disturbed? Where were the explosives delivered that morning? Was the man-car pushed rather than pulled by the motor, in violation of safety regulations? Why was Dave Turner, the head of Mine Safety, being kept out of the investigation?

Union spokesmen never got a chance to raise these issues. A CBC reporter interrupted to read aloud parts of a press release just faxed out by the police: "It has now been determined by the RCMP post blast team from Ottawa that the explosion that caused the deaths of nine miners at the Royal Oak Mine Yellowknife came from the side of the track and not from within or on the tram itself. As a result of this information and the fact that the blast was deliberately set, the police are treating this as a multiple homicide." Evoy and David sputtered, absorbing the shock. "That's all the more reason for a public inquiry," Evoy said lamely. "Of course we'll cooperate with the police," said David.

June Roberts and a friend were watching when the announcement was made. "I looked at her and she looked at me and [our] eyes swelled up with tears. 'Oh my God, they're going to get us now.' We were petrified," Roberts said.

Then the union leaders realized, to their dismay, that they had told the RCMP in advance about the noon press conference. Was the sensational police press release designed to distract the media from CASAW's questions about the blast investigation? Harold David pointed angrily at the first words of the police fax: "Not to be released before 11:50 A.M." The RCMP usually sent releases to the union just before they went to the media, but this one was an exception. "I better leave before I say something I'll regret," fumed Evoy. "The press conference is over." But the cameras were waiting for a killer clip, and mechanic Terry Legge provided it. He was having a particularly bad weekend. Answering the union's phone for most of the night, he'd fielded an endless series of hate calls, murder accusations, and threats. His hair was plastered down with sweat, his face hollow. When he heard the announcement of a homicide investigation, Legge cracked.

"It was an accident!" he bellowed. Other union men tried to calm him down. "You won't tell me to stop! That's the fucking truth, and if people don't start listening here somebody else is going to get hurt. We've been talking for four fucking months about safety here. Nobody's listening. There it is, right in front of your eyes!" Legge's outburst was played and replayed on national newscasts and documentaries about the Giant explosion, usually without the line about safety.

Legge's anger accomplished the near-impossible—he upstaged Peggy Witte's debut at the company's 5:00 P.M. press conference that day. "I'm here to put together a plan to reopen this mine as soon as possible," she declared. "We're going to help stabilize the community by getting the mine restarted ... Nine men have lost their lives to keep the Giant mine open."

Safety inspectors didn't see things Witte's way. At a meeting, Dave Turner demanded that all nonessential entrances to the mine be sealed and all others be guarded before the mine reopened. Inspectors and Royal Oak staff would do a full sweep of Giant's many miles of tunnels to see if there were more booby traps waiting to go off. He didn't say so, but Turner expected the job to take weeks. The sweep, in which shifter Keith Murray assisted, made some new discoveries. Strike-related graffiti had been painted in two places on the 750 level, on the way from Akaitcho shaft to active areas, and more were found in the surface lunchroom at one of the portals. On 750 and 1500, there were mysterious runes with the word "scab." This was presumably from various unreported break-ins during the summer; police now took paint samples. Inspectors also found explosives or detonators in about twenty improper locations, probably stashed by miners who hadn't bothered to take the material back to one of the mine's magazines.

That Sunday evening, union members and their wives crowded the hall for the first formal meeting since the blast. They were glum and scared. Accident scenarios and conspiracy theories about the RCMP and Royal Oak discrediting the union were discussed. But a question-and-answer session with union lawyer Gina Fiorillo was more important. Everyone knew that the RCMP would soon swoop down on them. She told them they could record their interviews with police or refuse to be questioned, but she recommended cooperation.

Gordie Kendall showed up at his first meeting in ages and apparently made a spectacle of himself. "His hair was fucking like a week's grease in it," says diamond driller Blaine Lisoway. "It was all yellowed from smoke, he hadn't shaved in a week and he had dirt ground into his skin ... Immediately I thought, the fucking guy's been camped out underground." Lisoway wasn't alone in suspecting Kendall or in noticing his disheveled state. When he lobbed nasty questions at Fiorillo, Harold David got fed up and shouted Kendall down. For months, he'd suspected that Kendall was an *agent provocateur*. It remains a mystery why Kendall insisted on being a devil's advocate in the face of suspicion from both the union and, later, the RCMP.

Disasters can bring communities together, but with the labour dispute still raging, that didn't happen in Yellowknife. Nonetheless, the deaths shook people out of their apathy over the entire Giant dispute. Now everyone wanted to do something to help—anything. The day of the blast, a local bank opened a relief fund for the victims' families. Donations flooded in from across the country. Public officials and community groups set up a twenty-four-hour phone-in counseling service at the hospital. Counselors called all the blast victims' families across Canada. They put the widows in touch with each other, and made sure all of them had friends or relatives to take care of them.

A local RCMP constable, Nancy Defer, was assigned the sensitive task of keeping the widows informed of the police investigation, ostensibly without releasing confidential information.

The widows and their families were swamped with calls from reporters. All of Canada heard about Chris Neill's career as a volunteer firefighter, Joe Pandev's plans to retire in a year, and Shane Riggs's happy-go-lucky nature. For some, the media barrage was too much. Bonnie Sawler stopped giving interviews. Other widows and close family members ducked out of sight completely. "I'm thinking a lot of crazy things," said Lynda Riggs. "I think [police] already know who's done it."

The pressure was almost as intense for men working at the mine when the blast went off, especially those who saw the carnage. "Everything makes me sick," said trackman George Samardzija. "I lose six best friends. I laughed with them, I talked with them. Kids miss fathers, wives miss husbands." His wife was tormented by grief and anger, and by reporters calling George late at night. "She cried all night last night. I cannot forget that forever," he said.

Townspeople were not satisfied with mourning the dead and comforting grieving relatives; they wanted a guilty party as soon as possible. The city contributed $20,000 to start a reward fund for information leading to the arrest and conviction of the killer(s).

The *Edmonton Journal* published a rumour-based story about an alleged CASAW "hit list" that included Chris Neill and Shane Riggs. More persistent was the story that Verne Fullowka was killed because he knew who had blown the hole in the satellite dish on July 21.

A federal government employee put up a poster at work: "CASAW—CAN YOU SLEEP AT NIGHT??? Nine innocent men are dead ... because they wanted to earn a living. The union said no, they had to die. You murderous CASAW fanatics. Nine ghosts will haunt you to the grave ... You are nothing but putrid murderers of your mining brothers ... The slain souls, their families, all good people, will share in stoking the hellfire of your eternal purgatory ..."

Bad feelings didn't stop at words. Picking up her children at school, June Roberts was stunned as a vehicle drove straight at hers, stopping abruptly just before colliding. The driver was one of the widows, Roberts says. Roberts and the rest of the CLASS membership suspended their fundraising activities, though many union families were scraping the bottom of the barrel. Roberts tried not to be too depressed, but privately she despaired. "I guess we can kiss adopt-a-family good-bye—guess we can kiss everything good-bye."

The men who died had many friends among union loyalists, who now felt awkward with their grief. Those who kept their feelings private were accused of being heartless. Those who expressed sorrow were branded as hypocrites, covering up a union murder. Striker Sylvain Amyotte had been a friend of Shane "Spanky" Riggs. "He phoned Spanky's sister [Lynda]—and she called him a murderer," says Amyotte's wife, Karen Fougère. "Sylvain has lived here all his life. He's feeling the whole community is against him."

For others, like Al Shearing, the issue was clear-cut. He spoke respectfully of Chris Neill, who had been with him on a mine-rescue mission to Grande Cache, Alberta. But when it came to the blast, "I didn't give a shit. Once they crossed the line, that was it. That was their own doing. If they would've never went in there, they would've never got killed. Period."

Regardless of their opinion of the dead, strikers felt they were getting a raw deal from the town. They became suspicious of any offers of help, as Dr. Ross Wheeler (who first examined the blast victims) found when he spoke at a union meeting. "Wheeler made a good attempt to talk about the hot line, whatever services had been set up for the community," recalls John Lang, secretary-treasurer of the Canadian Confederation of Unions. "And people jumped all over him. 'How come you're concerned about our feelings now? Nobody in the community cared what's happened to [us during] the strike.'"

Also waging a battle with his feelings and problems was Bob Robertson, the former Steelworkers' local president. He often drank with other miners—he had a twenty-five-year history of alcohol and drug problems, and had gone for treatment four times. "After the bombings, I was wracked with guilt," he says, because he'd heard about people breaking into Giant and had not reported it to the police. "My drug usage skyrocketed. I graduated into cocaine, it was like a $70,000-a-year habit. [But] I was still able to function. I was still doing my job." Within a week of the blast, Robertson says he contacted local lawyer Valdis Foldats. "I said, 'How do I get this information to the RCMP and preserve my anonymity?'" Robertson says Foldats acted as his messenger, passing on his story to the police, who were very eager to know the source. Foldats refuses to discuss the matter, despite having Robertson's permission.

HOT ON THE HEELS

Initial inspections of the mine and blast site yielded few obvious clues to lead the RCMP quickly to a suspect. There were the footprints at the Akaitcho headframe, and Corporal Dale McGowan had reported "evidence of access to an explosive shed" and some footprints there on the evening of September 18. It wasn't much to go on.

Mine foreman Noel O'Sullivan and several other Giant employees were enlisted to help search for anything that might be evidence. Besides the graffiti, there was another indicator of prior underground break-ins. Mine staff gave police a miner's lamp like those used at Con, found on the 750 level in July.

A major clue was found on September 23, when O'Sullivan and Sergeant Gary Christison noticed some unusual boot tracks near the 9-07 powder magazine, down B-ramp from 750. Plaster casts were made and photos were taken; the boot prints were like no others in the mine. If someone had used the misplaced scooptram to haul explosives, there could be more such boot prints at the 575 breakthrough, where the machine had been found on September 18. Sure enough, more boot tracks led away in the drift. The next day they found more, within 500 feet of the 7-12 scooptram shop, where line-crosser Milan Tuma had parked his scoop the night before the blast. The boot tracks were not continuous, but there were enough to suggest a route that a perpetrator might have taken in and out of the mine. The tracks appeared identical, so O'Sullivan concluded that one person had made them all. It seemed safe to assume that the prints were made by the killer, but there was no way to be certain.

Another clue was found along the way—a billy club made from a pool cue. With the union hall next to a bar with a pool table, this was taken as a sign that a union member or members would be responsible.

RCMP officers scoured local stores for footwear matching the boot prints. It wasn't done covertly, so word spread quickly around town. One store they checked was Wolverine Sports, owned by former CASAW president Dale Johnston. Police soon found a match in green rubber Kamik hunting boots, a popular brand, and other clones.

The police also made use of the media. Even before the boot prints were discovered, a great deal of information on the crime circulated all over Canada. The leaks were remarkably consistent. First, the NWT government was told that a detonator cap, B-line, and two bags of Amex were used in the blast. The *Globe and Mail*, Canada's only nationally distributed newspaper, reported that the RCMP had labeled the blast "an act of terrorism" in meetings with the NWT government. Joe Pandev Jr., a replacement worker whose father was killed in the blast, told the *Toronto Star* that he knew there had been a blast within ten minutes, an hour and a half before the police. He spoke of B-line fuse being used and a trip wire strung across the tracks to trigger the blast. About two bags of Amex, "at least 100 pounds of explosives were used," Jim O'Neil told a local reporter. "It appears the explosives came from down the ramp. They used an electric motor," and it looked as if two men were involved. Milan Tuma's scooptram had been moved and left up on the 575 level. O'Neil told the *Edmonton Journal* it was obvious that "whoever left that [train] motor left in a hell of a hurry." The *Globe and Mail* revealed on September 23 that a "homemade bomb killed miners," quoting Peggy Witte, John Smrke, and Jim O'Neil, who had a message, passed on by the RCMP, to phone Smrke the day before. They said that two bags of explosives likely ignited when the man-car rolled over a detonator (B-line, presumably) on the tracks. "It could have been an inside job," Witte speculated. "It could be an outside job." She told the *Toronto Star* that the bomber may have been a striker who had returned to work, "trying to scare our workforce off."

The RCMP resorted to extraordinary tactics in their investigation, due to the severity of the crime and the shortage of physical evidence. Fifty extra officers descended on Yellowknife to systematically interrogate union members. Police wanted alibis and tips on the summer's vandalism, as well as information on internal union politics, picket pay, who paid its lawyers, the identity of scrutineers for the strike vote, and how people had voted. Few union members, their relatives, or strike supporters were free from suspicion. As a result, the RCMP began a massive wiretapping campaign. On September 27, a judge sanctioned eavesdropping on more than fifty people,[1] including several southern trade unionists. A large room in RCMP headquarters was filled with tape recorders. Given the widespread belief that the RCMP were always listening, it seemed unlikely that this costly measure would provide evidence on the murder, but it might turn up other useful information.

Police also quizzed Royal Oak employees about their knowledge of union members. "We all sat around and made lists of guys that were causing trouble, would know enough about explosives to do it, know the area of the mine where the guy traveled, [and] where to get powder," shifter Keith Murray recalls. The boot prints and information gleaned from mine staff encouraged police to brag that they would break the case before Christmas. They placed bets on the date; Murray picked November 22.

The list of people considered union radicals and possible suspects by the RCMP included all but one member of the executive, some shop stewards and health and safety committee members, and other prominent leaders, such as bargaining committee chairman Bruce Bannister and former presidents Dale Johnston and Bill Schram. Rank-and-file members included miner Gordie Kendall, Jim Fournier (charged with offenses during the June 14 riot), and Terry Legge, the mechanic who lost his temper on national TV. Two men with underground experience and who had been involved in vandalism, Art St. Amand and Conrad Lisoway, weren't on the list, nor was Roger Warren. Just six of twenty-six men were miners, while seven didn't work underground at all.

Noel O'Sullivan's opinion carried a lot of weight with the RCMP, and the boot prints had led him to a theory. "The route that he took in and out tells me he never had to stop to figure out where he was going," O'Sullivan told police on September 26. The footsteps showed "calmness" and a "nonchalant step ... My number one suspect would be Al Shearing." In mine rescue and other dangerous jobs, "Al was always very cool under pressure. I think he wanted to prove to everybody that nothing shakes him." Three to eight people probably planned the explosion, but only one entered the mine, O'Sullivan deduced, fingering Tim Bettger as the man who dropped Shearing off at the mine. "It's common gossip that Shearing [and] Bettger are always together." O'Sullivan advised the RCMP to investigate some other men too, but not Warren or St. Amand. Gordie Kendall would not know his way around the mine well enough "unless he was really well coached," O'Sullivan said. He had no way of knowing if Kendall had been given such directions.

Roger Warren's name was not on the list of radicals, and after Warren's low-key interview with Constable Nancy Defer on September 25, the RCMP didn't even ask O'Sullivan about him. In the union hall the next day, Warren said that Defer had surprised him when she said the RCMP suspected that an outside union, the Pinkerton's guards, or "zealots" were responsible for the blast.

The RCMP quizzed Kendall for the first time on September 27. According to police notes, "he admitted that he was involved in planning the [June 29] entry into the mine, however did not go himself. The persons who entered the mine were

Arthur St. Amand, Al Shearing, and Tim Bettger." Kendall invited police to his apartment and gave them photos of the graffiti. Corporal Rod Douthwright told Kendall that "there's money available for people who can lead us to the culprits." The next day, Kendall set up another meeting with Douthwright, who reported that Kendall and his common-law wife feared for their safety if it became known he was talking to the police. He said that striker Luc Normandin had driven the graffiti painters to the mine on June 29. Kendall hinted that he knew more, and urged the RCMP to drop his arson and mischief charges from earlier in the dispute.

Interestingly, Kendall suggested that Royal Oak might have been responsible for the blast—a common theory at the union hall, where some thought the bomb was part of Witte's plot to discredit CASAW. "You could rule that out; of course they weren't involved," Douthwright answered.

Luc Normandin was soon in for a talk with the RCMP, as he was also one of O'Sullivan's picks. As Normandin drove away from the police station, he happened to meet Roger Warren. "His hands were vibrating on the steering wheel, he was so frightened," Warren says. "He said, 'These guys think I did this.' I said, 'Well, you know you didn't, so don't worry about it.'"

Recruiting informants was an important part of the RCMP's strategy. By his own account, former miner Bob Robertson was first called in for routine questioning about this time. Because of his picket-line activities in May, "I'd been seen to be an instigator, and they wanted to know what I was doing all that night [of September 17]." As soon as Constable Al McCambridge started to ask questions, "it was like the floodgates opened. He says, 'You're the guy we've been looking for!'," Robertson says. McCambridge had the information about the June 29 graffiti run from Robertson's lawyer. "I met [McCambridge] many, many times," Robertson says, but he was never asked to take a polygraph, though many men soon would be. "They trusted what I was saying, because I was so forthcoming in the first interview ... [It] kind of sidetracked everything he called me in for."

Strikers trusted him after his May 26 attack on Royal Oak's bus, Robertson says. "I paid my dues to the cause. That allowed me to get into more of an inner circle." He heard details about the graffiti run. In the Legion bar, Robertson says, Con miner Hank van Vulpen said that he'd smuggled miners' lamps to Al Shearing and others making incursions into Giant, and that "they had a cache of explosives. And that the sabotage was escalating to a certain point, and that there was more coming down the pike." Robertson says he told the police this, and that the cache consisted of about 300 pounds of Amex, and Powermex stick powder. "I don't know if they stashed it [underground]; I was under the impression they had brought some to surface as well," for use in earlier blasts. The B-shaft vent bombing was "sending the message they were prepared to kill," Robertson says.

The union executive was aware that a few men were involved in extreme vandalism, Robertson says he told police. "They didn't orchestrate, they didn't support it, they just quietly condoned it. That was all these individuals needed to continue. Then it became a war. And in a war, it's OK to take casualties."

Robertson says he was then hired by the RCMP, becoming part of "a network of informants" employed since the strike began. He was told to "target" Al Shearing, his former mine-rescue partner and a longtime acquaintance. Robertson says that his only pay was compensation for what he lost taking time out from driving taxi, his second job. "That would work out to about $200 a night, plus expenses for the booze, and buying rounds for the tables and stuff." His concern for mine safety, and that saboteurs like Shearing give unions a bad name, led him to work with the RCMP, Robertson says.

The RCMP called in Al Shearing on September 29. He was already the prime suspect. On September 17, he was in bed by about midnight, Shearing told Constable Al McCambridge and another officer.

McCambridge asked about Shearing's trustee position in the union executive, and who were his closest friends. "Did you know any of the men that died?"

"I knew Verne; I knew Chris [Neill]; I know Joe Pandev very good; Norm [Hourie], just to see him. Shane Riggs, he was a personal friend of mine. He wanted to go to the Wet Spot [*sic*] strippers bar and we'd go ... Dave [Vodnoski] was a good friend of mine too."

"When was the last time you were down on the 750 level?" McCambridge asked. "Honestly."

"Honestly, yeah let me see, it was two weeks, maybe three weeks before the strike," Shearing lied, unwilling to concede anything.

"Al, are you responsible for the murders of these men?"

"No, no. I hate to be even considered to be one that could do anything like this."

"When the police find out who set the bomb, what do you think should happen to that person?" McCambridge asked.

"I think that whatever the system is, it should be action; [he] should be taken up and castrated."

"Would there be any reason for your fingerprints, your hair, to be found at the blast scene?"

"No."

"Who do you think had the best opportunity to plant the bomb?"

"Somebody that was inside. They got better access to it. Pinkerton's could have done it."

"When was the last time you were up or down [Akaitcho] shaft?"

"Oh my God, maybe fifteen years ago ... I'd lose my way in there now."

The officers referred to the blast as an accident several times, correcting themselves once. They also confronted Shearing about his lies, but he admitted nothing.

"Put yourself in our shoes ... Who would be your number-one suspect?"

"Peggy Witte. If she did want to get rid of the union, this would be a good way of doing it ... We've done a lot of research, and I would put nothing past this woman."

"Have you been involved with any bombing explosives at this mine since this started?"

"No."

The officers then launched into talk of different-coloured fishing line and what kind Shearing used. The obvious implication was that police had found fishing line at the blast scene.

"Are you sure that one of the people in CASAW, a lone wolf, didn't go down and do this?"

"Your next-door neighbour could be a maniac or something. I can't say, 'cause I don't know."

"Someone in this room could be a murderer."

"No, I don't think so, no." Shearing remained calm, despite the accusation.

"Al, murderers don't have 'murderer' written on their forehead. We have to try and eliminate as many people as we can, and we're going about it as competently and impartially as we can," McCambridge said.

"Oh, I can see that with the questions you ask."

The RCMP's one hope of cornering Shearing was to strap him to the polygraph, also known as a lie detector. The test results would not be admissible in court, but might extract a confession or take Shearing off their list of suspects. Shearing agreed to take a test, but only if a lawyer were present and the questions were limited to the September 18 blast. "Ask me if I done it. If you stick to that, you'll get a negative reading."

Constable McCambridge told Shearing that he couldn't have a lawyer present for the test, adding, "if I had the RCMP on my ass, I'd want to be eliminated" as a suspect. Shearing was not convinced, and never took a polygraph test.

Tim Bettger says his first interrogation was by Bill Farrell, a fiery officer from Edmonton. "He brought it to a peak four times," while his companion "gave me an extremely compelling soft sell. After two and a half hours of being grilled by these guys, we were practically knee to knee, eyeball to eyeball," Bettger says. "[Farrell] looked me square in the eye and said, 'Do you know who did it? Did you have anything to do with this blast?' [He] tried to get me to believe some people fired from the mine will never be rehired." Farrell also gave Bettger some legal advice—he should get a lawyer more versed in criminal law than Austin Marshall, who was also too closely connected with the union. Gina Fiorillo was dismissed as "a broad." Bettger did not confess to anything.

The same day, police recruited striker Terry Regimbald to take them on a tour of the Giant mine property. En route, they inquired about his finances and offered to pay him as an informant. When Regimbald said he'd give information freely if he had it, they asked him to take a polygraph. Eventually he did, despite legal advice to the contrary—he got tired of police phoning his wife at work. He also owned a pair of size 10 Kamik boots, which were eventually seized by the police.

The RCMP naturally turned to Gordie Kendall for more ammunition against Shearing and Bettger. Shearing says that, after his arrest in October 1993, he made verbatim notes from a transcript of Kendall's interview of October 1, 1992, provided by the Crown prosecutor. Kendall told the police that finding the way in and out of the mine would be difficult, "unless they could give me, a guy, an awful good map," Shearing read. "[Constable] Douthwright: 'I think, Gordie, you can give me the key that's going to turn this all, blow it wide open. I think you can give me that key without me having to burn you ... They understand how to use explosives, Bettger and Shearing?' And Gordie answers, 'They are the best.'" Shearing laughs. A twenty-year miner, Kendall's knowledge of explosives was far superior to Shearing's.

RCMP documents reveal that Kendall described a trip-wire device that could trigger a blast, using a spring, a nail, and a piece of wood.

Shearing says that Kendall also told police that he had warned miners about a blast underground. "He come out and said it. Right to the cop. That he warned 'em. They didn't even flinch about it," ask who he had warned, or how he knew there would be a blast. Kendall was offered, but refused, a witness-protection program, Shearing adds.

Part of that story soon appeared in the *Edmonton Journal*. Jim O'Neil said that he knew a miner who had been warned when he went past the picket line that a bomb was going to go off. The man didn't take the threat seriously because he'd heard such threats before, O'Neil said. Police confirmed that miners had given statements about warnings, but "they were only rumours, nothing factual."

When CASAW president Harry Seeton was interviewed, he says he was asked who among his membership might have set the blast. They got mad when he said he didn't think anyone would. "It smells of a big, big cover-up. You mention 'accident,' they blow right up ... I said, 'You haven't given me anything to show it's murder.'"

FAITH AND POLITICS

My worst fear is that they won't find who did it. Then what do we do?

—Jim Evoy, September 26, 1992

I hope the union never gets back in the mine. How could I ever trust them?

—Jim O'Neil, September 26, 1992

Before the blast, the political tide had appeared to be turning against Royal Oak. Labour Minister Marcel Danis was about to order an industrial inquiry, and his officials were working on the commission's mandate. Strike coordinator Harold David says that, on the morning of September 18, he and Labour Canada's director general of mediation, Warren Edmondson, laid the groundwork for discussion of an industrial inquiry commission between Danis and Bob White, president of the Canadian Labour Congress. Danis remembers the day vividly. "It was one of my worst days in politics—in ten years ... The blast put an end to my discussion with White." Solicitor General Doug Lewis had told Danis about the deaths. "The first guy I called was White. He knew, he was feeling bad ... We talked about binding arbitration, too bad it wasn't done." Danis also spoke with Prime Minister Brian Mulroney that day, and the heads of several prominent unions.

Resolving the dispute looked more difficult than ever. Since the RCMP was conducting a murder investigation, Doug Lewis became very involved, Danis says. Lewis received regular reports from the RCMP, which may have been shared with other cabinet ministers. "We discussed the investigation, what we should do now, all the while trying to remain very careful never to link one with the other," Danis says. But Lewis was a member of the ad hoc labour committee of cabinet that dealt with Giant, along with Justice Minister Kim Campbell, House Leader Harvie André, and the chairman, Senator Lowell Murray. Indian and Northern Affairs Minister Tom Siddon sat in as a nonvoting member. Mulroney's entire cabinet also talked about how to solve the problems at Giant, Danis says, probably on Thursday, September 24.

Politicians were busy behind the scenes, but said very little before the blast victims' remains were taken from the mine on September 21. Jim O'Neil "brought the boys up" in the cage, and a prayer was recited at the collar of C-shaft; a crowd of relatives and workmates watched in silence. Joe Pandev Jr. smoked, and paced like a nervous cat. Sheila Fullowka sobbed. Doreen Hourie shifted her weight from one foot to another and wrung her hands. Then political jockeying resumed, more ferociously than ever.

In Ontario, NDP Labour Minister Bob Mackenzie argued that the deaths proved the need to ban the use of replacement workers. If that had been done, "the strike wouldn't have lasted this long, they would have avoided this kind of violence, and nine people would be alive," asserted a member of the provincial legislature from Sudbury. Their remarks sparked a backlash from opponents of Ontario's proposed law.[2] One editorialist called it "the bill for murderers," an appeasement for terrorists.

NWT Premier Nellie Cournoyea lambasted federal Labour Minister Marcel Danis in the legislature. "As the responsible minister he must find a way to get labour and management talking in a manner that will end the strife," she said.

In an emotional interview on CBC radio, Western Arctic Liberal MP Ethel Blondin-Andrew said she felt guilty about not having done more to settle the Giant dispute earlier. But she mentioned pleading with Peggy Witte early on not to hire strikebreakers, and asking Danis for help. "I ... begged him to come here and meet with all parties concerned," she said. "I mentioned that it was extremely volatile, that people could get hurt."

Marcel Danis still refused to go to Yellowknife, but asked Royal Oak and CASAW to meet him in Edmonton on Thursday, September 24. CASAW cobbled together a delegation. Local president Harry Seeton brought another executive member, plus Harold David and Roger Crowther, another CAIMAW veteran, then with the CAW. Jim Evoy represented the Federation of Labour. CASAW national president Ross Slezak invited himself, vexed that more CAW help had been summoned without consulting him. They were all tired and under stress, and no strategy emerged for dealing with the minister.

Danis, flanked by senior officials, wanted to try some shuttle diplomacy, meeting alternately with CASAW and Royal Oak. With the mine closed and the union beleaguered, the pressure was finally on both parties. Danis's list of ways to end the dispute included only three that remained viable. An industrial inquiry commission could take months, so he promoted voluntary binding arbitration, something his officials had long wanted. Or, a new mediator could try to break the ice between the parties.

CASAW's team debated bitterly in private. CASAW and the CAW had always opposed binding arbitration, claiming that it benefited employers. Jim Evoy argued that it was time to accept Danis's proposal. "There's nine guys fucking dead, we got cops all over us, and you're talking about the principle of refusing binding arbitration," he snapped. Besides, Evoy pointed out accurately, Peggy Witte could be counted on to refuse arbitration, so the union's public image would improve. Evoy lost the argument.

Meanwhile, Danis pitched voluntary binding arbitration to Peggy Witte and Vice President John Smrke. Witte's response was to pull out a list of strikers she wanted fired—fifty-two names, according to Danis, though Royal Oak had terminated only forty-three men. "I can agree to bring back the other workers," Danis remembers her saying. "Not these fifty-two. There's the list. If you can work out something, talk to me." Danis says he tried to persuade Witte to accept temporary suspensions for some of these men, but she refused. Then came the real blow. Danis casually asked Witte when she'd be able to reopen the mine, figuring he'd subtly remind her that production was being lost. "Oh, sometime tonight," she replied. "I was shocked," Danis says. "I thought it was going to stay closed for a while, either voluntarily by the company or on orders from the [NWT] government." Phone lines sizzled as Danis's officials tried to find out why Yellowknife hadn't told them what was going on. A NWT cabinet official says that the federal government was informed.

Witte and Smrke told reporters that the mine would open within hours. "We had an option Monday morning of laying off all those people ... until some future date when the mine did reopen," Witte said. "We didn't feel on the heels of nine deaths that we wanted to do that to the community." She said that Royal Oak hadn't ruled out binding arbitration or anything else, but she and Smrke then left town.

Danis broke the news of the reopening to the union. Seeton was astounded, and union representatives made some frantic phone calls. Harold David reached Premier Nellie Cournoyea, who said that, if the union wanted Giant to stay closed, they should ask the federal government to step in, which Ottawa had little, if any, jurisdiction to do. On the phone with Cournoyea, Seeton alternately begged and shouted. "Harry went berserk," David says. "I've never seen Harry so distraught."

Witte flew to Yellowknife after the meeting with Danis in Edmonton. Shortly after, she met with a soft-spoken, sixty-year-old picketer, Kurt Lehniger, who was trying to kick start negotiations. He had emigrated to Canada from Germany after the Second World War, and is a man of simple but refined tastes. A boxer in his youth, he was now gray-haired and hobbled by knee and lung trouble. Most of Lehniger's working life was spent at Giant, and he was proud of it. He was deeply hurt by being deprived of his job, but crossing the picket line was unthinkable. "I was very saddened, especially after the blast," Lehniger says. "I asked the union for permission. I made arrangements with Ms. Witte [and] we had a very friendly meeting, over an hour. She said she would like to get four or five people from the union, and start talking with them. I flatly denied this because we have an elected executive body. She understood very, very well. We came to an agreement to start talking without any preconditions ... to begin new. Ms. Witte agreed [to] contact the union and talk to Harry Seeton." Lehniger said he'd inform Seeton and phone Witte back, but his diplomacy produced no results.

Rumour circulated that Witte had secured permission to reopen the mine by threatening the NWT government with permanent closure. An informed insider says that "incredible pressure" was exerted. In a jurisdiction with just 55,000 people, Giant was crucial to the tax base. But Mine Safety chief Dave Turner denies that Witte made threats. Royal Oak met all his conditions for resuming operations, and he was obliged to approve, Turner says. The mine reopened at 5:00 P.M. on September 25, a week after the explosion. The RCMP's postblast team left the mine earlier that day.

Danis and CASAW's delegation stayed in Edmonton overnight to discuss the appointment of a new mediator. A few days later, Danis appointed Vince Ready and Don Munroe, titans in the BC mediation business and among the best in Canada. They had no power to force their will on CASAW or Royal Oak, but were authorized to publish their final recommendations.

All the union leaders left Edmonton disgruntled, and Ross Slezak was fed up with Harold David. Slezak was going to Ontario anyway, so he had a dinner meeting with Buzz Hargrove, the national president of the Canadian Auto Workers, and his special assistant, Hemi Mitic. Slezak described David as too bitter an adviser for CASAW, too inclined to decide things by himself. Hargrove and Mitic agreed that David should depart if that's what CASAW wished. But Slezak wanted Hargrove to come to Yellowknife, take control of the strike, and use his influence to force a settlement. Hargrove and Mitic almost laughed: the president of 170,000 members of the CAW was expected to drop everything to help out a local that wasn't even in his union? They agreed to send Mitic instead.

The cold rain that fell on October 3 did not cleanse, did not numb the skin, did not soothe broken hearts, did not make flowers grow. The temperature was just above freezing. It was Saturday afternoon, but Yellowknife seemed deserted. People either stayed home, or were among the 3,000 assembled in the new arena for a memorial service in honour of Giant's nine victims. Dignitaries were also there—Mayor Pat McMahon, Peggy Witte with John Smrke and Terry Byberg in tow, Premier Nellie Cournoyea, and Indian and Northern Affairs Minister Tom Siddon.

A stone cairn crowned with a miner's helmet sat near the podium. There was a stage for the choir. The Gumboots, a local folk group, sang "Farewell," a soulful and sorrowful lament for the past and future. Tears ran down the faces of friends and relatives of the victims. But many others also wept—acquaintances, children, off-duty reporters and police, line-crossers and strikebreakers. Five relatives of victims of the Westray disaster had come to help the Yellowknife families through their grief, remembering the expression of northern sympathy months earlier.

The town was in mourning, but not all its people could mourn together. Many mine workers who were friends of the victims but still on strike stayed away from the service out of respect, fearing tensions might erupt. Only one was present. Steve Moss, Chris Neill's friend and fellow firefighter, was a member of the honour guard, at the family's request. "I felt a lot better that they didn't feel I had anything to do with this," he says.

Moss ran into Nick Luzny, a CASAW member who crossed when the strike started. "I worked with the guy for ten years," Moss says. "He pointed at me, made a remark, and off he went. I thought, 'I can live with that.' Then he came back and kind of accused me. And I thought, 'Well, I can live with that too.' And then he stopped in the hall, and there's like ten counselors standing there, and he says, 'Spanky's going to get you for this.' And I [said], 'OK, Nick, let's talk.' He says, 'I can't, or I might strangle you.' His way of justifying what he'd done was, 'Well, you called him scab so you're just like whoever did it.' That really hurt."

Near the end of the ceremony, the arena was hushed as a Salvation Army captain read the names of the dead. With trembling hands, each of their families placed a red rose in the crags of the rock cairn. A member of the Westray delegation, Kenton Teasdale, added a tenth rose, symbolizing the losses of the two communities and their hopes for the future. The miner's lamp was lit. Teasdale made a plea for forgiveness. "If a few individuals have gone beyond what is reasonable, let us not blame groups, let us not make faceless the people who are our neighbours. Let's pull together. That's what helped us through in Westray."

Teasdale's words did not have the emotional impact of Tracey Neill's plea after the ceremony. "Chris and I were together for three and a half years. We had many hopes and dreams and they all ended when he was murdered. Chris and eight of his friends were doing what they felt was right for their families and community. To the people out there who know what happened, please come forward. I don't think I'll ever come to terms with the cowardly way it was done. There are eight widows, eighteen fatherless children, grieving mothers and families, all as innocent as the men that died."

The day of the memorial service, striker Marvin Ferriss became an RCMP agent, according to police documents. His "maintenance package" provided a regular income. In his first sessions, Ferriss confirmed what police already knew about the graffiti expedition into the mine, including the names of those who had participated.

The police confronted miner Art St. Amand on October 5 with their knowledge of his part in the graffiti run. He was cornered. His choice was to confess and escape charges, or eventually be arrested, and be hounded over the murder. So St. Amand confessed, and showed police the open window in the Akaitcho shaft house where they had entered. Police also searched his porch-workshop, apparently with his permission, but found "nothing of importance."

Hemi Mitic, the new envoy from the CAW, arrived in Yellowknife on the morning of October 6. Grim attitudes in the city had been deepened by forty-two lay-offs at Con mine, and well-founded suspicion that Royal Oak was still trying to buy it.

Meetings with special mediators Ready and Munroe were to start that night, so Mitic had to work fast. He would speak for CASAW, but knew little about the union's bargaining position. So he had breakfast with the local's executive and the new bargaining committee—Harry Seeton and former local presidents Dale Johnston and Marc Danis. Mitic is suave and articulate. All that might have distinguished him at first glance from a young stock-market wizard was his leather jacket and lack of a tie. His schedule is relentless. He rushes from rail negotiations in Montreal to mines in British Columbia or union drives in Nova Scotia. He takes breaks from long meetings to make a "quick call" to a senior railway executive. Among Mitic's talents is an uncanny ability to assess situations and people quickly and decide whether to fight or give in gracefully and cut his losses. In this case, he got a hostile reception and took a tough stance. For some local leaders, the fact that Mitic was recruited by Ross Slezak was reason enough for suspicion. Then Mitic insisted that a CASAW national official join the strategy meeting: "You let him in or I take the next plane out."

Mitic was startled to learn that the local didn't have a defined bargaining position. There had been no mediation since July, and since then Bruce Bannister, the head of the old bargaining committee, had been dismissed. Jim Gauthier, another influential member of the old committee, had crossed the picket line. Worse yet, Mitic could find no trace of a signed tentative agreement in the union office. As far as he could tell, there had been handshakes and verbal agreements, but no full text, leaving him uncertain of what had been agreed to in April. Mitic had no firsthand word on why Royal Oak had demanded some of the concessions granted in the tentative agreement. The local leadership didn't want him to talk with anyone from the old bargaining committee, who some felt were traitors. Mitic had to develop a bargaining position, virtually from scratch, in a day and a half. Getting people to concentrate on negotiations was difficult. "There was a siege mentality," Mitic says. "People were looking for victories in the paper and on the news [rather than a collective agreement] ... And the scabs going in every day, it became almost a war to some people. They forgot about the dispute and the hate turned on the people who were trying to steal their jobs." Mitic finally forged a consensus that CASAW would demand something between the tentative agreement and the old collective agreement. But CASAW wanted to rescind some of the concessions made by the old bargaining team.

Ready and Munroe told Mitic that CASAW was being unrealistic, that after four months of a labour dispute the union was obviously losing, it was time to make major concessions. Mitic had no mandate to offer anything further. He wanted to know how much the concessions in the rejected tentative agreement were actually worth to Royal Oak, and why the company cared about some clauses that seemed minor. The mediators saw that Mitic was still getting his feet wet.

Royal Oak was better prepared for the mediators. Peggy Witte did a multimedia presentation on the history of Giant and the labour dispute. She tried to hammer home the point that Royal Oak had no choice but to act the way it did. Giant was bankrupt when Royal Oak bought it and there had to be a quick turnaround. That meant dealing with the "poor productivity, poor labour relations, and poor labour climate in Yellowknife as a whole," she claimed, according to Royal Oak's notes from the meeting. Witte stretched a few stories from the 1980 strike into a "history of union violence" at Giant.

Smrke criticized CASAW's local leadership, stressing the story about then-president Bill Schram denouncing company executives as "fucking Americans." Of course, Witte and Smrke offered their theory that Dale Johnston and Harry Seeton had hijacked the local and forced a strike.

Hiring strikebreakers was essential, Witte claimed. "We knew that we had standby costs of $800,000 to $1,000,000 per month to shut the mine down," she said, inflating the $500,000 figure previously given to the media. Witte played a Pinkerton's video of picket-line incidents to show how dangerous CASAW was; she shared Pinkerton's' low opinion of Harold David. "When he showed up on the scene things really started to get nasty. There was the blowing up of the satellite dish, the explosion of B-shaft, and all of the threats downtown," she charged.

Finally, Smrke advised that no mediation should occur as long as there was "at least one killer walking the streets of Yellowknife." To take any other position would be for Royal Oak to shirk its duties under the Mine Safety Act, he said.

Ready and Munroe were not impressed by such arguments. They wanted to resolve a labour dispute, not review ancient history or pass judgment on each side's behaviour. They certainly wouldn't wait until an arrest was made, they said. "What issues are deal-killers?" they wanted to know.

Witte immediately brought up the fired strikers that she would not take back. She wanted more concessions, beyond those in the tentative agreement. And it had to be a long-term contract, not just for two or three years.

Ready and Munroe relayed Mitic's questions to Witte and called it quits. They were not making progress.

RAT IN A MAZE

Let's face it, I'm a rat. You know what happens to rats in prison?

—Gordie Kendall to the RCMP, October 8, 1992

He's got the knowledge ... Gordie's crazy enough to do it, but he's not physically capable of doing it.

—Al Shearing, August 13, 1994[3]

I never ratted. Right from the start, I admitted my own involvement ... There were several entries—same way we went in. Akaitcho.

—Gordie Kendall, June 13, 1994[4]

Corporal Vern White joined the Royal Oak Task Force after a sojourn in the tiny Inuit community of Lake Harbour. Thirty-four years old, big and balding, White leaped at the chance to get into the Giant fray while he was on a trip through Yellowknife. On October 6, "I volunteered to work a couple of days," White told the *Edmonton Journal*. Five weeks later he was still around; he was destined to become primary investigator. His father had been a coal miner in Cape Breton. "The way I look at this file, it is probably the greatest experience you're ever going to get as a policeman in any force," he said. "I look at it as a challenge." Intensely competitive, White loved to fight and did so with spirit. He keenly enjoyed his authority as a police officer.

The RCMP's immediate challenge was to sift fact from fiction in Gordie Kendall's statements. Officers pressed him to take a polygraph test, emphasizing that money was available. On October 7 and 8, Kendall bargained hard to have his charges dropped in return for details of a conversation he'd had which might provide vital information. Police insisted on a polygraph first. "They're piddly ass charges," Kendall argued. "If it's four or three or two people involved, there's always one weak link. And you always offer that one guy a deal. Reduce the charges or, in some cases, no charges. Long as they testify to hang the rest. Why would I give that away? ... I wouldn't have given up for myself, if I was involved. I'm not that dumb."

Kendall tantalized his questioners by hinting that he was involved, and a "weak link" at that. On the one hand, he said "they ... never told me anything about the killing"—whoever they were. "You're wondering if I planned this thing and sat at home and waited for the outcome ... I had absolutely nothing to do with it." On the other hand, Kendall insinuated that he could point police in the right direction, and dropped hints about explosive residues that the RCMP might have found at the blast scene. He hinted that Royal Oak might have been warned, and said, "I would have phoned in a bomb scare—if I had known ahead of time. Because we discussed this blasting many months ago."

The officer asked no questions about that. Later, Constable Rod Hamilton offered Kendall witness protection, an identity change, and a move to somewhere else in Canada. "Are people threatening you?" he asked.

"Ah, it has been veiled, you know, 'Keep your mouth shut ... Don't tell 'em nothing. Don't take polygraphs.'" Kendall kept up his half-flippant, half-mysterious manner even when discussing his alibi for the crucial hours of September 17 and 18. "Thursday afternoon I have no idea what I did," he said, and, that night, "I have no idea except watching TV all night. Not sure what time we went to sleep, somewhere between four and six ... I don't remember going out all evening ... Seems to me I remember one thing though, I remember [my wife's] daughter coming downstairs at 6:30 in the morning."

The police asked if he remembered saying good night to his wife.

"Must have, if you want me to." Kendall chuckled. He snapped his lighter continuously during his account of hearing the news of the blast, according to the police transcript. He shifted attention to Al Shearing, who he said told him at the union hall to get rid of any explosives he had.

"Why would Al say that to you?" asked Hamilton.

"Well, a lot of people had explosives, I think."

"How did you feel when Al said that?"

"I'll be honest with you. Cold shiver ... I was feeling a lot of things."

"What were you thinking?"

"I was saying to myself that little incident [June 29] that we're involved in is going to come back to haunt us ... Of course a cold shiver went through my back. What the hell do you think?"

"This is good, Gordon. Did Al say anything else to you?"

"No. I was scared to ask. I was scared of the answers."

One aspect of the June 29 raid that Kendall says really worried him was the bolt cutters Shearing, Bettger, and St. Amand left underground. "My prints are on there. So's everybody else's." Kendall said he also worried the police might "fuck up" the investigation from the start, and, like many other men, he had wanted to see the blast scene himself to figure out what happened.

"What about the dead miners?"

"I have mixed feelings. They were my enemies in a way. I feel bad for the children, they're not going to have fathers. I also feel ... these guys were the cause of prolonging the strike. And they were being used, which also made me angry ... I talked to a few of them. I said, 'Don't you realize Miss Peggy is just paying you to do her dirty work?'"

Kendall admitted advocating trouble at the mine. "It escalated from there," he said.

"And now we're dealing with the murder of nine men," Constable Hamilton said.

"I told all your guys that, first couple of days of the strike."

"What did you say, Gordon?"

"Someone is going to die. This strike is not going to end without somebody dying. I didn't know who was going to die. Anybody getting killed on the picket line is usually a striker. Often shot down by police."

They eventually got to the big question. "Gordon, if you had to speculate, who do you think did this [murder]?"

"Tim Bettinger [*sic*]."

"Can I ask you why?"

"If he didn't, he's involved in some way."

"Oh, no doubt," agreed Constable Hamilton.

Kendall talked about Bettger's rifles. "I got the impression he's kind of a frustrated soldier." He chuckled.

"Are you aware he did anything? What did he say, Gordon?"

"I can't tell you that. I'm holding back pieces of information."

"Why?"

"Because I didn't want to have it in the first place. I got it before the blast. It wasn't until after the blast that I thought about it."

"This information came from Tim," Hamilton probed.

"It doesn't matter where. It came from a horse's mouth, put it that way ... A detonation device was described to me for the ventilation shaft [explosion]."

Within days, Kendall moved to Vancouver.

Hoping for tips from the public, the RCMP unveiled the wrecked man-car, and the billy club they'd found underground (which Shearing says was his, but Art St. Amand claimed he'd forgotten on the 750 level on June 29). Photographs and the RCMP's explanation of the blast were reported nationwide by the media.

Roger Warren was still a bit player for police. On October 16, three weeks after his previous interview, they talked to him again. They wanted to look at the clothes he'd worn on September 17 to see if he was the man that shifter Brian Broda had seen on the highway on the morning of the blast. The clothes were piled by the door when the RCMP arrived at Warren's apartment: a pair of blue denim coveralls, a greenish shirt, a green ball cap with the crest darkened, the hood of a parka, and a pair of green Kamik boots. The boot soles had been blackened with a felt-tip pen, maybe as camouflage. They were cut and melted in some spots, but looked fairly new. "The boots surprised us. They were size 11," Constable Nancy Defer says. "We were looking for a boot like that. The same size and type." Before the soles had been scarred, they might have matched the prints in the mine.

Warren said that his parka had disappeared after he'd spilled fuel on it and hung it on his balcony. The officers took Warren's things with his permission, and photographed the boots, and Defer made marks inside with ink visible only under black light.

An hour later, the police returned and asked Warren to don his clothes and show them where he'd been on the picket line. He pointed out the spot where he'd jumped into the ditch when a car passed, and where he said he saw two people on mine property at Gate 5 1/2. They photographed him standing there. He said he'd heard in a bar that a pressure switch had been used to trigger the blast.

In the police car, the officers gave him the standard police warning. "I was surprised," Warren says. "I didn't think they did that unless you were a suspect." When they questioned him, he denied involvement in the blast and agreed to take a polygraph. On October 19, Warren went to the Explorer Hotel, where Sergeant Pat Dauk had been camped for weeks doing interrogations and polygraphs. Like most people facing this ordeal, Warren was nervous.

"You've told me your wife is dead set against this thing," Dauk said to Warren in the pretest interview. The RCMP get into this good cop-bad cop routine, she'd said—don't go near the place. "You've got to realize, there's a lot of fear in this stuff," Warren told him.

Dauk pressed Warren, suggesting he was protecting someone. "At one point, [he] became very, very nervous and very scared," Dauk says. Warren's stomach heaved as his breathing became fast and shallow.

Something must be bothering you, Dauk said, unaware that Warren had a heart condition, as yet untreated. "I don't want you failing this test." He edged closer and closer to Warren, touching his knee.

"I think I'm going to have to exercise my right to refuse the polygraph," Warren said.

"Exercising your right—you're the one telling me you can't sleep at night—is not going to get these things off your chest," Dauk said. "I think you have a false loyalty built up ... Tell me what happened that night."

"I can't."

"Why not?" Dauk asked.

"Just fear of being implicated in this thing," Warren said.

"Roger, what did you do that night? Tell me."

"I did exactly what I said I did."

"Roger, are you a criminal?"

"I don't think so."

"I don't think so either."

When police took his picture by the road, Warren told Dauk, he'd had a terrible foreboding: "I just got the impression that these guys are sure that I did it ... That just scared the shit out of me, man, I'm telling you." He imagined the picture being handed around among the Pinkerton's guards, fearing one would finger him. Under pressure, Warren said that one of the men he saw on mine property the morning of the blast resembled Conrad Lisoway, another striker. Listening in the next room, officers Nancy Defer and Dale McGowan were excited. "He was turning into a key witness," Defer says. "He was reluctant in giving us the name."

On Sunday morning, October 21, Warren was stricken with chest and back pains that also shot down his arm. His wife, Helen, and her sister checked him into the hospital. Corporal Dale McGowan phoned the same day and got the news from Helen. It wasn't a heart attack, but Warren's doctor kept him in the hospital for several days and put him on a drug to control irregular heartbeats. Word got around about his illness. There was a friendly note in the union's strike bulletin, and he even got a phone call from his old friend Keith Murray. They hadn't talked since Murray crossed the line at the beginning of the strike.

Warren and other men worried about dissension within the union. Terry Legge, the outspoken mechanic from Labrador, had been pressured into promoting the polygraph for the RCMP after taking it himself. He thought if everyone in the union took a lie-detector test that the police would stop their harassment. But he was unable to convince June or Derek Roberts to take it, or Warren, at first.

When Warren got out of the hospital, he told Corporal McGowan that he would not take a polygraph test. The police then said they would have to talk to his wife and daughter. This was a common pattern; some wives had already been questioned. So Warren eventually spoke to his doctor about taking the polygraph.

EXECUTIVE FLIGHT

You can go anywhere in the world, and you run across a miner, you got a friend.

—Bob Robertson, March 22, 1995

Mediators Ready and Munroe ordered a face-to-face encounter between CASAW and Royal Oak, so CAW troubleshooter Hemi Mitic went to Vancouver on October 19, 1992. Mitic and John Smrke didn't hit it off and Mitic soon dismissed him as a perpetual whiner. When he complained about picketers pounding the windows of a company bus, Mitic threw up his hands. "If that's the only thing that's holding this thing up, we'll buy you a goddamn bus!" he exclaimed. Smrke recited further vandalism against the company. When Smrke told Mitic who had sabotaged the satellite dish, he concluded that the company must have been getting information from the RCMP. Witte and Smrke complained about CASAW's local leaders, and Smrke repeated the "fucking Americans" anecdote, by then a year and a half old.

All the more reason to expect a hostile reaction to your demands for concessions, Mitic fired back, adding: If you needed concessions, you should have worked hard to improve relations before bargaining even started.

Witte and Smrke wanted to know how long the CAW would support CASAW's strike. "Until they get a collective agreement," Mitic told them. They didn't seem happy about it.

After less than two hours, Ready and Munroe gave up and adjourned again, having been unable to get the two sides to talk about a contract.

The memorial service did not bring harmony to Yellowknife. People shunned each other in church. Holes were punched in strikebreakers' tires. Two cooks from the mine got drunk, went to the picket line, and beat up a sixty-year-old striker. Picketer Mark Eveson says his brake lines were cut. He says he informed the police, who told him they weren't interested, but, if he pressed it, they would charge him for driving an unsafe vehicle. Bar fights erupted every few weeks.

They were sometimes spontaneous; but on some occasions strike supporters and strikebreakers hunted for targets. Pinkerton's guards appeared in town too. "The Pinkerton's are hoping to suck someone into fighting in the street. Don't fall into their trap," a union bulletin advised. Yellowknife's mayor fumed, and speculated publicly about the need to declare martial law.

In late October, picketer Kurt Lehniger was roughed up at Gate 1 by Karl Tettenborn, the hulking Pinkerton's guard hired just before the June 14 riot. Lehniger, who had personally implored Witte to bargain, had known the Tettenborns for twenty years. So he was surprised to overhear Karl report on the radio that Lehniger had threatened a taxi driver at the picket line. In fact, Lehniger said, his talk with the driver was very amiable. After alerting other picketers, Lehniger walked over to Tettenborn's security shack to confront him. "Are you the one who accused me?" Lehniger asked. When Tettenborn said that he was, Lehniger said, he turned in disgust to leave. "He grabbed me from behind, swung me around, and said, 'You're under arrest for trespassing.' I felt a sharp pain and fell down. He jumped on top of me, pushed my head down, and had my parka right across my face. I called [to] him, 'Let me free, I need my medicine, I can't breathe.'" (Lehniger suffers from angina.) Instead, he was handcuffed. He says he yelled for help and another guard ordered Tettenborn to remove the cuffs.

Pinkerton's guards and picketers both called the police. By the time they arrived, there was a crowd of twenty to thirty men. A constable on the scene feared more violence but found both sides cooperative. Lehniger was arrested, taken to the hospital for treatment, then released.

At home two days later, Lehniger was embarrassed and indignant as his ugly scrapes and bruises were photographed for the union by Marvin Ferriss, by now a police spy. Lehniger walked with pain, but still served excellent coffee in china cups to his visitors, in a tidy dining room, surrounded by memorabilia from his hometown in Germany.

Lehniger was charged with criminal contempt for breaking the injunction and was banned from the picket line. He was eventually found guilty, appealed, and lost.

Tettenborn was arrested but wasn't charged. The police investigation was thorough, but the Crown chose not to lay charges.

Royal Oak had its own problems after the blast. From senior executives to supervisors at Giant, many were angry with the company and tired of the labour dispute.

Royal Oak vice president Mike Gross had been the first to leave, in May, but he had been pushed. In September, treasurer Steve Manz, architect of many of Royal

Oak's financial coups, quit after a disagreement with Witte. For Kim Cornwell, Giant's human resources manager, the blast was the last straw. She and Brian Hagan, the mine's safety superintendent, were in Las Vegas when it happened. Cornwell resigned when she returned to Yellowknife. "A lot of people felt that they had to go on for the sake of the fellows that were killed. But I wasn't so sure [the mine] should be opened," Cornwell says. She and Hagan left for Toronto in late October, starting a trend that cost Giant much of its staff over the following two years.

Royal Oak replaced Cornwell with Bill Heath, who had extensive human resources experience, none of it in mining. Coincidentally, he'd bargained with Hemi Mitic before and the two got along well. Heath's relaxed manner and willingness to listen to subordinates' complaints, perhaps over a beer, shored up one of Royal Oak's weaknesses. Heath was manager of human resources for the entire company, but spent much of his time in Yellowknife.

June Roberts knew that CASAW could not survive without more financial support, but worried more about people than about the mounting legal bills. Her family knew the pressures firsthand because she and Derek weren't good money managers. The hounds of fiscal hell were howling outside her door and ringing her RCMP-bugged telephone. She was convinced police were spying on union members to find vulnerable areas in their personal lives for use in interrogations and to gauge how long the union could hold out. It was winter. Fuel and electric bills were climbing, and the kids were looking forward to Christmas. The four-year-olds she saw among the union families she'd come to know and love wondered how Santa was doing. It cost a fortune to live in Yellowknife, and the picket line would not hold if many more people had to leave to survive. Some of the wives from CLASS had a table at a local craft sale, but under their own names. "The women that show up to the meetings, a lot of them are scared and none of them want to be in public representing CLASS or CASAW," because it's too risky, Roberts said at the time. "If this doesn't end soon, a lot of them will want to leave town ... People are just afraid [and] feel guilt by association, even though there's no proof."

Roberts knew that union families had the heart to stand up to Royal Oak, and even the RCMP, but they needed help. Flyers for CLASS's adopt-a-family campaign had been printed before the blast. Federation of Labour president Jim Evoy distributed 200 of these at southern union meetings, and told Roberts that the response was good. Encouraged, she spent days writing letters, mailing flyers, chatting on the phone with supporters from other union locals, making hundreds of red and black end-the-strike ribbons to sell at union functions, and presiding at CLASS meetings. A dedicated group of people worked with her. In mid-October, Roberts launched the adopt-a-family campaign locally, describing it as a plea to unions across Canada "to take a family through the strike."

Her husband, Derek, was just as busy. The $9 an hour he earned as an electrician's apprentice wasn't much, but it was bread and butter. He set out early every morning after getting the kids ready for school, and, when he got home, his wife took off on union business, often not returning until after midnight. Between meetings, June spent time at the union hall, or visited the picket line and strikers' families. She seldom showed a trace of the pressure she was under. The admiration June inspired strained her relationship with Derek. He was just one of the guys, while June was a star.

Southern unions asked that June Roberts be sent to rally support for CASAW's cause. Recognizing her talent at last, the executive agreed. In October, she met with the Confederation of Canadian Unions' executive in Toronto, and spoke to members of the big Mine–Mill local in Sudbury. Both donated to adopt-a-family, helped with the Christmas party, and spread the word.

Eighteen families received a total of $12,000 through the adopt-a-family program in October, most of it from CAW locals. But June Roberts figured they had 116 families—out of almost 200 union members who hadn't crossed the line—who were still in town and in serious need. The adopt-a-family committee set up a system for distributing money to the most needy. Top priority went to those who kept the strike alive by doing picket duty, a decision that soon caused friction.

There were only seventy-nine active members on the picket line and in the office by late October, due to job demands and disgust with life on the line. As summer jobs ended, more men signed up for picket duty. By early November, with snow on the ground and the waters of Yellowknife Bay freezing over, everyone knew that the line would be manned all winter. "The boys" insulated the picket shacks for the inevitable weeks of minus 30 degrees Celsius weather. In mid-November, a small house trailer became a mobile picket shack for the overflow. Two gates were no longer enough, given the court-imposed limit of five picketers per gate.

Families living on credit-card overdrafts and informal loans from relatives made drastic decisions. Some moved to smaller apartments or sold possessions. Some men couldn't afford housing at all. Mark Eveson, for example, slept in the warehouse of a local business where he was temporarily employed. With the construction and summer tourism seasons long finished, short-term jobs were scarce.

The news was not all bad for CASAW. Early November also brought CASAW's first big court victory. Royal Oak had charged twelve strikers for blocking traffic on June 11 at the muck crossing, where picketing was forbidden. The judge ruled that ten of the twelve men had broken the injunction, but he did not impose penalties. Though there were still almost 100 charges outstanding against strikers, the ruling was a forerunner of many union victories in court.

Men behind the picket lines watched in disgust as the number and boldness of picketers increased. Line-crossers and strikebreakers endured abuse as they ran the gauntlet to and from the mine. They couldn't shop in town without getting the finger, curses, or hard stares from a CASAW member or sympathizer. The only refuge was underground or in the mill, where it was almost as if there was no labour dispute and the blast had never happened.

Hostility to CASAW went beyond mere irritation for Jim O'Neil. He had a sense of mission, especially after the death of Chris Neill and the other eight men. It was almost six months since the dispute began, so he could legally form a rival union to unseat CASAW. Through O'Neil's efforts, plus those of two of the blast victims' families, the Giant Mine Employees' Association (GMEA) was born. O'Neil spent hours on the phone with Israel Chafetz, the Vancouver labour lawyer he had contacted in June and who now provided advice.

Under federal law, the signatures of at least 50 percent of workers in a bargaining unit are required to force a vote on whether to bring in a new union or displace an old one. The problem at Giant was that it wasn't clear who was in the bargaining unit. Was it only CASAW members at the time of the lockout? What about the men hired to replace strikers who had quit, replacements for the fired strikers, replacements for the six CASAW men killed underground, and a seventh, killed in a car accident? What about the strikebreakers, some of whom planned to stay in Yellowknife permanently? Nobody quite knew.

Jim O'Neil knew that he had to sign up as many members as possible, spread the word quickly, and create at least the appearance that the GMEA would win. He phoned local media and told them to be at Giant before the day shift arrived the next morning. At 7:00 A.M. on November 12, he was at the inner gate of Giant's main entrance with Doreen Vodnoski, one of the widows of the blast. They handed flyers to strikebreakers who arrived in the bitter cold, many still half-asleep and astonished that someone wanted them to sign up for a union.

O'Neil told reporters that CASAW had caused the strike and the violence, and an independent association could end Yellowknife's woes over Giant. The flyers made a direct appeal to replace CASAW with the GMEA, "to bargain with the mine and end this tragedy." A questionnaire asked workers if they preferred to be represented by CASAW, the GMEA, or no union at all.

Picketers watched with suspicion from the other end of Giant's parking lot.

They were angry when they heard what was going on. Strikers weren't legally allowed to go where O'Neil was passing out his flyers.

With a home computer and help from his wife, Jane, Doreen Vodnoski, and Lynda Riggs, O'Neil did a thorough mail-out to appeal to CASAW members. Each striker, even those who had gone home to Newfoundland to wait out the labour dispute, received the flyer. This was a hot topic at the union hall. Where had O'Neil obtained all those addresses? Most people were listed in the phone book, but men with post-office boxes received the flyer in their boxes, not at home. Bob Kosta, the local's secretary-treasurer, smelled a rat and got everybody to bring in their copy, with envelopes.

Union leaders had anticipated O'Neil's maneuver. Hemi Mitic devised a plan to head off the GMEA. The CAW would conduct a "friendly raid" on CASAW and become the official bargaining agent. Mitic reasoned that a CAW raid might even put an end to the Giant dispute. Under the Canada Labour Code, first contracts can be imposed by an arbitrator if the union and the company cannot agree at the bargaining table after a stipulated number of months. This is to prevent companies from excluding unions from their plants by prolonging bargaining indefinitely. CASAW lawyers Gina Fiorillo and Leo McGrady were skeptical. The first-contract rule had never been used at the federal level when one union was replacing another, rather than signing up a nonunionized plant. But Mitic said the trick had worked under the Ontario provincial code and was worth a try.

Federation of Labour president Jim Evoy and most of the local's leadership supported a friendly raid, and the prospect of a legal way to force Witte's hand. The catch was that the CAW would do it only with CASAW national's consent. The CAW wanted to pick up the whole union, including the big Alcan local in British Columbia. That meant enlisting CASAW national president Ross Slezak; he vetoed it. He agreed that CASAW was too small to continue as an independent union, but he was wooing another independent union, the Pulp and Paper Workers of Canada (PPWC). The two unions were closer in size, so it would be more like a merger than a takeover. The PPWC, like CASAW, was primarily in British Columbia, was part of the Confederation of Canadian Unions, and shared a similar spirit. In Yellowknife, Local 4's leadership was annoyed but decided not to tell the membership about the rejection of Mitic's offer to raid. It was no time to show weakness or lack of solidarity, and the members of Slezak's local didn't deserve to be slighted after sending Local 4 extra dues every month.

THE 100 PERCENT TRUTH

Few days passed without someone in the union being interrogated by the police. Wives, and even children, were dragged in, especially if their men resisted further questioning or the polygraph. Tim Bettger's kids were interviewed several times, he says. His son Jake was thirteen years old. "It's pretty rough on a kid to have a cop look at you and tell you that your father's a murderer, and they're going to prove it."

Loyal strikers and their families came and went in the union hall, sitting on a sagging couch and wooden school chairs, sipping coffee, and swapping the latest news and police tactics. Few outsiders understood what they were going through, and many people in town felt the union deserved the treatment it got after the summer's vandalism and the September 18 blast.

But CASAW local president Harry Seeton's patience had run out. With help from lawyer Gina Fiorillo, he lodged a lengthy grievance with the RCMP Public Complaints Commission, a body independent of the police. The complaint covered RCMP tactics after the blast and alleged a pattern of bias throughout the dispute. Picketers had been booked on flimsy evidence merely to assist Royal Oak, the union claimed, while complaints about Pinkerton's misbehaviour were ignored.

The complaint had no apparent effect on the RCMP, whose liaison to CASAW, Sergeant Bill Code, was also a valued member of the murder task force. The interrogations continued, and it was Roger Warren's turn again on November 5. Corporal Dale McGowan, who had also spoken with Warren's wife, Helen, took a soft approach. "You guys seem to be very family oriented," McGowan said. "I had a talk with [Sergeant] Pat Dauk. He thinks you're a pretty good guy—you've got good morals, good fabric as a man." They went over Warren's whereabouts on September 17. Then McGowan homed in on the alterations to the soles of Warren's boots, which he said he'd cut after stepping on a grill taken off a fire at a picket gate.

"You're telling me the truth?" asked McGowan.

"Yeah," Warren said. "I don't know what's the big deal."

"There was a murder that night. We're the ones that have to clear you. Jesus, everything's a big deal."

"I just never attached any importance to it."

McGowan was also curious about CASAW, who had come to visit Warren in the hospital, who wrote the strike bulletins, who did what on the executive. And he asked about Al Shearing. "What do you think of his involvement?"

"Oh, I don't think he was involved."

"We definitely look at him a little stronger, because he was active in that shit. What do you think of him?"

"He's a pretty sensible guy."

They moved on to the two men Warren said were on the property that night. Though he'd said one man resembled Conrad Lisoway, Warren was now sure it wasn't him. "I just haven't got any impression of a mustache on the guy's face."

"If they suspect that you know, you could be in some heavy danger," McGowan warned. "I want to take care of you, of your family."

"I have no concerns about that," Warren said. "I don't believe it's one of our guys."

"Look at what your mind is doing to your body right now; it's fucking up your ticker. Strictly stress," McGowan said. "Maybe you do know who it is. We don't want another death, or a couple of deaths to investigate, especially yours." He pressed Warren to take a polygraph test. "You say you didn't do it. If you didn't, you got no problems."

Warren told McGowan that he found the idea of a polygraph stressful, adding that he didn't agree with the principle of hooking up most of CASAW to a machine. "It's like you're guilty and you have to prove yourself innocent. It's like anybody in Canada who's a suspect right now has to take a fucking polygraph."

Usually the polygraph is used to incriminate someone, McGowan conceded, but this time "we had to take the fast track to cut guys out of the picture," so we're making history right here in Yellowknife. "Roger, Jesus Christ, I know you didn't do this, [but] there were a couple of hours when nobody saw you," McGowan said.

"I'm lucky I wasn't walking the road the whole night. Then I'd be really fucked," Warren retorted.

You might be involved in a small way, even by mistake, McGowan suggested.

"I'd never be able to do it in the fucking first place. There's nothing to talk about." As for taking the polygraph, "I had that chest pain, and that guy just jumping on me, pissed me right off ... I used to get these sharp pains in my chest," along with seeing black spots and feeling nauseated, Warren said. He'd had these symptoms at work while going up ramps and ladders.

"The guys that play[ed] hockey with you say you were a hell of a hockey player, you were in good shape," McGowan said.

"I give it up for now." Playing the RCMP once, Warren said, "Holy shit, I just about died by the end of the game." As the 4.5-hour session ended, Warren agreed to help a police artist make a composite drawing of the man he said he'd seen on the mine property.

The RCMP finally gave Gordie Kendall a polygraph in Vancouver on November 1. Sergeant Pat Dauk confronted him with the results. "You had problems with a lot of questions, not just some of them. Some were directly related to the things that happened down in the mine. What's your involvement in that graffiti run?"

"I organized it," Kendall claimed, and bought the bolt cutters that were left hidden at the bottom of Akaitcho shaft. "Are you convinced that I had nothing to do with that murder?"

"I can't say that I am," said Dauk. "I would have loved to be able to clear you, but I can't ... Just be honest with me."

"I have been honest."

"You haven't been ... Tell me everything you know."

"I'd rather face my charges."

"You will not be retaliated against."

"There are lots of groups of people involved here. Do you realize that there are tie-ins?"

"No," Dauk said.

"I know who's tied with who and who and who. And I know how the ties work. And some of these people may not, are not involved but would not be very happy if their friends got caught."

Kendall appeared to be suggesting that the murder was the result of a conspiracy, that he was in a pivotal position, and that some of the players had considerable power to retaliate against those who were disloyal.

Dauk steered back to the June 29 graffiti run, and Kendall said that explosives had been taken from the mine.

"Is that what was used for other explosions?" Dauk pressed.

"Some of it. I was given some of the powder."

"Where is it now?"

"I ripped it open and flushed it down the river ... I was handed twenty fuses and fourteen sticks of powder and some electric caps. The caps, I set them off."

"Who planned the route?" Dauk asked.

"That was part of the trip. Art [St. Amand] knew the mine inside out. We weren't sure of the route or the conditions. We weren't even sure of the condition of the track." Sergeant Dauk apparently didn't pick up on this broad hint. What track was Kendall talking about? The train rails on 750? Why was he talking about it? Anyone who knew an area of the mine well would know the condition of the track—it was like knowing the road between one's home and work.

"It was more or less a surveillance trip," Kendall continued. "We had planned to go back down again."

"The next time was already planned?" Dauk asked.

"We were working on it ... I had talked to a few other guys too. You know, 'Are you willing to come underground, do something? How far are you going to go, I want to know that too. I need a psychological profile.'"

"Is this something you discussed with Al and Tim?"

"Yeah, we had come up with ideas what to do next ... I mentioned going underground, using the equipment and hiding it ... I said one time, 'If this doesn't work, what does work? You have to do something a little bit heavier, and do it heavier until you get to the point where you're killing somebody.'"

"Who's there listening to that?"

"Tim must have heard me say that a couple of times. I even talked to Bill [Schram] about it. And then I found my excuse to bail out ... There was a problem with my strike pay, so I just told them, 'I won't be involved with union stuff anymore and you don't have to pay me.'"

Kendall appeared to be saying that he recruited saboteurs, thought about their psychology, and urged them to kill if necessary. Kendall implied a conspiracy beyond junior union executives like Shearing and Bettger. Then, having played the role of *agent provocateur*, he found an excuse to step back from the union.

In the course of the seven-hour interrogation, Dauk also got around to the September 1 blast. "You know something about the explosion on the vent shaft. Do you know who made the trigger?"

"I know one person offered to make me a trigger. He used to be a biker. He was up on charges, assaults on a police officer." Kendall was referring to diamond driller Blaine Lisoway, although there is no other evidence to support his allegation.

There was also the matter of the mysterious conversation with which Kendall had been tantalizing the RCMP.

"Who are you protecting?" Dauk asked.

"I have no intention of protecting anyone. Once my court cases are over ... I admitted before the [polygraph] test that I was holding back information."

"That's causing us problems."

"I'm totally convinced of who did it now," Kendall said.

"Yeah, I know," Dauk said.

"All I have is that conversation I had with one of the perpetrators of the air [vent] shaft [explosion]. I'm sure he'd be involved in the murder."

"Well, who is it?"

Kendall did not answer. "I'm probably the only person he told ... I'm withholding it."

"That's like a guy who shoots somebody and says, 'I saw it but I'm not going to tell you.'"

"He might have a really good reason for it. Probably be a Mafia hit. Then you'd think twice."

The police continued to focus on Tim Bettger and Al Shearing. People who associated with them were grilled repeatedly. "Every time I go in there, they ask me if Al Shearing is capable of killing nine men," said striker Marvin Tremblett in early November. He alleged harassment; the RCMP Public Complaints Commission much later found that the investigator had "come close to the threshold of harassment and intimidation [but] oppressive conduct cannot be substantiated on a balace of probabilities." The RCMP weren't above using macabre measures. CASAW vice president Rick Cassidy, whom most saw as a moderate, was quizzed for three hours. Apparently unhappy with his answers, officers showed him a videotape of the dead men's remains on a slab.

In the union hall, Shearing himself was adamant that the police were desperate, not just to nail him, but to prove the blast was union-sanctioned. The RCMP "told me there's a hole in my alibi from the time I went home to the time I got up," he said, adding that they'd interrogated his common-law wife twice and her son once. Shearing said he told the RCMP that their reliance on the polygraph proved that they were scraping the bottom of the barrel. "They just figure somebody's going to confess," he said.

The police got their last shot at Shearing on December 2, when he went to the infamous room 701 of the Explorer Hotel, home of the polygraph. At first, Shearing denied taking part in blasting the satellite dish on July 21. And the vent-shaft explosion, he claimed, was probably done by the Pinkerton's guards—he saw them shine a spotlight over there about five minutes before it blew up. He'd heard that Art St. Amand was on the graffiti run into the mine, but said no more. They covered Shearing's whereabouts on September 18 again, and told him there was no doubt he was responsible for the killing.

"No," Shearing replied. The officers grilled him, using themes about inner feelings building up in him like pressure in a pipe. They hinted that Peggy Witte was to blame, that Shearing's parents were to blame. Finally Shearing admitted that he'd lied to them, but not about the blast. He also confessed to going underground on the graffiti run, but would not admit Bettger's role. "You guys know who did this," he said.

After almost five hours, Shearing wanted to leave, but the police homed in on the vent-shaft explosion. Shearing said he could have been involved, and might know something about the satellite dish, but he had to go to work. According to a police report, Shearing "terminated the interview by walking out. His demeanour changed drastically toward the end, and he appeared antagonistic and agitated." The RCMP concluded that Shearing would not take a polygraph.

If Shearing was worried, he didn't show it. "From what I can gather in the interrogations, they don't have nothing," he said that evening in the union hall. "What it looks like to me, they're trying to frame me ... They keep saying, 'This is the only chance we're going to give you to come clean—tell us how you set this thing up, how it was done.'"

The police did not believe Shearing's denial, says informant Bob Robertson. "They told me ... his alibi did not stand up for that night. He got up in the middle of the night. He said he was attending to his sick [stepson]. That's never been confirmed."

After another interrogation, Roger Warren finally agreed to go for a polygraph. First, Sergeant Dauk had him fill out a questionnaire, which was given to no one else during the entire investigation. There was just one question: "We have reached the determination that the explosion was deliberately set. How would you explain this?" Warren's answer took him an hour and a half to write:

> The only explanation I could give is that someone knew the regular crew was going to be late and knowing this set a trap that would be activated by the ore train which would normally have been pushed in by a Titan motor. Thus probably no one would be hurt but it would've been very scary.

> I must add that no one as far as I know, knew where the six members of our union who had crossed the picket line were working.

> I have no idea what sort of mechanism would be used that would be sure-fire. A power source with sufficient amperage would have to be used to set off any detonator available in the mine. This would require experiments or trials to make sure it would work.

Warren's polygraph was inconclusive, so police were left to wonder if he was being completely honest. The polygraph examiner told another officer that "he didn't think that Warren did it, but that he certainly could be involved."

Even after Kendall's and Warren's polygraphs, RCMP spokesman Dave Grundy told the media that many people on both sides of the labour dispute had taken polygraphs and "everybody that's been given them has been 100 percent truthful." Meanwhile, the RCMP had started work on an operational plan for arrests, including execution of search warrants, of "all persons identified as having criminal offenses," wrote Sergeant Al Macintyre. The roundup was "somewhat contingent" on being able to "arrest and HOLD the persons responsible for the murders."

TRIPPING OUT

June Roberts and Harry Seeton set off in late November to stump for support from BC unions. For her, it was an escape from the pressures of Yellowknife; for Seeton, there was no relief. As president of CASAW, he had an impossible job—he absorbed everyone's troubles while his own marriage was falling apart. The situation was hard on his two children. The police hassled him; he'd received death threats and been branded a murderer. Sometimes he couldn't contain his anger and frustration, which just fed the cycle of suspicion. The media portrayed the union as more a band of terrorists than a workers' organization, and Seeton was their leader. Perpetual rumours that arrests were imminent never materialized. Jim O'Neil's "scab association" was trying to raid the union, with Peggy Witte's blessing and help, as far as Seeton was concerned. After a stressful series of phone calls and meetings, he put his head in his hands and lamented, "Holy fuck, holy fuck, I mean holy fuck." As usual, someone was waiting at the door of his office to see him. The strains he felt were obvious to the union executive. "He was very paranoid," remembers Al Shearing. "We told Harry, 'All you got to do is ask for help,'" and eventually he took some time off.

CASAW's bills were astronomical and there was no way to keep up. Seeton lived in fear that the time would come when there wouldn't be any picket pay, or that he might fail the people who counted on him. So this fund-raising trip to British Columbia was just part of the pressure cooker; it had to succeed. Seeton was a shaft lead hand, not a politician, negotiator, public relations man, strategist, lawyer, or magician. He probably envied June, who reveled in her rise to prominence. She had an important mission, but it was much less burdensome than Seeton's.

Their ten-day tour was sponsored by the CAW and CASAW national. In two days, they raised $10,000 at meetings of six union locals or umbrella organizations in the Vancouver area. Seeton and Roberts were pictured in the *Vancouver Sun,* showing photos of police with M-16s on the picket line. About 350 people came to a benefit shared with the Congress of South African Trade Unions, attended by Svend Robinson, the New Democratic Party's Justice critic in Parliament.

Seeton and Roberts were nervous making speeches. But, each time, Seeton relived events which were tearing him apart. At night, he was distraught and relied on everyone around him—especially lawyer Gina Fiorillo—to keep him in one piece. Fiorillo's friendship and counsel pulled Seeton through.

The tour was exciting for Roberts. She met veteran unionists who steeped her in labour history that opened her eyes to the wider world of trade union solidarity. She survived the grueling schedule "running on adrenaline. Man, I had fun! I was spoiled rotten." At a rally against free trade, she spoke to about 200 people, following a speech by Audrey McLaughlin, the federal leader of the New Democrats. "I got more cheers and longer applause!" At a meeting of nurses, "I never got to tell them the whole story, they were all crying." For union crowds, Roberts's story was a flashback to company towns of the 1930s, with paid thugs, merciless banks, and governments that sided against working people in favour of a corporate tyrant. People were all horrified, Roberts said. "People said we should be proud we've been able to endure—that we really opened their eyes to the system in Canada."

On they went to Prince Rupert and Kitimat, where CASAW Local 1 contributed $50,000 from its strike fund. The tour was a huge success, netting support for CASAW, CLASS, and the adopt-a-family program that lasted for the duration of the dispute. Roberts met people who she felt would be lifelong friends.

Roberts found her return to Yellowknife depressing. She'd left admiration and open-armed hospitality and had come back to a community in which she felt rejected. "I got off the plane and saw the snow and just about cried. In Vancouver, they're planting flowers." But there were rewards too. In the union hall that night, Bill Schram hugged Roberts affectionately. "You did good—real good. Thanks to being adopted, I got a place to live now," he said.

Based on the success of the trip to British Columbia, CASAW sent June Roberts and her best friend, Sylvia Imbeault, to a CAW convention in Toronto and to a gathering of the Confédération des syndicats nationaux (CSN) in Montreal. There, 1,200 French-speaking delegates assembled in the immense Palais des congrès. Imbeault was too shy to join Roberts on stage, where she was just a little speck. Roberts's face was projected on two huge screens, like at a rock concert. Her simple speech outlined events from the start of the strike. She appealed to brothers and sisters in the labour movement to help CASAW and CLASS stand firm against an American owner's union busting. "I got a standing ovation," Roberts says, and, in French tradition, "when I got up to leave, everybody on the panel hugged and kissed me."

"When I started going to meetings, I never, in my wildest dreams, expected anything like that to happen," Imbeault says.

While Roberts and Seeton were in British Columbia, Tim Bettger and Marvin Ferriss, RCMP agent G175, hurtled down the road to Grande Prairie, Alberta, in Ferriss's truck. He had been sidling up to Bettger for several weeks. "He needed to work on his snowmobile, so he showed up at my place," Bettger recalls. "I said, 'Yeah, I got room in the garage.' I'm from Saskatchewan, he was out of Manitoba. We both grew up in rural communities; we understood the work ethic. Like, you got to make hay while the sun's shining, or that nor'wester's coming, you got to thresh. And you give 'er, you just work. So we got along good." Bettger says he was a bit suspicious—before September 18, he had known

Ferriss only as one of the guys. And Ferriss seemed unusually eager to talk about illegal activities. "There was always this attitude among the guys, some things were just known and not talked about," Bettger says. "But after a while you just said, 'Well, OK. This anomaly is normal for this person.'"

Ferriss made hair-raising reports to the RCMP about things Bettger allegedly told him during the trip to Grande Prairie, some of which were included in Superintendent Brian Watt's reports to Ottawa. On their August trip to British Columbia, Bettger and Shearing supposedly met someone who said they could supply "rockets for a rocket launcher, as [they] have access to a rocket launcher, hand grenades, and nutcrackers (thin-walled fragment grenades)."[5] But attempts to get these items failed. Ferriss said the two men made about twenty-four "roll-over mines" fired by sharpened nails and shotgun shells, and tested them near an abandoned mining town south of Great Slave Lake. "There was no place on the [Giant] mine surface that Bettger [and] Shearing had not been," Ferriss reported to police. "They were in the headframe one night, and through the mill on another occasion."

But Ferriss reported no hint of a confession about September 18. Bettger suggested a mishap, "the company finding the accident and then setting off a further explosion to cover the initial blast. This second blast is what the police found." On the other hand, Ferriss said, "Bettger feels strongly it was not an inside job."

As if confirming their faith in Shearing's innocence, CASAW sent him and miner Dan Noel to Newfoundland and New Brunswick, their respective home provinces. They visited unions to promote the adopt-a-family program, and handed out lists of strikebreakers from the region. "Unions assured Al and Dan they would act on the scabs' names that were given to them," a CASAW bulletin noted. Since the start of the strike, Shearing had religiously kept track of "known scabs," compiling a list that eventually included about 400 names.

The Pinkerton's guards took a trip too—a permanent one, out of Yellowknife. In November, Royal Oak began to replace Pinkerton's men with guards from Minion Protection Services, though Pinkerton's boss Chris Morton says he stayed until at least December 21. RCMP sergeant Bill Code applauded the change. "The whole time the Pinkerton's were here it was tense. We're going to hopefully start on a new footing."

The departure of Pinkerton's was a boon to Royal Oak's bottom line. The company had begun to cut security staff well before the blast. In August, for example, Pinkerton's cost about $607,000, while October's budget was roughly $291,000 and the projection for all of 1993 was just $750,000. With only twelve Minion guards on duty, that figure and the $22-an-hour fee per man were probably reduced.

NAUGHTY AND NICE

Mediation was stalled while Jim O'Neil and Hemi Mitic planned their respective union raids. Mediators Ready and Munroe organized conference calls and jockeyed with both sides, but found no willingness to compromise. In mid-November, they carefully crafted a report that would corner both CASAW and Royal Oak. In Ottawa, Labour Minister Marcel Danis secured support from the opposition Liberals and New Democrats before the report was made public. The two mediators labeled Giant's "the most difficult labour dispute that either of us has witnessed." The biggest single issue wasn't contract language, or even the September 18 explosion. The main problem was an unbridgeable gap between the union's demand for a full amnesty for fired workers and Royal Oak's insistence that all terminations were final.

Ready and Munroe slammed both sides. The bargaining position patched together by Hemi Mitic "falls short of comprising a realistically concrete proposal sufficient to generate real momentum at the bargaining table." Their criticism of Royal Oak was more pointed: "The employer must restrain itself from taking bargaining positions which it surely must know would be unacceptable to virtually any organization of workers."

Mitic wanted the union to endorse the report immediately, believing Peggy Witte would reject it and appear intransigent. He flew to Yellowknife and called a press conference. There would be no disastrous outbursts like Terry Legge's at the previous media event on September 20. Mitic rented a meeting room in a hotel and kept strict control of proceedings. "We're leaning very heavily toward the report," Mitic announced, tactfully implying that CASAW would drop its demand for an amnesty on the firings. The union executive was not easily persuaded, however; several felt the union was abandoning the fired men. But there was barely a murmur of protest when the issue went to a membership meeting three days later. One man stood up and told the men "not to stay out on strike just because I'm fired."

Witte scrambled to find grounds to reject the mediators' report, as Mitic had predicted. Royal Oak hired a business professor from Queen's University, Donald Nightingale, to do a fast study on the issue of the firings. He sent a graduate student to interview some strikebreakers and supervisors. Predictably, most were against the fired strikers returning to work; several said they would quit if the men did come back. Mayor Pat McMahon and RCMP superintendent Brian Watt were also interviewed, probably to give the report credibility. McMahon said she advised Royal Oak to accept the mediators' advice; Watt refused to talk to reporters.

Advice to refuse the mediators' proposal was in Witte's hands by December

10. "Expedited arbitration would result in unacceptably high levels of risk for underground miners and possible closure of the mine," Nightingale wrote. Royal Oak's Toronto lawyer wrote Witte a letter claiming that Royal Oak could be liable to Mine Safety charges or lawsuits if someone was hurt underground after an arbitrator ordered fired strikers reinstated.

Witte and vice president John Smrke flew to Ottawa to lobby Labour Minister Marcel Danis. They gave him copies of the Nightingale report and the lawyer's letter and insisted that the mediators were wrong about binding arbitration. A lawyer himself, Danis didn't agree with the legal opinion Witte had obtained. "That struck me, that letter. That's when I realized, oh boy, we're in trouble here," Danis says. "If you read the letter, with her attitude combined, you said, we're not going to settle this."

"Do you realize the powers of the Canada Labour Relations Board?" Danis asked Witte, showing her a series of CLRB decisions compiled by his staff. If you stick to your hard line, the CLRB could impose a contract on you, and even levy a big fine, Danis warned. Witte didn't budge. "I think she understood," Danis says. "She's pretty smart ... Maybe she thought she's going to take her chances."

Witte and Smrke repeated their pitch to Ready and Munroe on December 20. The mediators were unimpressed, and wouldn't change their recommendations. The next day, four weeks after the mediators' report had been made public, Royal Oak officially rejected it. "To contemplate taking back the terminated employees would violate a commitment to those working employees that their safety was of paramount concern and would not be jeopardized," stated the company's press release. The Nightingale report was quoted at length, but the full text was kept secret for another year.

Marcel Danis finally set up an industrial inquiry (IIC) into the Giant dispute on December 22. Ready and Munroe became inquiry commissioners, with power to subpoena witnesses, compel the company and the union to talk, and, eventually, publicly recommend terms of a new collective agreement. Everyone but the company had been asking for an IIC for months, but Danis had trouble obtaining cabinet approval for it. Solicitor General Doug Lewis, the RCMP's ultimate boss, was at first opposed. Danis said that law-enforcement officials were consulted about the IIC's terms of reference to make sure its right to compel testimony did not interfere with the murder investigation. It was a sensitive issue in which Mulroney's Privy Council appears to have been involved, with officials from Northern Affairs, Labour Canada, and the RCMP.

The RCMP postblast team's massive report on the explosion was inexplicably dated Christmas Day, 1992. Only a small part of it was ever made public. Inspector Don Watson provided the report to both Superintendent Watt in Yellowknife and headquarters in Ottawa. According to RCMP spokesman Dave Grundy, the Federal

Bureau of Investigation (FBI) in the United States was waiting for it too, for use in a profile of the killer(s). Information on the RCMP's main suspects had long since been sent.

Box after box of Christmas presents, most of them paid for by southern supporters, were carted into June and Derek Roberts's trailer. There were so many that they also filled a room at another striker's house. Gift wrapping took two nights. "The night I was there, there must've been twelve of us," says June's friend Sylvia Imbeault. Every present had a child's name on it, and each child had a Christmas stocking. There were gift certificates for clothing, especially for families who couldn't afford to buy presents for their kids. Turkeys from the Mine–Mill local in Sudbury were added to food hampers from the Steelworkers at Con.

More than a hundred families were getting adopt-a-family checks, including the Robertses. CLASS paid for prescription drugs, glasses, and emergency dental care. The women of CLASS rushed around, and planned a Christmas party for December 20 in a high-school gym. "There's people here that I haven't seen for the whole strike. It's great," Karen Fougère said with a smile. Almost 300 people attended the feast, including about 170 children. They ran around and played games. Some people sang songs. Miner Frank Mills and his wife, Rose, whitehaired and beaming, were Mr. and Mrs. Santa Claus. They were helped by their suited elves, Sylvia Imbeault and June Roberts. The children climbed up on stage for pictures with the Clauses. For a few hours, people put the strike behind them.

Some union members were not at the Christmas party; they were on the picket line. Strikers did four-hour shifts on Christmas Day, except Bill Schram, who took a twenty-four-hour stint. He was single, and he wanted families to be together.

Jim O'Neil was practically frozen stiff in the Giant mine parking lot during the week before Christmas, signing up members for the GMEA, "every day and every night." The temperature barely moved from minus 30 degrees Celsius, but he seldom sought shelter as long as men trickled in to work. At this time of year there was little daylight anyway, and at 7:00 A.M. one didn't even think about it. After taking a card, men sat in Doreen Vodnoski's truck to fill it out. She saw the GMEA as the only way to resolve the dispute, and felt that she owed that much to her late husband, Dave. He had dreamed of becoming a miner, she said, and "Royal Oak did that for him."

It wasn't until December that O'Neil had a chance of signing up enough workers to replace CASAW with the GMEA. The odds improved as Royal Oak phased out Procon, the contractor providing short-term strikebreakers. From November to December, approximately eighty people were added to Royal Oak's payroll, neatly dovetailing with O'Neil's organizing efforts.

CHAPTER FIVE

HOOF-IN-MOUTH DISEASE (ANARCHY IN YK)

We used to have this thing in the army, you know, the worst thing about rumours is that most of them are true.

—Gordie Kendall to the RCMP, October 8, 1992

Yellowknife's Legion Hall is a reminder of the city's rough-and-tumble past, before shopping malls and fast food. This squat, nondescript concrete building straddles the corner of the main street, Franklin Avenue, and the road to the airport and Giant mine. Inside, beer and talk flow freely, without the rowdiness of the nearby Gold Range bar. People drop in for inexpensive, home-style food at lunchtime—a rarity in Yellowknife, where New York prices are the norm. Shoppers from outlying Dene villages share tables with darts enthusiasts, who hold long tournaments in the hall's dim light. The number of veterans declines yearly, but many of their children have joined the Royal Canadian Legion and organize the annual parade. Like most original Yellowknife institutions, the Legion was built up by miners, and many are still members.

The Legion branch elected a new president, second-generation member Wade Merritt, in November 1992. About that time, Merritt, a CASAW member, crossed the picket line. Many union loyalists were shocked, feeling it was like a soldier committing treason or flouting democracy. Over New Year's weekend, anti-Merritt graffiti was sprayed on the hall's wall. "Is nothing sacred?" old men wondered in the coffee shops, shaking their heads.

The graffiti attack was spontaneous. Al Shearing and a miner were at the nearby Elk's Hall when Shearing mentioned that a third striker was roaming the streets with a can of spray paint. They found him outside the Legion, where he had decorated a wall with the word "Wabe."

"What the fuck are you doing?" Shearing asked.

"I want to write 'Scab Club Wabe Merritt,'" the man said. He wasn't dyslexic; he had always called Merritt "Wabe." He sprayed Merritt's last name, without the final "t." Then Shearing, a Legion regular, grabbed the can and added "SCAB CLUB." They took off.

Early January is a grim time in Yellowknife, even in normal years. Residents have endured two months of snow and face four more frigid months of winter. The sun grants only five hours of real daylight; people stay indoors, visiting and gossiping.

One rumour had Gordie Kendall getting drunk in a BC bar over Christmas and boasting about setting the September 18 bomb. The RCMP were keeping his arrest secret while they searched for more evidence, the story went. It was denied by the RCMP, so reporters dropped it even though it was common gossip. The RCMP did not admit that there was a witness to Kendall's boast, or that Kendall was a major suspect. Kendall says the police told him that "180 people said I killed 'em." He claims that he told the police that whoever did "should be given a fucking medal."

The one bright spot for most Yellowknifers was the region's diamond rush. It had finally dawned on the stock market that billions could be made on treasure beneath the tundra, as informed locals had whispered for more than a year. Tiny exploration companies' stock shot up, in some cases by a factor of several hundred. The world's largest mining firms were big players, and a major Australian stock analyst commented that there would be no need for unions at a future diamond mine.

Jim O'Neil barely had a Christmas break. He worked nonstop organizing the Giant Mine Employees' Association, armed with a new computer, a fax machine, and Jane's writing skills. With the zeal of a true believer, he implored coworkers to sign up. Royal Oak was informed about the GMEA's progress, and told the RCMP that, "once the union finds out, the radical group will again be a real threat to violence on mine property." Show time came on January 13, when the GMEA applied to the Canada Labour Relations Board to replace CASAW as the bargaining agent at Giant.

It was also show time for Peggy Witte. Her cost-cutting heroics and promotional talks had kept her in the public eye, usually in a flattering light. But Witte planted her foot squarely in her mouth when she was interviewed for CBC radio's *Morningside* program, at Royal Oak's mining lodge in Timmins, Ontario. It sounded like a fireside chat, until host Peter Gzowski mentioned CASAW.

"CASAW has been a very radical Canadian-based union, a small, nonmainstream union without support," Witte declared. "When they first came to the table during negotiations they had asked for a 30 percent pay increase." (The correct figure was 6 percent.) Witte blamed CASAW for everything, including Giant's high accident rate. "The union elected to go out on strike," Witte added. "The union elected to beat up on the company ... The tentative agreement was agreed upon with the bargaining committee. [After it was voted down] we agreed to sit back down with the union and work out wording changes with Jim O'Neil and people."

CASAW's lawyers were ecstatic; Witte had practically admitted to bargaining with O'Neil instead of with CASAW, a clear violation of the Canada Labour Code.

Gzowski zeroed in on Witte's remarks about CASAW. "It's hard to believe you don't want to break the union."

"That's very, very far from the truth. We do not," she asserted. "If we wanted to break the union we would not have started to negotiate with them ... CASAW, Steelworkers, an employee association, it doesn't matter to me as long as they bargain in good faith, they understand the economics of the operation, they allow the operation to run, they allow management to control the operation ..."

Not content with disparaging CASAW, Witte went on to rebuke Yellowknife. "The community has brought a lot of this on themselves. When the strike broke out and our people were barricaded in the buildings because the mine was being overrun with striking workers with baseball bats and clubs, and we called the mayor for help, for her to declare her community in distress and call in the RCMP, she wouldn't do it ... It's just like a kid in a candy store. If he goes in and he steals a package of gum and gets away with it, he's going to steal something bigger and bigger."

Witte wasn't the only one talking herself into trouble. Al Shearing told the *Edmonton Journal* that the RCMP had informed him that he was their number-one murder suspect. He proclaimed his innocence and explained why he wouldn't take a polygraph test. "They've got me guilty and I shouldn't have to prove myself innocent," he said. When the paper hit the newsstands, lawyer Gina Fiorillo begged

Shearing to keep quiet. They didn't want any more trouble and, as a trustee in the CASAW executive, Shearing should be more discreet.

About this time Royal Oak's suppliers boosted the reward fund for the murder investigation to $307,000.

Royal Oak and government officials were puzzled that CASAW showed no sign of fading away. Many felt that the infamy of the nine murders and eight months without wages should have sapped rank-and-file support for the union. Instead, ostracism, hardship, and anger had welded strikers and their spouses into a resilient, fiercely loyal clan. The men had spent long, cold nights in picket shacks, sharing life stories and cursing the Pinkerton's patrols and their dogs. It had brought them closer together than years of seeing each other changing clothes in C-dry. Many wives had made the union the centre of their lives. Through CLASS, they formed close friendships that replaced the ones they lost by being branded as thugs' accomplices. Sylvia Imbeault and June Roberts, for example, became inseparable. Early in the strike, Sylvia's friendship cooled with the woman who had been maid of honour at her wedding: her friend wouldn't support a CLASS petition against bunkhouses for strikebreakers at Giant. "All she said was, 'No, because scabs have a right to feed their family too.' It didn't ruin our friendship, but it's not the same."

Families, especially in Northland trailer court, took care of each other's children and shared what they had. Union tradesmen, such as Tim Bettger, pitched in with free house and car repairs. "Everybody was doing what they could," he says. Older couples, such as Frank and Rose Mills, offered advice and vowed to hold out until the strike ended. Roger and Helen Warren were much the same, supporting people who were in real difficulty. Many simply needed to share their feelings and troubles with someone.

CASAW's resolve came across with special force at a CLASS benefit dance at the Elk's Hall on January 22. The CASAW crowd was alone, except for a few stalwarts from other unions, so the several thousand dollars raised simply went from poor strikers to poorer strikers. The real benefit was a big boost in morale. Friends socialized and danced, until the lights were dimmed for the first public singing of "Ballad of the Royal Oak Giant Mine Strike." Everyone knew the words; it was the first song on a fund-raising cassette for CASAW. Many families had been playing it for weeks:

In Yellowknife
The flame burns bright
Of solidarity
In the cold and long dark northern night
It burns
There's working families on the line
For the right to work safely
A tiny flame against the northern night
They need our solidarity to keep it bright.

Locked out of the mine
They're on the line
Fighting for mine safety
'Gainst court injunctions, scabs and dogs
And against the RCMP
That's the Royal Oak special detachment
Paid for by your taxes
A private army for the Royal Oak company.

It was a night of shared escape from fears of hostile intrusions and snooping. One woman raised her fist in the air with the promise that, in the end, "The Pig" would not win.

If you offered to roll back your wages 10 percent, you couldn't get an agreement here. I'll try and hit the target; you tell me where the hell it is.

—Hemi Mitic, January 30, 1993

"Here comes The Pig!" someone blurted in a raucous whisper as Peggy Witte walked into the first session of Vince Ready and Don Munroe's industrial inquiry commission (IIC) on January 29. In a crowded hotel banquet room, strikers, line-crossers, and supervisors rubbed shoulders for the first time in months. The air was heavy as opening statements were made.

CAW envoy Hemi Mitic had encouraged some soul-searching by CASAW's leaders, but they did not soften their goals for a contract. They still wanted most of the terms of the 1989 collective agreement, scrapping the April 18 tentative agreement entirely. It hardly mattered, because Peggy Witte's position had not softened either, and she added a new obstacle. "We face the real possibility that a new bargaining agent will be substituted for the current [one] in the relatively short term," she announced. "We will not be called upon to advance new bargaining positions" until the resolution of the GMEA's application to raid CASAW. Union lawyers were stunned. Witte seemed ignorant of the Canada Labour Code, which imposes a duty to bargain even through raid applications, and confident that CASAW's defeat was at hand.

Ready and Munroe's subsequent backroom arm-twisting was to no avail. CASAW rejected a proposal for a massive wage cut, while Witte wouldn't hear of allowing any fired strikers back to work. The next morning, the commissioners admitted defeat.

Royal Oak dug itself deeper into legal trouble at its press conference. Reporters asked about the company's bargaining position; vice president John Smrke said executives had been too busy to think about it, and the company didn't have one.

And what about the legal obligation to bargain in good faith? "How can you be considered to be bargaining in bad faith if you're not bargaining?" Smrke asked, looking puzzled. There would be no talks with the official bargaining agent, CASAW, but "should there be a different association, a different union, that comes in and raids, and there are several, we would be prepared to enter into negotiations with them." It was the *faux pas* of the year, and Royal Oak's high-priced legal help must have been horrified.

A few weeks later, Ready and Munroe suspended future IIC meetings until a ruling was made on the GMEA's raid application. Their decision was delivered the same day the RCMP proclaimed that postblast experts knew that the September explosion was caused by a homemade booby trap, just as Witte and Smrke had told reporters on September 22.

TRIP WIRES

Scientifically, we can show it's not an accident ... The blast was the result of an improvised explosive device activated by the man-car, using a substantial amount of explosives. [We] know how much ... [We] know how it was made.

—Sergeant Dave Grundy, February 24, 1993[1]

The criminal investigation, both administratively and operationally, is of excellent quality.

—Sergeant K.E. Colonval and Inspector G.D. Bass, February 8, 1993

The RCMP had tapped phones, and cajoled and threatened possible witnesses. Townspeople were disillusioned, and CASAW's leaders even suspected that the police had stolen two files that had been locked up in the union office—one containing financial records, and the other on the RCMP. But behind the scenes, police reported that the case was solved. "Through circumstance, previous conduct, statements and technical knowledge, it was determined that two subjects were principally responsible for causing the fatal explosion." But they had not arrested Shearing, Bettger, or Kendall.

RCMP agents Marvin Ferriss and Bob Robertson resorted to increasingly aggressive tactics to entrap or gain the confidence of union radicals. Ferriss encouraged Bettger to "develop a plan to make a skiddoo go flying," according to police documents—a plot to set off explosives under a company snowmobile. Ferriss said Bettger proposed using a trip wire to flip a toggle switch, fueling a police theory that one was used on September 18. This method of triggering the blast became very important in the murder case, because miner Roger Warren would claim that he had used it.

Ferriss and Bettger made another trip to Grande Prairie, Alberta. Bettger says that Ferriss claimed to be picking up another shipment of cocaine for a user in Yellowknife.

Probably to bolster his reputation as a never-give-an-inch striker, Ferriss appealed a minor conviction for impeding traffic outside the mine in June 1992. The fine was $180, but his appeal cost the union almost $3,000 in legal fees.

Ferriss also collected information on the June 29 graffiti raid. Bettger reportedly told him the billy club hadn't been forgotten, but had been left "as a sign." And Bettger talked of having brought bolt cutters out of fear "that they might get locked inside," but left them behind because they were heavy and no longer needed, Ferriss told police.

The RCMP must have found this intriguing. Were the bolt cutters left underground for future use, perhaps to cut a lock off a gate like the one in the 1-38 portal? Was the billy club a message to an uninitiated intruder not to take the next raise down to 950? Or a sign that the bolt cutters were nearby? Or a stash of caps and B-line? A stick of nitroglycerine-based explosive that wouldn't require electricity to set off? This would have interested the RCMP, who never found a battery that might have triggered the explosion.

Later, both Ferriss and Bettger were physically attacked by a strikebreaker. Charges were laid and then dropped. The RCMP refuse to comment, and the entire 137-page file was exempted from public review under provisions of the Access to Information Act. Bettger says that he learned from RCMP files he reviewed that the Crown prosecutor assigned to the case told the investigating officer that "it wasn't in the public interest to prosecute replacement workers."

Bob Robertson says the police developed plans to maintain his image as a tough guy. On one occasion, two strikebreakers came to the union hall while Robertson was in the bar next door with some Steelworkers from Con mine. He says he chased one of "the scabs" down the street and watched as the other was beaten up. After the police picked up Robertson and the others, he says he told a surprised officer, "'Look, you better call my handlers. Here are the numbers to call them at home.' They got the story, 'Bob's doing this for us.' I was supposed to follow the trouble, wherever [it] went ... Behind the scenes, a lot of the Nerco [Con] guys were the real instigators causing a lot of the trouble [and] the scab hunting."

Steelworkers were angry over the use of strikebreakers, but also because Royal Oak was trying to buy Con mine, which had been up for sale since June 1992. In July, Chris Neill said that Witte had just spent three days at Con. From August on, Royal Oak staff and various government officials talked about Royal Oak's plan to acquire Con. The Steelworkers' contract would expire in May 1993, and there were rumours of a work stoppage. Negotiations started in February. Nerco's demands for concessions were not well received.

Police had been collecting information about Con and its employees since at least November 1992, and, in June, Superintendent Watt had noted that using a new file-management system for Giant material "[will] be good practice for next year's Con strike." Robertson says that the RCMP told him to spy on his former workmates at Con. "They wanted to know who all the radicals were ... These guys were talking about bringing their guns. Blowing up the headframe. Whether it was just talk or not, I felt an obligation and a civic duty to convey that to the RCMP." (In May 1993, Royal Oak was outbid for Con by another company, and a contract was later signed, with no strike or lockout. RCMP documents reveal that they had "well-placed" confidential sources, and information about union strategy.)

Meanwhile, Yellowknife was awash in rumour about the September 18 blast, footprints in the mine, and various suspects' names. RCMP spokesman Dave Grundy said that "there's so much misinformation going around it's getting dangerous ... We haven't released to anyone what evidence we have." But

Gordie Kendall says that he was given other people's statements to read. Confronted with them, he says he knew his own story "wouldn't hold up—and I'd change it and change it."

The RCMP lured Roger Warren into taking another polygraph test with a free trip to Winnipeg to see his mother and sister on Valentine's Day weekend. After the test, which was again inconclusive, Warren was questioned by Sergeant Pat Dauk.

"Do you know who set that explosion? I believe you do," Dauk said.

"I told you and told you and told you, I haven't got a clue who went down in that mine," Warren replied.

Dauk then claimed that footprints in the Akaitcho shaft were an exact match to Warren's boots—the ones with soles that had been cut and melted. "I didn't think they did match my boots," Warren replied, and he didn't change his mind after another two-hour grilling on February 16. Police believed that Warren was hiding the identity of the two men he said he'd seen on the mine property the night before the blast, and "he was potentially the best witness the entire investigation had." Harping on the boots might break Warren's loyalty.

Warren agreed to see a police hypnotist in Edmonton on the way back to Yellowknife. The hypnotist was instructed to probe Warren's memory of the two mystery men, but Warren failed standard tests on his willingness to follow orders. "Hypnosis would have been inappropriate," the hypnotist concluded.

Publicly, the RCMP nurtured the idea that the net was closing around the killers. The postblast team's final report was completed on February 16. A week later, the RCMP claimed they knew the blast was triggered by a homemade device, how it was made, and how much and what type of explosive was used, but they wouldn't release details—and, in court in late 1994, postblast experts would say the exact opposite, that they didn't know how the device was made and couldn't be sure what or how much explosives were used.

Better progress was made on solving the September 1 vent-shack blast, however, which RCMP saw as the final warning before the murders. Corporal Vern White, the primary investigator, had been cultivating Terry Legge at a gym where they both worked out. Legge had taken part in the vent-shack blast, and White was armed with details. Gordie Kendall had told the RCMP that Shearing and Bettger were responsible; debris found at the scene seemed to be part of a quartz clock; and Tim Bettger's Visa slips showed that he'd bought six quartz clock movements in Vancouver. According to Legge, White laid out the evidence and said, "'Unless you want to be implemented [sic] in a murder, Terry, I want to know what your part was [or] we'll nail your ass to the wall.'" On the one hand, Legge wondered if he knew something that could solve the murders and end the labour dispute, and, on the other, he feared that what he

(L. SELLECK / THE PRESS INDEPENDENT)

The O'Neils' house was vandalized on August 5, the day after Jim crossed the picket line.

(C. LOCKERBIE / NNSL)

Pinkerton's manager Chris Morton hands a $3,200 cheque to Carol Atkin of Alison McAteer House, a women's shelter, in early August.

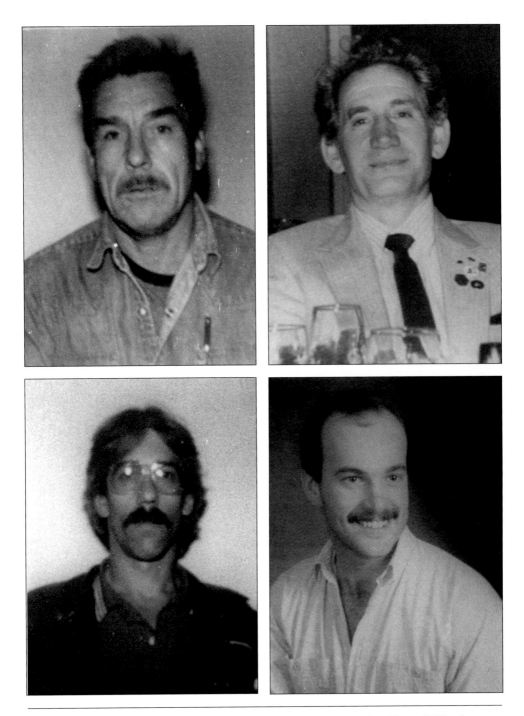

Victims: *(clockwise from top left)* Norm Hourie, Josef Pandev, Verne Fullowka, David Vodnoski. For profiles, see "Notes" in the Appendix.

(l. to r.) Shane "Spanky" Riggs, Chris Neill and Jim O'Neil are dirty but happy after completing a successful mine rescue in Alberta before the Giant mine strike. Riggs and Neill were killed in the Giant mine blast. (Editor's Note: Photographs of the three other victims—Robert Rowsell, Arnold Russell, Malcolm Sawler—were not available at press time.)

Royal Oak vice-president John Smrke *(l.)* and mine manager Terry Byberg hold the company's first press conference after the blast on September 19, 1992. Smrke said he'd been led to believe that the RCMP's investigation would be "lengthy," and promised that the mine would not be closed for long.

Peggy Witte arrived in Yellowknife from Hawaii in time for Royal Oak's press conference on September 20, 1992. "Nine men lost their lives to keep the Giant mine open," she said.

John Lang, secretary-treasurer of the Confederation of Canadian Unions; Harold David, strike coordinator; Jim Evoy, president of the NWT Federation of Labour; and Harry Seeton, president of CASAW Local 4, just after the RCMP issued its press release on September 20.

(Left) Terry Legge, a mechanic, loses his cool at CASAW's September 20 press conference after the RCMP announced that the blast was a homicide. Legge's outburst was aired and re-aired on television for months.

(Below) Tracey Neill was in tears after the memorial service on October 3, 1992. She appealed for people with information on the blast to help the RCMP.

(S. MUISE / NNSL)

(G. GEE / NNSL)

(Left) Late December 1992 was particularly cold with temperatures dipping to minus 30° Centigrade. GMEA president Jim O'Neil doggedly recruits members from the strikebreakers and line-crossers as they arrive at Giant for the day shift.

(L. SELLECK)

(A. KRUSE / NNSL)

The Royal Oak team at the opening of the Industrial Inquiry Commission (IIC) in the Explorer Hotel on January 29, 1993. *(l. to r.)* Bill Sheridan, lawyer and director of Royal Oak and Pinkerton's of Canada; Erik Watt, local media relations consultant who wrote a letter to the *yellowknifer* noting that "pussycats don't run gold mines"; Peggy Witte, Royal Oak CEO; Bill Heath, human resources manager, hired just before the September 18 blast.

(A. KRUSE / NNSL)

(Below) Judit Pandev gestures during an interview in the kitchen of her home in January 1993. On September 25, 1992, she said Giant should re-open—"the sooner, the better ... otherwise, these lives are gone for nothing."

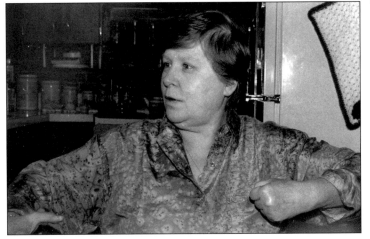

(Above) Mine foreman Noel O'Sullivan at the opening of the IIC. Of any civilian, he was the most important to the RCMP's murder investigation, being the first to arrive at the scene of the blast. At first he thought it was some kind of prank.

(NNSL)

Mill oiler Kurt Lehniger and Jayne Regimbald, a CLASS activist, talk in CASAW's hall. Jayne's husband, Terry, took the polygraph so police would leave her alone. Lehniger visited Peggy Witte on September 24, 1992 in an attempt to restart negotiations between CASAW and Royal Oak.

Miner Marvin Ferriss at the Canada Labour Relations Board's hearings into the Giant Mine Employees' Association's bid to replace CASAW as the bargaining agent at Giant. By this time, March 1993, Ferriss had been an RCMP agent for at least five months. Also pictured are Martha Codner and Judy Russell.

Hoistman Derek Roberts peeps out of the Gate 3 picket shack in March 1993. He was also working on construction jobs as an electrician's apprentice while his wife June headed CLASS.

Television news related to the labour dispute always had an audience in CASAW's hall, this time in late April 1993. *(l. to r.)* Rob Wells, CASAW recording secretary, who found explosives in his tent trailer; Alex Lacroix, vice-president of the Steelworkers' local at Con mine; Gina Fiorillo, labour lawyer; John Lang, secretary-treasurer of the Confederation of Canadian Unions; Mike Doyle, timberman.

knew might send innocent people to jail for murder. "In the meantime they've got my kid in the fucking [interrogation] room, questioning him because he's out drunk. They could slap the cuffs on him, maybe kick his ass," Legge says.

Legge told White the whole story, and described the detonator made from a quartz clock. He said that he guarded the scene the first night when the bomb didn't go off, but didn't go back the second night to reset the timer. The other three men involved, he said, were Bettger, Shearing, and Conrad Lisoway. Legge told Corporal White he wouldn't testify against them; he wanted his statement used only to clear up the murders. Legge thought he had a deal, but a year later he found himself testifying about the incident.

LOBSTER SEASON

We were running around in circles, saying, "What are we going to do?" And all this turmoil, this political infighting among unions, even our own union, even our own executive, eh. Harold [David] pointed us in the right direction and coached us, sometimes reluctantly. We would've been lost without Harold.

—Mark Eveson, April 13, 1994

Canada Employment Centre staff had been summoned to CASAW's hall early in the strike/lockout to take applications for unemployment insurance. It looked like a publicity stunt to protest the posting of strikebreaker jobs at employment centres. Nobody could remember a strike where anybody got UI, and payment was denied.

Harold David's interest was piqued when he became strike coordinator in July 1992. He was familiar with the Unemployment Insurance Act and some case law. UI payments are denied during a "work stoppage," which is deemed over when production and employment reaches 85 percent of normal without taking "temporary, exceptional or extraordinary measures." David submitted Royal Oak's frequent claims that production was normal or better to the Unemployment Insurance Commission to show there was no longer a work stoppage at Giant. The first appeal was denied in December 1992, on the basis that Royal Oak was using "extraordinary and temporary measures" to maintain production.

When David appealed again, he noted that Peggy Witte had publicly stressed that "fired" strikers would never return to work, and vice president John Smrke had stated that permanent replacements had been hired. Royal Oak had also provided financial assistance to strikebreakers and their families to move to Yellowknife. CASAW's appeal presented a dilemma for Royal Oak. After reassuring investors that Giant mine was running well, it was hard to tell a government tribunal exactly the opposite. Royal Oak barely bothered to fight the case. Roger Warren assessed the situation and said that Royal Oak didn't fight because they wanted people to use the money to leave town. Even union stalwarts like the Robertses would have been tempted to leave if Derek had been eligible for UI benefits. They were far behind on payments for their trailer and truck. "We don't know what to do—sell, or just lock it up and walk away," June said. "Walking away sounds good." But starting over isn't easy, and it was not a good time to move. June was pregnant with their fourth child and her doctor had ordered her to take it easy.

A tribunal ruled on February 17 that CASAW's strikers were entitled to UI payments, retroactive to July 1, 1992. It was ninety days before the checks arrived, but, when they did, it was like money from heaven, more than all the picket pay the most diligent men had earned in almost a year. "They were cheeky," Harold David says. "Somebody had a relative in Bathurst, New Brunswick. It was lobster season, so he went around town and took orders ... They ordered 1,200 pounds of live lobsters to be flown in to Yellowknife." David teased people about wasting money on lobster, but he admired them. "How the fuck is Margaret [Witte] ever going to starve you guys into submission if you're sitting around eating lobster?" he asked one man. "You're supposed to be eating porridge."

When you're dealing with corporations like Royal Oak, or Peggy Witte, you need something with a bit of clout.

—Jim O'Neil, February 4, 1994

The curtain rose on the labour dispute's first big "courtroom drama" on March 9, 1993. It was not actually a court, but a hearing of the Canada Labour Relations Board on the fate of CASAW and the Giant Mine Employees' Association. It was held in the same room at the Yellowknife Inn in which CASAW members had debated going on strike ten months earlier. For CASAW, it was a struggle for survival as a union; for Jim O'Neil, this was a chance to avenge September 18. A small group of strikebreakers and their relatives huddled in one corner, trading glares with the union crowd. As lawyers wrangled over legal principles, the CASAW men displayed the patience they'd learned in long, boring shifts on the picket line.

Lawyer Gina Fiorillo had done much of the research for CASAW's case, working day and night in the union hall and her hotel room. In the process, she'd forged a deep bond with the local's membership. She marveled at their spirit, and uncanny ability to ferret out information that was indispensable to the case. It would be presented by her colleague Leo McGrady, a veteran labour lawyer. Tall and thin with wire-rimmed glasses, he looks more like an academic than a legal pit bull, sounding gracious and polite, even as he demolishes a witness. By contrast, O'Neil's lawyer, Israel Chafetz, is short, round-faced, and nervous. He had clashed several times with McGrady before, and there was no love lost between them.

CLRB chairman Ted Weatherill, an old hand at labour matters, presided. As an arbitrator, and later on the Ontario Labour Relations Board, he'd gained a reputation with unions as a right-winger. Lately, as head of the CLRB, he was in the thick of administrative problems and open revolt from some board members over everything from principles of labour law to workloads and scheduling. Weatherill had caused more internal strife by naming himself to the three-member Giant panel. He wanted to be on it; only later did it become clear why.

Had the GMEA's attempt to dislodge CASAW been a normal raid, it's unlikely that a public hearing would have been held, due to the threshold percentage of bargaining unit members that must be signed up. But in this case, nine men were dead, reporters were swarming, and the numbers were interesting. Some of the original 234 CASAW members had quit, forty-three more had been fired, and forty-two had crossed the picket line, of whom six had been killed. Jim O'Neil claimed that some CASAW members who hadn't crossed had also signed up with the GMEA. It was at least arguable that all strikebreakers in the jobs of dead, fired, or resigned CASAW members should be considered permanent employees, with the right to vote in a union election. Indeed, it was arguable that *all* replacement workers should vote—as often happens in the United States. It had also happened in Alberta. A four-year strike ended on January 26, 1993, at Zeidler Forest Industries when the Alberta Labour Relations Board allowed replacement workers to vote and they decertified the union. Chafetz and O'Neil took hope from the decision, much as CASAW had from a February ruling on a strike at Nationair. The CLRB had upheld its precedents that strikebreakers could not vote. But what mattered most is that the Zeidler decision must have aroused Weatherill's interest.

McGrady had no way of knowing how many signed cards the GMEA had, so he attacked O'Neil's credibility. CASAW was certain that the GMEA was propped up by Royal Oak, and company-dominated unions are illegal. CASAW had a lot of circumstantial evidence that O'Neil had received improper help from the company. Terry Legge had recruited two line-crossers as witnesses for CASAW. Morris Sadowy had signed a GMEA card, but didn't think much of O'Neil. He and another worker testified that O'Neil had pestered them regularly about the GMEA, on company time, on Giant's property. They had seen GMEA pamphlets on supervisors' desks, and circulated openly in the locker-room area. At least one GMEA notice had been pinned to a company bulletin board. Sadowy said that he'd finally signed a GMEA card because he was afraid he'd be fired if he didn't. He said he'd seen O'Neil get special treatment, such as not having to work night shift and getting time off to organize the GMEA.

The really damning evidence came from envelopes O'Neil had sent to strikers, containing GMEA circulars. CASAW had collected sixty or seventy of them, and compared them with official letters mailed by Royal Oak. The address labels matched—same size, same lettering, same long form of names (Luideo instead of Louie, Allan instead of Al), same postal-box numbers instead of street addresses. For legal reasons, CASAW had given Royal Oak the new addresses of two strikers who had moved away. Oddly enough, the GMEA had them too.

Jim O'Neil was the last witness. His lawyer had no way of knowing how much information CASAW had on O'Neil. So Chafetz introduced the damaging evidence himself. First was the issue of how O'Neil had chosen his labour lawyer. O'Neil said he'd tried in early June, while still on strike, to find someone in Yellowknife. None of the lawyers he talked to knew anyone local who had labour experience. So he phoned Terry Byberg, then Giant's acting manager, and asked, "Do you know any good labour lawyers?" Byberg provided a list of four or five names, one of them being Chafetz's.

CASAW loyalists in the audience gasped. "How more company-dominated than that can you get?" they whispered to each other.

As for the addresses, O'Neil said he'd stolen an employee list from Giant's photocopy room. "I found a list on the cutting board, and some pages were in the garbage can. So I scooped them up."

Jane O'Neil hid her nervousness as she watched the hearing. She feared the intensity of the stares some of the union men gave Jim, especially Tim Bettger's, she said. None of them sat in the same row as Jane until the room was packed. She didn't want Jim to lose, but "if the association wins this hearing, or if they come out as the bargaining unit—to me, that's really scary." She feared both reprisals and the weight of responsibility that would shift to her husband.

Leo McGrady cooked Jim O'Neil on cross-examination, as more than 100 people, mostly CASAW members, watched. "Did this miraculous discovery [of the list] just happen as you were about to mail out your first bulletin?" he asked. O'Neil couldn't remember.

"It's an organizer's dream, isn't it, to walk into a photocopier room and have it in your mind to organize a rival union, and, lo and behold, there is a full company list," McGrady taunted him.

"Yeah, you're right," O'Neil replied, sounding crestfallen.

McGrady presented a pile of Royal Oak time sheets, showing where each man had worked while the GMEA was being organized. Time sheets and minutes of GMEA meetings showed that O'Neil was off work frequently during this period, and was "sick" on the very days he chaired GMEA meetings or reviewed labour law to discuss strategy with Chafetz. "What were you sick with, please?" McGrady asked sweetly.

"After the explosion ... I found myself very stressed out and I just had a hard time carrying on, so I requested a leave of absence," O'Neil answered. It was sweltering in the hearing room. The session went on for hours, with McGrady grilling O'Neil about his "good buddy," mine manager Terry Byberg.

When McGrady stopped for a break, his hands trembled from the excitement of extracting so much damaging evidence from O'Neil. The majority on the union side was ready to go out and party. The one skeptic was Hemi Mitic from the CAW. He trusted his instincts, and Weatherill gave him bad vibes. An outsider like Weatherill might decide that letting the GMEA win would be a quick, if dirty, way to end a horrible labour dispute.

"I was so tired that I didn't care if it went on forever," O'Neil said after his interrogation by McGrady. "I'm glad it's over—but I feel confident, I feel we've got a chance at this."

Luckily for O'Neil, the sources of some of the GMEA's funds had not been revealed. From Byberg's secretary, O'Neil received $5,000 in cash in an envelope with a note claiming it was from anonymous CASAW members who supported his efforts. O'Neil says the GMEA received a similar amount from an anonymous businessman. Later, when someone phoned Royal Oak about making a donation to the GMEA, the company's address was given.

In his closing argument, Israel Chafetz did his best to salvage O'Neil's case. He noted that the line-crossers and strikebreakers didn't need to be pushed by the company into disliking CASAW; the deaths had done that. The GMEA wasn't company-dominated, it was just on the same side of a nasty picket line as Royal Oak. Chafetz also had a novel legal argument in support of strikebreakers voting. The Canada Labour Code gives all workers the right to form unions, he said, and the Charter of Rights guarantees freedom of association. So are strikebreakers supposed to form separate unions, even though they work side by side with members of the striking union who crossed the picket line?

McGrady insisted that the interests of strikebreakers and union loyalists are opposed, not shared. Canadian courts and labour relations boards had ruled against strikebreakers on the voting issue since the 1960s.

Weatherill and his CLRB panelists returned to Ottawa to consider the case. Witness Morris Sadowy, who was given his first weekend off in months, was promptly quizzed by the RCMP. Royal Oak had complained about information leaks to CASAW, suspected several employees, and even asked the RCMP (unsuccessfully) to give six polygraph exams.

CASAW members celebrated their apparent CLRB victory, their euphoria heightened by a big win in territorial court. For more than two weeks, a judge had reviewed the case against twenty-one men charged with rioting on June 14. By the end of the preliminary hearing, the Crown had dropped some charges, and the judge threw out eight more, including Roger Warren's, leaving only nine men to face a trial.

Coincidentally, CASAW had planned a dance for the next night, March 12. It was a swank affair in the largest ballroom in town. The main organizer, Blaine Lisoway, had billed it as a "Let's Reunite Yellowknife" event, and naively hoped to attract some strikebreakers. They didn't come, but there were some local businesspeople, about half the city council, a Catholic bishop, and several national union leaders. The place was packed, netting $18,000 for CASAW's strike fund. To Lisoway's annoyance, many union supporters saw the evening as a union/political rally. New Democratic Party MP Svend Robinson gave a rousing speech for antiscab legislation, and former CASAW president Dale Johnston led chants of "NDP, NDP, NDP!" The fiery speeches and increasingly enthusiastic crowd drove away a few dignitaries, but the event was a big step forward for CASAW. Six months earlier, just after the blast, few NWT politicians or entrepreneurs would have sipped beer at a CASAW function.

Bob Robertson and his wife, Wendy, attended the dance, courtesy of the RCMP, who had instructed him to zero in on Al Shearing's common-law wife, Kara. They suspected that she knew Shearing was responsible for the deaths on September 18, or at least that he had gone out that night. Wendy was annoyed at the attention paid to Kara, who was very drunk that night, Robertson remembers. "I think she's carrying a lot of guilt ... If Wendy hadn't interceded, I'm sure I could've gotten it out of her."

They've got to get their upper management in line. I can't have my liveli-
hood jeopardized because the company is not acting professionally. There
are too many bosses running the mine.

—a contract miner at Giant, March 1993

CASAW's public relations coup with the dance was overshadowed by an accident at Giant at noon the next day. Two strikebreakers, one operating a scooptram, the other a 13-ton haul truck, fell 10 yards through a roadway over an old working. The scoop operator narrowly escaped death. He was thrown clear of his vehicle, which landed on top of the truck, and then pinned by fallen muck for about an hour. He spent days recovering in the hospital. The other man, a twenty-six-year miner and supervisor, miraculously walked away from the fall with a minor injury.

Some men on the picket line felt vindicated. For months they'd talked about unsafe conditions at Giant, saying that, with no union inside, anything could happen because nobody knew where they were going or what they were doing. Indeed, Mine Safety found that the accident was caused by a careless mistake. The roadway the men took had been roped off and should have stayed out of bounds.

Mine foreman Noel O'Sullivan, the RCMP's top contact in the mine, was made manager of "special projects" soon after. It was not clear if this was intended as discipline, but Mine Safety did not carry out its threat to lay charges.

It was evident now that the mine had serious production problems. In the heat of the labour dispute, Royal Oak had reduced its development mining (making tunnels to get at new ore bodies). This resulted in a shortage of quality ore. To compound the problem, costs were over budget.

Royal Oak was feeling the financial pinch. In addition, 1992's strike-related costs, for such things as security, were $3.5 million, according to published figures. Internal corporate documents give a figure of $5,160,904. Witte's cost-cutting miracle was in trouble.

Giant's problems were so serious, in fact, that a few weeks earlier Royal Oak had recalled Mike Werner, the manager who'd been transferred to Newfoundland after throwing rocks early in the strike/lockout. Terry Byberg was unceremoniously demoted to the number-two job at Giant.

PSYCHO-BABBLE

*There was a time I would have said to my son, "I would like to see you be
a police officer." I would never say that today. I'd just as soon he'd belong
to the Mafia, because I believe that they're as noble as the law.*

—Terry Legge, October 9, 1993

Throughout the dispute, CASAW accused police of subverting them in the
media every time events started going the union's way. A startling case in
point occurred on March 18, days after O'Neil's struggle in the CLRB hearing and the dismissal of riot charges against eight men. The RCMP released a
"personality profile" that they believed would fit the principal man responsible for the September 18 blast. RCMP spokesman Dave Grundy played up the
profile on national television, emphasizing the role of FBI experts in its cre-
ation. The profile stimulated a lot of talk, intercepted by wiretaps as police
had hoped.

*The dominant offender in this case will be a white male in excess of thirty
years. His childhood years will reflect a disruptive rearing environment. He
will have a deep-seated need to seek respect, recognition and social accep-
tance. While he may present a facade of confidence, he suffers from well-
hidden insecurities.*

Local wags pointed out that this description probably fit most miners in town,
and quite a few policemen. But the RCMP also claimed that the murderer had
set off the smaller explosions on July 22 (satellite dish) and September 1 (vent
shack). As to motive, "the anger which perpetuated [*sic*] this offense is mostly
depersonalized and is directed at 'scabs' generally and not toward individual
persons." In other words, the blast was committed by union members or sympathizers. The profile pointed fingers at Al Shearing and Tim Bettger, and put
pressure on their accomplices in vandalism short of the murders.

CASAW local president Harry Seeton and lawyer Leo McGrady jumped all
over the RCMP. "We think a number of members of the RCMP have an ax to
grind," McGrady said on television. The RCMP had quickly assumed the blast
was the work of union men, and didn't explore other options, he alleged—and
six months to the day after the explosion, the police appeared to have had little
to show for their efforts.

If the RCMP had hoped to flush out their prime suspect, Al Shearing, they
failed. He says he was told by Corporal Vern White that police had solved the

two smaller blasts, and were certain he was the murderer. Shearing says his reply was, "Vern, you got all this information. Look at me, I'm a free man."

CASAW's recording secretary, Rob Wells, got a nasty surprise on March 24, when his children helped him clean out a tent trailer he'd brought home from the picket line shortly after the blast. "My oldest one, who was four, passed me a plastic bag. I looked in, it was stick powder," bound with black tape, and a detonator cap. Wells was sickened by the thought of what might have happened if the powder had exploded, unlikely as this was. "I visualized everything everywhere, including my kids. I locked it up in my shed and left it there. I was nervous, scared; I didn't know what to do." He thought it was the same bag he'd told Tim Bettger to get rid of on the picket line on September 19. Wells says his lawyer advised him to give the explosives to the police, but he held off. A charge of possession of explosives could have dire consequences for him, and the union. The RCMP may have been privy to this information anyway, as Wells was on their wiretap list.

In the meantime, up to thirty RCMP officers made a daylight raid on the Bettgers' home. Sergeant Dave Grundy talked to reporters outside while cameras filmed officers roaming about in bulletproof vests and fatigues, with guns in leg holsters. Grundy refused to give a reason for the search, but noted that Vern White, the primary investigator of the murders, was present. Police peered down the chimney of Bettger's garage/shop and carried plants out of the house. A dog handler's animal sniffed the engine of Bettger's truck. An officer checked the truck cab with an explosives-vapour detector, pausing to read a letter from Bettger's lawyer, Austin Marshall. Inside the house, police crawled in the attic, unpacked boxes, and fiddled with Bettger's computer, he says. Vern White stood guard over Bettger to record everything he said, using a body pack.

Marshall was out of town, so CASAW hired a Vancouver lawyer to outline Bettger's rights in such a search and seizure. The police had three search warrants. Two alleged that Bettger, Shearing, and Conrad Lisoway had blown up the B-shaft vent shack. The third accused Bettger of committing murder on September 18.

The haul from the search was suggestive, but apparently inconclusive. The RCMP collected a sawed-off shotgun for which a new barrel was on order; a clothespin that had been modified, perhaps to make a trip-wire device; some gloves; tools and bits of wire; some yellow blasting wire; monofilament fishing line, useful for fishing, casting metal leaders to short out power, or making trip wires; metal rings and hooks; and wire cutters. The RCMP found five of the six quartz movements Bettger had bought in Vancouver; a search warrant reveals they expected to find only four. They were sure that one had been used as the detonator for the vent-shack blast. They assumed another was used on

September 18 as a timed arming mechanism, a safety device to prevent accidental detonation of the booby trap while it was being set up. An expert from the postblast team concluded that Bettger had everything he needed to make a bomb, except explosives.

The public had no idea what the police seized, and rumours flew that Bettger's arrest was imminent. His two children went to live with their grandparents in Saskatchewan.

Agent Bob Robertson claims that the RCMP said that some items found at Bettger's matched debris found at the 750-level blast scene. "They told me they had direct evidence linking those guys [Bettger and Shearing] ... They told me they had bits and pieces of the switching mechanism. I believe it was a toggle switch of sorts." Terry Legge heard something similar. "They have one piece of hard evidence. I got that listening to Vern [White], but it's not enough. They're putting the puzzle together, but there's pieces missing," he said.

Two days after the raid, Rob Wells gave the RCMP the bag of stick powder he'd found. Some union men were shocked by Wells's decision to hand over the explosives, given the RCMP's intent to charge Bettger with murder. "Anybody could have put that there," Roger Warren said later. "[Giving] the police something like that is like waving a flag in front of a bull." Indeed, police wanted Wells to gather more information. He says he declined an RCMP offer to pay him, pay all his bills, move him and his family away from Yellowknife after the investigation, and get him a job. Similar offers were made to others.

The RCMP kept up the pressure. On April 7, they released an expanded "psychological profile" of the murderer.

> Prior to these crimes, this offender felt pressure (internal and/or external) to impress those around him with his dedication to "the cause" ... This would lead him to take a vocal stance advocating acts of violence and revenge against his perceived enemies ...
>
> He takes great pleasure in hearing, talking, or reading about the crime and his philosophy is "the best defense is a good offense." By proclaiming innocence to a wide audience he can draw attention to his "achievements" while attempting to create doubt in the minds of his peers and accusors.

Al Shearing was the only striker who had proclaimed his innocence to the media, so everyone knew the police were referring to him. "They forgot to mention that he prefers a mustache," Shearing quipped in the union hall. Marvin Ferriss, who was there to observe reactions, reported to the police that Bettger said, "They got it all wrong."

The profile was no surprise to Shearing. The day before its release, the RCMP had questioned his sister in Ontario, who opened the pages of their family history. Neither she nor Al knew their natural parents before age twenty-one, Shirley Shearing told the RCMP. Just a year apart in age, Al and Shirley were separated as children and suffered beatings and shocking abuse in various foster homes before they were reunited with a good family. Despite their troubles, "I don't recall Allan complaining about anything," Shirley said. "Allan was always small for his age. I would protect him. I remember Allan did something wrong once and I took the blame for it ... I looked after him because he was my younger brother." Shirley named her first son Allan. After their marriages, their relationship remained close, and they lived near each other in Timmins, Ontario.

Bob Robertson says he also contributed information that went into the profile, and "the cause" is a phrase he often uses. "I was specifically tasked to give information about the psychology of Al," he says.

Despite Shearing's unconcern, Hemi Mitic from the CAW worried that Shearing and Bettger would be charged. He approached CASAW's leadership about getting them off the local's executive. They resigned without complaint.

The RCMP were up-to-date on CASAW's internal politics. "We have been receiving information from a member of the CASAW executive who feels that our suspects are responsible for the murder," Corporal Vern White reported on April 19. "He has been passing on information which is assisting the investigation."

A deputy sheriff knocked at June and Derek Roberts's door at about 10:00 P.M. on April 22, as a tow truck backed into their driveway in Northland trailer court. "Ma'am, I'm here to seize your property," said the deputy, who stood about 6 foot 4 inches. The bank wanted a $4,500 payment on the Robertses' trailer and truck. Tears ran down June's face as she spoke with lawyer Gina Fiorillo on the phone; Derek removed tools, tapes, papers, and a baby's seat from the truck. One neighbour screamed at the sheriff's deputy and another shouted at Derek about friends she'd lost on September 18. But the Robertses had no money, so the tow truck lumbered down the lane with their Ford Ranger.

Inside, June cried out in pain as she sank to the floor. Her friend Sylvia Imbeault had arrived, and rushed to June's side. "You better take her to the hospital. Take my car," she told Derek. June was admitted with premature contractions caused by high blood pressure. The doctor released her the next day, but ordered her to stay in bed for several days. Derek and CASAW president Harry Seeton went to the bank, which had given no notice about the seizure. The Robertses were given fourteen days to come up with the money, or move out.

June had a sister in town, Norma Michelin, but couldn't turn to her for support. Norma had nagged Derek to take the polygraph, which he refused to do. When she called him a murderer, June and Derek told her not to visit anymore, they said. In addition, Norma's relationship with their third cousin, Corporal Vern White, was far too chummy to suit June.

June was tired and worried sick. Walking was painful. After raising well over $300,000 for adopt-a-family, her own family was in danger of losing everything. But union members came to their rescue. Within three days, fifty-two people contributed from $40 to $200 each to raise $4,500. That amount brought their payment schedule back to where it had been in May 1992. "The money was strictly from donations," said CASAW's vice president Rick Cassidy, proud of the local.

There was still an urgent need to raise money for other families. At the end of March, twenty-two families were cut off the adopt-a-family roll. The union's legal bills were astronomical, so Imbeault, another CLASS member, and two CASAW executives set out for British Columbia to raise money.

DR. WEATHERILL'S SPECIAL ELIXIR

There's never been a decision like that in the history of Canada.

—Roger Warren, May 5, 1993

A revolutionary ruling on the GMEA was released by the Canada Labour Relations Board on May 5 as Decision 1010. CASAW remained the bargaining agent at Giant, but chairman Ted Weatherill ruled in the GMEA's favour on crucial legal issues. The GMEA was deemed a legitimate trade union, not a Royal Oak front. "One item of evidence, the 'discovery' of an employee list, is particularly suspicious," Weatherill wrote. "It is possible that the list was left for discovery by an office employee, not a member of management, who was sympathetic to the applicant."

Second, strikebreakers had the right to vote in a contest between the GMEA and CASAW. It was a reversal of thirty years of Canadian case law on the subject, including the Nationair ruling by Weatherill's own board a few months earlier. Instead, Weatherill followed a contrary Alberta Labour Relations Board ruling in the Zeidler Forest Industries case.

Jim O'Neil and his lawyer, Israel Chafetz, called Decision 1010 one of the biggest labour rulings ever, heralding the CLRB's entry into "the modern era."

CASAW remained the bargaining agent because O'Neil hadn't signed up enough men to reach the 50 percent threshold needed to force a certification vote. Ironically, Royal Oak lawyers may have inadvertently helped CASAW by stalling separate CLRB proceedings on the fired strikers, which had been scheduled for April. Weatherill counted more than forty fired men as part of the bargaining unit; if Royal Oak had enough evidence and the CLRB had confirmed most of the terminations, a vote might have been close.

At the union hall, some people celebrated O'Neil's apparent defeat. But Mark Eveson was angry the moment he read the decision. He walked out of the hall in disgust as Roger Warren came in. "Roger, I respect your opinion," Eveson said. "Why are they celebrating, is there something wrong with the way I'm thinking?"

"No, you're right," Warren replied. "They're nuts. This is a big defeat." There was nothing to stop O'Neil from signing up more members and reapplying in six months.[3]

Across Canada, the news spread like wildfire among labour lawyers and unions. They had known that Weatherill was at odds with much of his board, but not that the differences included such fundamental issues as the status of replacement workers. They saw disaster ahead if a company intent on union busting could hire replacement workers, lure a few strikers into crossing the line, and decertify the union with strikebreakers' votes. The practice is common in the United States, where the level of unionization is only half that of Canada's. MPs and federal ministers received complaints from Canadian unions, suspicious of the motive for this CLRB ruling so soon after Ontario and British Columbia passed antiscab legislation like that in Quebec. Union lawyers started writing submissions against the decision.

Federal Labour Minister Marcel Danis was dumbfounded too. "We expected a decision similar to Nationair," he says. "We had a meeting with my deputy minister and my chief of staff about the decision ... But there's nothing you could do about it."

Canadian Labour Congress president Bob White spoke with the NWT's executive member, Jim Evoy. He says that White told him to take a personal message to Harry Seeton: "You tell him to appeal. You tell him they are going to win." Fiorillo and McGrady had an appeal ready in three weeks.

CASAW vice president Rick Cassidy chuckled about an absurd aspect of the ruling. "Most of the scabs have not even stopped in to say hello. Now that we are their bargaining agent, they might stop in to see us."

CASAW deployed its most powerful legal weapon at the same time as the appeal of the GMEA ruling, a complaint to the CLRB that Royal Oak had bargained in bad faith. The duty to bargain in good faith is the linchpin of North American labour law, dating back to 1935 in the United States, and 1944 in Canada. Before that, companies could break unions by refusing to bargain and firing organizers. Ever since, both sides have been obliged to discuss contract issues rationally, though there is no guarantee of agreement. The good-faith rule is difficult to enforce, however. After sixty years, employers have refined the art of prolonging talks, making tough but legal demands they know the union won't accept, and making occasional small concessions to appease labour-relations boards. Such "surface bargaining" is also illegal, but even harder to prove. Consulting firms and lawyers provide sophisticated advice on "counterunion campaigns."

Fortunately for CASAW, subtlety was not Peggy Witte's strong suit. Her public insistence that the "fired" strikers would *never* return to their jobs and her refusal to bargain while the GMEA application was pending were major gaffes, as were equally damning statements by John Smrke.

With more than a hint of impertinence, Fiorillo and McGrady asked the CLRB to order Royal Oak to reimburse the strikers $1 million in back pay for each month of the dispute, since September 1992. The gesture made the point that people had sacrificed a lot to remain on the picket line for a year.

Royal Oak added to CASAW's legal ammunition within the week. The GMEA was sidelined for now, so IIC commissioners Ready and Munroe demanded written bargaining positions from both sides. Bill Heath, Royal Oak's human resources manager, said that Royal Oak would not put its position in writing, in part fearing that it would be made public.

The RCMP bolstered Royal Oak's decision behind the scenes. Superintendent Brian Watt reported to Ottawa on May 23 that Ready and Munroe were "under tremendous political pressure to try to resolve the dispute by June 21." Prime Minister Brian Mulroney wanted "the matter cleared up" before he was replaced by Kim Campbell in the run-up to a federal election. "Evidently, [Witte] is aware that she is likely to be forced into a situation where she has to settle or close the mine." Royal Oak asked the RCMP if they had concerns about any strikers not yet fired returning to work. "We have indicated that we have concerns," without disclosing specifics, Watt wrote. Intentionally or unwittingly, Watt had given Royal Oak an excuse to refuse the return of Giant's entire unionized workforce, and subverted the IIC's efforts. Company executives would assume that the RCMP's opinion would have strong backers in Ottawa.

Instead of providing a written position as the IIC had ordered, Royal Oak met with CAW president Buzz Hargrove and his assistant, Hemi Mitic, in Toronto on May 31. CASAW wasn't invited, and President Harry Seeton wasn't informed about it or the new demands made by Heath, Witte, and Smrke. The highlights included the following:

1. Royal Oak would not sign a contract with CASAW. The Canadian Auto Workers would have to sign the agreement.

2. None of the fired strikers would be reinstated.

3. There were up to thirty additional, as yet unnamed, strikers whom Royal Oak wouldn't take back.

4. Men not covered by demands 2 and 3 (above) would have to be vetted by the RCMP before being allowed back to work.

5. Even if a collective agreement were reached, it wouldn't come into effect until the RCMP assured Royal Oak that they had made all arrests related to the dispute, including the September 18 blast.

6. Returning workers would be on a one-year probation for any actions related to "lingering resentment" from the strike/lockout, and would not be allowed to file grievances if they were fired.

7. The union had to drop all prestrike grievances, including those on behalf of men fired by Royal Oak under its new disciplinary system.

8. The term of the contract would be at least five years, with no strike or lockout for seven years.

9. Wages for some jobs would be reduced to the rates the strikebreakers were getting, and some benefits would be cut.

The demands were worse than unreasonable; several were illegal, and strong CLRB ammunition for CASAW. But Heath and Mitic had promised to keep the meeting off the record, so even CASAW didn't hear about Royal Oak's demands for another two months.

Mitic wasn't sure that the Giant mine dispute would ever be resolved. His pessimism deepened when CASAW sent its "official" bargaining position to the IIC, on the same day as the Toronto meeting. Harry Seeton wanted the old collective agreement renewed for one year—the union's toughest proposal since the dispute began. It seems Mitic convinced Ready and Munroe that this was merely posturing, that he could persuade the strikers to make some concessions.

Union busting is a North American phenomenon ... The amount of money that was spent on lawyers and consultants and protection in Yellowknife would have more than bargained a settlement.

—Leo Gerard, Steelworkers' national director, May 22, 1993

They always underestimate the solidarity and resolve of the workers.

—Darrell Tingley, president, Canadian Union of Postal Workers
May 22, 1993

Mitic's pessimism didn't infect the strikers. The end of winter brought a surge in their morale. They had weathered adversity and were determined to soldier on, at least until fall.

It was nonetheless a blow when Al Shearing was sentenced in mid-May to six months in jail—five of them for possession of a slingshot which he denied owning. There was little doubt that Shearing used a slingshot regularly, but he hadn't been caught in the act. He was widely admired for his pluck, ingenuity, and calmness under intense pressure. Many thought the police were trying to frame him for a murder he hadn't committed.

At a protest on May 21, union supporters demonstrated their view that Shearing's sentence was unduly harsh and motivated by the court's antiunion bias. "You only get one day for rape in this town," one union member griped, but five months for having a slingshot.[4] The turnout of about 250 people was larger than at most rallies early in the strike, swelled by big-name guests at the NWT Federation of Labour's annual convention.

There were some quiet dissenters, behind the scenes. "I wasn't about to show him support, because I didn't agree with the stupid fucking things he was doing," says diamond driller Mark Eveson. "Al just couldn't figure out any other way ... He did something and he got away with it, he thought. So he got braver and braver and stupider and stupider."

The next day, May 22, was the first anniversary of the strike/lockout. To mark the occasion, CASAW and the Federation of Labour marched to the mine, in defiance of the picketing injunction and a warning from police that they would arrest Harry Seeton and Jim Evoy. Police did not intervene or arrest anyone, perhaps because the crowd included an impressive array of national union leaders. A few officers waited nervously at the main gate, while many more donned their riot gear and took up positions out of sight—alerted, Bob Robertson claims, by him.

CASAW passed out awards for "scab of the year." Jim Gauthier topped a secret-ballot vote for crossing the picket line after serving on CASAW's bargaining committee. Gauthier was "honoured" with a billboard depicting a large, bright pink pig in repose with his name on it. For runner-up Jim O'Neil, union artists painted a smaller billboard showing the back end of a pig.

The crowd dispersed peacefully, in high spirits. The frustration that had been so evident a few months earlier seemed to have crossed the picket line with the strikebreakers. Angered by insults and the immense "Scab on the Run!" sign the union had erected at the main gate, some strikebreakers would recklessly gun their cars through the picket line. At least two picketers were hit by vehicles driven by men coming to and from work. In the case of CASAW's most vociferous picketer, the driver was fined for leaving the scene of an accident.

BLITZED

We had something like forty or fifty people who were classified as agents throughout the investigation.

—RCMP superintendent Ross Grimmer, July 30, 1996

The RCMP unleashed a "blitz package" against Shearing and Bettger in mid-June. It had been planned for some time, and it was designed to convince union members that police were closing in on the killers and would lock up anyone who was withholding evidence. Blitz information included the Akaitcho shaft entry into the mine, boot prints in and out, the case against Shearing and Bettger for lesser crimes, and photos of the explosives found in Rob Wells's trailer.

RCMP pressure had already taken its toll. One distraught man told another union member's wife that police had threatened him with murder charges. "He told me he's going to kill himself if they charge him," she said. Roger Warren and many other men understood such desperation. "You're talking to these guys, after an hour or so, you wish you did know something," he said. "They just get you in [and] browbeat. They want to know everything you even think—especially what you think."

Traveling in pairs, police went unannounced to people's homes and workplaces to "blitz" them. This sent waves of rumour through the town, often about multiple arrests. Police apparently hoped to shake loose eyewitness evidence that would solidify their murder case against Shearing and Bettger, and sow seeds of suspicion among CASAW's most faithful. "I'm really beginning to wonder about Tim Bettger," agonized a union stalwart. "I don't know where he fits. My idea was that he wanted to get in the courts and challenge the cops. Maybe he's the one [working] with the cops. Is this guy trying to destroy our union?" On the other hand, from what people saw of Bettger and his family, it was hard to believe he was a murderer, or that they would be able to hide it.

Inspector Al Macintyre, recently promoted and heading the murder investigation, worried that some union members were refusing to be interrogated further due to CASAW president Harry Seeton's attitude toward the RCMP. So

Macintyre issued a "courtesy" warning to lawyer Gina Fiorillo. "I ... outlined some of the advances we had made in the investigation, with the key issue that CASAW can deny any union involvement in the bombings, but that subsequent court process will prove them very wrong, and their continued public denial of it ... may not be wise," Macintyre wrote on June 16.

Police badgered union recalcitrants to take the polygraph. Joe Ranger, for example, says he was shown photos of the victims' mutilated bodies and threatened with a charge of conspiracy to commit murder because he had shared information from an RCMP publication on explosives with Shearing and Bettger. Ranger eventually gave in and says he passed the test. Others were in no mood for polygraphs. Skip tender Terry Coe says he refused a test despite a $2,000 incentive, afraid that results would be tainted by the blitz information. He'd been on the picket crew that started its shift on the morning of September 18. When he visited his father in Ontario in June, Coe says, police appeared on the doorstep the next day to ask if he was looking for work.

Desperate to solve the crime, the RCMP tried to coerce strikers into getting others to confess. The police insisted that miner Dan Noel had driven Shearing and Tim Bettger to Giant on September 17. They approached Noel's friend Wayne Campbell. "If you can convince Dan to tell us his involvement, we shall guarantee his not being charged and you shall receive money," Campbell says he was told—and that from "the stuff they found at Tim's house, they reconstructed an explosive device exactly like they found underground [in] bits and pieces."[5]

Strikers' children felt the pressure too. One CASAW man recalls his seven-year-old daughter coming home from school and asking him, "Daddy, do you know who murdered those men? ... If you knew, would you tell the police?"

On the picket line, some crews were raucous and some were subdued, but there was a general feeling of disillusionment. Many men were depressed, but stubborn. "This country is so fucked up you almost want to become a Commie," said one man in his 40s. "We're not in a labour dispute. We're in a power struggle with a lot of fucking politicians ... I don't want to fight with the cops, I want to fight with the [owner of] this mine. I'm not leaving. I love this town."

The RCMP seized Roger Warren's green Kamik boots on June 18, the same ones they'd borrowed months earlier. He and his wife were on a holiday in the United States, and heard about it when they phoned their daughter at home. The search warrant alleged that the boots would afford evidence that Bettger had murdered nine men. "I am extremely sorry I was cooperative," Warren said when he came home. "I haven't heard from those guys for months, and as soon as I go on holidays they come and take my boots."

Police agents were busy too. Marvin Ferriss took Bettger with him on a trip to British Columbia's Lower Mainland to buy a motorcycle, and, supposedly, more drugs. RCMP documents state that Bettger told Ferriss during the trip that after the June 29 incursion into the mine, he and Shearing gave Gordie Kendall "a written rendition of their entry into the mine to the 750 level."

There was more. Ferriss tried to get Bettger talking about the two men that Warren said he'd seen at Giant the night before the murder. "I said I had been listening to Roger Warren talking one night ... and he was sure it was you and Conrad to the point where he almost called out your names," Ferriss said later in court.[6] By that account, Bettger had subtly confirmed that he had been at Giant on September 17, but not that he'd been with Lisoway or had anything to do with the blast.

July rolled around, and the blitz had further antagonized the union. "We don't want to talk to you bastards any more," newly elected CLASS executive Karen Fougère told police at one stage. Striker Marvin Tremblett says he told police to "get the fuck out of my garage. They wouldn't leave ... And they said, 'We got tracks down underground and it's believed to be Al and Tim's.'" On the other hand, Corporal Vern White noted that, as a result of the blitz, a "well-respected" member of CASAW had agreed to "gather intelligence from some of our suspects," and would be introduced to the investigation team. According to Inspector Macintyre, new evidence showed the "culpability" of the prime suspects.

Bettger and Shearing would obviously be arrested; the only question was whether they'd face murder charges. A review by experienced officers in British Columbia concluded that "we [have] enough evidence to charge both suspects with the murders," Macintyre reported to Superintendent Watt on June 22. Ten more CASAW members were to be arrested on other charges during a "roundup" in early August. "All of our statements have been typed, witness 'can states' prepared, physical evidence analyzed, and we are ready for court. This includes the murders, the other bombings, B & Es, theft of explosives and the possession of weapons." It was a strong statement from a veteran of about eighty homicide investigations.

Peter Martin, a top-notch Crown prosecutor from Alberta, was assigned to handle the case by the assistant deputy attorney general of Canada, says Pierre Rousseau, head of the federal Justice Department's NWT branch. Inspector Macintyre had recommended Martin; according to Macintyre their first case together was in 1979.

Martin flew to Yellowknife on June 22 to review the case with Macintyre, White, and other officers. Presumably, Martin identified weaknesses in the case, one of which was that most of the evidence was circumstantial. Police apparently had little or no proof that Bettger and Shearing had been at Giant the night before the blast, and their wives would testify just the opposite. It seemed unlikely that Bettger and Shearing would crack, but maybe Roger Warren or Gordie Kendall would incriminate them further. Warren looked like "reasonable doubt" personified, and had yet to be blitzed. Kendall appeared to know more than he would admit in his interrogations.

Charges were not laid on the other serious offenses because confidential sources of information would have to be revealed, and because charges were the RCMP's only real bargaining chips in the murder case. According to striker Marvin Tremblett, "Vern White made me an offer—if [Bettger] took the lie-detector test, they would drop the charges on the satellite dish and the vent shack, and put it in writing."

Ottawa could help to intensify the pressure on the strikers, and did so within days of Martin's visit. In late July, Canada's deputy attorney general endorsed the extraordinary step of direct-indicting seven of the eight men whose rioting charges had been dismissed for lack of evidence, back in March. Preferred (or direct) indictments are usually reserved for high-profile cases. They allow a trial to proceed without a preliminary hearing to review the Crown's evidence before a judge. But in this case, the preliminary hearing had already taken place and the men whose charges were dropped thought they were home free. Among the seven sent to trial were Roger Warren, Conrad Lisoway, vent-blast accomplice Terry Legge, and two other men who were on the picket line on the night of September 17.

To most union members, the federal government and the police were a "relentless force," as Warren would put it later. But Bettger says that "Al and I were saying, 'Let 'em come.' We knew things that everybody else didn't want to believe, and the cops weren't sabre-rattling anymore, they were brandishing." They expected to be arrested and charged with murder; if so, they would plead not guilty.

Agent Marvin Ferriss made one more attempt to coax Bettger to confess. It was an elaborate, dangerous scheme that tried to turn Bettger's loyalty to fellow strikers into a liability. Ferriss took Bettger to some motorcycle races in Edmonton on July 17. On the way home, Ferriss made his move. "Marvin starts talking to me about the blitz-package stuff and how he's so concerned, and about how a guy should start considering doing something nefarious that could never be traced," Bettger says. "If a second explosion happened in the mine, they'd have to say that it was an accident ... [and that] horrible scabs, doing stupid things, made their own problems."

Police documents confirm that Bettger and Ferriss discussed details of a plot in which Ferriss would blow up an easily accessible powder magazine in the mine near the 1-38 portal. According to the RCMP, Bettger suggested using a clothespin to construct a switch, advising Ferriss to use a circuit tester to make sure he didn't blow himself up. On July 25, Bettger allegedly handed Ferriss a trip-wire device made from a clothespin. The rest of the conversation was taped and transcribed:

"How do you guarantee alignment?" Ferriss asked about the clothespin.

"Simple ... Just line 'em up close as you can and ... put the wedge in there like that."

"Work good," Ferriss said.

"Oh yeah," said Bettger. "Vern White personally delivered a message from their demolitions and explosives guy. He said it was a very classy little piece of work."

"If you open up that battery ... and discover a nine-volt only in there ... don't trust it," Bettger advised.

"No, I'll test it," Ferriss replied. "I'll be using the red caps. We set them off on three and a half volts." Another type of cap, DCDs, take "a lot more amperage," he noted, perhaps told by the RCMP that fragments of a DCD cap had been found at the blast scene on 750, and that another had apparently been used in a test north of the blast site.

Bettger did not seem to know much about blasting caps, but he was not a miner like Ferriss.

"Just one more thing. The main ... reason for doing this is to [give] a good cover ... And ah, you're not telling me what I want to hear. If as you say it's true that it wasn't you, then there's no point in taking that big a risk right now."

"I don't know how to put this any more succinctly," Bettger replied. "I can tell you a hundred times that it wasn't me ... And, that's all I can say. I have to tell you the same thing that I told Izzie [his wife]. I'm not going to tell you anything where I'd end up perjuring myself. And then ... anything that I don't tell you can never be pried out of you."

"I get the feeling you don't trust me," Ferriss said. "It's nothing they're gonna get out of me. 'Cause you got enough on me to fuck me royally anyway ... I thought you were going to ask me on our last trip. I thought you noticed ... I be bringing back little parcels ... And these are worth about $2,000 an ounce to me, product ... Were you wondering about that?"

"To be honest, no ... I trust you. You telling me I shouldn't?"

"No," Ferriss said. But setting off a powder magazine was a big risk. "Under the circumstances, I ain't going to make it happen."

"It's your call."

"You're not denying my suspicions, anyway."

"I can tell you a thousand times I had nothing to do with it ... [But the cops] can't prove that I had nothing to do with it because ... the last time that I was supposedly seen was at 1:30 [A.M.] when [Marvin Tremblett] dropped me off at the house ... They won't believe Izzie. The next time they can account for [me] was at approximately ten o'clock the next morning, walking down Franklin."

Bettger says he thought it was the last he'd hear about blowing up a powder magazine, but Ferriss soon had a new scheme. Both men were planning to leave town again soon—Bettger to a wedding in Saskatchewan, Ferriss to Manitoba. Bettger says Ferriss planned to booby-trap the 1-38 magazine on a Friday, after Bettger was gone. With any luck, nobody would go to the magazine until Monday, so Ferriss would be gone too. When a bag of Amex powder was taken off the pile, it would trip a switch and "1-38 would've been part of history," Bettger remembers. "As far as I'm concerned, it's an academic exercise," he recalls saying. "Hey, it sounds like a hell of a plan. It would definitely take 'em by surprise. But don't do it on my account. Don't need it."

Someone with "a very military bearing" followed him and his wife to his small hometown in Saskatchewan, Bettger says. The fellow stood out like a sore thumb, and "Dad picked up on it right away. 'Oh, there's a weird guy.' I told Dad, 'Yeah, he's going to come at us from around the block.' And Dad says, 'Hey, you're dreaming, boy!' We were messing around with Dad's car, and a minute later, I said, 'OK, look over your shoulder and tell me what's coming up the street.' Dad said, 'What's going on here!'" Bettger's parents had known for some time that the police were after him. "Dad looks at me and says, 'Take care of yourself.' This was *far* and beyond the realm of any experience that he'd ever had. They didn't know what to make of it. They never sat me down and asked me, 'Did you do it?' They knew from talking to us that we were never involved in that kind of stuff ... The guys [the RCMP] sent from Saskatoon to talk to my parents—and the rest of the people in the town where I grew up—were treating this whole thing with a grain of salt. They seen the environment, the people that I grew up with," Bettger says.

Due to his holiday, Roger Warren was one of the last people to be blitzed. Officers Dale McGowan and Nancy Defer talked to him on August 6. Warren said he was surprised the warrant for his boots had Bettger's name on it. "I couldn't make much sense of it. I can assure you I never had nothing to do with those guys."

"Which guys?" McGowan asked.

"That were making incursions onto the property. I'm sure you know I was never in on that."

"I have to know, beyond a doubt, that Roger Warren didn't have anything to do with this ... Things are kind of coming to a close here," said McGowan. "Even though we have good evidence on a lot of stuff, there's still things we're looking for ... Minor players that are the first to come forward will be dealt with according to the law, in manners that are different ... I don't know if you've heard the phrase, unindicted co-accused." At the end, he warned, "you're going to see a lot of guys covering their ass."

McGowan then moved on to the two men Warren said he saw on the mine property in the early hours of September 18. Police had talked to Conrad Lisoway, who Warren had said resembled one of the two. Not only did Lisoway deny being on the property, he said he'd discussed the issue with Warren the next day.

"It hit me in the head like a ton of bricks," McGowan said.

Warren said that so much was happening on September 18, he'd forgotten the conversation.

"You know we have footwear impressions," McGowan said. "Did you borrow [sic] your boots to anybody that night?"

"No."

"Did you have anything to do with it?"

"No."

"I was talking to [former mine foreman] Noel O'Sullivan yesterday," and you're a hard worker who breaks a lot of rock, McGowan said. "He said [that] he couldn't see you being involved in a thing like this."

On the other hand, Nancy Defer piped up, one guy told police that Warren had said, "If you want to commit a perfect murder, all you'd have to do is do it by yourself, without telling anybody."

"What would be perfect about murder?" Warren replied.

"Did you mean it?" Defer asked. "If somebody did a murder by themselves, never talked to anybody ..."

"You know more about it than me ... I talk a lot ... Has anybody said ... did I kick the shit out of anybody ... in my whole life? ... Am I a psychotic person?" he asked.

"You guys were under pressure," McGowan said. "The union was in trouble. You had some high-profile strikers going back to work—Verne [Fullowka] being one. It was hurting the cause. There was anger. There was a lot of frustration."

"I would agree with you."

McGowan asked how members of the union would look at a murderer if he was one of their own.

"As a real piece of scum," Warren said.

But by confessing, the bomber might turn into a hero for the union guys, McGowan suggested. "We have a lot of guys that say, 'Enough is enough. This is what I did.' My feeling is the union wants this over with. The town wants this over with."

McGowan urged Warren to make a calculated guess about the identity of the second figure he'd seen on September 18. "You did see a couple people, and from day one, your story has never changed in that light ... Did you see Al and Tim out there a lot?"

"They were always moving around," Warren said.

McGowan revealed that the police knew who did the graffiti run of June 29, and that the culprits had gone down Akaitcho shaft. "When they left, they stole dynamite, they stole a bunch of stick powder."

"We know that Luc Normandin drove out, and Gordie Kendall planned it," Defer added.

"I know Gordie Kendall, I definitely heard him say he did it," Warren said. "He used to come out with some outrageous stuff."

"The gear used that night was supplied by a Nerco miner. The tape fuses and electric caps were cached by Bettger," continued McGowan, and Kendall was talking about hooking up a powder magazine to the central blast. "There was all kinds of plans": satellite dish, Bettger's clock mechanisms, the vent-shack explosion. "Terry Legge drove them out. Conrad was the lookout. It didn't go off."

"Somebody told me they used the wrong cap," Warren said, meaning they used a DCD cap instead of the lower-resistance red cap Ferriss had mentioned.

Miner Dan Noel drove the next night, and "there was a conversation a couple days before the murder when plans were made to set another explosion, with Tim Bettger ... The plans changed," and then the September 18 blast went off, McGowan rambled. He showed Warren photos of the stick powder from Rob Wells's trailer.

Bettger repeatedly showed disregard for life, Defer pressed. "Did you hear about these trip wires?"

"Guys were telling me some things they were using with flash bulbs or something."

So Defer described the trip-wire device. "I would've never thought of something like that," said Warren. "Jesus Christ," he said, remembering the little guy, Marvin, talking about that. No doubt it was Marvin Ferriss, but McGowan deflected attention from the agent. Tremblett? he asked, and Warren agreed.

The two officers trotted out the "progression of violence" theory, attributing its origins to former CASAW president Bill Schram, as Gordie Kendall had. It was a mind-set, the officers claimed, "which culminated in the death of those miners." The pattern was that Shearing and Bettger had used other players in each offense.

"My only involvement was being on picket duty, which I shouldn't have been, but I was," Warren said.

What about the alterations to your boots? McGowan asked.

"These tracks you got, they're the same size as mine?"

"Yeah."

"Exactly?" Warren asked, sounding incredulous. When McGowan returned to the topic, Warren added, "It definitely couldn't be the same boots you saw in those tracks."

McGowan raised an inconsistency. Some of the burn marks on Warren's boots were made after the cuts, but he'd always said the burns came from accidentally getting too close to a campfire. "That tells me these boots are the ones that went down," McGowan offered. "Now, whether you were in them ..."

"It doesn't tell me that," Warren said. "I never lent them to anybody and I definitely didn't use them."

They agreed to have the boots sent out for another expert's opinion.

"One thing bothers me," Warren said. "If there is a track, how can you tell when it was made?"

It was a question union men had wondered about for months. In areas underground where one might leave obvious tracks, there is very little to erode them and their age would be hard to determine.

"We know," McGowan asserted without elaboration.

Peter Martin, the Calgary-based lawyer chosen to prosecute the murder case if it ever went to trial, came to Yellowknife shortly after this interview. A decision was made to find someone to grill Roger Warren, preserving McGowan's nice-guy image in case damage control was needed. Inspector Al Macintyre says that the Canadian Police College's polygraph school was asked for names of their top interrogators, nationwide.

The RCMP also decided to get tough with Gordie Kendall. He was hauled in for eight or nine hours of questioning and a polygraph test between September 29 and October 1. "They accused me of doing it," he says. "At one point they told me, 'We know you did it—if you come clean, we'll go easier on you.'" Roger Warren would soon be told the same thing.

Kendall also claims police told him they'd recently got an anonymous phone call saying "Gordon Kendall told me he placed the bomb underground." After his second polygraph, "they said I was truthful." In the course of his dealings with police, they showed him a little ring with weights on it, Kendall says, but he didn't know what it was for. They also showed him photos of the man-car and the victims' bodies underground. "Two bodies were jammed into a little space barely above the track," he says. "The top of that fucking car was imploded. The blast had to come from the top. It came from above—I don't care what the experts say."

Peter Martin reviewed new information on the case in early October, an RCMP document states. He already had forty thick binders containing the "court brief" and was expected to "confirm our position in respect to charges."

STALEMATES AND ENDGAMES

In good negotiations, you never get everything you want.

—Peggy Witte, August 18, 1995

Through thick and thin, Royal Oak had kept the favour of investors, who liked Peggy Witte's style, despite her personal sale during the dispute of almost 1.4 million shares, over a third of her own holdings. Like her, investors profited, but the summer of 1993 brought another round of defections by managers.

Mike Werner bailed out in mid-July, almost certainly because of Witte's famous "hands-on" style. The constant second-guessing to which he was subjected had always infuriated him. Werner led a growing network of former Royal Oak employees who helped each other get jobs with other mining companies, particularly TVX Gold. Werner became a top executive at TVX, and promptly hired many supervisors wanting to escape from Giant. Terry Byberg refused a transfer to Royal Oak's mine in Newfoundland and went to a TVX mine in northern Quebec instead. Right on his heels was Giant's top mill supervisor.

Most of the supervisors who had been at Giant when the labour dispute started (and quite a number of those hired during it) would also quit within a year and a half. Morale was low among frontline supervisors, who were fed up with the labour dispute and its pressures. Many felt they'd been robbed of overtime pay on several occasions. Equipment was in poor condition, and getting permission to buy parts was like pulling hens' teeth. Pressure to produce was intense, but the support system was poor. CASAW was still outside the gate and it looked like the strikers might return to work someday. Giant was failing to meet pollution limits in its water license and was attracting attention from regulators and politicians. Without amendments to the license, the mine's operation was in jeopardy.

One night in late summer, a group of eight or nine current and former staffers hoisted beers in a Yellowknife bar. There was good-natured laughter, cigarette smoke rising, rounds of shooters and a table full of empty bottles. They disparaged Peggy Witte as crudely as men on the picket line. In the course of a year, many staff had lost respect for Royal Oak, in much the same way union men had in 1991–92.

Peggy Witte was angry about staff defections and probably wasn't aware of the morale at Giant. Her eyes were focused on the markets and, there, her skills are formidable. But with Werner's exit, she met with managers to determine why he had quit and what to do next. Human resources manager Bill Heath became acting mine manager until a permanent replacement was found. It was an unusual appointment, since Heath freely admitted that he knew nothing about mining.

To reverse the tide, Witte hired a new vice president of operations, Colin Benner from Curragh Resources, of Westray fame. Benner took over day-to-day supervision of the company's three mines. (He would quit a year later.) John Smrke became head of a newly acquired subsidiary, Geddes Resources.

In five years under Royal Oak, Giant would eventually have seven managers.

Breaking the stalemate between Royal Oak and CASAW proved impossible for IIC commissioners Ready and Munroe that summer. They brokered at least six meetings or phone calls between Hemi Mitic and Heath, who even had a pleasant dinner together. The commissioners offered binding arbitration for several issues, but no progress was made. Royal Oak wouldn't amend its demands or put them in writing, despite the commissioners' insistence. Union leaders believed the company was reluctant because its demands violated the Canada Labour Code.

Vince Ready phoned Superintendent Brian Watt on August 3, "seeking input on the [murder] investigation, in that it would help him determine what action he can take to bring the dispute to an end," Watt wrote on August 4. He told Ready that the RCMP had suspects, and planned to arrest ten to twelve others, "mainly CASAW," but that "a crucial ingredient is still missing" in the murder case. "We are not able to predict when charges will be laid."

The exasperated commissioners abandoned efforts to promote talks in late August and wrote a masterful final report. Its import and the delicacy of their task was reinforced by Kim Campbell, Justice minister when the dispute began, but by then Canada's prime minister. In a letter to Yellowknife's mayor, Campbell refused further federal intervention in the dispute, because the IIC was still at work, and the RCMP hadn't wrapped up the murder investigation.

Meanwhile, the Canada Labour Relations Board finally made another decision, this time by all board members. They met in Ottawa to reconsider Decision 1010 on the GMEA's application to dislodge CASAW. Legal arguments from trade unions had poured in, denouncing the original ruling. Employers had been invited to make submissions, but none did. Chairman Ted Weatherill's Decision 1010 was unanimously reversed by the board, including Weatherill and the original panelists. Strikebreakers should not have the right to vote on the choice of a union to represent workers. "Simply put, in the US, a striker may lose his or her job to a replacement worker during economic strikes," the board wrote. "In Canada, the position is different and ... generally to be preferred. In this country, when they are not banned, replacement workers are only recognized as having a temporary, precarious status." Unions had actually made a small gain, in that the plenary decision was a precedent that could be overturned only by another plenary.

On the issue of whether or not the GMEA was a company union, Weatherill's colleagues ruled that he had applied the wrong legal test, and instructed him and his panel to reconsider. It would take months.

Ready and Munroe's final report was issued on September 14, ten months after their appointment to the IIC. Essentially, they recommended a return to the tentative agreement of April 18, 1992, which union members had rejected. "Neither side has offered a good reason why the terms of the tentative agreement ... should not prevail," the commissioners wrote. They advised that Royal Oak and CASAW be given one last chance to negotiate several major issues. These included the wage scale, the minimum number of days of safety inspections per month, the duration of the collective agreement, and other benefits. The parties should have thirty days to agree before Ready and Munroe would intervene to set the terms, through a process they shrewdly dubbed "mediation to finality."

Ready and Munroe were asking union men to admit they'd lost the strike/lockout, and to make further concessions to Royal Oak. In return, the commissioners offered speedy arbitration for all the men who had been fired, and to resolve all prestrike grievances.

The most significant statement came near the end of the IIC report: "Neither side should be permitted to treat this report as being simply another chapter in a dispute without apparent ending. If either party approaches this report in that unproductive manner, it should be seen as raising serious issues of good faith." Ready and Munroe were as blunt as any mediator is ever likely to be in public. In their view, Royal Oak had already shown bad faith by stalling talks, making unreasonable demands, and refusing arbitration for the fired workers; if the company missed this last chance, they deserved to be penalized by the CLRB.

He did fuck all, threw a few rocks, that's all I saw.

—Major Ralph Sinke, speaking of striker Garth Beck,
September 15, 1993

[196]

A big, bald man with a deep booming drawl stood in the foyer of Yellowknife's courthouse, waiting to testify in three trials against men charged over events during the infamous skirmish of June 14, 1992. He sported a stylish blue suit with a red kerchief in the breast pocket, US Marine pins in the lapel, and yellow-tinted aviator glasses. On adjacent fingers of his right hand were two huge rings.

"How long are you here?" someone asked Major Ralph Sinke, the former Pinkerton's boss.

"Until they're all fired," he boasted, nodding at a group of union men nearby, including two of the accused.

James Mager's and Jim Fournier's cases were partially linked; many of the witnesses were the same. But Mager pleaded not guilty and had a jury trial, so verdicts and sentences came at different times.

Jim Fournier pleaded guilty to an assault with a rock on Eric Melançon, the guard who had fled into the catchment pond. After the preliminary hearing, the Crown had amended the charge to attempted murder. At this time, the testimony of Melançon and Fournier provided input for sentencing arguments. Fournier's frank and thoughtful statement impressed Justice Mark de Weerdt. Fournier had a long history at Giant, had two sons, played hockey and fastball, coached a kids' team, and believed strikebreaking was immoral. "I thought then and I think now that ... Pinkerton is a strikebreaking, antilabour organization."

By this time, de Weerdt had heard Sinke's flamboyant testimony, rife with speculation and unsolicited comments. "While you're probably used to command, you now have to obey," de Weerdt had finally ordered Sinke.

The Crown prosecutor asked that Fournier get a jail sentence "in excess of two years."

"One of the questions I'm asking is how far this individual is being scapegoated," de Weerdt said, noting the RCMP's inaction to avert the entire incident. "It may trigger an appeal, but I think I have to do what is right." De Weerdt sent Fournier to jail for three months and fined him $1,000.

James Mager was punished more severely. He was charged with assaults with a weapon on Sinke and four other Pinkerton's guards, plus a police officer, while his face was hidden by a balaclava. The evidence revealed how chaotic the June 14 incident was, but when the dust cleared Mager was found guilty of concealment and assaults against Eric Melançon and the policeman. De Weerdt chastised Mager for not showing remorse or admitting his guilt, and sentenced him to fifteen months in jail. His wife and daughter left the court arm in arm, crying. Mager still insists he did not assault Melançon and several eyewitnesses support his claim. By the time Mager learned who they were, he'd served some of his time and didn't want anyone else to go to jail if he appealed the case.

Garth Beck fared better. He was charged with rock-throwing assaults on Sinke and fellow Pinkerton's boss Chris Morton. They were the Crown's only witnesses, while Beck and June Roberts testified for the defense. The issue came down to their word versus Sinke's and Morton's. The jury quickly acquitted Beck, who was relieved and elated. He'd worked at Giant since 1976, was married with young children, and didn't want to lose his job. (He'd been fired but thought he'd get his job back through arbitration.)

"We are paying heavily for the June 14 'riot,'" noted CASAW's strike bulletin. "Thousands in legal bills; worry and fear of being jailed; much valuable time given up that could have been used more productively." But payment for the June 14 melee was just beginning.

THE CHOSEN ONES

The article is a work of fiction.

—Crown prosecutor Peter Martin, November 10, 1994

It has all the earmarks of an article fed by sources of information which may or may not have been accurate, but fairly close to the investigators.

—Justice Mark de Weerdt, December 1, 1994

I think the cops are trying to shake us up, and raise a lot of shit here.

—Terry Legge, September 17, 1993

The approaching first anniversary of the fatal blast was an embarrassment to the RCMP. Thousands of interviews and wholesale use of the polygraph and electronic surveillance hadn't resulted in arrests, and public assurances that the police were making progress were wearing thin.

To mark the anniversary, the *Edmonton Journal* promoted a special feature. Reporters David Staples and Greg Owens wrote a long article on the police's theory of how the blast was carried out. "RCMP believe Coyote and the Goblin committed the most troubling and wicked crime in the history of the Canadian labour movement," they wrote, using false nicknames for Shearing and Bettger instead of their real ones, Weasel and The Bear. Though they weren't named directly, their identities were obvious to hundreds of people in town.

Some investigators must have leaked critical information to make the article possible. Owens and Staples say that sources were pointed out by Inspector Macintyre and Corporal Vern White. The RCMP hoped a graphic description of the crime would trigger a confession or at least some helpful statement from a union witness. The article also named mechanic Terry Legge as one of the men who helped set the vent-shack blast.

The local newspaper *yellowknifer* got a copy of the article, "Footsteps of the Murderer," days before its publication. The editors were shocked, considering it irresponsible to accuse people publicly of crimes before they had been charged. Innocent people could get hurt; this article was like a bomb dropping on a war-torn city. Trying to scuttle publication, the newspaper copied the article for CASAW, Royal Oak, the RCMP (who sent a copy to Ottawa on September 16), and territorial and federal officials. All of the media had the story within hours, and reporters with TV cameras roved around outside the union hall and downtown. CASAW lawyer Gina Fiorillo flew to Yellowknife on September 17, and government officials telephoned the *Edmonton Journal*.

At least twenty people were in the union hall when Fiorillo opened the door. It was her first appearance since the big win with the CLRB. Two men scurried over and knelt on the ground in front of her. "Allah, Allah," they chanted, adding a blush to Fiorillo's dusky face. Jokes and welcome aside, she quickly joined the summit meeting in President Harry Seeton's office. He did not mince words: the cops were using the newspaper.

RCMP agent Marvin Ferriss watched closely, pretending to be a loyal union man. "We just got our heads out of the noose, and somebody kicked the chair out from underneath us," he said to another striker known as Ghostrider. Rick Cassidy, CASAW's vice president, emerged from Seeton's office for a coffee. "We're trying to see if we can get the paper pulled from up here," he said. "We're scared. We don't want anything to happen. It could be a very dangerous town tomorrow night."

Sergeant Dave "Hollywood" Grundy was on television again. "We're not really comfortable we have enough to go to court," he said.

Terry Legge was furious. "They must've got it from the cops ... I called Vern White. I was fucking excited. [He] denied it. I said, 'Vern, they quoted what I told you.' The editor called me today. I said, 'You could jeopardize my family, me—I applied for a job in this town and when they open up the paper ... 'Hey, this guy here admitted blowing up the vent shaft.'" The Legges had already sold their trailer in Northland and were living in subsidized housing.

At the last minute, the editors deleted Legge's name and the nicknames from the story—but then published the names separately, a week later. *Journal* and *yellowknifer* editors did some public mudslinging, but ignored the issue of the *Journal* becoming a tool of the RCMP.

Bob Robertson says the RCMP assigned him to watch Bettger's and Shearing's reactions to the release. "When the story broke, I was sitting right between [them] in the bowling alley," he says. "When it hit the national news, [Shearing] was in seventh heaven. It was on the TV set in the bar, eh. Just the look on his face—he loved it."

This was his last official job for the RCMP, Robertson says. "I was struggling with my addiction ... I was a basket case. I was about to crack. And they decided to give me a holiday of sorts." He went to Edmonton for an alcohol and drug treatment program.

The next day, September 18, one of the widows called Al Shearing, whose phone and apartment had long since been bugged. Tracey Neill now lived in Alberta, but kept up with the blast investigation. She had written Shearing, and enclosed some photos of Chris, as well as a typed article titled "When I Die," penned anonymously by Jane O'Neil. Neill and Shearing had a polite but odd conversation. "It's Tracey," she said. "What did you think of my letter? Did you read it?"

"I read it," he said, then explained that he couldn't reply because there was no return address.

They talked about the *Edmonton Journal* article, in which Shearing was quoted. "I like what you said about castrating whoever is responsible," Neill said. "What is the atmosphere up there?"

"I've had a few prank phone calls."

She asked him if he was going to the memorial service that night.

"We were advised to stay away from it," Shearing said.

Neill wanted to know what he thought had happened underground, so he gave her the theory that the blast was set by the Pinkerton's guards, perhaps to show the need for more security and extract more money from Royal Oak. She asked him a few times if he was sure the murderer wasn't a union member. She couldn't imagine how the murderer lived with the guilt.

"There's nobody who's breaking down," he replied, "and you'd think you'd see some signs if someone had done it."

"Do you think Peggy had anything to do with this?" she asked.

"I don't know ..."

"Do you think you could ever work for Peggy again?"

"Oh yeah ..."

"How long are you going to last up there?"

Shearing said he'd stick it out until the end.

Even when Neill brought up difficult memories, her voice betrayed no emotion.

"Did you read that article I sent you, 'When I Die'? So truthful."

"Yeah," Shearing said.

Reminding him he said he'd write, Neill said, "that would sure make me feel better ... Thanks for talking to me, Al." They said good-bye.

Tracey's friend, Jane O'Neil, says that the police were involved in the phone call. And "When I Die" was not intended for distribution, she says—her husband, Jim, gave a copy to Tracey, who sent it to Shearing without permission.

Despite the *Journal* article, the anniversary passed quietly. About 150 people attended a memorial ceremony at the mine, where its new superintendent played "Amazing Grace" on the bagpipes.

It was a trying time for the O'Neils, who were worried and hounded by reporters. "There's a lot of tension everywhere," Jim said that night. "There's guys that are hurting big time, guys on our side. We're talking about psychological breakdown. [I tell them,] 'Don't do nothing stupid. You don't know what's going to happen.'"

After reading the *Journal*'s story, O'Neil wondered about Legge. "I know Terry quite well. Pretty good guy. I used to fly him out in the bush with his family."

O'Neil said that Owens and Staples had interviewed him for their story, but he wasn't the main source. "They're going to presumably get a Canadian award for it ... They were picked, it looks like."

The story stirred an assistant commissioner of the RCMP to send his compliments to Superintendent Watt.

CONCESSIONS

A fair collective agreement is our destiny.

—CASAW strike bulletin, September 2, 1993

So many hurdles, you run out of acreage to run it.

—CASAW picketer Dennis Moraff, September 18, 1993

The second winter of the strike/lockout was looming, and with it the prospect of hunching around heaters in chilly picket shacks. On September 27, CASAW members agreed to make concessions to Royal Oak, something they'd vowed never to do. The vote was 94 percent in favour of the IIC report. They had little choice: a rejection of Ready and Munroe's report would make them guilty of bad faith. "If we'd have known what was coming, we'd've never had a strike," President Harry Seeton said a few days later. "But if we'd have accepted the tentative agreement [in April 1992], we'd have been gone in three years, [died] a slow death."

Royal Oak waited ten days before rejecting the IIC report, claiming that the two parties were trying to reach a negotiated settlement. "If the appetite ... for a deal is not there, the endless meetings and telephone conversations would not have been initiated by the Company," Peggy Witte wrote to Bernard Valcourt, who had replaced Marcel Danis as minister of labour. "The fact that the Company has taken a tough bargaining stance seems somehow to offend the Commissioners."

Royal Oak revealed the summer's off-the-record meetings with the CAW as proof of Royal Oak's honourable intentions. In the picture Witte painted, Royal Oak and Mitic had bargained hard, but, in the end, "CASAW was still not prepared to entertain the proposal put forward by the Company." The proposal was the notorious thirteen points that had been presented to Mitic orally on May 31 and that he had given to CASAW in August, calling for major wage cuts and CASAW's elimination as the bargaining agent. It was hardly a bargaining position.

Valcourt said that he was disappointed, but the dispute would soon be heard by the Canada Labour Relations Board, which might be able to resolve it.

Out on the road between picket gates, the sturdy boss of Minion Security tried to chase away a reporter who was taking pictures. CASAW's guys want their jobs back, he said, and the company wants the strike to end—the problem is the forty-five guys who were fired.

CHAPTER SIX

JAWS OF THE TRAP

We give 'em the bait. And then they fuckin' took it. They were just taking that fuckin' lollipop and they were sucking right on it.

—Al Shearing, October 20, 1994

"Something has to be done, but what? If this dispute drifts into another winter, The Pig will win. The line won't hold, and the scabs will have our jobs forever. If it does hold, who wants to sit here day and night, in rotting chairs, going broke and getting flabby? Just because we are in a territory, they can get away with it. They are going to crush us." Many men on the picket line that fall had such thoughts, including Roger Warren.

On the afternoon of October 14, he agreed to yet another talk about his boots with Corporal Dale McGowan. That evening, Warren and Al Shearing met in the Polar Bowl Pub. On their table were a couple of beers, the *Edmonton Journal*'s "Footsteps of the Murderer" article, and a copy of the uncut version, Shearing says. The previous day, a bold headline, "Arrests before talks," screamed on *yellowknifer*'s front page. Wry jokes were made in the union hall about confessing to the murder to become the hero who'd end the strike.

"Myself and Roger [had] a discussion about the article," Shearing says. "[We were] saying, 'Maybe we should get somebody to be arrested, and see if we'll get the talks going.'"

According to Warren, Shearing said, "Geez, I know enough, Rog, you know enough ... I just couldn't go for this because they got enough on me already."

"We figured the best one to get arrested would be Roger," Shearing says.

[203]

"They had [Tim and me] as number-one prime suspects, so it'd be a little harder for us to dig our way out."

The police would have to be told something credible enough that they'd make the arrest. And it would have to hold long enough to kick government machinery into gear to end the strike.

Warren was disgusted by but intrigued with the *Edmonton Journal*'s story. It was obvious that the reporters had been fed information aimed at nailing Al Shearing and Tim Bettger for murder. "I kept it by the couch, and I used to look it over every once in a while," Warren says. "I was trying to figure out what they didn't put in it. I thought that somebody could convince the police they had actually done this if they had enough knowledge."

A great deal of information was available, particularly if one had friends at Giant. When CASAW members visited in the union hall, bits and pieces of interrogations emerged. Shearing heard a great deal while he was on radio duty. Even a year earlier, RCMP spokesman Dave Grundy said that he'd never seen so much information released during an investigation in his nineteen years on the force, and that was six months before the blitz package. Since then, there had been an avalanche of information.

"We figured that most of the information was in that story from the 18th of September," Shearing says. "All we had to do was modify a few things to suit the scene ... Which was easy. We explained to [Roger] the route going down to [750] through Akaitcho. He didn't know how to get down there." That information came from the graffiti run in June 1992, he says.

Downhearted, Warren arrived at Gate 3 for his picketing shift at about midnight. "Every day seemed like an eternity," he says. He felt weak, like he'd never be able to manhandle a drill again. His linemates, including his younger friend Blaine Lisoway, and Cal Williams, were usually lively if not always upbeat, but that night they, too, were in the dumps. They'd all been interrogated many times by the police. Cal was bitter over his broken marriage and missed daily contact with his little son. Blaine's brother Conrad had moved back to Saskatchewan only to be hounded by the police, and their aunt, who worked in a local grocery store, wasn't speaking to either of them.

"I was feeling melancholy all the time, like something had happened that made me sad," Warren says. He went home with a movie, *At Play in the Fields of the Lord*, but couldn't keep his mind on it. The *Edmonton Journal* article didn't grab him either, so he dozed fitfully until his appointment at the RCMP's task-force office above Centre Square Mall. When Corporal McGowan answered Warren's buzz at the door, a surprise was waiting. It was time, as McGowan would later tell the *Edmonton Journal*, that Roger Warren got "hardballed by somebody."

Sergeant Gregg McMartin waited at a desk in the reception area. He looked important, with the smooth, bland handsomeness of a TV news anchorman. Warren shook his hand. The two officers left Warren alone in the reception room. Space dividers in a makeshift office featured enlarged photographs of boot soles and footprints in some mud, with red lines on them. File boxes were labeled "Shearing," "Bettger," "Warren," and "Court Documents." Warren's box was open, but the pictures caught his eye. "I wanted to see what they had found out about the boots, and I was worried about the next thing they were going to come up with," he says. "But I expected it to be a normal interview." Then he was told that Sergeant McMartin was working with the special prosecutor assigned by the attorney general to handle court matters for the case.

This was a major interrogation for forty-four-year-old McMartin, perhaps the most important of thousands he'd done in twenty-three years with the RCMP. The call to do it had come about a month earlier, when he was in Ottawa. McMartin's interrogation skills had been honed by giving polygraph exams, "sometimes a couple a day for a month." He has an almost frightening ability to tap into and manipulate emotions with the ebb and flow of his voice and the powerful psychological themes he'd adjust as he went along. And, McMartin resorted to threats and inducements with Warren, because he was regarded as a likely defense witness who could become a pivotal Crown witness. The investigators' hopes for a breakthrough seemed to rest on Warren, because Shearing and Bettger were no longer talking, Kendall had not cracked and was too evasive, and informants weren't getting much new material.

An Edmonton polygrapher had given McMartin a rundown on the investigation and a faxed copy of the "Footsteps of the Murderer" article, which he claims had provided his "main understanding of the investigation." He'd also discussed Warren's statements with special prosecutor Peter Martin, and read a transcript of one of Shearing's. Sergeant McMartin says he believed Warren was lying, and hiding something. In part, his view was based on "scientific content analysis," a technique developed by a former Israeli police officer to detect if a subject is lying during interrogation, based on language used. "I was sure, by the time I had gone over the material and the evidence, that Roger Warren was involved in this," even if other people appeared more implicated, McMartin says. He called Macintyre in Ottawa on the night of October 14, according to a later report in the *Edmonton Journal*. "What do you think?" the inspector asked.

"He's your guy."

"What do you mean, 'the guy'? Are you saying he's the guy who planted the bomb?" Macintyre asked.

"Yeah, I am," McMartin replied.

"What about Bettger and Shearing?"

"I can't say. I haven't even looked at that."

"Well, yeah. Good luck on your interview," Macintyre said.

McMartin began talking with Warren about mining, conveying no hint of study or preparation. Then he cut to the chase, determined to pry "the truth" from Warren. McMartin later testified that he considered anything short of a confession as untrue.

"I've been in contact with Peter Martin and this file. There are some problem areas," McMartin told Warren. "I would like to go over the evening of September 17. Go back in time, visualize what you can ... Tell me everything you did, everything that you felt, everything that you saw." Warren repeated the story he'd told for months. McMartin was indignant. "Roger, I don't believe you. The people you saw, Roger, that's not the truth." What you've said about going into the mine, and about your boots, that's not the truth either.

Warren said nothing. He sat in his chair, relaxed, arms folded on his chest.

McMartin raised his voice. "You've worked all your life for things you believe in ... These guys piss you off, cross the line." Shearing and Bettger are just a couple of screwups whose misdeeds shrouded the killer's, he said. "I have no doubt whatsoever that you are the person that did this." Warren sat, poker-faced. McMartin said Warren probably thought he'd be a hero after the blast, since he'd been man enough to do it, but now, "guys are moving away ... You guys are at an impasse, the union [and] the company. The mine is going again. Now, nobody gives a shit ... It becomes so bloody important for people to understand, why did it happen? ... It's like a boil—it's all coming to a head ... soon, totally. When you were little, when we do something wrong, what is the one question that was asked? Why did you do it? I don't believe it was done to kill. I think it was just to screw up the whole operation, which is fair enough when it comes to unions."

Warren remained silent. "It takes a very very big man to take that step and say, 'I'm sorry,'" lectured McMartin.

"You guys are arresting me, you mean?" Warren finally asked.

"No," McMartin replied, but "you aren't telling the truth." Your boots were cut first, then burned, not the other way around, as you said. "That has come back from the forensic lab." And, no one else saw two people on mine property that night," McMartin claimed. It's not clear whether McMartin knew about a hefty file of statements and composite drawings from Pamela MacQuarrie-Higden, who said she'd seen two strange men at Giant that night.

Warren objected mildly, but McMartin would hear none of it. "Maybe you don't give a shit," he blustered. "[Surely] you are not so cold, and not so callous that you don't give a shit about human life. It's a hell of a thing that you're going to have to live with ... We're all accountable, Roger. Maybe it does take a man to say, 'Jesus, this has gone on long enough, I'm sorry.'"

"If you guys are that convinced of this stuff, I'm just wondering why I'm not arrested," Warren said.

"This could go on for another six months. I'll give you a little bit of a hint what the attorney general's department is looking at ... Rest assured, Roger, there is an awful lot going on."

"I have to pick my daughter up for a therapy appointment," Warren stated abruptly. "Right now, actually." It was 3:45 P.M.

This took the wind out of McMartin's full sails, but he hurriedly cast another hook into the water. "There's a lot of things I'd like you to think about ... I'll explain a few things that are happening."

Amazingly, Warren agreed to return at 5:30 and walked out. After the first half hour, he had barely said a word.

"I was pretty terrified," Warren says. "I was glad I had this excuse. I didn't know if I could get out of there. It was like being on the edge of a precipice or something. I was tempted to step off it, and I pulled back just in time. I thought, 'I have to go, take the daughter to the appointment.'" She had broken her ankle playing fastball.

It was almost as if his daughter Ann, twenty-two, had called him back from ruin, the voice of love penetrating his subconscious mind. He was her hero, and the admiration was mutual. Her dad had taught her to pitch, but he'd lost a lot of his stuff in the last couple of years, and often played outfield, zipping the ball in underhand. After years of mining, he could no longer throw overhand, a teammate says. Even in Warren's prime, Ann had caught for him when he warmed up to pitch. Now, he picked her up at work, took her for physiotherapy, and went home.

His unexpected departure threw the Royal Oak Mines Task Force into a tizzy. Where was he going? What was he doing? Would he seek out Al Shearing? Go to the union hall? Several officers, including primary investigator Vern White, rushed to their unmarked cars to tail Warren. When he picked up Ann at about 4:30, she noticed more police cars than usual on the way home. But Roger just poured himself a coffee, sat down on the couch, and picked up a newspaper. "We're going [out] to have dinner for Mum's birthday," which was two days earlier, Ann reminded him.

He left to pick up Helen at her office, but the celebration slipped his mind. "Some guy from the attorney general's office is making accusations," he told Helen, who replied with a derogatory remark about Witte or John Smrke. On the way home, Helen went to the bank in the mall beneath the task-force office.

"I've got to go and see these guys for a few minutes. The guy said he had something to tell me," he said.

"I'll wait for you."

A LOT OF BALLS

You trust your instincts. You step back and, half a second later, 50 tons of rock drops exactly where you were standing. Working in that environment binds miners together. You put your life on the line to save your partner, knowing that he would do the same for you.

—Bob Robertson, March 22, 1995

Warren arrived at the task force's lair at the appointed hour, walked straight into the stark interview room, sat down, and crossed his outstretched legs.

Sergeant McMartin sat 4 feet away. "You're worried what this is leading up to?"

"Well—of course I'm concerned," said Warren.

"There's a lot of other things with a lot of other people, and I guess what the attorney general's department is doing is, do we take the great big picture?" McMartin began, hinting at multiple arrests or the union's involvement. "Or are we looking at individuality, where we look at things separately?" And then he launched into a repetitive, mind-bending monologue, asking questions and answering them himself. "It was not Roger against Joe [Pandev]," he railed, "it was union against company ... You got the hands of a hardworking man ... Scabs put you out of a job ... Roger Warren's not a violent person. Never has been. Never will be ... I consider myself to be a fairly good judge of character. What do you feel is the best way to deal with it, Roger?"

Warren chewed his gum and took a long time to answer. "If I was convinced that somebody was guilty, I'd just arrest 'em and lock 'em up."

"I don't think that's fair to you," said McMartin. "Are we talking about a bad judgment call, a bad mistake? ... There are a lot of people saying, 'This was deliberate!'" he shouted. "I said, 'Bullshit!' We're not talking about the hardened criminal. We're talking about something that was running on an awful lot of adrenaline ... and if there weren't any miners hurt, you'd be able to walk around with a smile on your face." On and on he droned; he spoke of disciplining a daughter, of the families of the dead, of manhood, of being a false hero abandoned by his friends. Powerful officials down south had directed him, he insisted, "'You go see Roger. Because we know what's happened ... see if he does give a shit.'" His voice soared and fell, arguing with himself for roughly two hours, a gospel preacher turned interrogator, asking, "Was it meant to kill miners? Or a tragic screwup?"

Finally, Warren interjected. "I don't see the point. A bunch of guys are dead. If you're going to nail somebody, fuckin' nail the guy. You got about eighty people affected directly ... Some guy's going to come up with an excuse for this, and people are going to feel sorry for him? Not too fuckin' likely."

"Feel sorry for the person?" McMartin asked angrily, pausing to build up steam for a tirade. "Depending on how it was done and why it was done ... Nobody is going to walk up to you and shake your hand and say 'Congratulations.' [But if it] becomes, 'I don't give a shit about them, I don't care about them...'"—his voice fell—"it can be dealt with, Roger. You have some compassion, Roger. Does it make it better to hear from a person who's got the balls to say, 'I'm sorry?' Does it not even bring you some peace inside? Look at what it's doing to you—you don't want to keep on living like this ..."

"I've got my wife waiting for me downstairs," Warren said.

"Do you understand what I'm saying?"

"Yeah, I understand. I just can't understand why anybody'd give a shit."

Judges give a shit, McMartin said, and have discretionary powers they can use "if they know what's in that person's mind."

Periodically, McMartin snapped his fingers as if he wanted Warren to snap his silence, or come out of hypnosis. "Do you not think your wife would give a shit ... hey? ... Roger, it would mean something to know what the truth is ... Was it set deliberately for the guys?" Silence. "I give a shit, you know why? Because all of a sudden we're not playing a game anymore ... Roger gives a shit—not only to those eighty people, but to himself ... I know how you're feeling. I know what you're going through."

"You are wrong there. I didn't say I affected a lot of people's lives, because I never did." Warren's voice was tinged with anger. "YOU can say that."

"Maybe I am being snowed," McMartin returned. "I can go back to Calgary and my words are, 'He didn't give a shit, do what you have to.' Things are happening, Roger ... [There's] no question about what or who, but why, that is the ONLY thing. That's all."

Warren did not respond.

Maybe you're not man enough, McMartin suggested. "I'm a little surprised ... I would hope you wouldn't [take] the rough road," he said quietly.

"I think all of 'em are probably going to be pretty rough if a guy's going to admit to this," Warren said.

"It might be a little bumpy along the way, but God, you know that,"

McMartin conceded. "Roger Warren made a very big mistake, there's no down-playing it. Goddamn it, nine people are dead ... But if it wasn't meant to be that way, then it becomes very important ..."

Warren was mystified. What was this guy talking about? Not meant for the guys? A blast that powerful would kill them for sure.

"Let that healing process start, for the community, for the people involved ... for Roger Warren," droned McMartin. "Why would you want people to think that Roger Warren was just playing the game? ... You know what it's like down there ... It was not a pretty sight, right—you couldn't take it ... Am I wrong?! Hey?!"

Silence. McMartin was referring to a terrible mine accident in 1987, in which one of Warren's fellow workers was killed and another was blinded.

"Can you not be a man yourself, Roger? ... And say, 'Goddamn it, I'm sorry?' You could not live with yourself, knowing that it was going to happen, could you? Eh?"

"No, I wouldn't be able to," Roger agreed.

"So it was done as an accident ... I'll tell you what, I'm glad you told me that," McMartin burbled. "It wasn't intended for the guys, it was only intended for the mine ... It's something that you'll have to live with the rest of your life ... Was it done the way they said that it was?"

Silence. "Hey?" Silence.

"The way those guys say it was done, if it was done like that, then somebody deliberately tried to murder somebody," Warren said.

This was a break. McMartin went back to Warren's boots and claimed they'd made the footprints in the mine.

At this, Warren bristled. He denied it.

McMartin was adamant. Those boots were the ones that went down inside the mine. There is no doubt about that whatsoever.

"Guaran-fuckin'-teed they're not," Warren stated.

"What boot prints are in the mine?"

"How in fuck do I know, but I know they're not mine," Warren snapped. "You guys are lying to me."

At that, the interrogator shouted and banged, attacked Warren's manhood, then appealed to his conscience. "The police will say, here's how it was set, and who cares?" he challenged. "Knowing that you didn't mean to ... It's become very rough for Roger Warren."

"It's not just Roger Warren," replied Warren. "Anybody, whoever is faced with this kind of stuff has got to think of a lot of things—your wife, your chil-dren ... If a guy was hypothetically going to make a decision, like what you are talking about, without getting advice from lawyers, which I never have done ...

Even if you could prove it was accidental, it's an act of terrorism. Anybody that's involved in this kind of stuff is going to get ten years."

McMartin pounced on the chance to explore this topic. "[We] got first-degree murder. We have second-degree murder. We have manslaughter. They all carry life." But a man might be able to serve a few years and come back out into society. "It's not for eternity, Roger ... And yes, a person's got to deal with their wife, with their children ... Roger, what was in your mind?"

"I've got to talk to my wife before I have anything else to say," Warren said. "If you don't mind, if I'm not under arrest or whatever."

"Roger, if you want to talk to your wife, fine. Do you want to bring your wife in?" McMartin asked. Warren had no intention of bringing Helen in, and, if he had, the session would have ended swiftly.

"I can understand what you're thinking ... to be able to talk to your wife, if we know what the truth is ... so that you can start your life, and get on with it," rambled McMartin. "Tell me what happened," he pleaded. "It wasn't done for the miners, and Roger, I know that ... You said so, and I know that in my heart, too ... Was the explosion set the way the police are saying that it was?"

Silence. "Mmmm?" Silence. "Hey?"

"We're looking at a trip wire. Does Roger Warren know that?" prompted McMartin. "I know you deal with explosives all the time, but not with trip wires."

"[You] never deal with stuff like that," Warren said.

"Was it set that way?" McMartin badgered. "And there just wasn't supposed to be guys in there?" Silence. "I think they're probably wrong."

"Well, I think they're probably wrong, too," offered Warren.

"How was it done, then? ... Hey? ... Roger? Deal with it, Roger ... If you want to show a little emotion, don't be afraid."

"The only thing I'm afraid of is ... somebody tricking me into an admission of something and then I find out after I didn't have to admit to that." Warren had read newspaper stories about people who had cooperated with the police and then been falsely arrested for the crime in question.

"Are you a sociopath?"

"I doubt it," Warren replied.

"I doubt it too. No one is tricking you," McMartin protested. "Say, 'I'm sorry.' For godsakes, if you are, say it."

"What's to stop you," Warren asked, "hypothetically, if I say I did this, you're going to say, "Fuck you, man, we know you meant to do this ... I can't understand how I could ever prove that it wasn't deliberate."

"Look Roger, who?"

"Could be anybody."

"When you tell me the truth ... I [will] not say, 'Fuck you.' You're not the type of person [to] deliberately try to take them out. You would not be able to live with it. I believe that."

"How am I ever going to prove that? ... The bottom line is, one wrong word and it's go straight to fuckin' jail," Warren argued.

"It's not a trick to make Roger say one wrong word. Be a man, what is the truth? It wasn't the miners, was it?"

"Of course it wouldn't be," agreed Warren. "I wouldn't be sitting here now ... Any sane person would go shoot themselves, or gas themselves or whatever."

"[Was it] just to disrupt productivity, or whatever?"

"I think anything that was done, that's why it was done," Warren said.

"Is that what was done here? Is that all? Hey? Roger? Roger, you're man enough to take that step," drummed McMartin. "How was [the explosive] set?"

Still, Warren stalled. "I'm going to have to do some heavy thinking about this kind of stuff. If I'm not under arrest, I'm going to leave."

"Can I get you to wait here just a moment?" asked McMartin. "Let me talk to the investigator."

"OK."

McMartin left the room, closed the door, and was gone for five minutes. McGowan and McMartin discussed making an arrest before he rejoined Warren.

"Roger, Nancy [Defer] is going to have a talk with your wife and send her on her way, so she's just not sitting here." Because the Warrens had been tailed, McMartin knew Helen was downstairs in the mall—but now it was about 7:40 P.M. and virtually everything was closed. Helen Warren was already gone.

"So I guess you answered my question: you're arresting me?"

"No, not right now," McMartin said, adding that he dealt with Peter Martin and the attorney general, and it would be up to regular investigators to make an arrest. There were two camps among the police, McMartin claimed. "I know Corporal McGowan; he's a very understanding person ... He and I are both on side against other people."

"You got to put yourself in my place too, you know," Warren said. "Would you sit in my place, talking to you, without legal representation? Would you?"

"Roger Warren wants to deal with this," McMartin countered. "How many guys have told the investigators to 'fuck off, go take a hike'? Hey? Roger Warren hasn't. There isn't one person who has cooperated more than Roger Warren. And that's why I've come up from Calgary. What I'm saying, Roger, is, let's deal with it all," McMartin begged. "We can sit here and talk ... Yes, it's a big step, but you're also a big enough man to do it. How was the explosive set, Roger?"

Warren said nothing. McMartin nagged again. Finally, Warren stood up and threw his gum in the garbage can.

"You can only chew gum for so long," McMartin said, and returned to a quiet attack. "You are sorry for what happened, aren't you?"

"I'm refusing to comment anymore. Unless I'm arrested, and even if I'm arrested, I'm not commenting without a lawyer."

"So you want to play the game, then?"

"It's not a game. A guy's got to protect himself, pardner. Holy fuck."

This was trouble. McMartin had to squash this, fast. Frustrated, he ranted that, if it makes it any easier, "we'll get ten lawyers here, I don't care." Again, he urged Warren to be a man.

"Oh, so you're just saying, being a man, I'm fucked," Warren shot back, after "half the shit that happened should've never happened. Twenty-one million people in Canada are protected from this shit" because they've got antiscab legislation, he said. There are double standards, and "I'd put a little guilt on the people that caused that shit too ... I don't really feel that I'd be guilty."

Now he's talking, McMartin realized. He agreed, swore more often and sneered at scabs, egging Warren on.

"Sure, there's a lot of mitigating circumstances, [but] nothing mitigates somebody [losing] their life," Warren said. "Only one person is going to take the fucking rap for it."

"Those guys are supporting what you did ... It didn't stop those pricks from going in there," McMartin said, evidently referring to Shearing and Bettger.

"That is a total fuckin' disgrace," Warren replied. "It's a stupid thing to use violence, especially if somebody deliberately used violence ... and then to do fuck all about it, that's the worst part ... Fuck, forty of our own guys were in that [mine]."

"They shouldn't have crossed the goddamn line," McMartin said.

"Oh no."

"It takes a hell of a goddamn man to stand up for what you believe in. Roger, you had a lot of guts," McMartin said, sounding like he was about to cry. "The only bad thing is that it didn't stop ... Maybe the end result is we get the goddamn governments involved ... Maybe, something can come from this. Do you think something could?" asked McMartin.

"I doubt it," Warren answered, pointing out that many people had tried to lobby the government.

"You've already got three provinces" with antiscab laws, McMartin said, and the situation at Giant was "a kick in the ass" for politicians. "I tell you what, the mine's not hurting! You know who's hurting, it's you guys ... Is that what the thought was, let's put an end to this? I'm sure a lot of strikers admired what you did."

"They admired it?!"

"Admired the balls ..."

"I don't think anybody admired that."

"For what you did, for the cause," McMartin argued, "Maybe get something changed in this bloody country. Wake some people up. Hey?" Silence. "You said before it wasn't deliberately put toward the miners, you wouldn't have been able to live with that. Are we talking the difference, they're not miners, they're scabs? It's their own fuckin' fault?"

"That's just semantics," Warren said. "I'm just saying, hypothetically, [if I] wiped out nine guys like this, I'd just go and gas myself, something gentle so my wife wouldn't have to look at a mess."

"Roger, cut out the bullshit here with the 'hypothetically.'"

"Look, to me, this is like fuckin' being grilled in an inquisition. I'm not under arrest, but I can't go ... I don't want to answer something."

"You want to go?" asked McMartin.

"Right at this particular moment, anyways."

McMartin spoke over Warren's objections. "Why don't you want to answer? ... The scabs shouldn't have been there anyways ... Boy, we're talking real conflict here."

"A guy can set something up, underground, hypothetically ...," Warren said. "An ore car has got something on it that no other car has. A fifth fuckin' wheel, eh."

Meanwhile, officers McGowan, White, Defer, and Ken Morrison were listening in the monitoring room, elated, according to an *Edmonton Journal* report. As McMartin preached, the officers fell to their knees, chanting a "team prayer" about a stress headache. "He's right there! Take him!" McGowan rooted.

McMartin ran out to get a photograph from the lobby, and "the old Pepsi can" for Warren to use as an ashtray. The Pepsi was found after the blast and was photographed by the police. If it was a clue from McMartin, Warren missed it, yet he'd often referred to having a Pepsi and an Eat-More chocolate bar on the picket line that night.

"This is a man-car, not an ore-car," Warren said, looking at the photo. It would be possible to trigger a device with the dump wheel protruding from an ore-car, he theorized. Normally, when the wheel hit a special ramp, the car dumped its cargo. Because of the wheel, ore-cars are wider than man-cars, which might pass safely by a trip wire. "Fucking harebrained, but not set to kill fuckin' nine guys." He made a diagram of an ore-car.

"Roger, cut the bullshit, OK."

Warren drew another diagram, showing a piece of steel wedged against the wall at an angle, with a string tied to the pipes at the top left of the drift. When pulled taut, the string would flip a toggle switch fastened to the steel, connecting a circuit fed by a 9-volt radio battery.

"Why didn't you tell us this before?" McMartin asked.

"Fear ... I can't barely sleep sometimes ... I was going to go out to the shaft and really fuck that shaft up—with nobody in it, of course."

McMartin grabbed the map from the *Edmonton Journal* article. He'd marked the route in and out of the mine with a yellow marker, and the blast site was clearly identified. He handed it to Warren.

Now, Warren was effusive. He told them there was a spot about 65 feet away from the blast site where the dump wheel scraped the wall of the drift, and that's where he'd measured the distance the trip line would have to be from the tracks.

"A piece of fish line was actually what was in there. Only this fuckin' wheel was supposed to hit the thing," Warren answered. "If the fuckin' thing goes off, the company's going to be in a lot of shit—it's going to be an unexplained explosion ... There's lots of room for that man-car."

"Is this your Pepsi can? This was found in one of the shops," McMartin prodded.

"No," said Warren. He paused and mumbled, "Ah, this is fuckin' pitiful ... how pitiful."

When did you cut the boots? McMartin asked.

A couple of days after the police went around town looking for boots, Warren answered. "But they aren't the fuckin' boots. I wore boots like that, but a size smaller," size 10. Later, he told them he'd bought them at Woolco a few days before the blast.

"Where are they?"

"I burned the fuckers," he said. Out at Cameron Falls, about forty minutes' drive out the Ingraham Trail.

And the coat?

"I just threw it in the garbage. It had a little bit of mud on it."

"Can I get Dale in?" McMartin asked, adding, he's a good guy. Warren agreed. "You took a big step, Roger. I congratulate you."

"Couldn't tell any more fuckin' lies," Warren said to Dale McGowan when he came in at 8:45.

"I didn't think you were the type of guy who would intentionally do something like that," McGowan said. "I knew something was churning in you." And they launched into more details.

"You can imagine the fuckin' haste," Warren said. "I'm not that young ... I was running out of time." For explosives, Warren said a DCD cap was wrapped in B-line and inserted into one stick of 20 to 30 pounds of powder, which fired a bag of Amex.

"Where would the explosives be?" McGowan asked.

"Must've been this side. I can't even remember now ... I had to be quite careful putting all this shit together ... I figured, this wouldn't be so bad, you know, scare the fuck out of somebody."

Warren told them he went straight from Gate 6 on the picket line to the Akaitcho shaft, took the plywood cover off the hole, and climbed down the ladders (see map D). He claimed that his lamp was made from a bicycle light with a brighter bulb held in with a paper clip and powered by a 6-volt battery, which he discarded in a swamp. He descended to the 400 level, then to 575, and at last to 750. Three-quarters of the way along the drift, he heard the central blast go off, he said. "I went in the [7-12] shop, got the scoop," and drove it down the B-ramp to the powder magazine, got a bag of Amex and a few sticks of powder, Magnafrac 5000, "the big stuff." It was about 3:00 A.M, he said. He'd looked at his watch. (Later, he'd say it was 4:00 or 4:30 by then.)

Here, something was amiss. Central blast went off that night at 3:16 A.M. (Later, he'd say that he was near the 9-07 powder magazine when central blast went off, another 2,000 feet down B-ramp from the 7-12 shop. And if Warren had not reached the shop until 4:00, setting a booby trap and climbing out to the Ingraham trail before 6:00 A.M. would have been difficult, perhaps impossible.)

He talked about collecting the explosives, DCD caps, some B-line, and then deciding to rig something on 750. "I checked the thing, everything was safe ... It was fuckin' scary hooking that up. That fuckin' man-car should've never set that off ... I figured it'd just derail the train." Before leaving, Warren put "one or two planks or a real thin [rail] tie" over the explosives, he said, so "you wouldn't hardly notice anything."

It was after 4:00 A.M. by the time he could start on his way out of the mine via the 1-38 portal, he said. "I was surprised there wasn't guards there ... I figured I got to sneak by this guy." Warren said he had crawled under the gate, climbed over the hill toward the road near Gate 6, and stashed his gear in the bushes. On the highway, a truck passed him. Later that morning when he went to pick up the bag, Byberg saw him on the road.

"Did you take your tin of Pepsi down there with you?" McGowan asked. Apparently, the police had not found the Pepsi's owner and believed it was related to the blast, so McGowan hoped that Warren would finally pick up on the hint.

"A tin of Pepsi?" Warren returned.

"That's not your Pepsi?" In the picture?

"Oh, fuck no."

It was 9:33 P.M. when McMartin parted with a handshake; their next encounter would be in court.

Other investigators besieged McMartin, the *Edmonton Journal* reported later, asking if he thought Bettger and Shearing were involved in the crime. "I don't know if they helped plan it," he asserted, "But they sure as hell weren't down in the mine." Special prosecutor Peter Martin was on the phone: "Congratulations. Gregg, you have absolutely no idea what you have just done." McMartin flew home the next day, crippled by the worst headache of his life. He laid on his couch with wet towels on his face for two days—and by January 1995 he said Warren's face still haunted him in dreams.

NO TIME FOR FUCKIN' LAWYERS

Under unusual circumstances, normal people do unusual things.

—Corporal Vern White, October 16, 1993

Roger Warren's confession was manna from heaven for the police, but did they dare accept it? Obviously, he wasn't going to implicate Shearing and Bettger, at least intentionally. The odds of convicting them of murder on circumstantial evidence had just evaporated. Now, the only hope for this investigation was that Warren was telling the truth, or something close enough to convict him. So task-force members planned to interrogate Warren virtually around the clock. The timing was perfect for the RCMP—9:30 P.M. on a Friday night, no arrest had been made, and Warren hadn't yet called a lawyer.

At 9:45, Corporal Harry Ingram got a call on his cellular phone in Rocky Mountain House, Alberta, outside a hotel during an undercover operation. He was told to drive to Edmonton and catch the RCMP plane to Yellowknife at midnight. Calls were also made to Crown prosecutor Ron Reimer and at least four other officers.

About this time, McGowan told Warren they'd go find the bag he'd thrown into the swamp, take a drive to Cameron Falls, and do a walk-through in the mine. Finally, he offered Warren something to eat, and went to make arrangements. McGowan returned with Vern White. "It'll be just be the two of us dealing with you," McGowan said.

"Just call me Vern."

"As of now, I'm obligated to indicate you're under arrest for murder," McGowan said. No reaction from Warren. When we take you through the mine, he added, "[with] respect to any difference in charges ... we want you to look at us as a vehicle to bring out everything to your advantage ... We are the collection agency."

"I knew I could've made the process way harder," Warren said moments later. "But there's a hundred some people that are fucked up already because of that shit."

"The strike might get back on the wheels here," McGowan said. "You're doing the proper thing."

"Is anybody going to notify my wife?" Warren asked. Nobody had seen her. Maybe send Nancy, he said, and tell her, "I didn't fuckin' mean to do that." McGowan spoke to Nancy Defer at 10:21, but she did not go to see Helen Warren until 12:55 at the earliest. Her sister Kathy Hrynczuk remembers saying, "It's 1:10, where the hell is he?" When Defer finally relayed McGowan's message, Helen asked, "What is this, some kind of joke?" She was horrified to learn that it was not.

In the task-force office, White and Warren talked lightheartedly about hockey, the "mystery meat" in their sandwiches, and hickory barbecue in Texas.

The police wanted former mine foreman Noel O'Sullivan as their guide underground. "As long as you guys can handle him," Warren said.

"He seems to know what he's talking about; he makes you comfortable," McGowan replied.

"He's a kind of funny guy," Warren said. "Pretty volatile."

RCMP superintendent Brian Watt tracked down Bill Heath, the acting mine manager and Royal Oak's human resources manager, responsible for dealings with IIC commissioners Ready and Munroe. Heath was at a pool hall with two men from work when Watt arrived. "We have a confession," Watt said. Heath and the mine superintendent picked supervisor Rob Moore to escort the police. Welders went to open the entry to Akaitcho shaft, sealed since after the blast.

"They got a cage in there?" asked Warren, back in the task force's headquarters.

"Well, ah, no," Corporal White answered, ignoring the implications of Warren's query. There had never been a cage or hoist machinery at Akaitcho, as anyone who had descended in the shaft would obviously know.

Warren was left alone while the officers prepared for the long hike to the blast site. He lit a cigarette and completed the crossword puzzle in the *Edmonton Journal* without a single error.

When the RCMP arrived at Giant around 1:00 A.M. with Warren, Heath was astounded. "There were two prime suspects, and I know what they look like. And this guy shows up that I've never seen before ... 'Who is this guy?'" Moore told him it was Roger Warren.

"This'll be the last time I'll go underground," Warren said as they walked to the Akaitcho headframe. "Next time'll be six feet under." Two more sergeants came along to videotape Warren's farewell. He loved mining, it had been his life, and now the police would be on his turf. Here, he was "The Ace," as some miners called him, tramping around with clumsy officers who wanted nothing more than to nail him to the cross.

"I entered through that window," Warren said on videotape. "I stood on the barrel and jumped in. It was already there. I found the entrance to the shaft. I proceeded to go down. I was alone ... I had a canvas bag. They use them for draegers, to carry tools." He said he'd used rubber mine gloves. Warren looked dour. The group descended ladder after ladder, landing to landing, to the 425 sublevel (see map D). There was a short jog there to a raise going down to 575, carved through the rock at about a 60-degree angle, and then another raise to 750. They'd descended the equivalent of seventy-five stories in the dampness, with Vern White leading, followed by Warren. They were all sweating heavily. Warren looked haggard, but it was still another 1.25 miles along the drift to the 7-12 scoop shop. They walked three abreast, with Warren in the middle.

Finally they came to the cavernous 7-12 shop. A battery charger buzzed loudly. "I picked up a scooptram here," Warren said, standing beside a big diesel machine. McGowan asked if it was a big scoop. Warren's subsequent description fit a big scoop, but not number 50, the small one used that night. Scoop number 50 seemed an unlikely choice for a knowledgeable intruder. It was probably the slowest one in the mine, and the earsplitting shriek of its engine was easily identified from a great distance.

The next stop was the 9-07 powder magazine, about 650 yards down B-ramp. Warren said he'd loaded a bag of Amex and some stick powder into the scoop bucket, then got caps and B-line on the way back to the 7-12 shop. He transferred the load to a Titan motor and went to set the trap, he said, stopping to test a cap along the way. Walking with the police, he stopped at a spot that had been cleaned up. Nine white crosses were painted on the wall, which was wet. "I'd already checked how far the [ore-car's] dump wheel was from the track," Warren said. "I hooked the string up to the pipes. It was right close to the wall." He said he tested the string, found it was too tight, and loosened it. "At the time, I figured, that was good."

"What was your mental state?" McGowan asked.

"Not too good," Warren said emphatically. "I'd put all this effort into coming down here, and I just wanted to get something done ... Probably would have been a lot better off if I'd've blew myself up ... I've been dreadfully sorry about it for over a year now ... Nothing's ever going to repay that."

Now he said he'd left at about 4:30 A.M., ridden the Titan motor back to 7-12, refueled the scooptram, and lumbered up the ramp, parking at the 575 breakthrough doors.

The police wanted to see where the dump wheel scraped the drift wall. Finally Warren stopped by some vertical scrapings in an area about 10 inches square.

"Before, it was even longer. Maybe there was muck against the wall," he said lamely. When police measured later, they found that the markings were beyond the reach of any dump wheel. Soon, Warren made another strange comment that seemed to go unnoticed by the police: "I never knew they were using this area to carry powder in."

McGowan saw there was no hope of trudging through the route out of the mine; besides, Warren said he was worn out, and looked it. They went back up in the cage at C-shaft, then to visit the 1-38 portal on surface. Warren was asked to describe his exit. After abandoning the scooptram, he had walked to the Muir raise, he said, and climbed to B-3 first level, passing the second level about 300 feet up. "I kind of panicked ... I could see a ramp down there. I kind of slid down the muck," and came out at the ramp leading up to 1-38. "I just rolled underneath the gate. It was locked." It was about 5:30 or 5:45 A.M. when he stepped out into the "early twilight," he said.

Here was another anomaly in Warren's account of his exit: the Muir raise doesn't go all the way to B-3 first level; that was a different raise. And he didn't mention going into the lunchroom on the second level, as the boot prints had when the police tracked them. Moreover, what would he have done if he had been unable to get past the padlocked gate at 1-38? Without bolt cutters, he would have been trapped. At best, he would have had to hide in the mine until he could escape, and everyone on the picket line would have known he was missing. These were not hallmarks of a good plan by a "lone wolf."

Problems with Warren's confession have never been acknowledged publicly by the RCMP, but they must have feared that either Roger Warren was not the murderer, or he was already planting inconsistencies that would be the seeds of his defense. The police acted as if they did not believe Warren, and kept questioning him.

McGowan got Warren to agree that no promises had been made, that he was not forced to do this "voluntary reenactment," nor was he refused a lawyer. "Nobody coerced me," he said. "It was my own decision."

Warren's entourage was still sloshing around in Giant mine when an RCMP plane touched down at the Yellowknife airport. Corporal Harry Ingram and prosecutor Reimer were whisked to a briefing chaired by a police crime analyst. Ingram knew he'd be put into police cells as a plant. He was told about the day's events by Warren's confessor, Gregg McMartin. Prospects looked dim, Ingram says, for watching the Toronto Blue Jays on TV in the World Series, an interest shared by Warren.

This was an unusual assignment, despite Ingram's credentials. First, he'd spent seventeen days in Yellowknife in 1992 with the riot squad from Red Deer, so there was a chance he'd be recognized. And Warren had confessed, hadn't refused to talk, and was already doing a "re-enactment" in the mine.

Ingram was told to be a passive but "inquisitive" listener, and to act disgusted with the government. "I would be lodged in cells for failing to pay matrimonial [support payments] and I was going to be escorted back to Red Deer in a few days," Ingram says. He was placed in a detachment cell at 6:00 P.M. on October 16.

"I can't believe I'm in here," Ingram said. "I didn't pay the old lady and I'm sitting here, beside you ..."

"Actually, you look a little more sinister," Warren replied.

"No, you." Ingram laughed, "Jesus Christ."

"Me?" Warren chuckled. "I'm going down big time."

—in RCMP cells, October 17, 1993

It was almost dawn when Warren and the police changed back into street clothes in the dry at Giant, but they did not call it a night. Instead, they drove west from Yellowknife, looking for the pond where Warren said he'd discarded his gear. At about 7:00 A.M. he pointed out a small ice-covered pond north of the road. He posed for the police photographer, pointing to where he'd thrown the bag. The next day, two divers found an old, brown canvas bag in about 2 feet of water. Its contents included a rock, two spools of fishing line, two squares of flowered bedsheet, two lantern batteries, three receptacles for 9-volt batteries, two pieces of plastic tubing, a plastic bag from Canadian Tire, a silver-gray bag simply labeled "Colleens,"[1] and a third from Home Hardware. There was no bicycle light, and no gloves, contrary to Warren's statement.

At last, Warren was checked into a cell in RCMP headquarters. He was to have no contact with anyone except the investigators; he slept for three or four hours. Two officers had been assigned to watch Warren's apartment, and surveillance was beefed up at Shearing's and Bettger's. The next step was to look for boots at Cameron Falls.

In the Warren home, Ann had just received the news, but she didn't believe it at first. "I took a shower and all of a sudden it hit me, 'Holy man, this man's in jail!' I come running out of the bathroom, 'Do we have lawyers? Do we know what we're doing? What are we doing? Let's get the hell down there!' I tell you, if I would've known that night, he would've NEVER, EVER been in there. I would've followed those cops right down there and I would've yanked him out of there." Helen and her sister told CASAW president Harry Seeton what had happened, so he set up a meeting with lawyer Austin Marshall. Back in his office, Marshall had a message to call his wife, and learned from her that the police had called about Roger Warren.

Around 3:00 P.M., twenty-five hours after McMartin began his interrogation, the police roused Warren and read him his rights, as they always did when questioning was to start. Finally, he showed interest in having a lawyer. "I got to get one, you know." They took him to a phone, but Marshall couldn't be reached, the only local lawyer he trusted. It was a blow to Warren. He felt alone among the wolves. "I just wanted to be able to contact my wife once in a while," he told the officers. He agreed to go to Cameron Falls, again hinting as they walked to a police car that he could be more difficult. "Yesterday, when I was having a coffee with my wife, she didn't know nothing about it, but I decided, 'Fuck, I'm sick of it.'"

"Sick of what?" White asked.

"Sick of this lying and bullshit."

"You just felt it was time to get it out in the open?"

"I just never did that before in my life, lying like that ..." Warren's voice cracked. He put his hand to his face and sobbed. "I hate lying. I did it for a year now. It's almost as bad as doing that, killin' those guys."

The consolation is, some guys do that kind of thing and never think twice about it, offered White.

"Most of the stuff I told you was true, but it didn't happen at that time," Warren said. He slumped out of sight as they drove past the picket line on their way to Cameron Falls. Two more cars carried members of an emergency response team for protection, McGowan says. It was a lovely, crisp fall day. Autumn leaves bowed over the boardwalk into the woods toward the river. They set off on the path, ERT officers ahead, armed to the teeth. They were almost to the falls by 4:45, when White was handed a message containing "some concerns" and instructing him to question Warren about his intent in committing the crime. White denies that it also stated that Austin Marshall was trying to reach Warren, and says that the group was out of radio contact with police headquarters.

Warren led them to a shady spot about 150 yards off the path. There was a stone fire pit right on the riverbank. "Here's where I destroyed the original boots I had when I set that blast on September 18, 1992," Warren said. "I cut them up with a gyprock knife and burned them," using a stick to fling the pieces into the water. It was sometime in late September or October, he added vaguely. The fire, he claimed, was started with some gasoline he'd carried in a plastic jug for windshield antifreeze. "I chopped it up and burned it." Moments later, he said he cut the jug up and sank it with a rock. Then he said the jug was used to put out the fire. The police did not pursue these inconsistencies.

En route to town in the car, White asked Warren if he'd like to contact a lawyer. "Not right at the moment," Warren replied with a hint of sarcasm. White then homed in on Warren's intent in setting the blast. Wouldn't 80 pounds of explosives kill the driver of an ore-train?

"It was dumb, I'll admit it, it was like reckless [and] stupid ... I didn't have any misgivings at the time. I had misgivings when I got to surface," Warren said. In retrospect, the guy might've been injured or killed, he conceded. That thought came to him as he was walking from 1-38 to Gate 6, and he considered phoning in a warning, he said—"but what if there was some lack of communication and something did happen, I'd be in a lot of trouble." He wished a million times he'd made the call, he said.

They ran through the items Warren said he'd used: braided casting line, toggle switches he'd bought for another project, some plastic tubing he'd bought at Canadian Tire "a couple of days before," forgetting that the store's grand opening was September 17. The Kamik boots were bought at Woolco about September 15, at around 11:00 A.M., he said.

On the picket line in the morning, seeing the police going into the mine, "I said, 'Holy shit, they've found this stuff.' I was heaving a sigh of relief," Warren said. Then picketer Terry Coe saw a cloud of smoke caused by a blast underground. "After that, it was total doom."

Again, Warren denied anyone else's involvement in the crime, and denied telling anyone he'd done it.

How do you feel? White asked.

"OK. Not too bad, tired."

And mentally?

"Deeply depressed," said Warren.

As the police cars passed the mine, Warren suddenly broke the silence that had fallen after White's questions. "Dale, what's going to happen to me now?" McGowan replied that prosecutor Peter Martin would come, and "we will probably lay the charge today." Your request for a lawyer and to meet your wife will be honoured, and we'll adhere to whatever your lawyer advises in your best interests, McGowan promised. "I told you that we would want to search your residence. We'll be taking a statement off your wife and family ... We will do so with the utmost compassion and professionalism." It was a good speech, but McGowan wouldn't be around to keep the promise. His lengthy sojourn in Yellowknife ended when he boarded a plane for the half-hour flight home to his wife and children in Hay River.

The car pulled into the secure bay at the detachment about 6:30 P.M., avoiding a band of reporters out front. McGowan noted that White was going to clear the interview room so Warren could call a lawyer. But it didn't happen. Some other officers and a postblast expert wanted to see Warren to clear up some things, White said, "That's OK with you?"

"I don't mind," Warren agreed. "But I would like to get hold of Austin [Marshall]." When the police asked Warren to continue, he "was nodding his head up and down, and his eyes were up," McGowan says. Then Warren said, "I got no time for fuckin' lawyers." This exchange was not taped. White turned Warren over to officers Dean Ravelli and Mike Brandford, who were waiting in the interview room with video and audio recorders ready. Brandford handed White a note, which he put in his pocket—without looking at it, he says—and then went for dinner with McGowan and Inspector Al Macintyre. The note stated that Austin Marshall had called; McGowan said as much in a taped memo made before he left the police station.

Marshall had done more than make phone calls. When he couldn't reach Warren by phone, Marshall went to the police station, where he was told that the members had Warren out for a drive and wouldn't be back until 6:00 P.M. "I asked Constable Steggles to contact those members," Marshall said. Steggles advised Marshall to leave a message. So Marshall explained that he'd had a call from Vern White, and wanted to see Warren. The reply was that "White is with Warren, and Warren hasn't asked for [you]," Marshall said. "I went back to my office." At about 5:00 P.M., Corporal Ravelli called and said that White and Warren were doing a re-enactment. Then Alex Pringle called from Edmonton. He worked with Marshall on another case against union members, including Warren. But the union executive had decided it was not wise for its lawyers to defend Warren, regardless of who paid the legal fees. The executive had only a sketchy idea of what had transpired.

Meanwhile, Brandford and Ravelli wanted "a pure virgin statement" from Roger Warren. "You have two lawyers retained—Mr. Austin Marshall and Mr. Alex Pringle," Ravelli said, and you can talk to them if you wish. But Warren agreed to talk to the investigators first, and repeated his explanation of how the explosion was set up. "I hate myself," he told them. "I still don't understand what compelled me to do it ... [I'm] definitely not a fuckin' killer, I can guarantee you that."

Then Jean-Yves Vermette arrived, the blast expert from Ottawa. A little nervously, Warren had just described the construction of the triggering mechanism to Vermette when the phone rang. It was Vern White, who'd interrupted his dinner after Inspector Macintyre told him that two lawyers were trying to contact "Roger." White says he tried in vain to reach Marshall before phoning Brandford. Finally, Marshall and Warren spoke on the phone for about fifteen minutes, after he had already spent about twenty-four of the previous twenty-nine hours talking with police.

"He said I shouldn't do any more talking," Warren said when the officers returned. "I guess my wife is quite distraught. I don't know if she wants to come and see me."

Nancy Defer has the warrant ready to search your house and car, Ravelli said. "Would you be willing to accompany us?" They left him alone while they made the arrangements.

Time was running out before Warren would have to appear before a justice of the peace, which must be done within twenty-four hours of an arrest, or as soon as practicable. JPs were available day and night. Seamus Henry was summoned, a real estate developer with just six months' experience as a JP. He walked in at 8:40, by his presence transforming the interrogation room into a courtroom. The interrogator, Brandford, represented the Crown. The JP asked Warren if he'd talked with a lawyer, and was told "one's supposed to call me," but none had been retained. Henry then read Defer's information, stating that the RCMP had grounds to believe Warren had murdered nine men, and read out the names. Brandford asked that Warren be remanded into custody until 4:00 P.M. on October 18.

"At this time, Mr. Wallace," Henry began, mistakenly using Warren's middle name, you've heard what they're asking for, would you like to have a lawyer?

"No, that's OK, I'll respond," Warren said.

"How do you feel on that?"

Warren mumbled a reply.

"OK, I will grant this wish of the Crown that you be remanded in custody." And that was it. Warren was officially back in the hands of the RCMP. Minutes later, Warren got a call from Glen Orris, the Vancouver lawyer who would joust with the system for the next several years.

Thanks to a warning from Austin Marshall, Warren's family was absent (but watching from the Hrynczuks' window across the street) while their cosy apartment swarmed with police doing a videotaped search. The camera's wide angle and crowded quarters made their home look stark, but the living room affords comfortable, intimate talk and a good view of a large television set. Most of their art is northern, by aboriginal artists. With Warren's help, the police seized his copy of the "Footsteps of a Murderer" article, a hard hat, a pair of jean coveralls, three rolls of monofilament fishing line, three pieces of plastic tubing, and a hunting knife. From his car, they took a circuit tester, a pair of pliers, a pocket knife, two toggle switches, and a roll of black electrical tape. Police described Warren as "cooperative" and "relaxed," but, to those who knew him, he looked nervous and ill at ease. Several officers searched alone after Warren's group left.

Just before 10:00 P.M., Warren landed in his cell—where Harry Ingram, the deep-voiced undercover operative, was already installed. Their cell was wired for sound; they would be together for nineteen hours. "When he came in, I would say he was stressed," Ingram says. Almost immediately, the two men bemoaned their lack of cigarettes, and Warren hadn't eaten since lunchtime. He yearned to be home, watching the ball game with Ann. But he soon asked Ingram where he was from, so the officer told his lame cover story. Pretending to learn that Warren was in for "homicide," Ingram wondered aloud how he'd "fuckin' sleep tonight. It's going to be scary." So Warren painted a quick sketch of the crime, and the labour dispute.

How did they lock you out? Ingram asked.

"They had security guards. They had fuckin' fifty riot cops from Red Deer," Warren said slyly.

Now, because of stupidity, nine men are dead, a tenth (CASAW vice president Ken Cawley) was killed in British Columbia, and "I'll be eleven. I know I could've stayed out of jail ... They had some circumstantial shit ... a hundred and some people that are left in the fuckin' union, but now I got to balance that off against my wife and two kids ... Hopefully I am not separated from my wife for the next twenty years."

Neither did Warren forget Bettger and Shearing. "There was a couple guys there, that's when they had that big story in the paper last month. Them guys had fuck all to do with it. They did a lot of other shit. Those guys didn't do it, but they tried to let on they did it. I talked to those guys. I told 'em that I wouldn't believe it, that's just bullshit."

Is there anything I can do for you, Roger? asked Ingram.

"Not much. Ha ha. Not unless you got a .22 there that won't hurt too much." Ingram was not concerned that the quip about the gun was another hint that Warren knew he was a police officer.

"How'd they know how you did it?"

"Ah, they didn't really. They got suspicious because I had these fuckin' boots. You'd be amazed how easy it is to get away with stuff if you really want to. The first thing you do is you refuse to talk to anybody, and nobody can do a fuckin' thing about it."

You can't tell nobody, Ingram agreed.

"I never did," Warren said. But that played into Witte's hands, he suggested. "The fuckin' cunt's got a reason not to take the people back, 'cause there's a murderer among us, eh. That's the only reason I [decided] to tell the cops, 'OK, I did it.' Otherwise I wouldn't have. I felt bad about the guys, and I'm responsible, but I know I didn't do it deliberately."

The next morning, Warren still hadn't heard from Helen. "Fuckin' pricks were supposed to bring my wife over to see me. I'd like to see her," Warren said. "Unless she is pissed off, I guess."

Warren's appraisal of Witte was caustic. He said that when geologist Toni Borschneck was killed by loose rock, Witte didn't care, and doesn't care about anyone. "Some guys thought she deliberately did that [blast] last year. I am not condoning any type of violence ... but none of it would've happened if it hadn't been for her ... She should stick to what she's good at, like making money ... She's not fuckin' stupid [but] she thinks she's in 1925 in Alabama or someplace. Even the Americans don't do that shit now." In Alabama now, "they're on strike but there's replacement workers. So the guys are standing out there in the fuckin' road, and a guy comes tearing out of the plant with a cop and killed two guys, eh." Finally, the cops got the replacement workers off the property, he said.

Warren complained that people were hurt during the melee of June 14, 1992, and it was "covered up ... It was collusion between this government, [the] federal government, right from the start because of this Mulroney bullshit, eh. Goddamn it, 'Canada's open for business.' Everybody's against you, the cops, the fuckin' courts and everybody; nobody's helping. That's why those other guys did stupid shit ... You get a mentality like it's a war, and you get so you think you don't have to think about the consequences."

Eventually, Warren's near monologue shifted to the tactics police were using on him. "They want to make sure you're not bullshitting, eh. But there was enough stuff in the paper ... that a smart guy could convince 'em that you did that shit ... And then a little later on, popping up with something to show that he didn't do it ... There is nothing that they can say, 'Well, this is the only guy that could've known this.'" Warren apparently feared that the RCMP did not believe his confession.

And on the morning of September 18, 1992, the company's behaviour was despicable, Warren railed. A truck passed him very slowly with two guards in it, he said. "So they knew somebody had probably been in that fuckin' mine." Workers had also gone down the ramp before 8:00 A.M., so someone had already seen the scoop that was out of place on 575, he said. "And instead of shutting down, checking ... the whole fuckin' mine," the company's concern was "get another day's production." If Terry Byberg had closed the mine for a day, Witte would have fired him, Warren said. Her attitude was, "Well fuck, it's only guys ... Just get to work, eh," Warren said.

"What the hell? Where the hell's Roger?" It was unheard of for Warren to miss a shift on the picket line without telling anyone, as he did at midnight on October 15. Blaine Lisoway was anxious about it, and kept bringing it up.

"Me 'n' Roger are as good a buddy as you're going to get in this union," he says. "I mean, I really love that guy. Roger'd tell me stuff that he'd tell nobody else; we used to do stuff together all the time, eh. We're mechanically inclined, we con-tracted, we worked all across Canada, the whole bit. I mean, a good fifteen years' difference, but Roger is ... like my father-figure." Roger was full of information and anecdotes. Picketing on graveyard shift wasn't the same without him. Lisoway finally went home to bed with no news because there was none to be had.

Acting mine manager Bill Heath wasn't so lucky; he got no sleep that night. After an early breakfast downtown with Rob Moore, the RCMP's guide for the evening, Heath called a supervisors' meeting. "The RCMP have a confession. I'm in a position to tell you who it was," Heath announced. He understood from the police that they would name Warren in a press release by 8:30 or 9:00 A.M. When the RCMP were silent, rumours spread at Giant that the man who confessed had implicated several strikers, that the RCMP had uncovered a huge conspiracy. Heath says he kept Warren's name from his staff, other than those involved the night before.

Constable Ken Morrison knocked on Noel O'Sullivan's door on Saturday afternoon, October 16. "We have to speak out of earshot of your family," Morrison said, according to O'Sullivan. In the basement, Morrison asked O'Sullivan if he'd heard what happened overnight. "No. What did take place?"

"After I take a statement from you, I will tell you," Morrison said, and went quickly to the point. "Who do you think set the blast that killed the nine people at Giant mine on September 18, 1992?"

"Roger Warren," O'Sullivan replied, and gave his reasons, based on his interpretation of the boot prints in the mine.

"We had a confession," Morrison said. "We took him underground last night and he has shown us what we want to know."

According to *Saturday Night* magazine, Morrison also asked, "Why didn't you tell us?"

"I have been telling you guys! You guys haven't been fuckin' listening," O'Sullivan said.

These things may have been said during Morrison's one-hour talk with O'Sullivan, but the RCMP's typed statement was only two pages long and did not include any such remarks.[2] The officer asked O'Sullivan about the boot prints in the mine.

"As I was walking them, it was as if I had walked behind this person before, as if I knew the person walked this style," O'Sullivan said.

"Who would that have been?" Morrison wondered.

"Roger Warren."

"What made you think these were Roger's steps?"

"The way Roger carries himself, he has kind of a hunch."

"What was unique about the stride, from the footprints?"

"They never seemed disturbed, very sure steps, didn't appear nervous ... I was visualizing how the person was carrying himself and the picture which came to mind was, I was walking behind Roger Warren," O'Sullivan said.

"Do you recall talking to anyone about your belief in these footprints?"

"Keith Murray, who was a personal friend, I talked with him and Keith felt Roger would do something like this."

This was a major turnaround by O'Sullivan. Eight days after the blast, he told the police that Al Shearing was his number-one suspect, referring to his "nonchalant step," and the sort of man he was. When the officers asked who knew the mine well, O'Sullivan hadn't even mentioned Warren.

Blaine Lisoway's reaction was total disbelief. "Saturday morning, I don't know who I talked to but they told me that Roger's nailed with the fucking murders. I couldn't believe it ... Roger's not looking well recently. I don't think Roger has a long time—he's not going to be around that long, and I think he knows," Lisoway said. "I can see him taking the rap, because Roger has such strong resolve. And Roger'd do anything to get the guys back to work. His family's all grown up and ... I could see him—maybe even turning himself in just to get it over with. We'd talked about it."

Lisoway wasn't alone. Terry Legge, who'd helped the investigators, now wondered what the police were doing. "I think they really blew it this time," he said hours after Warren's arrest. "The guy's saying that because he's had it with this shit. They would probably charge my ten-year-old, if he admitted to doing it ... Roger's health is not good. I don't think he's capable of doing it, physically—not by himself, anyway. [And] what was all this about Al and Tim? I can't believe it. It's bizarre, I've known this guy for fifteen years—he's good people." On the picket line, "he's into sitting back and having a game of crib. He would inspire me to play it cool." As he spoke, the RCMP were parked outside his home.

No details of Warren's arrest were public yet, and wouldn't be for another five months. Sergeant Dave Grundy confirmed the arrest, but refused to comment on rumours of a confession. He acknowledged that Warren's polygraph test had been inconclusive.

While people in the union hall were concerned that Warren was terminally ill, there was a new twist on the picket line. "The scabs are grinning today," said Alex Kiszenia at the main gate.

"I've dealt with Roger lots, underground," Derek Wiseman pitched in. "I've got a very bad feeling about this."

"It's very hard to accept," Terry Regimbald agreed. "Best miner I ever met. You ever see the drifts he cut? Smooth."

"I also think Roger was an attention-seeker," said Sam Pawluk. "He wanted people to listen to what he had to say."

Wiseman noted that the police had never mentioned Warren, always Al and Tim. "They told me I was a suspect."

"They told me I was a suspect," echoed Regimbald, and they had seized his Kamik boots.

"The cops are interviewing everybody who was on the line that night," Wiseman said.

Regimbald said the RCMP wouldn't lay charges against Warren "unless they had a noose around his neck. He has lived with this for such a long time, the conscience of us not getting back—can you imagine having to sleep with something like that? Maybe there is two innocent people he seen going down ... I know Roger's smart enough, if he did do it, he did it alone."

That evening, Helen Warren finally saw her husband. Forty-five minutes later, Constable Brandford interrupted. On Helen's heels was lawyer Gillian Boothroyd, in from Vancouver to help Glen Orris. Forty-six hours after his arrest on nine counts of first-degree murder, and fifty-four hours after his interrogation began, Warren met face-to-face with a lawyer.

DRAGNET

Dozens of reporters wanted a glimpse of Roger Warren. Over the weekend, they'd scrambled for anecdotes that would define his personality and image on TV and in the newspapers. Reporters considered Warren an enigmatic mass murderer, a man evidently so crafty that he'd been under the very noses of the RCMP on one of the biggest manhunts in Canadian history. The consensus was that the Mounties had finally got their man, and would leave little to chance on something this big.

The public learned little, and much of that was hard to reconcile with a murderer's conduct. Warren was a good ballplayer, hockey player, and coach. He liked to have coffee and talk with "the guys" in the old Miner's Mess on

Franklin Avenue. He wasn't a union activist; something must've gotten into him. So the stories went, and most were superficially accurate, though Warren was, and is, a strong believer in trade union principles.

Roger Wallace Warren was born December 17, 1943, in Toronto, Ontario, but grew up in Elgin, a small town near Kingston, with two brothers and two sisters. Roger's upbringing didn't fit the RCMP's psychological profile of the bomber; he'd had a normal family life. The family was short of money during Roger's final year of high school, so he quit during Grade 13 at age seventeen, despite being an able student. He went to work on a dam project for Great Lakes Power, a utility in the Sault Ste. Marie area of Ontario. He also worked on a giant traffic tunnel under the St. Lawrence River. A fellow worker took Warren under his wing, and taught him to use the big post drills that were the forerunners of the modern jumbos used at Giant and elsewhere.

As a teenager, Warren had a couple of run-ins with the law, typical of a spirited youth. On one trip to New York State in his souped-up car, Warren was arrested after a friend got in a fight over the exchange rate on the dollar. The penalty was ninety-nine days or $99, so his mother bailed him out.

He drifted around a bit, guiding on the Rideau Lakes and working as a bricklayer's helper in Sault Ste. Marie. In 1965, he drove drifts in an iron mine at Wawa, Ontario. "You blasted, removed the muck, extended the track, the pipe, you made the tunnel," he says. But he was only there about a year before returning to Southern Ontario for a stint in the sugar bush, guiding, and finally joining his father tending a marina. "That winter, we cut pulp," he remembers, "and in '67 I went to Montreal. My family had moved [there], so I went and got a job with Dow Brewery. In the spring I went out west, in '68. I got hired by Inco in Thompson [Manitoba]." There, he did production work underground, mining ore bodies and driving raises in the nickel mine. He met Helen's brother on the train to The Pas, and later went with him to Winnipeg, where he met Helen Hyrnczuk. "We started exchanging letters." Two years later they were married and she came to Thompson.

Keith Murray was working for Inco too, but not as a miner. His girlfriend and future wife used to baby-sit for the Warrens after Patricia, their eldest, was born. In 1978, Warren and Murray landed jobs mining in Snow Lake, Manitoba. They didn't stay long, but they were miners for good. They were hired on at Giant mine over the phone, and made the long trip in Murray's pickup. They were partners at Giant for another five years, earning a reputation as top-notch drift miners.

"He was my best friend for years," Murray says. "Quiet and intense would definitely describe Roger. Very opinionated. Always got to be the best at everything, and wants everybody to look up to him. He did a lot of reading, and always was up-to-date on what was happening." When Warren railed about the boss, however, it was more often Murray who tried to do something about it; Warren never filed a grievance through the union in his entire career underground. The ten-year difference in their ages and Roger's attention to family life led them in different directions, but the two men remained friends.

Warren likes to stay fit. He has an easy laugh and a lively wit. During the strike, he, Helen, and her sister Kathy were a frequent trio in the union hall. "Him and my mother are very close; they're always together," says their daughter Ann. "He was always the family type, stuck close to home. Anyone ever needed a hand, money or anything, my parents were there. And never asked for it back. That's the way my parents have always been. That's the way they raised us."

In his cell, Warren still hadn't had a shower or change of clothes since he'd gone to his interview on October 15, even after tramping through the mine. Before his court appearance on October 18, he finally got a shower. Helen had brought clean clothes.

Police at the courthouse were heavily armed that morning. The small courtroom was packed. Shane Riggs's family had arrived from British Columbia, and CBC-TV had sent a sketch artist. Warren looked tense in the accused's box, wearing his ski coat. Crown prosecutor Peter Martin introduced himself in deep, confident tones. Glen Orris, Warren's lawyer, also cut an impressive figure. A big man whose hair was but a memory, he seemed affable but very careful. For the first time, the nine first-degree murder charges were read in public. "For security reasons, it would be best if Mr. Warren were kept at the RCMP lockup," Martin said, and his request was granted.

Lynda Riggs looked as tense as Warren. "We wanted to see who this man is—we never heard of him before," she said outside, before the cameras. "I read about it in the newspaper." She'd left Yellowknife just eight weeks earlier. "You're hoping every day they're going to make arrests; you're living your life around that ... I'm not too relieved because they're going to arrest more."

Meanwhile, Ravelli, Brandford, and Warren sat in a courthouse cell to clear up a few more points. The officers had photos of the boots recovered by divers from Cameron River ("The soles were right at the foot of the rock where the fire was," a witness says. "[Warren had said] that they were heaved out into the current."); Warren seemed surprised that the pieces were so big. Tired and annoyed, he accused Royal Oak of negligence on the morning of the blast. "I came out of the portal. I knew every morning around 5:30 [or] 6:00, the truck used to come down there. I stayed until the guy came along, so they'd see me. This guy looked at me real good. Fuckin' Pinkerton's, do they give a shit? Fuck man, a guy walked out of a portal with a lamp on, I would check the place out." Besides the scooptram, he said he'd moved a Titan motor, and left all kinds of boot tracks unlike any others in the mine. "Why doesn't anybody look for anything?" The safety meeting the 750 crew had might have been phony, he said. "I'd like to know if [managers] wanted to do a few more checks before they sent the guys down." Warren's anger vented, the police returned him to his cell. It was several days before he was interviewed again, and then he told Ravelli and Brandford that he hadn't burned the boots at Cameron Falls until September 1993. He'd say the same thing in his trial a year later.

Izzie Bettger hadn't seen her husband, Tim, for two weeks. At last, he'd landed a good job as a mechanic at Buffalo Junction, south of Great Slave Lake between Hay River and Fort Resolution. It was good for him to get away from the stress and trouble in Yellowknife. While he was gone, police had continued to watch the house. Their number increased with Warren's arrest, but no one came to the door to explain. Izzie, no shrinking violet, was beside herself with worry; now the kids were back in town from their grandparents' and exposed daily to the RCMP's headlights.

The police made their move early on October 18. By 8:30, Constable Ken Morrison and a crowd of reinforcements were on their way from Hay River to see Bettger. By 9:15, four officers strode into a mechanical repair shop looking for him, while others guarded the exits.

"He's over there working on that loader," said Bettger's boss.

"What do you think I'm here for?" Morrison asked Bettger, who had a wrench in his hand.

"You're here to make trouble for me, or somebody."

"Well, you're under arrest," Morrison said, for setting the explosion at the satellite dish and the B-shaft vent. The police handcuffed Bettger and herded him to the backseat of their car.

"Morrison had this evil little spiel going on the car ride and on the airplane, about how he felt so sorry for the union," Bettger says. "He admired how I had set my life together and what a neat little family I had and how good my kids were and what a terrible mess I'd made out of all this, because they were going to do everything in their power to make sure that my life became an incredible living hell." In Hay River, a Twin Otter sat ready to fly them back to Yellowknife, normally a quick hop across the lake. But this time, Bettger says, "we were in the air for a little over an hour and Morrison is haranguing me ... At the airport, there's a small squad of guys on the tarmac, as if they figured that I intended to make the big run for it."

According to Morrison, "throughout the trip back to Yellowknife, Bettger was spoken to, however did not choose to return the conversation." If he had, he might well have simply replied, "Fuck off," as Constable Bill Farrell says Bettger did later, in the holding cell of the courthouse. "I knew he was angry," Farrell says. "I spoke to him about taking responsibility for his actions."

Meanwhile, "Little Buddy," as Bettger sometimes called Al Shearing, got similar treatment. He had seen extra police parked near his apartment all weekend, so he wasn't surprised when they snatched him at work in the boiler room of a Yellowknife high school. At about 9:30 A.M., "there were three uniform RCMP, three undercover RCMP, and one woman," he says. "They put handcuffs on me." Shearing was read his charges during the short ride to the RCMP cells. Among his effects was a list of license numbers of unmarked police trollers that he had noticed about town. "Doing some surveillance, are we?" Farrell asked.

Austin Marshall wasn't immediately available, so the RCMP said that "this was the only time I would get to come clean," Shearing says. "I said I didn't have anything to come clean for. They said I should take the bull by the horns and deal with it, like Roger Warren, that I should apologize to the membership of my union and their families for what I put them through. 'Other arrests are going on right now,' [Constable Farrell] said, 'even your own brothers from your union told on you and Tim.'" Shearing says that Farrell accused him of helping Warren set the blast, and couldn't understand why he wouldn't take the polygraph if he was innocent. "[He] said, 'You should have taken one so your name would not be on the suspect list.' I said that I would not help them, and that I would not give them the sweat off my left nut. This kind of questioning went on from 9:30 to 1:00."

Only two reporters saw Shearing enter the courthouse, wearing his leather mine-rescue jacket. "[The cop] asked me if I have ever been scared in my life. I said, 'I don't think so.'

"'Aren't you scared when you go down to rescue somebody underground?'

"'No,' I said, 'I'm trained for this and I would not put myself or any of my team in danger.'

"'What do you feel now?' he said.

"'I feel nervous because of the prefab information that you guys have put against me.'

"'That doesn't make you scared?'

"'No, I'll take my chances in court,' I said. Then Austin came. He said we should hold off until Monday for a bail hearing because of all the things that were going on with Roger, that the police are doing this Hollywood style."

The RCMP had a press conference in city hall at 1:00 P.M., announcing their arrest before Shearing and Bettger were arraigned. Besides reporters, most of the city's aldermen, some Chamber of Mines executives, Harry Seeton with labour lawyers Leo McGrady and Gina Fiorillo, and a few curious citizens were in the crowd. Sergeant Dave Grundy lowered the boom on the CASAW commandos with his list of charges, most of them for incidents in 1992. Both Bettger and Shearing were accused of breaking into the mine on June 29, painting graffiti, and stealing explosives; blowing a hole in the satellite dish with Magnafrac stick powder on July 22; and setting the September 1 explosion at the B-shaft vent shack. Bettger was also charged with possession of explosives on September 19, with intent to endanger life; possession of an illegal sawed-off shotgun on March 30, 1993; and threatening to kill a replacement worker on August 26, 1993. These and other charges were still under investigation, Grundy said.

Peter Martin was again at the helm for the Crown when Shearing and Bettger went to court that afternoon, still in their work clothes. Bettger's hair was flattened from wearing a ball cap and Shearing sported a CASAW baseball shirt and sweatpants. Again, the courtroom was packed.

Outside, Izzie Bettger sobbed. She and the kids had arrived early with a friend; Izzie wanted to see her husband. "A tall guy in a suit was shaking his head, no, no," she said. After going downstairs, they came back to find a long queue to get into court, and "they wouldn't let me in until after we caused a stink ... I'm only sorry I let [Constable] Ken Morrison see me cry." The harassment was minor but symbolic: the Riggs family arrived after them, but was ushered right into court, even though the charges were unrelated to Shane's death.

It was a banner day for the RCMP, the crowning glory of a $3.6-million investigation. As for the labour movement in the Northwest Territories, it was the entry into "our last stage of purgatory," said Federation of Labour president Jim Evoy.

CHAPTER SEVEN

"A CRUEL WASTE OF TIME"

I think we're sitting on a powder keg. Partly, it's psychology. These guys are taking the fall for the rest of us ... If it hadn't been for the violence, we would have been shut out, until it was too late—nobody would've paid any attention to us. That's a horrible thing.

—a union member's spouse, October 22, 1993

The union never condoned any sort of premeditated violent acts. Therefore, we can in no way be involved in the defense of our members who are accused of it.

—CASAW president Harry Seeton, October 25, 1993

There was so much pressure put on the RCMP, in conjunction with the anniversary of the blast. They were under tremendous pressure from Ottawa.

—Bob Robertson, March 22, 1995

Al Shearing and Tim Bettger were arrested a week before election day, as if Brian Mulroney's failing government was putting the lid on at least one can of worms. News from Yellowknife briefly replaced pre-election hype in the national spotlight before the Progressive Conservative party was all but erased from the electoral map.

In an October 18 press release, Bill Heath expressed Royal Oak's grief and sadness that "one of its former employees, Roger Warren, has been charged with nine counts of first-degree murder ... Two other former employees [were] arrested for seven acts of violence against the company during the ongoing labour dispute." Heath listed some of the charges and noted that Al Shearing had been active in CASAW's executive since 1980. Then he pulled out the stops:

> *Several other members and past members of the union executive, and shop stewards, have been charged either civilly or criminally for their activities during this labour dispute. There is still great concern about other ongoing criminal investigations. The RCMP has stated that everything from broken windows to more serious violent crimes continue to be under investigation. We cannot be entirely at ease until all crimes committed during the strike have been solved and charges have been laid. While it has not been confirmed by the RCMP, should additional arrests be made for other crimes, they too may involve CASAW members.*

> *Royal Oak wishes to express its sympathy toward other members of the Canadian labour movement who have stood squarely behind CASAW ... Particular concern is felt for the Canadian Auto Workers who have dedicated many of their resources in an effort to find a resolution to the dispute. Concern is also felt for those local unions who have supported the strike through the adopt-a-family program ... There is also relief felt for the families of the victims of the explosion. Royal Oak President M.K. (Peggy) Witte has committed to personally contacting family members over the next few days to express her personal relief that this tragic chapter can now be closed ...*

> *[On October 7th], the Company raised the issue of the tremendous violence which has been aimed at the Company by the union and its members. The company now takes the stance that until the RCMP can confirm all charges have been laid in conjunction with the outstanding acts, it would be inappropriate to discuss our position with respect to collective bargaining.*

> *... The Company feels vindicated that our concerns about returning to*

the bargaining table with CASAW have been legitimate. We believe more than ever that this union is not part of the mainstream of the Canadian labour movement and does not represent the true wishes of its membership. Royal Oak will soon call upon the federal Minister of Labour to undertake a complete investigation of this local union and its illegal activities during this strike.

With that, Royal Oak bid farewell to the labour movement's support for CASAW, may it rest in peace. Game, set, match to Peggy Witte, at long last.

The message was met with indignation. "When northern workers are on legal strike, we support them," said Jim Evoy at the NWT Federation of Labour. "We don't pick and choose what's trendy." Hemi Mitic of the CAW was no less firm. "They're trying to split the CAW from CASAW," but it won't happen, he said. "I'll be happy when we can ink a document that starts putting our people back to work."

Yellowknife's crisis atmosphere began to lift after the arrests. To most people "Giant" was again a labour dispute, not a murder mystery. If their neighbours weren't terrorists or killers, they should be allowed to work again. The picket shacks were full, and "the guys" were seasoned and hard to provoke. With the return of winter and the end of summer work, picket pay was again a crucial lifeline. But now, men on the line could visualize an end to it.

Union members could not shake the police, however. They were now re-interviewing men who had been on the picket line on September 17—or at least some of them. Picket captain Burke Driscoll was apparently never interviewed until after all the arrests, despite being in charge of the line. Terry Coe and Brian Drover, who had seen Warren on the morning of September 18, and another man who saw him at about 2:00 A.M. at Gate 3, were thoroughly and suggestively interrogated. They would eventually testify in Warren's trial. Corporal Vern White tried to get Harry Seeton in for an interview, but he refused. The RCMP also continued to interview Noel O'Sullivan about Warren's history at Giant mine.

In jail, Bettger and Shearing were kept apart on orders from the RCMP, while Warren was moved to maximum security in Edmonton. The police did it "just to fuck around" with him, he says. Helen Warren says the NWT's new justice minister, Steve Kakfwi, signed the paper approving the transfer. "It was comical when I got to Edmonton," Roger Warren says. "They looked at that order, and said, 'What fucking idiot signed this?'" Warren says he was held in "the tank" and inmates thought he was a sex offender. Guards finger sex offenders at Edmonton Max, he says, and inmates wrap catalogs around their midriffs to keep from getting stabbed.

In the week that Warren was gone, rumours swirled in Yellowknife. He had confessed, he had cancer, he was suicidal and had slashed his wrists, his wife wasn't told where he was for days after he'd been moved. Those who knew the truth kept quiet.

Warren, Bettger, and Shearing felt their isolation, right down to the issue of who would defend them in court. Helen Warren said that the RCMP didn't like the idea of hotshot Vancouver lawyer Glen Orris taking her husband's case. "They've made it quite clear they want a legal-aid lawyer," she said. Hanging over the heads of all three men were the costs, because there would be no assistance from CASAW. "The union would not put up bail for me and Tim," Shearing wrote in his journal. In court, Austin Marshall announced that he could not defend Bettger and Shearing, who urged their wives not to criticize the union. "We are still hunting pig," Shearing wrote. They also sent a note to June Roberts, who was upset about the union's position. "We appreciate your efforts. However, we want you to stop. All is not what it seems." It was signed, "Weasel and the Bear." Soon after, Izzie Bettger put their house up for sale.

The feeling that the labour dispute might end had sneaked across the picket line, but the GMEA and Jim O'Neil had not yet accepted defeat. His membership was "very uptight," now that the Canada Labour Relations Board had ruled that the GMEA was company-dominated and unfit to represent workers. O'Neil seemed shell-shocked. His lawyer missed the deadline for an appeal, but O'Neil claimed that it had been filed with the Federal Court of Canada after the labour board ruled that strikebreakers could not vote. After the employer-domination ruling, O'Neil insisted that it would be appealed too. But there was no appeal; the GMEA was finished.

The end of the labour dispute came at marathon hearings of the CLRB in early November. It was the same panel that had heard O'Neil's application against CASAW; led by the same controversial chairman, Ted Weatherill, in the same conference room in the Yellowknife Inn.

This time, however, Royal Oak was on trial, charged by the union with failure to bargain in good faith. CASAW's case appeared overwhelming. Even IIC commissioners Vince Ready and Don Munroe had slammed Royal Oak in their final report, released six weeks earlier. But union members kept their hopes in check, haunted by the CLRB's unorthodox decision in May. Union lawyers Leo McGrady and Gina Fiorillo were determined to unearth so much evidence that even the most procompany CLRB member couldn't deny it.

The lawyers had scarcely unpacked before Harry Seeton, Hemi Mitic, and Bill Heath huddled in the hallway of the hotel. When Heath left, they were joined by Fiorillo and McGrady . "The company wants to make a comprehensive offer," but the document wasn't completed yet, Mitic said. McGrady believed the company was trying to whip up some last-minute good faith, but off-the-record meetings dominated the first two days of the hearings. Royal Oak's proposal never reached union hands, but it was lying around in C-dry at the mine, according to a line-crosser who had a copy.

McGrady and Fiorillo had a formidable foe in Michael Coady, Royal Oak's labour lawyer from Vancouver. Coady worked at Ladner Downs (as had then-prime minister Kim Campbell), and had been around about as long as McGrady. They'd tangled frequently and respected each other's talents. Compared to the false politeness of many court proceedings, their honest rudeness over the nine days of hearings was almost refreshing. Their fencing was natural, given the tension in the room and the stakes riding on the hearing. Peggy Witte was there, sunny and casual, but not entirely at ease in a crowd of fifty to 100 union loyalists who detested her. At her side was board member and lawyer Bill Sheridan.

For the first day and a half, Coady seemed intent on stalling the hearing with procedural wrangling and requests for adjournment to examine new documents. The CLRB had scheduled only three days for the hearing. At first, Weatherill appeared sympathetic to Coady, but he suddenly curtailed delaying tactics. "These proceedings ... will now continue without adjournment until this matter has been concluded," Weatherill announced sharply. "As Christmas approaches we may change that view, but we are very serious about proceeding." There were smiles on the union side; for once, "CLRB" was not synonymous with delay.

McGrady called six witnesses in four days. Coady refused to accept newspaper articles as evidence, so McGrady subpoenaed three journalists (including the authors) to testify to some of the juicier statements by Witte, Smrke, and other Royal Oak officials. There was Witte's comment, in the second week of the dispute, that the use of replacement workers "could break a union," although that wasn't Royal Oak's intent. She had suggested to reporters in January 1993, right after the GMEA's application to dislodge CASAW, that CASAW didn't represent the workers at Giant.

Local CASAW president Harry Seeton spent a grueling day and a half on the witness stand, but most of his testimony was already public knowledge. The strain of having 200 people depending on his words was etched into his face, and he looked uncomfortable without his customary baseball cap. Coady tripped up Seeton several times, building one of his major lines of defense that Royal Oak may have been a hard-nosed bargainer, but the union had stubbornly toughened its negotiating stance when it should have known it was losing the strike/lockout.

The first revelations came when Hemi Mitic took the stand. Until then, few people knew the extent of Royal Oak's demands. The company's insistence that it would *never* sign an agreement with CASAW but only with the CAW, for example, had been a well-kept secret. So were demands that returning strikers would be on probation for a year and would have to be cleared by the RCMP before coming back to work, and that as many as thirty more unnamed strikers would not be allowed back.

For hours, Coady attempted damage control in cross-examination. Hadn't the company dropped some of its most provocative demands during the summer? Hadn't the union demanded an extension of the old contract, as late as May 1993? Mitic parried every question. And if Royal Oak had dropped any demands, that was news to him.

The highlight of the hearing came when Royal Oak called its only witness, Peggy Witte. She had joked with Sheridan, Coady, and Heath during the union's case; talked to reporters about Royal Oak's expansion plans; and asked about union members, such as Kurt Lehniger, who had tried to get her to bargain.

On the stand, Witte smiled and spoke with great conviction, almost as if she were selling the CLRB on a new investment. This labour dispute shattered her own daily life, she said. "I've had to live in fear ... I've received death threats in the mail [and] on the phone. My phone is tapped by the RCMP. My husband's life has been threatened. I've been phoned in the middle of a dinner party and told there's a bomb in my car outside. I can understand what my employees have gone through." She was on the verge of tears. To listen to Witte, all Royal Oak's actions from the day it bought Giant weren't just reasonable, they were essential. Anyone who disagreed with her was a bit slow-witted, and needed to hear her explanations again. A typical example came on cross-examination, when McGrady grilled her about Royal Oak's demand for additional firings of unnamed strikers.

"Are you not seeking the union's agreement that fifteen of its members in addition to the forty-five are terminated?" McGrady prodded.

"No, we are not seeking the union's agreement that those people be terminated automatically," Witte answered. "We are seeking someone from the union to sit down with the company and go over the list of people and discuss the lists and *understand*—take the time to *understand* what the company's concerns are about these individuals."

"And what if they don't understand, what will you do then? Will you fire them?" McGrady asked with false gentleness.

"Somehow it is up to us to make the union understand, put forth arguments so that the union will understand what our position is," Witte replied. The possibility that CASAW might understand perfectly but simply disagree didn't seem to occur to her.

McGrady extracted two interesting bits of hard evidence from Witte. First, she was personally involved in providing a list of labour lawyers to Jim O'Neil, just weeks into the dispute. But Witte said she had no idea who wanted the list or why. "It could have been for any employee or group of employees," she said. "Many times when an employee has a marital problem or has problems and comes to the company asking if we could refer them to the legal community, we do that."

"But you don't hire a labour lawyer for matrimonial problems, I would hope?" McGrady needled.

"That wasn't the point, Mr. McGrady," Witte replied sourly.

Second, Witte produced a list of additional strikers Royal Oak hoped to fire or get rid of with a severance package. The twenty-one people listed were a who's who of union activists who hadn't yet been fired. At the top of the list was Harry Seeton—a decision based largely on allegations that he had threatened Jim O'Neil in a heated argument at work, a month before the strike/lockout began. The list also included Seeton's predecessor, Bill Schram; the local's secretary-treasurer, Bob Kosta; the union cochair of the mine's health and safety committee, Bonnie Nordahn; her husband, Ben, a member of CASAW's original bargaining committee; and two more of the local's executives. And Kurt Lehniger, whose face went pale when he learned about it. He was insulted and hurt, and believed that the reason must have been his age and the toll that his work had taken on his body.

More damning evidence came with the insight Witte offered into her thinking about the union. McGrady asked her, for example, about Royal Oak's suggestion on June 6, 1992, that strikers could make up for the company's strike costs to date by working Saturdays for free. Witte insisted the demand was serious, not a provocation or an attempt at humour. "That's one of the suggestions I made, but I also suggested that somehow the relationship between the company and the bargaining unit should improve," Witte said. Not content to just answer the question, she volunteered, "That is what I thought was happening as a result of shaking hands and signing the tentative agreement. And when the tentative agreement was voted down, it took the *faith* away from us that the relationship would ever be resolved again." It was a poor choice of words for a chief executive officer accused of bargaining in bad faith, and it came early in Witte's cross-examination. She chafed under the ebb and flow of pressure from McGrady, and looked very grim. Her face and eyes grew red until she was almost in tears. McGrady sensed it, and eased his aggressive tone.

By November 10, after eight very long days of hearings, the lawyers closed their respective cases. Though both were exhausted, they might have gone on for several more days except that Ted Weatherill berated McGrady. "The facts of this case are not that contentious," he snapped. "Drawn-out hearings with repetitive evidence do not help us at all." Weatherill apologized to McGrady the next day, but the message was clear. So clear, in fact, that Coady and Royal Oak decided not to call any more witnesses.

The moment Coady and McGrady finished their closing arguments, Weatherill stated that this time the CLRB would rule quickly. He promised to have the decision ready by the next afternoon, November 11. "Uh-oh, I don't like the sounds of this!" Coady muttered to himself.

So, on Remembrance Day, most strikers still in Yellowknife crowded into the hearing room. It was a holiday and many brought their families. There was an expectant hush as the crowd braced for a half hour of legalese.

"It is our hope that the order which we will shortly announce will bring an end to the industrial dispute which has caused so much havoc in this community," Weatherill read in a precise, almost paternal voice. Allowing the suspense to build, he outlined the evidence. "The evidence is uncontradicted that [union] concessions were necessary if any realistic hope of continuing the mine's operations were to be maintained," he said, to a few grumbles. Nonetheless, union members had every right to vote down the April 18 tentative agreement, he added. "This would appear to have shocked and outraged the company, whose management, although experienced in achieving very good results in mining operations, were not experienced in collective bargaining."

Reporters scribbled furiously at the press table, while the strikers barely moved. The packed room was silent.

Weatherill threw in some barbs about the union's bargaining tactics, accusing CASAW of occasional bad faith and "irrationally optimistic and obviously unacceptable positions."

But the harshest words were reserved for Royal Oak, which was guilty of at least four bad-faith violations, Weatherill said. First, refusing to bargain during the GMEA's application was illegal. The CLRB, not the employer, determines which union represents workers. More importantly, Royal Oak's position on the forty-five fired strikers (and the extra twenty-one it wanted to dismiss) was also illegal. Witte's argument that she might be held legally liable if any of the strikers were arbitrated back to work and violence ensued underground was sincere but not persuasive, Weatherill said. "The fallacy in this argument ... is that it assumes the guilt of the persons concerned, or perhaps more precisely, it asserts the jurisdiction of the company to be both accuser and judge." There is a risk that an arbitrator might make a mistake and allow a dangerous worker back into the mine, Weatherill conceded. But, he decreed, the rule of law and justice for the fired strikers is more important, and it is not unusual for arbitrators to evaluate similar risks every day. As a seasoned arbitrator himself, Weatherill was probably offended by Royal Oak's distrust of his profession.

Royal Oak had bargained in bad faith on at least two other issues, by suggesting a probation clause that discriminated between strikers and nonstrikers, and by proposing a one-year probation clause, Weatherill noted. To be legal, all Canadian collective agreements must include access to arbitration to resolve union–management disputes. Royal Oak's probation clause would have denied arbitration for firings.

Generally, when a company is convicted of bad-faith bargaining, labour boards order the company to comply with the law and resume bargaining. To do that in this case, Weatherill said, "would be an unrealistic and even a cruel waste of time."

When CASAW first filed the bad-faith complaint, it asked for heavy damages from Royal Oak for prolonging the dispute. At the hearing, McGrady stated that the union's main goal was a collective agreement, and dropped the request for compensation. Weatherill told Royal Oak to accept Ready and Munroe's final IIC report, table a full contract proposal based on the April 18 tentative agreement, bargain in good faith with respect to four issues—including wages, benefits, and safety inspections—and prepare for arbitration hearings on the fired strikers.

"The violence and tragedy that has been associated with this dispute has had a devastating effect on this close-knit, openhearted and spirited northern city that is Yellowknife ... Good luck to all of you," Weatherill concluded.

The CLRB had finally quit its dithering. Errors and political infighting had worked against the union for months, and this realization probably influenced Weatherill's ultimate ruling. Internal CLRB documents on the Giant case and others reveal that, until then, he had played a disgraceful game of political football rather than take effective action—at the expense of workers and employers who depend on the labour board. The root causes of the board's near-paralysis were philosophical differences, personality conflicts, and poorly qualified appointments by the Mulroney government. But now, with the way paved by Ready and Munroe, Weatherill's panel had made a just solution to Canada's most tragic industrial dispute in decades.

There were no whoops of joy. But the strikers and their families, many of them crying quietly, rose and gave Weatherill what was probably the longest standing ovation of his career. Then they crowded around McGrady and Fiorillo, congratulating and thanking them. Fighting a terrible cold as well as the company's case, Fiorillo got dozens of long hugs. "I will always treasure that," she says. Fiorillo was riding a wave. This was her first big case, she had become a member of Local

4 at heart, and the decision was more than an end to a labour dispute. Combined with the plenary ruling on Decision 1010, she had helped thwart the legal use of permanent strikebreakers under the Canada Labour Code. Giant mine had almost become a domino in the history of union busting, along with President Ronald Reagan's rout of the air-traffic controllers in the United States, or Phelps Dodge's destruction of unions in the Arizona copper belt. This, in a northern land on the verge of a mining boom, where entire peoples had been colonized, let alone the workforce. There was no winning a labour dispute like Giant's, but in their arena Fiorillo and McGrady had won. The victory was so sweet because of what it meant to people Fiorillo loved.

Most union families were in a daze. After a year and a half, it was over. Maybe life would return to normal. They hadn't beaten Witte into submission, but they had survived with their union intact. Their broad smiles were more of relief than jubilation.

"There's no thought in our minds of going back and making hardships," Harry Seeton told reporters, the usual fire gone from his voice. "We're just happy to go back to work and we want to get back producing gold again."

On the company side, Bill Heath was depressed and annoyed. Not only had Royal Oak lost, but the only supervisor who'd even bothered to show up—despite the Remembrance Day holiday—was his secretary. "I thought that was a real sad comment," Heath says, something he never understood. Royal Oak had gone to great expense to bring in strikebreakers and security, in part so supervisors could keep their jobs, but they showed no gratitude. "I don't think that the staff truly appreciated the stance that Peggy took ... I don't think that they realized the toll that she paid."

BACK TO WORK

The IIC's final report, which set up the CLRB's ruling, provided for a last round of negotiations on wages, benefits, and safety inspections. Royal Oak still wanted concessions, including an across-the-board wage cut of 3 percent. Within hours the two sides decided to leave the final ruling to Ready and Munroe; union leaders say that Royal Oak still refused to bargain.

The two commissioners took several weeks to rule on the outstanding issues. Workers' benefits would be less than those specified by the April 18 tentative agreement. There were only two improvements. The length of safety inspections was doubled, and there would be recourse to Ready and Munroe if problems developed. Wages returned to predispute levels, except those for a few unskilled jobs; for those, returning strikers and CASAW members who had crossed the line would get the old rate. But strikebreakers who stayed on would be paid the lower rate that Royal Oak instituted during the dispute.

Royal Oak sent recall letters to the strikers on November 19. Two days later, the picketers took down their signs. The gigantic "Scab on the run!" rat sign was given a place of honour in CASAW's union hall, to the annoyance of line-crossers and strikebreakers who would soon pay union dues. Picket shacks were towed away and raffled off. Historic graffiti remains on at least one of the shacks. "Please remember, picketers, that the replacement workers are only in there to save our jobs!" one wag had written, in reference to Witte's line a year and a half earlier that strikers should be thankful the strikebreakers were there to prevent Giant's permanent closure. "The Termination of this Strike will be accidental," another picketer had predicted.

Malaise and unhappiness were common behind the picket line. Until the recalled strikers had all reported in, no one knew how many would actually return and how many strikebreakers would get walking papers. Witte promised to hire as many as she could at the Colomac mine north of Yellowknife, which she'd bought a few months earlier and planned to reopen in 1994. But few men relished working in an open-pit operation out on the tundra, where they would live in bunkhouses and not see their families for weeks at a time. Most shifters were uneasy, and some were afraid to work with the strikers again. For months they'd gossiped about the violence that was bound to erupt underground between union loyalists and "scabs." Two shifters quit before anyone even knew how many CASAW men would be back.

Acting mine manager Bill Heath, not normally a worrier, lay awake at night. He says he was sure someone would be hurt or killed, maybe even on the first day the workforces mingled. But on December 1, when the first strikers returned to work, nothing happened. Ready and Munroe had made it clear that using the word "scab" at the mine could get a man fired. Heath and other supervisors also gave stern lectures to strikebreakers about not provoking incidents. A couple of weeks later, Heath braced for the return of the underground workers. In the dark depths, where men are far apart and conditions dangerous, it would be easy to arrange an "accident." Witte herself had been saying so for more than a year. Shifter Martin Kolenko, a crusty Croatian Canadian, former union president, and best friend of blast victim Joe Pandev, told Heath not to worry. "Tomorrow will be like any other day. Nothing will happen." And he was right.

"It was very strange," says Bruce Bannister, head of the bargaining committee that signed the April 18 agreement, "just being able to walk through that gate ... Then go back to the hoist room, which I hadn't seen for a year and a half. Here's a scab who's been doing it for six months going to teach me how to hoist ... I just told him, 'Get off my hoist and stay off it,' and he did."

Things went better than everyone expected at the mine. Most of the union men who strode in and out of the security shack in the cold, predawn blackness looked as if this was routine, except that they toted their gear. But that wasn't how they felt. "It's weird," one said. "I never thought I'd be back in here again."

There were some minor, nonviolent incidents. Talk between strikebreakers and union stalwarts was no more than needed to do their jobs. But there were some ugly scenes downtown. CASAW's recording secretary, Rob Wells, was assaulted by a displaced strikebreaker he didn't know. Later, a contractor was beaten by union supporters and, according to some reports, stripped to his undershorts outside the Gold Range bar.

A few union loyalists were so disgusted at having to work with the "job thieves" that they quit after one shift, or stayed just long enough to bump a replacement worker out of a job before leaving. Several went to work at Con mine; one operated a locksmith business. Others kept their new jobs with the phone company, computer store, or cable TV, satisfied to accept much lower wages than they could get at Giant in exchange for their escape.

The union's huge legal bills had to be paid, and now strikebreakers and CASAW's line-crossers would share the cost of squashing the GMEA, among other things. At a CASAW membership meeting just before their return to work, union dues were boosted to ten hours of pay per month. It was a drastic but commonly used solution. CASAW spent over $4 million during the dispute, including the adopt-a-family program and strike pay. Bob Kosta, a shaft maintenance man, accounted for it all to the auditors.

The dues hike sparked a last attempt by CASAW opponents to decertify the union. Nick Luzny, a CASAW member who crossed at the very start of the dispute, followed in Jim O'Neil's footsteps and set up the NWT Miners' Association. Their meeting was attended by many CASAW loyalists. Tense arguments ensued, but it was a step forward—the two sides were talking. When the new group applied for certification, the CLRB dismissed the raid attempt. Raids are allowed only in the absence of a collective agreement, or three months before an agreement expires.

Even as strikers returned to work, Royal Oak maintained that no collective agreement was in effect, and that the CLRB's order ending the dispute was illegal. Royal Oak's lawyers asked the Federal Court of Canada in Ottawa for a stay of the CLRB's order, the same day that most of the miners returned. The judge threw the case out of court.

Harry Seeton resigned as CASAW Local 4's president in mid-December, after some union friends gave him a rousing birthday party. Seeton had endured the stress of leadership for too long and finally gave it up, but his swift retirement could have been construed as a peace offering of sorts. Vice President Rick Cassidy assumed Seeton's post, which helped soothe the feelings of supervisors and strikebreakers. Cassidy, an even-tempered Nova Scotian who worked in the mill, was on the bargaining committee that originally recommended the April 18 tentative agreement, and he had maintained his reputation as a moderate.

When the dust settled after the arbitrations, CASAW loyalists accounted for about 65 percent of the workforce. CASAW's leaders seemed confident that the union's effectiveness in dealing with Royal Oak would win over the strikebreakers. Unionists claimed that several "scabs" approached CASAW loyalists after returning to work to say that working for Royal Oak without union protection was "hell." To add credence to the union claim, even strike-breakers who left Giant for the Colomac mine became union members after a few months. The Steelworkers organized Royal Oak's latest mine—the first fly-in, fly-out operation in the Northwest Territories to get a union, and the first of this type in Canada for the previous ten years. Fly-in operations are particularly resistant to unionization because it is difficult for organizers to set up shop at the campsite. Steel's success heralded an era of increased union organizing in the Northwest Territories, but collective agreements were slow in the making. Colomac's workforce finally ratified a deal in late 1996.

THE QUEEN'S COWBOYS

The labour dispute was far from over for the RCMP and the courts. Dockets were clogged with strike-related cases. One man was jailed for a failed attempt to set fire to a power pole in June 1992, another was fined for throwing rocks at a car; the same strikebreaker whose runaway truck ploughed into an occupied security shack was arrested for impaired driving in town.

Tim Bettger and Al Shearing had a hearing for a bail release on November 22. Before their arrest, "both of the accused had been subject to continuous twenty-four-hour surveillance, both visual and electronic," at tremendous public cost, Crown prosecutor Dennis Claxton told the court. The RCMP had deemed that necessary for the safety of the community. After nine men were killed on September 18, Bettger "continued to make bombs and prepare war. Mr. Bettger has shown himself to be a violent person," fully supported by Mr. Shearing, who "has no respect for court orders [and] is a dangerous person." Claxton predicted that they would be convicted of most of the charges against them. He said that Shearing had admitted doing the graffiti run of June 29 to an investigator with the RCMP Public Complaints Commission, confirming that information from the independent tribunal was obtained by the RCMP. In June, before Shearing and Bettger were arrested, they had the "unmitigated gall" to do "countersurveillance" by recording RCMP license-plate numbers while sitting in a pickup in the City Hall parking lot.

Bettger's and Shearing's lawyer pointed out that the two men had been free for months before their arrest, and had done nothing wrong since their alleged crimes. The judge from Alberta took a month to decide to keep them in jail. His decision, made on December 22, was not relayed to the two men until Christmas Eve.

If agent Bob Robertson could have spoken, he would have agreed with the judge and Claxton. Robertson returned to Yellowknife soon after Warren's arrest, and was dumbfounded by what had transpired. "Right up until Roger's arrest, the [police] were gearing for Shearing and Bettger, based on all the evidence they had collected ... In my discussion with my handlers, they were expecting Roger to implicate the others. They didn't want Roger, they wanted Al! He was the bigger fish they wanted. And they had wanted him from day one. Roger was a mistake. He dropped into their laps. They took him because there was so much pressure, they had to go with something.

"Right after they arrested Roger, I was in the Gallery [bar], and they were in there celebrating, all the RCMP. [Constable] Morrison comes up, and puts his arm around me, he was really pissed. And I says, 'Are you fucking nuts? Showing that you even associate with me, in a place like the Gallery!' It was packed. But they were patting themselves on the [back]—a job well done," Robertson says. "This is bullshit, guys; the emperor's got no clothes on. Maybe you guys are buying it, but I've been working too closely with you all these months to buy it. And you're telling me all of this stuff now is bullshit, what you were telling me? No way! You wouldn't have given me this information if you thought it was bullshit."

Gordie Kendall, the jaded ex-con, was arrested in Vancouver on November 12 and popped into jail in Yellowknife with some other strikers, including Bettger and Shearing. The group had many visitors and the mood was initially amiable. Shearing and Bettger say that Kendall bragged to them and several others about smuggling guns and cigarettes across the Canada–US border, and about links to the Hells Angels in BC's Lower Mainland.[1] Shearing says it sounded like "more bullshit" from Kendall, except for the missing Hells Angels insignia on the jacket of the man who had met Bettger in the mall in BC and taken the envelope.[2]

Soon after this, "Al was working in the kitchen. I'd done my morning shift, and I was sitting on a window sill reading a book," Bettger says. "Kendall comes along and makes the most incredible offer—he said, not everybody had to go down for this thing. He said he could guarantee me $3,000 a week if I would go along with him, and basically sell out Al. And all I had to do was drive back and forth across the border up in the mountain passes with a snowmobile and a sled, hauling cigarettes one way and guns the other." Bettger says he wrote all this down and gave his notes to his lawyer.

Then things cooled off, Shearing says. "When [Kendall's] lawyer come in with the disclosure materials, he put two and two together—'Well, if I got the disclosure material, those guys must have the disclosure material.' So he never talked to us again." Bettger and Shearing suspect that Kendall's two-week stay in jail before he went to court was a police ploy, probably to implicate them in the murders, with or without Roger Warren's involvement in the crime. Kendall insists that this was not the case.

Kendall appeared in court on November 30. Crown prosecutor Dennis Claxton struck a different note than he had with Bettger and Shearing. Kendall pleaded guilty to a charge of break and entry for planning the June 29 graffiti raid; a charge for theft of explosives was dropped. "Mr. Kendall began to recruit fellow members of the union to enter the mine," Claxton said. "The plan was they would paint slogans on various equipment and the walls." Kendall bought some bolt cutters and "there were meetings between the accused and people he recruited." Kendall also pleaded guilty to throwing a rock that broke a window of a Royal Oak truck on June 14, 1992, the day of the riot. Claxton asked for a six-month sentence.

A legal aid lawyer pointed out that Kendall had been interviewed by the RCMP six times and they "have been in constant communication. He has been candid and forthright and cooperative. He's saved the Crown and the justice system considerable time and effort and resources. Mr. Kendall has shown remorse."

Kendall was sentenced to three months in jail. Bettger, Shearing, and another man who'd backed out of the graffiti run were perplexed by Kendall's guilty plea. He had not planned the raid, so why confess to it? They wondered what Kendall was up to.

Meanwhile, the RCMP interviewed people about Roger Warren, such as his former partner, Keith Murray. Warren had some visitors in jail, but not many. His lawyer warned that visitors were likely to hear from the police, and that was an effective deterrent. "The first little while, guys would say they didn't think I did it, but if I did, they didn't give a fuck," Warren says. He was thankful for the visits, and the support shown to his family.

Shearing and Bettger were repeatedly refused visits with Warren by jail officials. Finally, they passed him a note through an inmates' inspection committee. Four days after the union's underground crews returned to work, Warren sent a reply to some of their questions. It was December 24, the same day Bettger and Shearing learned their own bail had been refused.

Dear Tim & Al.

All I can say, guys, is that I've tried to see you guys since your first message. I put in requests too and was flatly denied.

I feel responsible in part for your predicament as well as mine. I don't know how much I can say, as Glen [Warren's lawyer] is still studying everything.

I will say this much. I think we would still be on strike if I hadn't "confessed." I could have walked away anytime I felt like it and did on [sic] 3:30 on Oct. 15, because like you guys they wouldn't arrest me.

I went back at 5:30 fully intending to get the joke over with, but the thought of another winter of this bullshit was just too overwhelming. I won't say any more except to say that most, if not all the "evidence" I gave them is bullshit and based on stuff I'd learned over the past thirteen months, including the Journal story. I just hope I haven't buried myself by being too convincing.

If I'd have known the Union wasn't going to help with costs I'd be home with my family now. I never thought this shit through, which was stupid.

The ROMPs [RCMP] were pretty suspicious of some things a few days later, but I wouldn't say any more to them. I don't think they really care. They just wanted somebody.

On the "guided tour" I had to look around for manways and went the wrong way but it didn't seem to bother them.

Also we never traveled up and out 1-38 because I would have been lost as well as dead climbing despite listening to people talk about it for a year.

Anyway bye for now. Hope to see you soon.

Roger.[3]

Shearing sent word that he and Tim Bettger wanted to meet with the union's executive, so President Rick Cassidy and at least three others visited on December 29. Cassidy read Warren's letter, and several days later shared it with the others. He'd copied it word for word through the glass of a visitation booth.

Neither prison officials and police nor the Crown knew about Warren's denial of his confession. The few other people who knew about it were sworn to secrecy. Warren's lawyer, Glen Orris, had not even been told yet because he was in Vancouver and telephone lines could not be trusted, with good reason. According to a prison official, Warren's visits were carefully logged and "all calls are monitored, of course." This went on well into 1994.

By mid-December, at least fifty people associated with the union had received letters from an agent of the Solicitor General of Canada confirming that their private communications had been subject to interception by the RCMP since the second week of the murder investigation. Among those notified were union lawyers Austin Marshall and Gina Fiorillo,[4] CCU secretary-treasurer John Lang, CAW envoy Harold David, Mine–Mill president Rick Briggs, Harry Seeton, Rick Cassidy and many other CASAW executives, June Roberts, Kurt Lehniger, former strike coordinator Dale Johnston, as well as many other, more direct suspects and quite a few of their acquaintances.[5]

SWEET FREEDOM AND BITTER FRUIT

Nineteen months after the June 14 skirmish, it came to roost in court. In late January 1994, fourteen CASAW members faced trial for allegedly participating in a riot, a charge that carries a maximum sentence of two years. Canadian prosecutors rarely use the charge nowadays, since it involves proving group intent, not just individual intent, to damage property, commit assault, or mischief, and so on. Two men charged were spared going through the trial—Roger Warren and another man who had been hurt in an accident driving a transport truck.

In this case, the Crown's evidence was inadequate. The prosecution knew about secret meetings before June 14 when some strikers discussed occupying C-dry, or the mill, or the kitchen. But the Crown could not prove a direct link between them and the pandemonium that occurred, and there was some evidence that no such link existed. It was even touch-and-go whether the chaos legally constituted a riot. After three weeks of viewing videos and hearing from witnesses, the jury apparently concluded that the Crown had not proved that the confrontation was a riot, and all fourteen strikers were cleared.

The Crown had erred and the RCMP's investigation was sloppy. Crown prosecutor Sandy MacDonald had to root out some witnesses himself. Royal Oak staff had made identifications on videotape in multiple group sessions with Pinkerton's guards involved, but not the RCMP. Many identifications were made in the trial only after repeated replays of the video; in one instance seven replays failed to produce the desired identification. Royal Oak staffers were determined to nail each man accused, a point driven home by the presence of an unhappy Noel O'Sullivan in the gallery. As "special projects coordinator," he had been assigned to monitor the case, but disappeared after the defense pointed him out to the jury.

The accused men, most of them longtime Yellowknife residents fired from their jobs, had a lot at stake in this trial. They would probably be out of work if they were convicted. Some feared they would be blacklisted as well. Their wives, families, and friends attended when they could. They felt the company and the Crown had a vendetta against the union men. "It seemed like it was a personal thing between the Crown and us," said Rick Cassidy, CASAW's president. The lawyers were uptight too—so much so that during a recess, MacDonald belligerently approached a defense lawyer in the courtroom. They were separated by a sheriff.

The jury deliberated for fifteen hours. "I was a bundle of nerves that whole day. When they went out for the verdict, I felt like somebody had their fist in my stomach," says Sylvia Imbeault, whose husband, Robbie, was on trial. When the names were read out, none of those cleared uttered a sound until the last man had been freed. Then cheers and claps of jubilation swept the courtroom. Seconds later, the eyes of all the men glistened with tears as they clasped hands, hugged wives and friends, and breathed great sighs of relief. "I didn't know how much pressure there was," said Terry Legge, one of the accused. As the names were read out, "I could feel it rise off everybody like a heat wave." At the party in the union hall that night, spirits were sky-high.

Even some of the union men who got off admit that illegal acts were committed on June 14. But by charging the strikers individually with mischief, assault, and possession of a dangerous weapon, then dropping the charges in favour of a single riot trial, the Crown was left empty-handed. Cassidy labeled it a huge "waste of taxpayers' money," but it was very costly for the union as well. The only man to do any time for a riot charge was an unfortunate striker who broke ranks and pleaded guilty in March 1993. He'd been arrested on other charges, unrelated to the strike/lockout, and decided to get it all over with.

In fact, the Crown was singularly unsuccessful at convicting strikers of anything throughout the dispute. The conviction rate on 244 criminal charges was 18 percent, including the results of six appeals. The rate was about 19 percent in fifty-two contempt-of-court charges, most of them alleged violations of the picketing injunction, brought by the Crown or Royal Oak.

Roger Warren's preliminary hearing was held at the same time as the riot trial. Anticipating throngs of media and local spectators, the court rented the cavernous former Legislative Assembly chambers and put in 300 chairs, most of which were never used. The victims' families had a protected enclave, counselors were numerous, and people close to the families or the Warrens wore "support group" tags. Warren was hauled to court in the back of a seatless van like a dog, but well dressed, in a suit. He was furious and complained to his keepers. The shoddy treatment was planned "higher up," a jail official said. "Somebody is influencing the RCMP."

Blast victims' families and union loyalists found themselves together for the first time in many months at the preliminary hearing. Before long they heard that Warren had confessed. His successful interrogator, Sergeant Gregg McMartin, noted that Warren "at one point suggested there should be some guilt put elsewhere."

"Oh God!" exclaimed Doreen Vodnoski, whose husband, Dave, had been killed. She strode out.

Bitterness and anger were never far from the surface, particularly when people lined up together to pass through the security scanner in the lobby. Near the end of the hearing, another widow, Doreen Hourie, went at Harry Seeton with her fists. He'd come at the request of the Warrens as a member of their support group.[6]

As usual at preliminary hearings, reporting of testimony was banned, and few people showed up to hear an outline of the Crown's case against Warren. Details of his confession did not come out, so the most dramatic statements were made by former mine foreman Noel O'Sullivan. He said that, a week after the blast, he told the RCMP, "Your suspects are not my suspects and you should change your tactics." O'Sullivan said that he suspected Warren by the evening of September 18, and then thought about it "as I went through the scene [and] the route of travel." He said that the boot prints in the mine reminded him of Warren's swagger. "On different occasions, I followed those tracks again, on my own."

O'Sullivan's testimony was a flagrant contradiction of his statement to the RCMP on September 26, 1992, when he said that tracing "the nonchalant step ... I would have to think it was Al Shearing." Of course, Warren didn't know about that statement when he wrote a note to Shearing and Bettger in jail:

Al and Tim.

So far in testimony the worst guy against me was N. O'Sullivan. This guy is nuts. He said right from the start he suspected me. He followed those tracks and he just knew!! I find out now the guy lost his way on 425 and 575 and also walked past the Muir raise before doubling back. I can tell you, that me and a few others after June 30 knew the route into that mine if you know what I mean. I hauled gear up the Muir raise.[7] I now think for sure there were two or more people. The boots were used to make it look like someone not a miner. Also where the blast was is totally illogical. Why? [...]

This was pointed at the guys who did the graffiti no question. I don't think some of the stuff was done on that night either ... The distances and extra effort to do something stupid make it hard to believe. Also, central blast went off at 4:10–15.[8]

"Any bandwagon there is, he jumps on it," Warren said of O'Sullivan in mid-1995. "I think seeing that [blast scene] just traumatized the guy." O'Sullivan talked a lot of guys into crossing the picket line, Warren said.

While lawyer Glen Orris was in Yellowknife for the preliminary, Warren finally told him that the confession was a fraud. There was a lot of work to be done. Talking to reporters, Orris coolly dismissed predictions of a June court date. "I don't think that's realistic," he said, refusing to say what Warren's plea would be. "This matter will go to trial," he said, preempting any questions about a plea bargain.

CASAW's fortunes were predictably the exact opposite of Warren's. A month later, the union scored another big court victory. The Federal Court of Canada rejected Royal Oak's argument that the CLRB ruling ending the strike/lockout was illegal. The company promptly applied to the Supreme Court of Canada for permission to appeal.

All this still left about forty-nine CASAW members in limbo: the men Royal Oak had fired during the dispute—including Harry Seeton, at the very last minute. The men had baseball caps made up, dubbing themselves the "49ers." Arbitration on a single firing can take months, but Ready and Munroe promised to do them quickly. It nevertheless took until April 1994 for the first hearings. CASAW's executive complained bitterly about delays, but was overjoyed by the result of the first round, a clean sweep for the union. Ready and Munroe ordered Royal Oak to reinstate all twenty-nine workers. In Harry Seeton's case, the commissioners ruled he didn't deserve any discipline and ordered Royal Oak to pay him from the end of the strike. Several other men were suspended for periods ranging from two weeks to ten months. Even the man who pleaded guilty on the riot charge was ordered rehired.

The first batch of twenty-nine were informally known as the "easy" cases that the union had the best chances of winning. But, even in the second batch of hearings, held in May, CASAW did almost as well. Ready and Munroe upheld only the dismissal of James Mager, who'd been convicted of several offenses during the melee of June 14. He felt like a scapegoat, but took it philosophically and was hired by the Department of National Defence.

Gordie Kendall, the striker suspected of being an *agent provocateur*, couldn't be reached and didn't show up for his arbitration, so the commissioners let his firing stand without hearing evidence. Kendall blames CASAW. "They could contact me; they didn't want to," he says. "They fucked up my arbitration."

Thirteen of the strikers were reinstated with back pay for at least some of the time since the end of the strike/lockout. In the cases of Dale Johnston and five or six others who did not want to return to Giant, the commissioners ordered the company to pay severance and change their employment records to show they had resigned, not been fired.

That left Roger Warren, Al Shearing, and Tim Bettger, all in jail awaiting trial. Ready and Munroe postponed any ruling on their cases, though it seemed obvious that none of them would ever work at Giant again.

Over the next few months, the union won all nine arbitration hearings for workers fired before the strike/lockout began. Among them was the man known as the mouthpiece of the picket line, happy to end a sojourn at a discount store.

Inside the mine, life was tolerable but trying. Workers complained they couldn't get parts to repair equipment and that they were being cheated on their bonuses. Even one of CASAW's line-crossers said that shifters were picking on returning strikers.

That view was strengthened when Witte appealed to the Supreme Court of Canada to strike down the collective agreement, made as the CLRB had directed. Witte's action angered even some former strikebreakers, who saw it as just another irritant in their workplace. One said that some would join CASAW on strike if Witte won her case, everyone was being treated so badly. He said her methods were worse than those used at the Gainers meat plants in Alberta.[9]

Peggy Witte got her wish on one point. The workers at Giant soon joined the "mainstream" of Canadian labour. After heavy campaigning by the CASAW leadership, members voted on June 2 to merge with the Canadian Auto Workers. There was some resistance within CASAW's biggest local in Kitimat, BC, but the overall vote was 73 percent in favour. In Yellowknife, where strikers had received more than $1 million in support from the CAW, the vote was 98 percent in favour. CASAW Local 4 became CAW Local 2304, and most members were proud of it.

Strangely, one of the first proponents of joining the CAW now fought against it. Jim O'Neil mentioned both the Steelworkers and the Union of Northern Workers as alternatives, and petitioned CASAW before the vote to allow the Yellowknife local to break away as an independent, to determine its own fate. But his campaign sputtered and died.

Al Shearing and Tim Bettger were back in court on June 13 for their preliminary hearing. Their legal aid–funded lawyers came from faraway Iqaluit and had no links to other Giant cases. Most of the charges were related to the June 29 graffiti raid and explosions at the satellite dish and B-shaft vent shack.

Crown prosecutor Dennis Claxton wanted the public excluded from the entire hearing, in addition to the customary publication ban. He argued that several witnesses now back at work at Giant mine could be fired once they admitted their illegal conduct under oath. It was a legitimate fear. Bill Heath, the company's head of personnel, had told a CAW representative during Terry Legge's arbitration that Royal Oak would just wait and fire him after he testified in court. Legge panicked and went to Corporal Vern White, who said he'd take care of the problem. Others potentially on Royal Oak's chopping block were Art St. Amand, Luc Normandin, and Rob Wells, all former strikers. Banning the public would also prevent anyone from hearing the testimony of civilian agent Marvin Ferriss, who was reportedly under the RCMP's witness-protection program.

It was an ironic situation. Royal Oak was the injured party in the case, but was exerting pressure that made Crown witnesses reluctant to testify. Over defense objections, the judge decided that civilian witnesses would testify in secret, except Ferriss. None of the witnesses was fired by Royal Oak, and Ferriss had quit. Shearing says that in opposing secret hearings, he wasn't trying to get anyone fired; he wanted as much of the story of the labour dispute as possible to become public knowledge.

Shearing and Bettger were freed on bail after the hearing. Despite his skills as a mechanic, Bettger was unable to get a job. Shearing had no problem finding one, but watchful eyes were still upon him. "It was right when Peggy Witte was appealing the CLRB decision," says Bob Robertson, who was driving cab when he picked up Al Shearing and Kara Rodrigue. "They were talking. He was really pissed off that Peggy Witte was appealing the decision, and the way he put it, he said, 'We will just have to kill some more scabs, then.' And he said it convincingly."

Robertson says he was much more excited about this information than the police, not surprisingly. Even if it meant Shearing was involved in the explosion, the "we" in the statement did not preclude Roger Warren's involvement.

Beyond the tentacles of the police, another person also said that Shearing has admitted setting the blast. One source described the moment vividly, and named people who were nearby but out of earshot. Shearing denies saying anything of the kind to Robertson or anyone else. Even if he has admitted involvement in the blast, no link has been proved, and his saying so doesn't mean he did it. Furthermore, there might have been motives known only to Shearing to say that he was involved.

Meanwhile, there was no money to pay Roger Warren's lawyers. Immediately after his arrest, Warren qualified for legal aid. But he was denied his choice of lawyers according to a rule that they had to live in the Northwest Territories. Warren was convinced he needed an outsider to get a fair trial, and insisted upon Glen Orris and his associate. They finally persuaded the NWT Supreme Court to order the federal Crown to pay for Warren's defense, opposed by the Crown and the NWT government. But that didn't happen until four months after Warren's preliminary hearing in February 1994. Rather than delay it, Warren's family scrambled to make funding arrangements. "Because of that, my wife and I have exhausted all personal resources," Warren stated in a legal affidavit. For an eight- to ten-week trial, the estimated cost was $250,000, but his trial would last four months.

While the defense tilted with the system, the RCMP and the Crown's legal team prepared their cases. Vern White, newly promoted to sergeant, was in charge of the 100 legal file boxes of printed material related to the homicide, about twenty of them pertaining to Al Shearing and Tim Bettger. If needed, the boxes on other Giant mine offenses filled 17 feet of shelves. And there was more on computer.

The labour dispute was over, with just a few workers' suspensions yet to end. The cost of policing the dispute, including the murder investigation, was almost $6 million "and rising," according to a local newspaper. Nine men had died. The price of the entire fiasco was astronomical, but, on the eve of Warren's trial, there was hope that most of the remaining questions would be answered.

CHAPTER EIGHT

WHEREIN LIES

I was after the truth. The only thing I had in my mind is that Roger Warren was responsible for setting the bomb.

—Sergeant Gregg McMartin, September 14, 1994

I hate lying ... I did it for a year now ... it's almost as bad as killin' those guys.

—Roger Warren, October 16, 1993

The cops are trying to make everybody believe that he broke down, relieved and all of this. What the fuck did he have to be relieved of? He never even fuckin' done it.

—Al Shearing, August 3, 1994

Most people in Yellowknife had bridled their passions by the time Roger Warren went to court on Tuesday, September 6. None of the rumours were as dramatic as the story about to be heard. Crown prosecutor Peter Martin went into court with a mind-boggling confession supported by sensational but tenuous circumstantial evidence. His cocounsel, a Calgary defence lawyer, avoided the limelight. Warren's lawyers, Glen Orris and Gillian Boothroyd, were outwardly calm but must have feared being outflanked by police, who were unresponsive to their requests for information but scurried for the Crown. Warren's lawyers were not given transcripts of Gordie Kendall's interviews.

Justice Mark de Weerdt, at age 66 the most senior NWT Supreme Court justice, would hear the case, since the other two resident judges were former partners in the local law firm used by Royal Oak. Soft-spoken and perceptive, de Weerdt is considered a conservative judge. He had presided over injunction hearings, various riot-related trials, and many others, and was thus familiar with the labour dispute. He had spent only nine years practicing outside the Northwest Territories since 1958, but had once headed a fifty-five-lawyer office of the federal Justice Department in British Columbia. His experience included five years as a prosecutor and five more as a defense lawyer.

Court security was tight. Only police, lawyers, and court staff entered unchecked by metal detectors. Two policemen in red serge, with shiny brown boots and guns in leather belts, guarded Warren as he entered. He looked much healthier than at the preliminary hearing. His thinning gray hair was brushed straight back to a little ducktail that curled above the collar of his white shirt. He wore a silk tie and steel-blue suit, and appeared as composed as ever.

Silence fell when de Weerdt arrived to arraign Warren. "You stand charged that, on the 18th day of September, 1992, at or near Yellowknife in the Northwest Territories, you did unlawfully kill Verne Fullowka, and did thereby commit first-degree murder," de Weerdt began, repeating the charge eight more times with full dramatic effect, naming the victims in alphabetical order.

"How do you plead?"

"Not guilty," Warren replied quietly.

Prosecutor Peter Martin's first job was to prove to the judge in a voir dire, a hearing in which a judge rules on the admissibility of evidence in a trial, that Warren's statements to police were voluntary. This was not an issue in the first interrogations when Warren denied involvement in the crime, but the confessions beginning on October 15, 1993, were vital to Martin's case. Without them, the Crown had no chance of a conviction.

Orris challenged the legality of the confession. First, he charged that Sergeant Gregg McMartin had shouted down Warren's requests to have a lawyer during the pivotal interrogation of October 15. The officer's threats to use the full force of the attorney general, and promises that the RCMP would help Warren if he said he was sorry and confessed, subverted his rights to both silence and counsel. Then he was told that it was to his advantage to help Corporals McGowan and White collect information, a lie that compromised his right to remain silent. The justice of the peace's remand that put Warren back into the hands of his interrogators was illegal, Orris claimed. And throughout the previous year, Warren had been told he had to prove his innocence, and that any refusal to cooperate would be used against him. Trying to clear himself of suspicion, he submitted to two grueling polygraph tests. Because Royal Oak and the RCMP appeared to be working hand in glove, and both insisted there would be no end to the labour dispute until arrests were made, Peggy Witte should be considered a person in authority under the law. Her pressure amounted to a threat. Stalling a collective agreement served the interests of both the RCMP and Royal Oak, Orris argued.

"She [Witte] was a former employer, at best," Martin retorted, describing the RCMP's conduct with Warren as "exemplary." The investigation after Warren's arrest was not overzealous, considering nine men were killed, he added.

Orris also charged that the "the police used the judicial system for their own purposes" by delaying Warren's remand so they could interrogate him further. After his arrest, they kept Warren on the move, away from lawyers, he said.

Peter Martin staunchly defended the police and grew annoyed with Orris's attacks. Inspector Al Macintyre said he was surprised the first time Martin's voice quavered with anger. He'd only seen that happen once before.

The Crown's case for the voir dire began with Nancy Defer, now a corporal. She portrayed Warren as "very constructive and open ... very honest" in his first contact with the RCMP. As the evidence unfolded, spectators finally heard Warren's account of what he had done on the picket line on the fateful September night, and much more. There were tapes his of interrogations by police, including the one in which he experienced heart trouble.

Sergeant Gregg McMartin sat in the witness box on September 12, following the transcript of his amazing interrogation of Roger Warren, who made some notes. The content of McMartin's message was similar to Corporal McGowan's on August 6, except for the degree of threats and inducements, and McMartin's claim that he was the envoy of the attorney general and special prosecutor Peter Martin. That was false, they had never met, and it was one of the lies he'd told Warren, McMartin conceded.

The first task for Warren's lawyer was to discredit his client's initial confession. Orris grilled McMartin until he couldn't remember the date of the explosion. Orris asked if, during an interrogation, McMartin would put a gun to someone's head and say, "Confess, or I blow your head off." When McMartin said no, Orris asked if the threat of a murder charge wasn't the equivalent. No, McMartin replied, he was "trying to find the right key to unlock the truth." He offered an insight into the way his interrogations unfolded. "While you're talking, sir, you have absolutely no idea what's coming up next. One thing leads to another."

Police officers testified that, in interviews before the confession, Warren sat with his eyes lowered and arms folded, rarely showing emotion. But when he spoke of entering the mine, he was animated and held eye contact. It was "an outpouring of information," Corporal Dale McGowan said, and Warren had seemed relieved. McGowan described Warren as "strong-willed. [He] had opportunity. He had motive, being in the strike position that he was. He had capability. And he had knowledge." But his cooperation "was inconsistent with other people that had committed crimes."

The primary investigator's testimony in the voir dire exposed the ham-handedness of the RCMP's dealings with CASAW, despite Martin's deft handling of Sergeant Vern White. A big man with a jutting chin and deep-set eyes capped by unusually bushy eyebrows, White was disliked by people he interviewed, because of his "very cold and detached, but aggressive" style.

White denied that the RCMP had stalled a settlement of the labour dispute, but admitted that he used the liaison officer, assigned as "a mediator of sorts" with the company and CASAW, to persuade union executives to submit to interviews with murder investigators. He also denied RCMP collusion with Royal Oak, claiming that the company was not privy to details of the investigation. This seemed inconsistent with former mine foreman Noel O'Sullivan's testimony in the preliminary hearing that "the RCMP used to come see me often," once or twice a week, sometimes more. (It did not come up in the trial, but Royal Oak negotiator Bill Heath also heard from White or Inspector Macintyre two or three times a week, and played squash once a week with Superintendent Brian Watt.) White also agreed that The *Edmonton Journal*'s blast-anniversary article set out the RCMP's evidence and theories on the murders, and he described his role in the article as "stopping disinformation." For most of the material, he said, "I believe there was a source at the mine." Orris ended his questioning of White with the comment that police witnesses "are not very reliable."

Spectators bristled with electricity when Warren was called to testify. The crowd soon swelled to near capacity. Most people were surprised to hear from him in the voir dire. The blast, Warren said, "cast a pall over everything. The whole focus was on the union ... We were besieged by the police ... I never had any unfavourable dealings with police at that time." That, and the pressure to eliminate himself as a suspect, led him to do whatever the police asked, he said. By the time Sergeant McMartin arrived, "this strike was starting to get to me. Like a lot of people, I was depressed. It was getting overwhelming." Depriving a person of a job "is a profound thing to do to a human being."

McMartin's hint that he'd reveal what was going on, as the agent of the attorney general, "piqued my curiosity," Warren said. "Sure, I was fearful. He's almost above a police officer, this guy. I wanted to leave a couple times, but I got the impression I couldn't ... I was 90 percent sure I was under arrest ... The minute you mention lawyers to this guy, he went ballistic. Really, what I wanted to do was get the hell out of that place ... It was getting frightening, I was getting alarmed by myself ... It was like two personalities—my personality was not in great shape, and his was. [I was] despondent, depressed. I didn't fight back the way I'd usually fight back. The main thing in my mind was, 'What's convinced this guy?'"

But Warren heard nothing new, except McMartin's refrain about the blast not being meant to kill. "I started out to tell him how it could be set up ... Finally, I did it, I admitted it. I thought I'd get another response—'You didn't do it, we know you didn't.' As I kept talking, they just kept accepting it ... I was drained of emotion by [then]." Warren said he thought that the police would eventually realize there were things he didn't know. "By that time I was just committed ... It was a strange feeling. I confessed to the thing, but why would I confess if I was like what this guy said I was," but now full of remorse? "To me, it started as a problem to solve. 'Can I fool these guys?' Yeah, I could, apparently quite easily."

The videotaped mine tour seemed unavoidable, Warren said. "I'd come to the conclusion that any attempt to contact lawyers would be held against me. I'd be charged with first-degree murder ... It'd help me out a lot if I helped these guys. I was fearful of not helping them ... But according to McMartin, I could get as little as two years."

Warren described his feelings when he woke up after tramping through the mine all night with the police. "I was devastated by what I'd done. I was horrified ... The worst thing was what I'd done to my wife, kids ... I thought they'd disown me." Then officers had come to get him, and he tried phoning his lawyer. "What I really wanted was Austin to talk to my wife. I wanted to talk to her in the worst way ... have Austin come to see me ... I remember feeling abandoned." When he broke down and cried briefly, "that was mainly because I couldn't speak to my wife. I was wondering what she was going through. This is the biggest lie I ever told in my life ... ruined her life, ruined my own."

The boots were thrown into the river just weeks earlier, Warren said, and he thought the police would find that out.[1] By the time Corporal Vern White questioned him in the car coming back from Cameron River, Warren said, "I wanted to make sure I could get it through his head, what I was talking about. It was becoming more difficult, because it was ludicrous to start with: 'If everything would've went according to plan, nobody would have got killed,' which was actually ridiculous."

Peter Martin tore into Warren when Orris finished his questioning. After showing that union members got free legal advice from Austin Marshall, Martin asked Warren if he had a phone book and knew how to spell "Marshall." Then Martin poked into the family finances, showing a joint income of close to $150,000 a year—enough to afford a lawyer.

Why stay in Yellowknife? Martin asked.

"My wife was working here," Warren replied, but that wasn't the answer that Martin wanted.

Why didn't you go to Winnipeg? You had your garage, and your wife's family was there.

"The same reason as a lot of other people didn't go—they became committed," Warren said. "It was just the principle."

You were profoundly disturbed, but you stayed on principle? Martin asked, incredulously. This was the opinionated man he wanted to get at. You knew as a Canadian citizen you didn't have to talk to the RCMP?

"To me it was just semantics," Warren said. "In this situation, we were told you have to clear yourself."

Talking with Sergeant McMartin, you just chose to be stubborn? Martin asked. Warren agreed.

You knew he was a special policeman, connected to the attorney general, and your reaction was to get up and take your daughter to therapy at 3:45, Martin stressed. But he soon zeroed in on the bag in the pond where Warren had guided the police.

"Those items had been put there sometime in May of '93," Warren said. "I decided if a CASAW member was charged with this, I would show it wasn't a CASAW member." He said he was convinced no CASAW member was involved. "I guess you could say I planned to obstruct justice."

Why did you want to screw up the police investigation? Martin wondered.

"If they'd investigated it properly, [I wouldn't have]. I figured I knew more than they did."

Did you do anything else like that? Martin asked.

"Yes. In early September of '93, I'd taken a pair of green boots out to Cameron River and burnt them and threw them in. That's the ones that were recovered ... I don't think they were Kamik boots."

And these boots didn't have a lace to tie at the top?

"No, they didn't," said Warren.

Where did you get these boots?

"At the auto wrecker. They were in a '77 or '78 Mercury ... They looked fairly similar," but they had a lot of tar on them.

In your confession, did you intentionally tell police things that you knew were inconsistent with the evidence they had?

"I was misleading them about everything, but I wasn't intentionally misleading them about anything [in particular]," Warren said.

The reason you confessed is your overwhelming sense of remorse, Martin offered.

(L. SELLECK)

Al Shearing plays darts in CASAW's union hall in April 1993. He did not think the RCMP had hit the bull's-eye with their psychological profile of the Giant mine murderer, released earlier that month. He saw it as a pressure tactic, and not as a true profile.

(L. SELLECK)

On the anniversary of the strike/lockout, about 250 people march to Giant, led by delegates to the NWT Federation of Labour's convention. Arm-in-arm at the head of the column are Leo Gray, national secretary of the Canadian Merchant Services Guild; Jess Succamore, a founder of CASAW and the western area director of the CAW; Dave Morris, a CLC representative; NWT Federation of Labour president Jim Evoy; Darrell Tingley, president of CUPW; and Harry Seeton, president of CASAW Local 4. The march took place despite warnings from the RCMP of arrests. No arrests were made.

(L. SELLECK)

Kelly Rhodes with CLASS executives Sylvia Imbeault and June Roberts
in CASAW's hall, May 1993. At the desk behind them is Terry Regimbald,
whose Kamik boots were seized by the RCMP.

(L. SELLECK)

Picketers on Yellowknife Bay (part of Great Slave Lake) in June 1993 temporarily
turned back a tugboat and fuel barge headed for the Giant mine.

CLASS takes part in the Canada Day parade.

(Above) Roger Warren, Garth Beck, Kelly Rhodes and James Mager on the picket line at Gate 3 on August 27, 1993. Rhodes became a key witness in Warren's trial, testifying that he'd seen Warren at 2 a.m. on September 18. The jury rejected Rhodes' testimony, because if it was accurate, Warren could not have committed the crime as it was described.

(Left) The Akaitcho headframe is up on a hill and surrounded by bush, a short hike from Ingraham Trail or Vee Lake Road. This is the entry point where Roger Warren allegedly went underground to set the blast, and also where intruders entered for the June 29, 1992 graffiti run.

(Left) Author Lee Selleck stands beside a ladder on 1100 Level. Roger Warren allegedly descended the equivalent of 75 storeys on steep, narrow, grime-covered ladders like this one, obtained explosives and set a deadly trap, refuelled a scooptram and drove it a distance, ascended several hundred feet on ladders, and walked out of the mine on a steeply graded ramp—all within four or five hours in the early morning of September 18, 1992. Note the air and water pipes on the right, just above head height.

(Right) Corporal Dave Grundy shows the chassis of the blasted man-car to reporters on October 14, 1992.

(S. CAMPBELL/NNSL)

(L. SELLECK/THE PRESS INDEPENDENT)

(Left) As the RCMP's senior officer in the NWT for most of the Giant dispute and the murder investigation, Superintendent Brian Watt was in a pivotal position. He briefed his superiors in Ottawa as well as ministers of the NWT government.

(NNSL)

Sergeant Gregg McMartin extracted a confession to the September 18 blast from miner Roger Warren.

(NNSL)

Former Con miner Bob Robertson, a service officer with the Union of Northern Workers, was used as a paid informant by the RCMP.

(NNSL)

NWT Supreme Court Justice Mark de Weerdt was the territory's most experienced judge. He issued the injunction limiting CASAW's picketing, presided over several trials related to the June 14, 1992 skirmishes, and Roger Warren's murder trial.

(NNSL)

Sergeant Vern White and Inspector Al Macintyre with files on the Giant mine murder investigation.

Roger Warren is escorted by RCMP officer Jim Barr from court to a waiting police car to return him to jail during his trial. Warren is carrying a bag from Yellowknife's book store.

(Left) Early in November 1993, during hearings called by the Canada Labour Relations Board, CASAW's team huddle in a hallway to discuss Royal Oak's intent to offer CASAW members a contract. The CLRB's decision would end the labour dispute. *(l. to r.)* Lawyer Leo McGrady, Harry Seeton, CAW advisor Hemi Mitic, Dale Johnston and Gina Fiorillo.

(Above) In April 1995, CLASS members threw a party to thank those who had supported CASAW during the labour dispute of 1992-93, and for the months after, while suspended union members returned to work. CLASS raised hundreds of thousands of dollars so union families could remain in Yellowknife. Izzie Bettger is on the far left.

(Left) Glen Orris defended Roger Warren against the murder charges. The verdict was appealed in January 1995 and an appeal is scheduled to be heard in May 1997.

"That's not true," Warren answered.

Martin played the tape of Warren sobbing before the trip to Cameron Falls, when he said lying was "almost as bad as killing those guys." That was the truth? Martin asked.

"The emotional part was," Warren said. "The reason I broke down was concern for my wife, and my child, the one that was at home ... I just kept playing along with it. It was a false thing."

Even then, you could lie, and lie convincingly?

"Yeah, I would say so," Warren said.

Local lawyers were flabbergasted that Warren had testified, and found his story hard to believe. Some said that psychiatric and psychological experts should have been called to shed some light on Warren's mental state when he confessed.

Warren's testimony cast a new light on the whole case. Some of it undermined his lawyers' arguments that his confession was not made freely. Here was a man who said he had intentionally lied to police for more than a year and planted false evidence he might have used to obstruct justice, a man who thought the RCMP would frame a culprit and considered doing something about it. A man who now said he'd lied as he sacrificed himself, and claimed innocence. To most observers, that took a lot of balls—or Warren had delusions of grandeur. Or both. Some, including the victims' families and the police, obviously shared Sergeant McMartin's view: "Roger Warren is very cold, very cold and callous," he told *Maclean's* magazine in January 1995. "He's a cold-blooded killer."

The five-week voir dire was the longest in NWT history. After hearing the evidence and lawyers' arguments, Justice de Weerdt's eighty-one-page ruling offered no comfort to Warren. "The evidence shows that he was enormously self-confident and self-controlled ... His conscience was clearly troubling him deeply ... His confession was the result of a carefully considered decision dictated by his stubborn will and not by any promise, threat or inducement held out to him by the police."

In the videotaped "re-enactment," de Weerdt stated, "there is no indication that [Warren] may have been inventing details of the tale ... The accused's demeanour is very convincing as to the truthful intent of his statements and his utter sincerity." The recovery of the canvas bag in the pond and the boots below Cameron Falls reinforced de Weerdt's opinion. He rejected Warren's account about planting the items. He offered his observations with a disclaimer: "It is not my function, on this voir dire, to reach a determination as to the truthfulness or otherwise of the confessions."

Justice de Weerdt concluded that Warren had understood his right to counsel, but didn't want a lawyer until just before going to Cameron Falls, and then he just wanted to contact his wife. When he mentioned a lawyer during his session with McMartin, it was "more as a tactic in his verbal fencing than a genuine expression of his need or wish to [obtain] counsel," de Weerdt wrote.

Errors made in Warren's remand hadn't compromised his rights, de Weerdt ruled, concluding that the administration of justice would be brought into disrepute if any of the evidence was excluded from the trial.

Warren's lawyers didn't give up. They argued that his boots had been seized illegally on October 16, 1992, without a warrant. The fact that Warren let the police have the clothes he wore on the night of September 17 and his boots didn't make the seizure legal, said lawyer Gillian Boothroyd. Constitutionally, police had no right to take Warren's boots without a warrant or advising him that he was a suspect, she said. Then, when the boots were seized with a warrant on June 18, 1993, as evidence against Tim Bettger, Warren was not implicated in the affidavit supporting the seizure. Boothroyd asked de Weerdt to throw out all evidence obtained as a result—much of the case against Warren.

It was a long shot, given that Warren had let the police have the boots, and testified that he would have surrendered them for lab tests, believing they would clear him of suspicion. The Crown argued exactly that, and won the day. De Weerdt ruled that the RCMP had taken the "prudent and appropriate course" on October 16, and the June 1993 search warrant was valid but "could have been done more elegantly."

RABBITS IN THE HAT

Marty, as Inspector Al Macintyre calls Peter Martin, is a legal prodigy. Since becoming a Crown appeal lawyer in Calgary, he hadn't had much call to do jury trials, but he'd been very effective, making the most of the court's process in his cases. "He comes across as the tough guy, [but] he charms that jury," says one Calgary defence lawyer.

Lawyers who have tangled with Martin in Alberta say he's very close to his family and unimpeachably honest. "If I were an innocent person charged with a murder, the last person I would want prosecuting me would be Peter Martin," says Noel O'Brien, a lawyer and friend of Martin's who has argued murder cases against him to the Supreme Court of Canada. "He puts his heart and soul into a case that he firmly believes in ... He will avoid nothing [of what he's properly allowed to do] to achieve what in his mind amounts to the proper administration of justice. And in this case, it would be a conviction ... There are very few people who can boast of the type of ethic that Peter displays, not only in the courtroom, but in his everyday professional life," O'Brien says.

In the Warren case, Martin obviously planned to leave nothing to chance. Less than a month before the trial, he went to the NWT Supreme Court to have Glen Orris, Warren's lawyer and a fellow Queen's Counsel, removed from the case. According to Martin, Orris had to go, to avert a mistrial or an appeal, protect the high standards of the legal profession, and ensure that Warren was well represented. Martin argued that Orris "was a compromised lawyer" because he had advised Shearing and Bettger in March and April 1993. Justice de Weerdt ruled that the brief consultation on searches and seizures, at CASAW's behest, would not hamper Orris's defense of Warren.

The man Martin wanted to dump was known for thorough and determined defense work. A high-school football star, Glen Orris won a scholarship to attend Simon Fraser University at age sixteen. The Winnipeg Blue Bombers signed him after graduation, but he continued studies in law at the University of Manitoba. He turned forty-six years old during Warren's trial, and got a spoof present—a pair of Kamik boots signed by many of the people involved in the case (some police refused). Orris, over 6 feet tall and quite bald, has a voice to match his impressive figure. Where Martin is short and small-boned, Orris is powerful. A regular spectator in the gallery said that Orris and Martin fit their names: Orris the bull, methodical, and seemingly oblivious to scurrying underfoot; Martin the ferret, pinched and intense, darting this way and that to survey all the angles.

The biggest threats to the Crown's case were Al Shearing and Tim Bettger. If all went as Martin planned, these two "rabbits," as Noel O'Sullivan had dubbed them, would get nowhere near the witness box, and evidence related to them would never pop up in Warren's trial. Of course, Warren's lawyer would want the jury to see everything that led the police to believe so strongly in Bettger and Shearing's guilt for so long. Orris had repeatedly demanded disclosure of the RCMP's investigation on Shearing and Bettger, to no avail. Martin was familiar with that evidence, as the original prosecutor assigned to their case, and before that as an adviser to the task force. Orris had finally asked the court to order disclosure in August 1994.

Warren had claimed sole responsibility for the blast in his confession, Martin argued. He declared that he'd rebut any hints that Shearing and Bettger were involved. In fact, they might be Crown witnesses. "My friend [Orris] cannot cross-examine those two."

The unlikely prospect of Shearing and Bettger becoming Crown witnesses amazed people who'd perpetually heard the RCMP accuse the two men of murder.

On August 26, de Weerdt ordered full disclosure of the RCMP's material on Bettger and Shearing to Orris, days before Warren's voir dire was to begin.

When Martin emerged from the voir dire on October 24, he was still fretting about Shearing and Bettger. That very day, Martin announced in court that they would waive any solicitor-client privilege they had with Glen Orris. Martin had made arrangements with their lawyers and had Bettger and Shearing subpoenaed to appear. It was their right to waive privilege, but the court had already ruled that there was no conflict of interest.

This was a brilliant stroke by Peter Martin, and almost risk-free. Shearing and Bettger believed they were helping Warren by ensuring his lawyer's continued service, but it would also help protect them should anyone try to implicate them in the murders. Shearing testified that he'd been wrongly suspected, and Bettger said, "I had nothing to do with the homicide in any way." Both men waived their right to privilege with Orris. Martin asked for a publication ban and got it. What he had probably feared was that Bettger or Shearing would testify for the defense and one of them would admit setting the September 18 blast, free from prosecution under the law. Now if that happened, Martin had previous statements to the contrary, made under oath.

Warren's jury heard none of this, of course. The trial began the same afternoon with de Weerdt's address to the jury.

Jurors had been selected in the town's largest banquet room during a break in the voir dire. From a record 793 potential jurors, about 250 cleared the initial screening and joined a long queue outside the door of the Explorer Hotel. The numbers dwindled as de Weerdt asked questions. It was graphic evidence of how much the crime and the labour dispute had affected the town. Among the potential jurors were relatives of the blast victims, friends of their families or the Warrens, their former coworkers, relatives and friends of witnesses, and many people who could not afford to be away from work for the duration of a long trial. Seven women and five men were finally chosen, one of them a former police officer, to pass judgment on Roger Warren.

It was a trying time for the widows and families of the nine men killed. The Riggs, Doreen Hourie, Tracey Neill, and Judit Pandev had returned to town for the voir dire. They felt some anxiety at being back, sensed uneasiness around them, and wondered what people were thinking and feeling. Carol Riggs's grief was etched into her downturned mouth. There was some support and sympathy, but it seemed hollow after all this time. Yellowknife was still suffering the strain and anguish of the murders and the labour dispute.

IN THE FIELDS OF THE LORD

A trial is a solemn inquiry to determine truth.

—Crown prosecutor Dennis Claxton, September 15, 1993

As scarce as truth is, the supply has always been in excess of the demand.

—Josh Billings (1815–1885)

Only one person's going to take the fuckin' rap for it.

—Roger Warren to Sergeant Gregg McMartin, October 15, 1993

Peter Martin's deep voice lacked its usual confidence when he spoke to the jurors for the first time on October 25, but they were rapt nonetheless. "This man, Roger Warren, caused the death of nine other men and thereby committed first-degree murder," Martin said. He compared his case to a puzzle. "I will now show you the cover of the box so you will understand how each piece fits together." He sketched in the mine and outlined the labour dispute, deepened by the use of replacement workers and security guards. By the time he slid into his version of September 18's events, Martin had warmed to his topic. Pulling a midnight shift picketing on September 17, "Mr. Warren walked to [the] abandoned Akaitcho shaft. He entered the mine. Alone, he went down a long series of ladders ... He began walking." Miners noticed nothing unusual as they left work, believing the mine was empty. "They were wrong. Roger Warren was in the mine." He got everything he needed and assembled "a large bomb designed to be triggered by a fishing line." He left the mine through the 1-38 portal and "scampered over a hill," where he hid his gear near the road. "He was passed by a mine employee named Broda ... For the next two and a half hours, no one knew there was a bomb in that mine besides Roger Warren."

Meanwhile, workers going to the 750 level had a safety meeting, Martin continued. Eight men got in the man-car; a ninth drove the motor pulling it. "They could not have known that waiting for them, a few hundred yards ahead, was death."

By the time Noel O'Sullivan found the disaster an hour later, Warren had returned to the picket line, said Martin, but had left behind unusual footprints made by size 11 Kamik boots. Warren owned size 10 and size 11 Kamik boots, Martin said. "Mr. Warren has confessed to committing this crime," and his words are confirmed by his "intimate knowledge" of what happened, the boots, and a bag of items used.

The first police witnesses were not sure that the footprints found in the Akaitcho headframe were left by one person. The shaft was covered when it was found, and police had not checked to see if the hinged grate and plywood cover could be replaced by a man descending. One officer said he thought it could be done.

Boot prints, found underground at Akaitcho five days after the blast, were followed. They disappeared mysteriously on the 750 level, about 500 feet from the 7-12 shop. Witnesses did not speculate why, but the implication was that someone had come down the track on a motor and given the boot wearer a ride.

Sergeant Wayne Locke testified that boot tracks found in the mine were consistent in size and tread with Warren's Kamiks, but no direct link was made. And such boots were common. The Woolco store sold identical boots in 1992; someone had made a matching track on brown paper at the police station in late September 1992; and soles of Black Arrow boots matched as well.

With Noel O'Sullivan as guide, Locke had followed another set of matching boot prints in the mine. He had gone to photograph the number 50 scooptram on 575, and found more footprints on the other side of the breakthrough doors, near a red wooden box containing explosives. The only electrical caps in it were DCDs—the type police believed had been used in the blast.

Locke also introduced photographs and videotape of the blast scene, including the man-car and some of the victims' remains. A day and a half after the explosion, the site looked gray, misty, and wet. A miner's helmet was found near some pipe stacked in a cutout (known as a slash) in the drift wall. Arnold Russell's body was lying between the tracks, face up. The colour of life had left him and he had become an exhibit, a ghost to haunt the future and shock the jurors into realizing the enormity of the crime, and their task.

After some simple questions about the "re-enactment" video made by Locke, Orris paused. You understand, he asked, the defense is that these confessions are false? Martin objected, but the point was made. Minutes later, Orris asked if there were concerns about Warren's physical ability to exit the mine to complete the "re-enactment," and Locke said yes. "That's not so," Martin protested.

Martin's next witness was Max Dillman, the striker who had driven Warren to the picket line on the night of September 17. Dillman said he hadn't seen Warren for the rest of the night, including a drive along the line at about 4:30 A.M. This weakened Warren's claim that he had walked the line that night. But, in cross-examination, Dillman said that Warren was wearing coveralls and rubber boots, "black, with a red stripe around the bottom." Boothroyd produced a worn pair of black rubber boots and showed them to Dillman. "They look to be about the same type as he had on," he said. Martin was furious. "Pulling these black boots out of a bag, like a rabbit out of a hat ..." He wanted to know if defense lawyers had shown Dillman those black boots, or if someone else had suggested that to him. "No," Dillman replied. The jury was sent away as the lawyers sparred; Martin won the right to cross-examine his own witness. His aggressive questioning brought a humbled Dillman to admit that he was not certain about the colour of the boots. De Weerdt cautioned the jury about the value of answers obtained in this way.

Former mine manager Terry Byberg had been waiting in the wings for some time. He wasn't in the witness box long before saying that, on the first day of the strike, only managers, six regular employees, and security stayed on site. Byberg didn't mention time sheets showing that strikebreakers were also on the property. On the morning of the blast, he said, he'd joined the 750 crew's safety meeting. Then, shortly after 9:00 A.M. he and Vice President John Smrke learned that air pressure in the mine was off. When Byberg responded to an emergency call from a surface worker near Akaitcho, he saw Warren's car stop on the Ingraham Trail, at about 9:30 or 9:40.

Men who were sucked into the maelstrom of events after the blast gave jurors a glimpse of life underground. Milan Tuma, a union stalwart during Giant's 1980 strike, described his work the night of September 17. His scooptram had broken down, so he used scoop number 50 for the last forty-five minutes of the shift, but had forgotten how much fuel was in it. When he left the 750 level, everything looked normal. The big Titan motor was parked in the charging station, as always. When Tuma left for home at about 3:15 A.M., he noticed a small, dark-coloured car parked at the main gate. This detail would be significant; the RCMP had not located the car's probable owner and it would slightly bolster Warren's testimony.

The Crown's expert miner was Keith Murray, Warren's former partner. Murray has the lean body of a man kept fit by strenuous work. He described the pneumatic jackleg drills that rotate and hammer a drill bit, weighing more than 100 pounds. The drills inject water into the hole to suppress dust, so miners get wet. Like Warren and many miners, Murray has whitehand. "You lose nerves in your hands [and] a little control in your fingers. It'll get worse if you keep working. When your hands get cold, they get white." Warren, said Murray, "was a good miner. He was careful ... I learnt a lot from him." Both men were very experienced users of explosives. The chance of surviving a detonation of a bag of Amex and thirty sticks of powder 70 feet away was "zero," Murray said.

Orris asked Murray about explosives used at Giant that contained nitroglycerine. "Nitro" is sensitive to shock, friction, and heat, and can be set off without using electricity. Unlike Amex, nitro is not water-soluble, so it's good in wet conditions—where it would be detectable after an explosion. Murray said that he had seen Forcite and Xactex at Giant. Both contain nitroglycerine.

With the jury absent, Martin asked that they be taken into the mine, to the blast site and the 7-12 scoop shop. It would help them understand the environment, the darkness, and the degree of planning involved in committing the crime, he said. The prospect of the jury rolling along a rough little railway into the blackness, perhaps imagining themselves the blast victims, didn't thrill Glen Orris, who had already been there. "I listened carefully to my friend. I don't hear anything about the interest of justice." Putting the jury in Royal Oak's hands as guides and hosts "introduces the mine as a party to the proceedings [and] closely associates the prosecution with the mine."

"There's a danger we could derail the proceeding," de Weerdt quipped drily.

"The jury should see that, when Warren said he set this blast up with a surgeon's precision, that's impossible," Martin persisted.

"The matter has come before me as a surprise [and] raises many more questions than it's likely to resolve," de Weerdt said the next morning. "I remain unpersuaded that the view is necessary ... [or even] desirable."

With that, the jury was back on the job, and Noel O'Sullivan described the carnage on the morning of the blast. His mouth drew taut and he held his breath for a long moment before describing the scene. "Bodies were missing from the waist up ... The track was covered with water." He recalled leading investigators to the 9-07 powder magazine and finding unusual boot prints, some right between the shelves of powder. He and the police found more boot prints at the 575 breakthrough. Contradicting the testimony of at least two officers, O'Sullivan said there were boot tracks on both sides of the breakthrough doors. "We noticed that the footprints took a shortcut under a timbered area leading to the 575 drift." They were easy to follow, 75 feet past the Muir raise and back—implying that the person had missed it. Climbing up, they found the tracks again on B-3 second level, going into a small lunchroom, then 200 feet beyond the man way leading up to the first level. On B-3 first level, the boot tracks went towards the 2-34 stope before petering out on the rocks. O'Sullivan said he'd been in the area two or three weeks prior to the blast, but saw no strange footprints. The theory was that the boot wearer continued past 2-34 to the ramp from the 1-38 pit and hiked out, but no more prints led to the surface, a distance of about 2,000 feet. There were other possible routes out.

No experienced mine worker at Giant would unknowingly leave such footprints behind. No evidence revealed when the prints had been made, beyond the dates they were found, and opinions that they were recent.

O'Sullivan had also guided the RCMP's inspection of boot prints leading into the mine from Akaitcho. They backtracked the steps from a bit north of the 7-12 shop, out the long 750 drift. They climbed the man way to 575, where they found prints going 200 feet in both directions, though there was no apparent reason to exit the man way. Up on 425, there were footprints on the 40-foot jog over to the bottom of the man way in Akaitcho shaft. "We didn't think it was possible for somebody to get lost" on 425, O'Sullivan said, and that's why it had been a week before additional boot prints were found on 425 by an engineer working in that area. The boot tracks led about 1,000 feet past the man way to 575, and back.

Time was another critical factor for such a strenuous journey into the mine. On May 10, 1994, O'Sullivan and a rangy sergeant followed the same route as the footprints, except for the extra 2,000 feet on the 425 level. Neither did they build a dummy booby trap or use scoop number 50. From Gate 6 to the Akaitcho headframe and back out to Gate 6, it took them three hours and six minutes, including a fourteen-minute break. This was longer than the three hours Corporal McGowan had told Warren (in an interrogation) that his whereabouts on September 17 couldn't be accounted for. But in the trial, no Crown witnesses had seen Warren for about six hours. Some of that time would be accounted for by defense witnesses.

In O'Sullivan's cross-examination, it finally became public that two Procon men had worked overtime on the night of September 17, probably in areas that did not have to be evacuated during central blast. Martin was startled when Procon's time sheets—signed on September 18 by O'Sullivan—showed that mechanic John Springthorpe and miner Larry Bather had laboured an extra hour. Springthorpe could have been anywhere, O'Sullivan admitted. Bather had moved sixty-four scoops of muck, working close to the bottom of the 1-38 ramp, the murderer's alleged exit route. Most likely, it was never mentioned because their overtime violated the NWT Mine Safety Act, but it also showed that it was a guess to say that the mine had been empty.

Two other overtimers, shifters Denis Morin and Gordon Edwards, testified before the jury heard the taped voices of Roger Warren and the police. This began a procession of officers, each providing more pieces of the Crown's puzzle. Of Warren's preconfessional statements, Martin had chosen to air for the jury only those of September 25 and October 16, 1992.

There was Nancy Defer, who got Warren talking. From day one, he'd told her about green boots, the khaki parka he'd worn, and two men he had seen on mine property. The police were interested in them. Warren had described in detail a man who had passed him in a truck. When Defer asked to see the clothes he'd worn, he had also produced his boots.

When Defer was cross-examined about covert taping of Warren's other interviews, Martin objected, saying that Warren himself dismissed the statements as lies.

"We want to show that there's ongoing police contact," Orris stressed, and that Warren was aware that his interrogations were secretly taped.

"This would be most unfair to the Crown," Martin insisted. De Weerdt ruled that the dates, times, places, and names and ranks of the interviewers were admissible. With that, the jury heard about two more interviews.

Sergeant Gregg McMartin swore to tell the truth, opened the Bible, and kissed it. "So help me God," he said. The jury then heard his extraordinary interrogation of Warren for the first and only time. The lies McMartin told were "to impress on Mr. Warren that I know more about the investigation than I really did," McMartin claimed. "I presented different ideas. The idea is to present themes or ideas as to how something may have happened. A truthful person will categorically deny them." Many of McMartin's threats and promises were exposed for the jury, but perhaps none was more powerful than the suggestion that, if Warren confessed, the strike could end and there would be antiscab legislation for the Northwest Territories. "That's certainly what I said, sir," McMartin agreed after the passage was read to him.

After listening to tapes for a day and McMartin's exam-in-chief, Orris tried to get all Warren's previous statements before the jury, saying they affected his state of mind when he confessed. This could have added days or weeks to the trial. In the interviews, police had described theories and evidence against Bettger and Shearing, and Martin didn't want the jury to hear those. Nor did he want to "confuse" them with Warren's repeated denials of involvement. De Weerdt compromised; material from earlier statements was admissible only if it shed light on Warren's state of mind when he confessed. Piece by piece, his lawyers tried to enter key points from the other statements, but Martin usually fended them off.

Martin and Orris battled again over the *Edmonton Journal's* "Footsteps of the Murderer" article becoming evidence. The Crown was against it because the story was framed around Shearing and Bettger as the killers. "The article is a work of fiction, anchored by a few facts," Martin said, offering to give the jury a much-edited version. The lawyers failed to reach a compromise, so Orris temporarily withdrew his request to admit the article that had had such an impact on the case and the community.

It may have been McMartin who had pushed Warren over the edge, but videotape of the so-called re-enactment was a jury-breaker. Warren was earnest and downcast, even morose. The police, like de Weerdt, apparently believed that Warren was face-to-face with the demons of his guilt. But there were some discrepancies. Picking up on a hint from Corporal McGowan, Warren had described the wrong scooptram. The times he said he'd been at various locations didn't make sense, and he didn't know when the central blast had gone off. This was a critical matter he could not have ignored if he had been in the mine.

McGowan described the trips to the pond and Cameron Falls; the jury saw videotape and heard White's interview with Warren in the car.

It was time to introduce Warren's boots, but the Crown didn't want to cover the search warrant because it alleged that Tim Bettger was the murderer. The police had left the warrant because they were obliged to, and now the Crown wants to hide the evidence, Orris charged. When de Weerdt ruled that the warrant was admissible, Martin introduced it himself.

In case the jury thought there was something to Warren's story about tramping the picket line on the fateful night, McGowan said he'd been back "many many times" to check if it was possible to see people walking along the road to the tailings retreatment plant at Gate $5^1/_2$. Only silhouettes were visible, not details, McGowan said. He admitted that he hadn't told Warren that someone else had seen two men on mine property that night, and had even denied it under oath in the voir dire. The witness, Pamela MacQuarrie-Higden, had not only seen two men, but McGowan had interviewed her and compared composite drawings she and Warren had done independently with a police artist. This information was not given to Warren's lawyers until they specifically asked for it.

Warren spent about twenty-seven hours in interviews with police between November 1992 and August 1993, jurors learned. Content was not revealed, but Orris did point to links between statements, especially the August 6 session, which included McGowan's pressure to turn Warren into a witness against Shearing and Bettger, hinting that Warren could become "an unindicted co-accused" by making a deal. Warren would never have been charged. Orris wanted to make this point to the jury, even if only obliquely.

In addition, McGowan had not asked picketers in their interviews if Warren's clothes had been dirty the next morning. It was impossible for a man to have set the blast and stayed clean.

Other problems with Warren's confession surfaced. He said he'd used Magnafrac 5000 stick powder in the blast, taken from the 9-07 powder magazine, and postblast experts had found a piece of Magnafrac wrapper in the blast area. But when McGowan checked the 9-07 powder magazine on September 22, there was no Magnafrac, only four full and some half-full boxes of Superfrac, and twenty bags of Amex. The magazine had been marked out-of-bounds, but when Sergeant Gary Christison took inventory on September 23, he recorded thirty-five bags of Amex, eleven boxes of Superfrac 3000, five sealed boxes of Superfrac 4000 and an open one, a box of Magnafrac 5000 that was one-third full, and some B-line. The discrepancy was never explained. Neither was it mentioned in the trial that, on May 6, 1992, Terry Byberg had told supervisors that Magnafrac was no longer available and would be replaced by Superfrac at Giant.

When Brian Broda stepped into the witness box, it was twenty-six months since he'd seen a man walking along the highway, north of the 1-38 pit at about 5:55 A.M. on September 18. As a mill supervisor, Broda drove along the tailings pipelines twice every twelve-hour shift. He came out Gate 7 and turned left on the highway, down the hill toward Gate 6. "It was still dark, although there was some light coming from the east." The man he saw was walking in the same direction, wearing brown and green camouflage coveralls with a matching cap. Broda said that, as he drove slowly by, the man put his right hand up to shield his face, but could not hide his pale complexion and short, light hair. Broda reported it to mine security at 6:05 A.M. A session with the police hypnotist hadn't helped Broda's memory. The RCMP apparently did not show him the photos of Warren taken at the mine on October 16, 1992, in the clothes he'd worn on the night of September 17—probably because they didn't match Broda's description. When Broda was interviewed by the RCMP, they were probably happy that his description better fit Al Shearing than it did Warren.

Former striker Alex Mikus's testimony was delayed after Martin's squabble with picketer Max Dillman. Martin seemed to be having doubts about calling union loyalists as witnesses. Perhaps he also recalled a conversation he'd had with union president Rick Cassidy at a restaurant, along with Vern White. They'd met at Martin's request; he said that he would not smear the union in Warren's trial. Cassidy says he told Martin that most of the local's members didn't trust the RCMP or the Crown, and believed Warren was innocent.

Now, Mikus, dressed in a three-piece suit, described his picket duty the night before the blast. He had slept in the camper trailer at Gate 5 until about 4:00 A.M. When he got up, the radio's battery was dead, so he drove his truck to Gate 3 for an exchange. He saw two vehicles leave the mine site. "I was kind of suspicious what they were doing this time in the morning, so I followed them," Mikus said. There was a small vehicle in front of him until he turned around at Gate 1. Back at Gate 2, the men hadn't seen anyone go by. In the bus at Gate 3, Mikus spoke with Leo Lachowski, who hadn't seen the vehicles either. Then Mikus returned to Gate 5. He hadn't seen Warren at Gate 3, or recalled anyone walking along the road.

A thirteen-year mechanic at Giant, Mikus was familiar with scooptram number 50, the one found on 575 on September 18. Mikus's description of the controls differed from Warren's on the videotape. "Scoop 50 is an especially slow scoop." It is not one that a knowledgeable man would pick for his escape, if he had a choice.

Corporal Mike Brandford, recently promoted, was called to launch more confessional tapes, starting with the "virgin statement" joined in midstream by blast expert Jean-Yves Vermette. Now the jury saw the sketches Warren did with Vermette of an ore-car and a triggering device. But Brandford had also helped search Tim Bettger's house, and Orris was keen on revealing what was seized. The Crown was opposed, so jurors had a long break. "This evidence is not insignificant," Martin insisted. If it went to the jury, "we will be scurrying to disprove Mr. Bettger's involvement." De Weerdt ruled against Orris, but Martin's statement raised some questions: What had been seized that showed Bettger's involvement? And if it could be disproved, why had the RCMP pursued him for the murders, right to the end?

Results of the search of the blast site were the domain of Superintendent Don Watson, promoted after heading the excavation. As an RCMP explosives technician, he'd occasionally worked with US, British, and Israeli bomb experts. His crew included the postblast consultant (Vermette), a computer specialist, a forensic chemist, a photographer, and an exhibit man. They had set up a 3-foot grid extending 45 feet south of the blast's crater and 150 feet north. About 5,000 artifacts were collected after painstaking sifting and cleaning.

Photos and multilayered charts showed where the victims' bodies were found. The blast crater was 3 feet out of place, and Watson had to redraw it by hand during cross-examination. The only evidence of the type of explosive used were two pieces of Magnafrac label and pieces of clear plastic consistent with Amex bags. Neither could be definitively linked to the blast. Both explosives are water-soluble, and broken water pipes had drenched the area, so Watson had no chemical evidence.

Wire fragments of a DCD detonator cap were found near the seat of the blast, and another with much less damage was discovered 118 feet north of the crater. The date of their detonations was unknown. The caps were the blast team's most damning evidence against Warren. In his confession, he said he'd used a DCD cap to trigger the explosion and that he'd tested another one north of the blast site. Bettger and Shearing had also used DCDs to blast the vent shack, although other caps requiring less voltage to fire would have been a better choice. Coupled with the confession, the cap fragments implied that either Warren had used DCDs to make it look as if it wasn't a miner who set the blast, or he knew that someone else had used the wrong type of cap—as Shearing and Bettger had for the vent-shack explosion.

From the man-car's position relative to the blast, "we came to the conclusion that the device was activated by movement of the man-car," but no pieces of the mechanism were found, Watson said. His team tested a triggering device based on Warren's confession, but neither a man-car nor an ore-car would set it off. After moving the trip wire about a foot, the device worked, but failed once when the drill rod fell, with the toggle switch attached. As for a drill rod at the blast site, Watson remembered seeing one, but he hadn't examined it. It was not collected for exhibit or mentioned in the team's massive report. The rod hadn't seemed important at the time, and now it was lost. There also appeared to be a discrepancy in the man-car's position in relation to the explosives, if they had been set up as Warren described.

More unanswered questions emerged. From the location of the crater and the angle of the wall behind the explosives, one would have expected damage in the drift to be greater north of the blast site than south, but the opposite was the case. The postblast team had no idea why. Neither did Watson know if bits of wood driven into the ceiling—protected from water—had been analyzed for explosive residues. No such tests were included in the team's report. According to Warren after the trial, RCMP hadn't looked for traces of nitroglycerine either. This was important because it is not water-soluble and can be set off without electricity.

No power source to fire the blast was found, police testified. This undermined the RCMP's theory (and Warren's statement) that a battery had been used, because Vermette was able to reconstruct eight of the victims' lamp batteries, and had parts of the ninth. Watson and Vermette said that there was nothing inconsistent between their findings and Warren's version of the "improvised explosive device," but this opinion contradicted their report, completed early in 1993. Vermette wrote that the 3- by 5-foot crater was probably made by a charge set up off the ground,[2] with about two bags of Amex and a stick or more of Magnafrac, surrounded by wood. In Warren's confession the explosives were on the ground, but Vermette now claimed the result would be similar because Amex and Magnafrac burn with different velocities.

After seeing the postblast team's report, Warren said later, he thinks Vermette was right the first time about the explosives being off the ground. "If those bags were on the ground, there would've been a big hole," he said. In the RCMP's tests on 575, the track rails were blown off the ground and the hole was larger, Warren said. Only one bag of Amex was used in testing on 575, according to the police.

Data from the Geological Survey of Canada's seismic station outside Yellowknife, while inconclusive, suggests that the September 18 blast was larger than could be produced by two bags of Amex, or one bag and some stick powder.

At the blast site, a huge boulder sat just inches from the track, obstructing free passage. It was so heavy it took some "big guys" to move it, Vermette said.

He didn't know where the rock came from or if it had moved in the explosion. This large block of evidence elicited little comment from the postblast experts, but the rock could not have been there when the night shift left the mine early on September 18. It was either blasted there, or had been left there on purpose, perhaps to stop a man-car. It was possible that the explosion was triggered manually by someone hiding in another slash farther north (maybe with a Titan motor for a fast getaway), or even to the south, around the corner, towards B-shaft.

In the trial, there was no evidence of a trip mechanism, but in a short voir dire Vermette said that a small hook and black plastic line were found. They could have been used in a trip mechanism, or for a line to signal the arrival of the man-car to a hidden assailant. (There was no mention of the ring and small weights that Gordie Kendall says the police showed him.)[3] The RCMP apparently concluded that a trip wire was used because it seemed more practical for a saboteur than lingering in the mine. Yet, the abundance of yellow blasting wire present, the rock, and the lack of a battery to fire the explosives tend to support the theory that someone may have been on 750 when the blast went off. Or, if the assailant had left, nitroglycerine could have been used to ignite the blast.

According to primary investigator Vern White, the theory that only one person set up the blast was based on the unusual boot tracks in the mine. It was apparently not considered that the tracks could have been made intentionally, as a distraction. The theory was that an intruder entered via Akaitcho, and no thought was given to an entrance via the 1-38 portal or any of the other possible entries. But such an oversight is unlikely. An RCMP document states that, during the summer of 1992, "Bettger and Shearing advised [Conrad] Lisoway that they had entered the mine via the 1-38 portal [and] gone to a lunchroom."

It appears that the only people with experience in underground blasting who were consulted by the RCMP were from Giant mine. The postblast team had no such experience themselves, and there was no evidence that independent expertise was sought. The police already depended on Royal Oak employees to get around the mine, and a number of employees were used in supporting roles by the postblast team. Some had an interest in the outcome of the labour dispute. Information leaks were inevitable, perhaps intentional.

Except for gory details, however understated, much of the evidence uncovered by the postblast team seemed divorced from the rest of the case. Reporters on duty were unable to assess it, and its significance was not well explained to the jury by the defense or the judge.

Roger Warren raised his eyebrows after looking at the charred remains of boots recovered from the water at Cameron Falls, introduced by Sergeant Locke. There was part of a lace in one piece of boot. One sole was almost completely intact and appeared to be size 10. Due to the size, Locke did not think these boots had made the tracks in the mine. They smelled of petroleum when they were retrieved, but he didn't know how long they'd been in the water. Debris in the fire pit was near the surface. It had either been unmoved by fast-moving water in the spring, or had been put there later.

Robert Carroll, the only witness on record as having applied for reward money, had seen Warren, an old acquaintance, in The Diner on the morning of the blast. "He came in ... scanned the room, and walked to a table where I couldn't see him," Carroll said, fidgeting. Warren appeared "very fatigued. Tired-looking. Stress. Preoccupied look." Carroll used to have coffee with Warren a couple times a week, but said he hadn't asked Warren if anything was bothering him that morning. Later that day, Carroll heard about the explosion and handed a note to the RCMP at about 3:00 P.M.—before a reward was offered. He said he suspected that the blast was sabotage.

How much is the reward? Orris asked.

"Three-hundred-and-eight thousand dollars," said Carroll. "I'm not sure if there's interest in that fund."

The Crown shrewdly split Warren's endless interviews with other witnesses, highlighting the confessions and breaking the monotony. Now, a month after the trial began, the jury heard the tape of Warren's overnight conversation with undercover man Harry Ingram. It was a profane, four-hour sledgehammer of a session culled from nineteen hours of tape. It was often hard to understand the two men; the aid of a transcript was required.

The last Crown tape was of the October 18 interview in the courthouse, in which Warren said he'd taken steps to make sure the bomb on 750 would be discovered, and insisted that the boots he'd worn in the mine were size 10, not size 11. His gloves weren't in the bag from the pond, officers noted. Warren said he must have thrown them away. Two pieces of cloth in the bag were to wipe away fingerprints. He couldn't remember if he'd used a toggle switch with plastic or aluminum casing. It was on such details of Warren's confession that Peter Martin closed the Crown's case.

Gillian Boothroyd opened the defense by casting Warren's confession as the main character in a play, without whom there is no story. Every fissure in the confession will be lit, she claimed, "and you'll be able to see it for what it is ... nothing but a fraud." She promised an electrifying drama, complete with the twists and turns of psychology, physiology, and circumstance that had led Roger Warren to martyrdom, charged with a diabolical crime he did not commit. Stepping into the witness box, Warren knew that even his sex life with Helen would be laid bare to all.

Justice de Weerdt was impatient with Glen Orris within minutes. The guided tour of Warren's life included his first brush with the law in 1963. Martin objected that this was irrelevant, and de Weerdt seemed inclinded to agree. "It seems improbable that what happened can be tied to what happened in 1992," he said. "We've already been here for five weeks and ... it's unfair to the jury for us not to keep this trial within a proper compass." But he reluctantly allowed the story, as it had influenced psychological evidence to come later.

Warren had gone drinking one night, left the bar with a man he didn't know, and wound up accused of stealing a Volkswagen that was wrecked in an accident. Warren was drunk and didn't believe he'd done it, but couldn't remember what had happened. His father and a probation officer advised Warren to plead guilty to car theft, so he served a month in a jail.

In the middle of one of Warren's answers, a woman wandered into the courtroom and burst out: "I hope the fuck you die a slow death!" She appeared drunk, and was removed by a sheriff.

"It's OK, Roger," said Orris, and they ploughed into the wear and tear Warren had suffered as a miner—a ruptured disk in his back in 1983, whitehand, carpal tunnel syndrome in his left hand, and substantial hearing loss.

On the picket line, Warren talked a lot but didn't cause trouble, so he was surprised when he was charged after the rumble of June 14 and fired for "action inappropriate for an employee," he said. "I was there, anyways." He and Helen used to visit picketers in the evenings and take them doughnuts. "I never did picket duty until [September] ... Bill Schram called me, saying he was short of guys. He talked me into doing picket duty." Like some other men, Warren sometimes walked between gates to break the monotony. He went on graveyard shift on September 14, he said. On the night of September 17, "I wasn't going to go. Then Helen asked me a couple of times, 'Are you going, or not? I'll make your thermos.'" Going out, he donned his old parka, "I think the green rubber boots [and I] took one Pepsi out of the fridge and one Eat-More chocolate bar," and rode to Gate 6 with Max Dillman.

Warren said he had walked south toward Gate 5 at about 1:00 A.M. "[Just] before Gate 5, I went on the [west] side of the road ... You could skirt the whole picket system, and the guards, by going around on the B-shaft side, until you come to a little trail running across from the mill over to B-shaft."

He pointed out his route on a large photograph. He cut back to the road and walked to the bus at Gate 3, Warren said. At about 2:30, he saw Leo Lachowski asleep, and Kelly Rhodes getting ready to sleep. "I went outside and sat on a chair. I remember dozing off, because when I woke my hands were cold. I got up and went over [to] the parking-lot fence. A couple of vehicles went by," one of them a white truck. "This is close to 4:00." He kept going toward Gate 2, he said, and was down in a gully when something went by that sounded like a little sports car. At Baker Creek, he turned back north.

In this regard, Warren's testimony was consistent with those of Crown witnesses Alex Mikus and Milan Tuma.

Past Gate 5, Warren said he saw lights coming from the north. "I went in this sway-out here, it's a little swampy. I scrunched down, and got my elbow and knee wet because I tried to keep my hands out of the grass, it was frosty." He thought the car might be the Pinkerton's guards, who "used to patrol up and down the road two or three times a night." Instead of stopping at Gate 6, Warren said he followed a road toward the 1-38 pit. "I had done this a couple of times, it was pretty safe ... It's around 5:30 at least."

On the other side of the pit, someone laboured up the bank, Warren said, so he ducked down to watch. "I could see the whole portal." Minutes later, he heard someone swear, and he saw movement at the portal's gate, he said. "It startled me ... The first thing I picked out was, the guy takes his coat off and shakes it. He come toward me ... stopped, put stuff down on the ground and took his hat off. He had a hard hat with a light. He wiped his face and it looked like he was wiping his hair off, put the hat back on ... He put the coat back on—I got a glimpse of maybe a checkered lining. He had coveralls on, a battery for a lamp. And then when he turned, he had a small bag, a satchel or something with a long strap. He put it over his left shoulder ... He had a bony face. He seemed clean-shaven, very slim, and [had] a sharp-boned build ... In his left hand he had—to me, some type of assault rifle, something three feet long. It looked thin, and seemed to have a clip on it, something sticking down like a handle[4] ... He got not quite to the bottom of this roadway, and then there was tires spinning behind me and I got this impression of lights ... There was a vehicle going up the side of the pit ... It went quite fast up the hill toward the TRP (see map B). This didn't seem to disturb this guy, he just went up that same steep bank, really fast, effortless ... As soon as I lost sight of him, I tore up out of there as hard as I could go. I went back onto the Ingraham Trail right away." Warren said he thought the man in the truck had seen him, or the other man in the portal, and would report it. "I thought for sure I was caught in the pit."

Back on Ingraham Trail, "somebody stepped up on the road ... quite a ways from me, maybe 200 or 300 feet. I started to cross the road and he stopped, then turned around and come back to the edge of the road real quick ... He made a motion with his right hand as if somebody was behind him ... [Then he] started walking very slowly toward me. He's on the 1-38 side. Then I see this truck with just parking lights." Warren demonstrated how the walker shielded the side of his face with his hand as the truck pulled up beside him. "It was like a signal ... 'OK, I'll watch this side and you watch that side.' I figured these guys are looking for me. The truck continued down, turned into the Vee Lake Road ... then turned toward town, now using full headlights. I thought it was a Pinkerton guard truck.

"This guy on the road, he comes a little closer ... and I started hearing a loud car, a small white car or maybe a Toyota, quite fast. When the car started to appear around the corner, this guy dove into the bush. The last thing I seen was him disappearing through the little willows there ... I just got up out of there and walked back to the picket. It would've been shortly after six, five after." Warren said he thought the man on the road was a Pinkerton too; he did not see the hard hat, satchel, or rifle again. Back at Gate 6, Brian Drover, Frank Woods, and Tom Krahn told Warren that they had heard a diesel engine start in the pit or portal. Warren said he didn't talk about what he'd seen, but fished for a little information. "I might have made some leading remarks, but nobody bit."

To explain his year of silence about this story, Warren said that he had seen pictures of the graffiti trip into the mine, and heard about other explosions and vandalism. "I thought it was making the strikers look bad in the eyes of the public" and harmed the chances of government intervention to end the labour dispute.

In The Diner for breakfast on September 18 (where Carroll had seen him), Warren said, he was mulling all this over. "I knew if any of our guys were carrying firearms or any of that stuff on either side, somebody better stop it. That was an escalation." Warren drove back to the picket line, turning around at Yellowknife River. The car's engine quit just before getting to the corner beyond Gate 6, he said, and then mine manager Terry Byberg drove by in a hurry.

"From the start [the blast] was the worst thing that ever happened," Warren said. "It was devastating ... Right away, accusations and stuff against the union ... The place is on strike, they're using scabs, replacement workers, and they are running the place like a feudalist, eh ... We've got all these guys uptown, fights in the bars and everything. It seemed totally irresponsible ... And a police officer telling the guys to tell certain guys to stay off picket lines because the guys inside were threatening to shoot them. I mean, arrest them. It just wasn't the normal way for people to act. I don't care what kind of disaster happened, somebody has to be in control."

"Were you angry about the replacement workers, the fact that they were there?" Orris asked.

"Not anything personal. I didn't like the idea of it, but my anger was more against the powers that be. It's a small community, the thing should have been nipped in the bud. I was pretty sure that the whole thing was orchestrated from start to finish. You have your replacement workers. You have volatile guys on the union ranks, the next step is injunctions. The next step is get as many guys as possible off the picket line and [lure them] back to work, because they have no fear of driving through a picket line that's only got five guys on it. It was the Mohawk Valley scenario right from the 1920s or '30s." Union leaders didn't have the power of generals to control members' actions, Warren said.

By the time of his first interview with Nancy Defer, Warren had already heard about "pretty accusatory interrogations ... I decided to tell them I walked up and down the road and that was it ... I didn't want to be charged with trespassing on top of these riot charges ... I was starting to have a bad attitude toward authority." Then Warren told Defer much more than he had intended. "She mentioned that the Pinkerton's were the prime suspect. I took that with a grain of salt, but it was basically my idea too. Describing where I had went, I had this urge, 'I've got to tell this woman something.'" So he described seeing two men by Gate $5^1/_2$, as he actually had a few days earlier, "but I put this person's face on it that I had seen in the 1-38 pit." He didn't want to tell Defer about the path he'd taken around Gate 5 that night, because it was on the property and too close to B-shaft (a convenient exit point from the mine), Warren said. Fearing he'd been seen in the 1-38 pit, Warren told Defer he'd stayed on the Ingraham Trail, and pretended to be the man walking down the road. "I figured it would put the Pinkerton guard in the truck, on the road at a specific time so if there was anything underhanded going on they'd have a hard time denying it; and it put me on the road and not in the pit. That was my reasoning, flawed as it was ... After the interview, I was cursing myself. It was stupid to tell about guys at the wrong time in the wrong place."

By the time Defer and Corporal McGowan came to his apartment on October 16, he'd spilled diesel fuel on his old parka and thrown it away, Warren said—it hadn't gone missing as he'd told them. The clothes he'd worn were right by the door. "Dale McGowan picked up the boots and looked at them and said to [Defer], 'Oh, these are 11s,' in a dismissive fashion which intrigued me. He made up some story, that he wanted to take these and the parka." Warren still had its hood, so they took it. The green boots were different too, Warren said. The pair he'd worn that night had steel toes, were bought many years ago, and had soles that had melted next to a fire on the picket line. "They were cracked and I had got a wet foot with them." The new boots he bought at Woolco looked similar to the old ones, which he'd thrown out. When McGowan and Defer took his new boots, Warren figured, "Green boots are green boots, what's the difference?" and didn't say anything.

Later, a Woolco employee produced receipts for the court which showed it was likely that a pair of boots were sold at the Smokeshop's register (where newspapers were sold) on October 9, 1992. The store sold eighty-six pairs of green Kamik boots from August 1 to September 29.

The new boots hurt his feet, Warren said, so he cut the shank after wearing them once. One afternoon he went hunting outside Yellowknife, near a microwave tower. "I lit a little fire. My sandwiches were hard from sitting in the cold ... There had been talk [that] they were looking at clothing and boots ... I got to thinking, if they're checking everybody like that, I better make sure everything lines up with what I told [Defer], which was that I had burnt these boots." He found a piece of galvanized steel near the tower, heated it in the fire, and marked the soles, he said. "I even put black stuff on the bottom so it would look the same as the original boots."

"Did you know [then] that those boots were the kind the police were looking for?" Orris asked.

"No. I doubt if I would have had them sitting there in plain sight if I had any inkling that they were that important."

By the time he met Sergeant Pat Dauk on October 19 to take a polygraph, "I was starting to get fearful. I had misled them and I felt guilty about it," Warren said. "That's one of the reasons I wouldn't refuse to talk to them."

"Why didn't you tell them that there had been a misleading statement?" asked Orris.

"Fear of being implicated somehow. It looked too suspicious so I stuck to the same story." That was the session when Warren had a bout of heart arrhythmia. "I'd had this for a long time. At least a year. It didn't seem to happen under major exertion, it always seemed to happen just after ... A few times I just leaned against the wall for a while and it would go away. But in this instance ... the guy is right on me, [he] started touching my knee, which just sent me right through the roof, but I couldn't respond ... That's the first time I mentioned [this] to my wife, and she phoned her sister (a nurse). They put me in the hospital." From then on, Warren had medication to regulate his heartbeat. Only once previously was he tempted to see a doctor, he said. "This was maybe January or February of '92 ... The cage was down, so I started climbing from 750 up to surface. And I made it up just about to five [575] and I ended up fainting ... I was just out for a minute or two." Warren said he finally lay down in a lunchroom, where a shifter saw him, but he said nothing about his attack because he didn't want to be told to stop working.

The medication caused side effects, Warren said. "It started off like a mild depression, as if you had been drinking the night before ... Usually I was a little bit hyper and it just kept me toned down ... After a while they told me I could play hockey, and I couldn't get going."

Warren described the pressure he felt to continue being interviewed and to take a polygraph. He didn't want the RCMP to bother Helen and Ann. "I didn't want anybody even thinking I was involved in actually doing something to, to kill guys," he said. "I knew quite a few officers. I didn't want those guys to think, 'Here's a guy that's involved somehow.'" By the time he and McGowan flew to Winnipeg in February 1993, "I was really depressed. I just went, and whatever you want to do, I'll do it. I think McGowan realized it."

The police relentlessly hounded other union members, including Tim Bettger, whose house was raided on March 30. "I felt a little guilt over it. They didn't deserve to be harassed like that. I figured a lot of it was because I wasn't forthcoming about where I had been [in 1-38] and what I had seen. We definitely had the impression that there is nothing ever going to happen here unless somebody gets arrested for this ... I can see it from [the police's] side [but] I found it very unjust."

Meanwhile, Warren said, the effects of his medication worsened. "I had very little sensation sexually." With the medication and depression, "it just went way down ... In February when we were playing hockey, I had a horrendous pain in the groin. I checked myself. Where there should be two testicles, I had three. I figured this might have had a lot to do with other things that were happening, more so than the [medicine] ... but I am too terrified to go and find out ... My personality was changing ... I wasn't my normal self ... [Before], I could work all day and go play sports at night. I just didn't have it any more. Where there used to be a flame, there was just a tiny spark ... I figured eventually I'd get my body to acclimatize itself, but it didn't happen. I noticed—I was starting to get angry. It was something like a regular anger but it was way colder, it was relentless ... That was the strangest part—I just couldn't get up enough determination to do anything or try to find out anything about it. I found myself talking to myself a lot in my mind, just as if it was really two people talking ... I started referring to myself by the word, 'Meat.' I would say, 'Well Meat, what world-shaking events are you going to shape today?'"

Warren said he didn't even share his troubles with Helen. "We were very reticent in that area ... I figured, 'She is the one that's working and doesn't need any guy whining about what is wrong with him.'"

On the picket line, "guys still treated me like I am exactly the same as I was before. I couldn't believe they couldn't see the difference. I remember one guy said, 'As soon as we get back to work, I am going to push to get you to go training with me,' and I was astounded."

Such was his state, he said, when he saw McGowan on August 6 to hear the evidence against Shearing and Bettger, and about his own boots. "These guys are going to find out if I put marks on them after I cut them. Who cared, you know? ... I just figured I had to keep cooperating to get them to realize that [they were] wasting time on me ... If you were the person that actually perpetrated this crime, you definitely wouldn't be having dealings with the police if you could avoid it." He was afraid to admit where he'd really been because he might face more charges. "You would end up blackballed in the industry. You would never get a job again. With no work, my identity was fading. It was a weird thing. When you are approaching 50 years old in that industry, you don't want to stop [or] you will never get started again." Before the labour dispute, "I figured I could hack it another three or four years." With the prospect of never mining again, "I was feeling melancholy all the time." He said he'd hoped the June holiday in the United States would change things. But it didn't, and the RCMP had seized his boots, somehow accusing Tim Bettger of murder in the process.

The *Edmonton Journal*'s blast-anniversary article was so full of information that "a guy could fake it and get away with it," Warren said. "I was constantly scanning it ... It was almost like they were words through a spell ... A lot of people were angry about it, because they knew that a lot of that information had to come from the police ... I was intrigued by it. I figured there had to be something significant left out."

"Why were you concerned about that?" Orris asked.

"In conversations with myself ... I figured I was quite worthless anyways, so if you are going to go down, why not make it count?" He had a conversation along those lines with Al Shearing, Warren said. He believed the police would arrest Shearing and Bettger, who had both been members of the union executive. That "would probably be the end of the union," Warren testified. "There would be intimations that the union executive had some type of input into this event ... the blast. And it would basically destroy the strike." Warren envisioned all the men out of work, their families leaving Yellowknife, and fanfare for Peggy Witte the union buster.

Before planting the bag in the pond, "I was on picket duty and I came up with a scenario that would be pretty accurate. I didn't know how accurate it would be, but it ... would actually work. I started thinking of stuff to make this look like it was clues ... Maybe a guy could throw a wrench into the works." Warren said he laughed at himself and thought he wouldn't have the nerve to actually thwart the authorities, but "at the time it seemed like a rational idea. Now it seems kind of ludicrous ... I was convinced [Shearing and Bettger] never did anything ... I felt kind of responsible for not telling the real story about what I had seen at 1-38. And that's why I did it."

On the night shift of October 14, after meeting Shearing, "I thought about what Al and me talked about, put an end to this, get this strike over. Because there was never going to be a letup. There is no other force you can bring on them. I had read the article about charges before talks ... You can't count on politics to save you. I wrestled with ... the idea of admitting to this just to make a false confession. I thought of all the things I knew. I didn't think it would bother me too much, being arrested. What was the difference, sitting in a picket shack or sitting in a jail? And then I got this voice all the time telling me to go for it. 'You are going down anyways, you are not worth too much any more. You will probably never be able to work like you used to.' Every time I would think, 'Yeah right, and then what about your wife and family?' And then I would say, 'They are better off without you. You are just a glorified chauffeur.' That was the state of mind I went into the interview with."

So on October 15, Warren went to see the police about the tests on his boots. Instead, McMartin came at him with double-barreled accusations from the attorney general and Peter Martin. What Warren felt, he said, "was like fear. I remember thinking, 'You are arrested now ... Better to be arrested than to make a confession,' but that's not what happened. It was just your typical threats and intimidation ... I got this voice telling me to do it, do it. Then a more sane part took over and I thought of—I had to go, take the daughter to the appointment. I was quite surprised I walked out. The guy had actually given me the impression the jig is up. But it wasn't ... Then I picked up Helen. I figured, that's it. When I get home, I will tell them, 'I won't be seeing you any more.' But I talked myself into talking to him again ... A small part of it was curiosity ... about these boots."

When Warren went back, he couldn't make much sense of McMartin at first, he said. "I was having my own conversations ... One voice is whispering in a raucous manner, 'You have the stones. Go for it.' And I was outside myself sometimes, watching. I was over against the wall. A couple of times I looked over and expected to see somebody standing there. I could see through my coat, I could see the wrinkles in my shirt. That was the strangest thing, the image kept coming to me of this huge guy talking to me ... I seemed very insignificant ... I remember having the conversation with myself that the only important thing is that he is here, this McMartin. The voice tried to tell me, 'This guy is a cur, he is licking at your heels.' Another strange thing was when I looked at the guy's eyes. It looked like holes, like black holes ... I finally started to get what he was trying to say. The theme was, this doesn't have to be first-degree murder. Then the voice is saying, 'See Meat, what are you scared of? Go for it. Take these guys down.' It was eerie. The worst thing was thinking what the effect was going to be, in your rational mind, on your family. Finally I kept edging toward this precipice, and the voice is telling me, 'Look, you almost done it.' I remember mentioning a lawyer ... I don't know if this is the time he started yelling, 'I will get you ten lawyers.' By this time I was pretty well over the brink. I could actually look at the guy and it wasn't terrifying anymore. My rational side made a hypothetical scenario, and I forget what the key question was he asked[5], but that's when I took the step. I was off, off the cliff. I didn't really understand much of it until I read the transcript ... because I was having this Herculean struggle in my mind ... It seemed there was two forces. One huge army and one little one, and the one guy that had got separated. He is lost. He can help his army—he is going to end up probably getting wiped doing it, but maybe it would be the one thing he could do right. So he did it."

"Who was the little guy in that image?" Orris asked.

"I would be the guy between the two armies. If you don't get totally destroyed, you could win. I was telling myself this. You are going down in flames, but you might rise like a phoenix from the ashes. You triumph anyways, no matter what happened because you would affect a change."

"A change in what?"

"Well, you would actually subvert the system. I knew if there was an arrest that they would probably resolve this labour dispute. I wasn't doing much good for anything, so I might as well go down for something real. And I guess I did. The labour dispute, for all intents and purposes, is over. The other thing I kept telling myself, 'Don't get carried away here. These guys aren't stupid ... Just act like your normal low-key self and no whining. People hear this stuff.' And the fear was there, but it was also a euphoria. I remember having a feeling of playfulness, which is one reason why I done this crossword puzzle. But I didn't want to get too cute; people don't normally act like this when they confess to killing nine people. And all those thoughts were there, and the rest is history."

Sergeant McMartin influenced the story about the blast, Warren said. "The biggest thing was that if there was some way you could show that you didn't mean it, it [might] make a difference in charges. It was like the sane part of your psyche is going to try to preserve yourself when you are throwing yourself off a cliff."

"When you stepped off the cliff, were you thinking about what you might accomplish?" Orris asked.

"Yeah, I might end up with twenty-five years in jail, but in the end I would win, because I did it for a principle. The system is not for a certain group of people. It is for everybody. If it doesn't work for everybody, then you have to do something to wreck the system. As far as I am concerned, I wrecked the system. I can guarantee you the strike would still be going on ... They would have just kept on using that excuse—it is charges before talks. And in my state of mind, I said, 'No, that's it ... Lady, the last thing you want is charges, but that might be the first thing you are going to get. You stretch that elastic too far and I am going to be the little razor that's going to cut that sucker.' This is the voice telling me, basically, but it is really me ... I wasn't my same self and I didn't want to be around too much if I wasn't. I figured my wife could adjust. That will tell you how irrational I was. Concern about her didn't bother me until the next day ... Whenever this happened, I looked into the abyss, to use a phrase from Nietzsche, and the next day the abyss was looking into me. It was like being in a horror movie."

"Roger, did you remember before the start of this trial actually how this came about, how you talked your way into this?"

"Not really, no. I couldn't remember, 'Did I say I did it?' I did not know until I read it. It was foreign to me. I was amazed at the words."

After McGowan and White showed up, "I just try to convince them—try not to arouse suspicion. I was forcing myself to be as relaxed as possible ... The peripheral reason is the strike, and the other one was fear. The best-case scenario would be to get charged with manslaughter, so I was trying to convince them of this. McMartin kind of laid it out for me, and I tailored my admission within the parameters that he laid out. 'Was it meant for the guys?'—Well obviously it was meant for the guys, to me it was because of the amount of explosive ... It had to be meant for human beings ... I spent a lot of time thinking about that ... Maybe [it was] some type of holdback information."

The triggering mechanism and the items in the bag in the pond went back to the questionnaire he'd filled out for the RCMP in December 1992[6] and a disabling switch he'd once made to discourage snowmobile thieves, Warren said. The bag and phony boots, "I wasn't planning it for myself, but I had those plants in place, so I used them."

The first time he'd ever been down the Akaitcho shaft was on October 16 with the police, Warren said. The notion that a 9-volt battery would fire a DCD cap came from Blaine Lisoway, who later testified that they'd talked about it several times, all after September 18. The first time, Warren seemed surprised it would work, Lisoway said.

Warren also explained the selection of DCD caps for his false confession. "If I was going to do something like that, I would have just stole a couple of caps off the picket line and took them out someplace and tried them. But I used that as part of the story to make sure there was no attention pushed onto anybody else." A DCD cap "would be a stupid thing to use," due to its high resistance.

Warren had a theory related to the postblast team's work: the boulder near the tracks had probably been very near the seat of the blast, been heaved about

10 feet, hit the wall, and landed near the track. He estimated its weight at 500 to 600 pounds, and it could have reflected the force of the blast, causing extensive damage south of the site, and so little north of it.

One of several ways he'd identified the blast site when he went there with the police, Warren said, was that the new pipes were chained up, rather than pinned with metal forged in the blacksmith shop in the 1950s.

The exertion from the first part of the walk through of the mine on October 16 had left him too exhausted to climb out to the 1-38 portal, Warren said.

No sooner had Orris finished questioning Warren than Peter Martin asked for an adjournment to seek a psychiatrist to assess the testimony. De Weerdt refused the adjournment after a long argument.

Roger is the ultimate martyr, a martyr for the cause ... I could probably be accused myself of having a martyr complex.

—Bob Robertson, March 27, 1995

Bob Robertson came to court on December 1 and heard Warren's account of Sergeant McMartin's interrogation. Robertson believed that while Warren testified, "he was in a daze. But one thing he wasn't going to do was rat on the others. He would go to his grave with that ... I said to myself, 'This guy is a puppet. He's not the player,'" Robertson says. "Roger is the extreme loyalist ... He thought he was dying, and he was prepared to take the fall ... Number one, there's no way physically Roger could have done it."

The next day Robertson met with Glen Orris to say that "you should have the same information that the prosecution has." He revealed his role in the murder investigation and what he knew about it, especially its focus on Shearing and Bettger. "I told him, 'I don't know if Roger's part of it or not. But I do know Al Shearing is.'"

"He wanted to put me on the stand," Robertson says. "[Orris] says, 'But I won't subpoena you, Bob. That goes against my grain.'"

Robertson says he was then in a tight spot. "I've just burned my RCMP [witness] protection program." Working with the RCMP, he'd insisted on anonymity and hoped not to testify in court. So he consulted his lawyer, Valdis Foldats, who advised him to "let your handlers know what you've done and beg forgiveness."

"I phoned [Constable Al] McCambridge. I says, 'I think we better talk.'" They met in the interrogation room at the task-force office with Sergeant Gary

Butts, Robertson says. "I wasn't going to let them intimidate me. I says, 'You guys have got the wrong man on the stand. You know damn well it's Shearing and Bettger.' We talked a lot about the conspiracy thing. How they had told me that the investigation was ... focused on that, and now all of a sudden Roger drops in out of the blue and he's never had anything to do with the previous bombings or anything, and you believe that crap?! We talked about [them knowing] damn well they couldn't get a conviction without either a confession or an eyewitness statement, and they couldn't get the confession out of Al and Bettger. There was lots of circumstantial evidence, but that's all. We discussed how they wanted Roger to implicate the other two. And McCambridge said, 'I give MY WORD that Al didn't do it.' I thought to myself, 'Yeah, right.' He had to cover his ass. Right up until the day Roger was arrested, all guns were pointed at Al, and now all of a sudden he tells us, 'No, they didn't do it.' Only on the strength of Roger's confession, that's it. [I says,] 'You TOLD me, time and time again you wouldn't make arrests until you had all your ducks in order! Now all of a sudden this drops in, right out of the blue, coincidentally timed with the anniversary. You guys are full of shit here!'

"And I says, 'Furthermore, I know DAMN well that the Crown was putting all sorts of pressure on you guys to make an arrest at the time.' You could see the colour draining from their faces. I knew that they were going to [tell] all this to [Peter] Martin, that Orris is now privy to all their cards. I told them that Orris wanted me to go on the stand. And they said, 'We don't want you to go on the stand.'

"I says, 'Look at it from my point. I kept quiet a long time ago and nine guys died as a result. Right now, there's potentially an innocent guy's going to be spending the rest of his days in jail. And I'm not going to keep quiet a second time ... Because you guys have been withholding evidence from [Orris].' They said, 'Well, what are you going to do, Bob?'

"'I don't know. If I go on the stand, I'll never be able to live in this town again. And I don't have the resources to leave town right now.'

"'Well, there's nothing we can do for you anymore.' They cut me loose" from the witness-protection program, Robertson says.

He'd be branded a rat, he'd lose friends, he might lose his job, his days in the union movement would be over. He phoned Warren's lawyers and told them, "I've now told my RCMP handlers that I've talked to you guys."

Robertson did not testify. His role as a police informer and his reasons for believing in Shearing's guilt were not made public.

Robertson's allegations were never tested in Court and remain, to this day, as allegations only.

The move may have kept Robertson out of the witness box. He says that, if he had testified, the Crown would have used his drug addiction to smear him and imply that he had psychiatric disorders. The Crown warned Orris, Robertson says.

Orris confirmed that he'd spoken with Robertson, but refused to comment further.

About sixty spectators were in the gallery on December 5. Police officers and Crown lawyers filled an entire row on the defense side of the room, behind Helen and Patricia Warren, Bill Schram and some other union supporters, and two reporters from *The Militant*, a US-based leftist newspaper. The victims' families and friends, as ever, were nestled in the first two rows near Martin, with most of the media behind them. Warren's psychiatrist was present.

"I would like to clarify some matters," Martin told Warren, repeating a phrase used by his interrogators to launch a series of tricky questions. Warren finally resorted to answering, "That's what I told them." No matter what Warren said, Martin made it clear that he didn't believe it, and regularly reminded Warren he was under oath.

The psychiatric defense was recently manufactured, Martin charged. Why didn't Warren seek help immediately after making a false confession, assuming that's what it was? "Yeah, I never asked for treatment," Warren said. "I understood the next day ... that it was totally irrational. After this confession, I didn't think I had much of a defense. I wasn't even going to bother with lawyers. I figured, 'I am down for the count, so who cares?'" The first time he'd told anyone his confession was false was in a note to Shearing and Bettger, after they'd asked him, Warren said.

Martin accused Warren of murder, and charged that any alibi he had now was fabricated. "I deny it," Warren responded.

Martin pressed hard for the "leading comment" Warren said he'd made to Brian Drover at Gate 6 on the morning of September 18.

"I remember mentioning something about a guy coming down the road in a truck with the lights off," Warren replied.

"Did you make mention of the word 'scoop'?"

"I might have. I am not sure. It is possible."

"Did you mention that you had been driving one?"

"I don't remember that."

"Did that happen, or did it not?"

"No. I can't remember making a remark like that."

"Did you mention powder magazine?"

"I don't remember it ... It is quite a while ago."

So Martin asked about leading comments to Tom Krahn. "Could you have mentioned scoop?"

Warren said he might have referred to machinery starting up in the 1-38 pit, and was surprised that men went to work before anyone checked on reports of seeing something there. It is unlikely that either Krahn or Drover had said anything to police about Warren driving a scoop. If they had, they would have been important witnesses for the Crown.

Boots were another hot topic. Martin made no secret of his contempt for Warren's story that after the blast, he'd thrown away the pair of boots he wore and had owned for fourteen years, spoiled his old parka and chucked that too, bought new Kamik boots and marked them up, and let police think he'd worn those.

"You didn't care if they solved this crime or not?" Martin asked.

Warren said the crime was used to legitimize the use of replacement workers.

"The question was, did you agree it was a priority for the police to solve this crime?"

"The answer is, it seemed that the priority was to make sure it was a striker that did the crime."

"Did you think it was important that the police solve this murder of these nine men?"

"Yes, I thought it was important."

Yet, Martin said, "The first time you were asked by the police to help them, the first words from your lips are lies."

"I wouldn't say the first words, but during the course of my description, I did lie."

"Yes ... Let us count the lies, Mr. Warren," Martin said. "You told us that Corporal [sic] Defer told you that the Pinkerton guards were prime suspects. I suggest you are lying about that, sir."

"I suggest that I am not lying about it ... That is one of the first things she said to me."[7]

In view of all the lies Warren told, he could hardly claim to have cooperated with the police, Martin said. On August 6, "all you have to do is say, 'Listen, Dale [McGowan], I have to tell you something. I lied. Here is why.' Did that ever cross your mind?"

"Yes. I was feeling—I told such a tangled web of lies that it is hard to get them back now."

"Did you ever tell the police this boot story you are telling us now?"

"No, that's the one thing I was going to tell them that day. I come close to it, but I didn't."

"Sir, you told us last week, Mr. Orris was questioning you about this interview ... 'I had explained it and did everything I could do to try to resolve it.' Mr. Warren, that statement was a lie ..."

"Well, it is false, but it was inadvertent. I didn't contemplate lying under oath. I was taking it in the context at that time."

"You like inadvertent rather than casual?"

"It wasn't a deliberate lie. I was describing the effects of various interviews."

Now Martin was ready to deal with the *Edmonton Journal* article. He asked Warren just what he'd used in his confession. The main things were the map for the route out of the mine and taking the scooptram to the 9-07 powder magazine, he replied. So Martin recapped the story for the jury, beginning with the descent in the Akaitcho shaft, concluding, "'The time was likely 3:00 A.M. The climb had taken about 30 minutes.' This is also roughly what you have said in your story to the police?"

"Yes," Warren said. "I put some stuff in there about it taking longer than what it really did."

"And getting lost at both levels," Martin added.

"Yeah. The chances of me getting lost in a mine would be fairly slim."

"And that was not in the article."

"No, I put it in to make it more realistic," Warren said.

"Right," agreed Martin.

While Warren rejected illogical things from the article, Martin pointed out that Warren added descriptions of an explosive device with a toggle switch, fish line, B-line and drill steel (none of which were supported by any hard evidence), and the DCD caps and their number.

"You used almost nothing in this article, Mr. Warren," Martin said.

"No, just the basic outline. I made up a lot of the rest of it a long time before that."

"But Mr. Warren, you told us the idea was that you would falsely confess and convince them you were the guy to bring this strike to an end."

"I think I did a fairly good job," Warren suggested.

"Why did you tell them that you got lost coming down Akaitcho?" asked Martin a few minutes later.

"Because if you left where I said I left and went straight there, you would be sitting around down there waiting for an hour and a half, waiting to get rid of the central blast ... It would be pretty hard to get lost. It is almost straight down there."

"How would you think of all these details?"

"If you have got nothing else to think of for a year, it is pretty easy."

"So over a year you [had] been thinking about confessing falsely to this thing?"

"No, I am saying over a year's time when this is on your mind a lot, this stuff is on all our minds a lot. For example, you really thought how could this be done, and then you start to think how you could convince somebody it could be done, then you take a whole bunch of different facts and tie them in. That is the way I did it."

Why, Martin asked, when the police thought your size 11 Kamik boots were the ones that made the prints in the mine, "why don't you then also lie about the boots" and agree they were the ones?

"I bought them later, after the blast ... I figured they knew they weren't the boots."

Throughout his questioning, Martin accepted nothing as the truth unless it agreed with the confession. And he always returned to the boots, the only real piece of physical evidence that might be somehow linked to the mine. "When it comes to lying, you are a convincing liar."

"I guess so. If I have proper motivation."

"Right, and there is no question that this week and last week you have got proper motivation to lie."

"Yeah, the last couple of years, I suppose," Warren said dejectedly.

Martin hashed through the story about planting the bag in the pond and the boots in Cameron River. "There was a tremendous amount of black smoke that went up when you burned these boots?"

"Yeah, it was pretty ridiculous," Warren agreed.

"It was like a signal that someone was there and burning something?"

"Yeah, it was, just like a sacrifice to the rubber gods." There were muffled snickers in the gallery.

"If somebody had come by and saw you and reported that to the police, that would sure heighten their suspicion, wouldn't it?"

"I suppose it would ... It wasn't very risky. There was nobody there."

Martin opened the book of Warren's voir dire testimony, given under oath, digging for lies. "You told us last week about your mental state when you confessed, about the medication, the depression, your testicular problem, the voices in your head, the split personality, seeing McMartin's eyes as black dots, one tittle of that, did you tell us about in the voir dire?"

"No, nobody asked me about it." Which was not strictly the case, as Warren would soon admit. Neither was it true that he hadn't mentioned it—he had, but not in such detail. Martin alleged that Warren withheld information "to deceive us."

"I wouldn't say that. I just didn't want to admit to being so screwed up."

"But Mr. Warren, you were in a court of law, not a union hall. So why didn't you tell us the truth, if this is the truth?"

"False pride, I guess. I just couldn't bring myself to bare my soul that much. [The reasons I gave for confessing were] all true."

"Right. So the answers were not the whole truth and nothing but the truth. Is that right?"

"No, it is not the whole truth and nothing but the truth. You just about have to analyze yourself on the stand. I didn't do that. I hadn't written any of this stuff down, what I had been feeling ... You feel stupid talking about stuff like that ... I couldn't articulate the whole truth at the time."

"But you had no difficulty last week going on and on about your third testicle, about the sex life with your wife, about the—"

"No difficulties?" It seemed to come as a surprise to Warren. Only now was he showing some emotion. During Orris's questioning, he seemed as cool as ever, preserving an inner privacy even as he revealed his feelings, bit by bit. "I was having a hard time keeping from breaking down a few times," Warren said after the trial. "I had to steel myself."

Martin was bent on piercing Warren's armour. He acted as if Warren's story was the raving of a desperate liar; the truth, the whole truth, and nothing but the truth was anything that would cast Warren down to atone for a terrible crime, the crime of murder, the crime of playing God.

Finally, Orris could take no more. "My friend is cross-examining Mr. Warren with respect to what wasn't said." The jury should be told that the issues in the voir dire related to the voluntariness of the statements, not the substance of the entire defense case. Justice de Weerdt spoke to the jury, but Martin was not deterred. He proceeded to ask Warren if, awaiting trial, he had ever applied for bail. Orris objected. Such decisions, made on the advice of counsel and based on the offense, the community, and where it occurred, "should not be held against Mr. Warren." The question was allowed, but the entire argument took place in front of the jury anyway. And Martin did not ask if the Crown had offered to reduce the charge to manslaughter in return for a guilty plea.[8]

The audiotape of Warren crying before going to Cameron Falls was replayed. "So even in that emotional moment, you were able to lie fluently and apparently convincingly, is what you tell us now?" Martin asked.

"Yeah, and you notice just before that I was talking about sitting with my wife for coffee."

"That's right," Martin agreed.

"And this here goes together with it too," Warren added. "Sure I was lying then. I had been lying all night. I had been lying all year. As far as killing the guys, no, that's the problem, you see. A guy lived forty-nine years and never even slapped anybody, and all of a sudden you have to convince people he killed people. It's a toughy."

"It is not a toughy at all," Martin retorted. "The only part of what you have said in this case is true is the confession. Everything else is a lie. You lied at the voir dire. You are lying to us now. Do you agree?"

"You can say whatever you like. I am denying it."

"You have an intense dislike for replacement workers and the laws that permit that," Martin charged.

"The idea of it, I have got an intense dislike. I talked to replacement workers. I didn't pound them or swear at them or nothing."

"You also had an intense dislike of Peggy Witte?"

"Actually, I admire the woman, but the way she was operating the labour relations I didn't care for. It is a step back in time."

"The way you described her to Corporal Ingram——"

"I am ashamed of referring to her that way. It was a derogatory thing to do. Just because she is female has nothing to do with it."

"But you clearly demonstrated an intense dislike of this woman?"

"Of what she was trying to do, yes."

"Which you thought was to break your union?"

"Yes, I am sure that was the plan."

With that, Martin quoted Warren about principle and wrecking the system, but said that's what he was doing when he entered the mine to kill people.

"I don't think you are going to gain much by doing acts like that," Warren replied.

"I am going to tell you something else, Mr. Warren. The reason that you are here admitting that you lied, and the reason that you committed perjury was to hide from us the fact that you are also a murderer."

"You can suggest whatever you like. I am just denying it."

"Those are my questions, milord," Martin said.

Roger Warren was in the witness box for seven days, three under cross-examination, and he was undoubtedly happy to get out. His daughter Ann was next. On the morning of the blast, she said her dad was just as he always was after a night on the line. His parka smelled of diesel, she remembered. "I asked him to take it out." Ann didn't notice any change in her father's behaviour until the fall of 1993. "He wasn't communicating, he wasn't talking the same, he wasn't eating as well ... He had something on his mind." His drinking "had increased a bit. It was very unlike him." Occasionally, he came home drunk. After the arrest, she didn't see her father for weeks.

Warren's medical problems were reviewed by Dr. Andrew MacMillan, who had treated Warren for pain in his chest and arm on October 21, 1992.

Warren had extra, irregular heartbeats every third beat, "a very high frequency," MacMillan said. Warren probably hadn't suffered a heart attack. Another doctor's records stated that Warren had complained of "no other episodes of chest pain, as related to exertion, [just] similar, milder, momentary distress through the summer." This supported Warren's statement that his ailment wasn't new, but cast a shadow on his account of fainting in the mine. The cause of Warren's arrhythmia could not be determined with certainty, but MacMillan believed anxiety was a factor.

Warren was put on a drug that dulls the electrical excitability of all heart cells. It also suppresses reactions of the central nervous system, such as sweaty hands, and can cause light-headedness, nightmares, drowsiness, impotence, and even depression. The prescription was written by a specialist, so MacMillan didn't know if the potential problems were explained to Warren, but he didn't complain about any side effects. MacMillan said that such silence was common, at least for the first several months.

Warren also had a five- or six-year history of whitehand, and pain in his shoulders and elbows, ailments common to miners. "Usually people in that situation have other problems with the nerves at the same time," MacMillan said. In December 1992, Warren was put on an anti-inflammatory drug often given to sufferers of tendonitis and carpal tunnel syndrome. In almost every visit, he was told to quit using heavy equipment.

The first time Warren sought medical help for his testicular problem was January 5, 1994, when he was in jail. "He said he'd had it since the previous March [1993]," a nurse said. Tests revealed a nonmalignant lump that did not require treatment, she said. He was also asked about depression, "but Roger said that he was OK."

Danny Mino, 38, described Warren's character. They two men had been mining partners for two years. Warren "was number one as far as some of the boys were concerned," Mino said. A formidable man with a bushy mustache, he was helped into court by a Seeing Eye dog. Mino had moved to Montreal after he was blinded in an accident at Giant in 1987; Warren was one of the first men on the scene, and Al Shearing led the rescue team. Mino described what happened. About Warren's work habits, Mino said, "Roger seemed to have more concern [for] aesthetics and a properly done job" than most men, taking pains to get smooth floors and prevent loose rock. Warren "figured most second men were extra baggage. He had a grumpy attitude, like an old coot" who cursed the ground and the machine, and spit on the drift walls. "I think that was when he was at his happiest ... It was just get the job done, and we'll talk later when we reach the lunchroom ... He was always at least two weeks ahead of the project." By colour and smell, "half the time he was telling the surveyor where the ore was," and even if they were put into a "rat hole, he would turn it into a money-making proposition." Warren and Mino had become friends, but after his accident, "the air seemed heavy. We wanted to speak, but, we didn't know what words."

When the police visited Brian Drover in Stony Plain, Alberta, soon after Warren's arrest, they wanted to hear about scooptrams, 1-38, and powder mags. "They kept pressuring me ... Roger mentioned something about 1-38 and being down there ... setting wires to a scoop so it would blow some powder." Unbeknownst to Drover, this was an echo of a plan espoused by RCMP agent Marvin Ferriss.

But Drover had also seen a Giant truck drive by a man walking south on Ingraham Trail toward Gate 6 around daybreak. Then Warren returned. He wasn't unusually dirty or tired, as he would be if he had been underground. Drover remembered that Warren was wearing green boots with a lace at the top, and a solid green work coat. "He didn't do anything abnormal. We talked. I mentioned how busy the Pinkerton's were around our gate that night." Usually, they showed up about twice per shift, but on September 17 they came about every half hour to the top of the hill. "They were down in the portal entrance, shining their lights around," between 3:00 A.M. and 4:00 A.M, which was unusual, Drover said. The Pinkerton's guards generally sat in their trucks at the top of the hill for better surveillance.

It was not news to Peter Martin that Warren had an alibi in Kelly Rhodes, the only man on the picket line who said he'd seen Warren after 1:00 A.M. From Rhodes's first session with police on September 28, he'd said that just as he was going to bed about 2 A.M., Warren came into the bus at Gate 3 and sat down. Then, Rhodes saw Warren again when he returned with Tom Krahn sometime after 6:00 A.M. The police "threatened me to come in on [October] the 20th" after Warren's arrest. "I was afraid of being arrested—they told Dave [Madsen] they were coming to get me if I didn't come in."

Were you ever suspected in this investigation? Boothroyd asked.

Yes, Rhodes replied. "I had my phone lines tapped and I was harassed." Martin implied that Rhodes was lying or mistaken about seeing Warren the night before the blast.

Unlike the RCMP, Warren's lawyers left no stone unturned to find the little car Warren said he'd heard just south of Gate 3. It turned out that Gino Orsi, a mechanic from Con mine and a former police officer in Italy, had visited the picket line driving a blue Pontiac Fiero. He said he arrived at about 4:00 A.M. after his shift ended, and talked with Leo Lachowski for about an hour. He did not see Warren that night, or anyone walking along the Ingraham Trail. "It was a little bit after five when I left."

The police didn't contact Orsi until about a week before the trial, when they learned he would testify. He told them he'd answer every question in court. Once there, Martin tried to impugn Orsi's credibility because he had supported CASAW. He didn't provide a direct alibi, but his sports car could have been the one that Warren, Tuma, and Mikus mentioned.

Leo Lachowski couldn't remember if he'd seen Orsi that night or not. When Lachowski got off shift on the morning of the 18th, he gave Warren a ride home. Roger wasn't dirty, Lachowski said.

Tom Krahn drove to Gate 3 with Warren that morning. "Roger mentioned he'd almost been seen on the property," and had been 100 yards into the 1-38 portal, Krahn said. "I found it a little unusual to be on the property, but I didn't ask for particulars." Krahn didn't tell Warren's lawyers about this until November 30, after Warren had stated his whereabouts on the witness stand, and he had never told the RCMP. "I wasn't under oath. I wasn't happy with the way the interviews went," because officers spent so much time insisting that a union member was the murderer.

Martin pressed Krahn, who was sporty and confident. You lied to police to help Mr. Warren? demanded Martin.

"That's correct," Krahn said.

Did the police ask you if there was conversation between you and Warren?

"That's correct." In a series of questions and answers like this, Krahn was unruffled. He was a damaging witness for the Crown, but for one detail: he'd been at Gate 3 until about 2:10 A.M, and he hadn't seen Warren. Neither had they seen each other on the Ingraham Trail after parting earlier that night.

If Martin challenged Krahn, he belittled Terry Coe, who was respectful and direct. At Gate 3 on the morning of the 18th, Warren said something about seeing "a couple guys around Gate 5 or 6," Coe said, and he'd told police about the conversation. He was hounded mercilessly during the investigation, because police thought the two men were Bettger and Shearing.

Pamela MacQuarrie-Higden was not a CASAW member, but had been harassed by police nevertheless. The RCMP interviewed her many times about the two men she had seen just before 6:00 A.M. on September 18. One was close to 6 feet tall, the other about 5 foot 7 inches. They wore camouflage outfits, but the shorter also wore a tan jacket. "I believe the tall one had a beard. The shorter one was kind of skinny and scrawny ... the taller one was in good shape." They were south of the Vee Lake turnoff, between the 1-38 pit and Gate 6. She passed within about 40 feet of them that time, she said, but she'd seen them on September 12 between Giant's main office and A-shaft. She'd had a session with the RCMP hypnotist. And with her help, a police artist's composite drawings were a fairly good likeness, she said.

Martin pressed her hard, suggesting that she hadn't seen the men on the 18th, that it was too dark to see their faces, that she was confusing different days. "I might not be able to give you as much description as you would like, but they were there on the 18th and they were there on the 12th," she replied.

In your statement of November 5, 1992, you said that some days you weren't even sure if you saw people at all, Martin told her.

"I was under an awful lot of stress and I was not being treated well by the RCMP."

You were hospitalized for stress in November of '92?

Yes, she agreed, some of it caused by the police.

Martin couldn't shake her from her account, but he managed to cast some doubt on her memory by asking when she was contacted by the defense. "I believe in September," she said. "There was no snow on the ground, but it was cold." Her memory of the 18th had probably been affected by intense, repeated interrogation. If Shearing and Bettger had been charged as the RCMP planned, MacQuarrie-Higden would have been a key witness for the Crown.

It was now mid-December and only Luc Normandin would testify before a Christmas break. In late October 1994 he was building a bulkhead in the B-3 man way so it could be used for ventilation. No mining had taken place in the area since before the labour dispute. Normandin was wandering around to keep warm during a break when he noticed a yellow slicker jacket tucked behind a sheet of plywood used to anchor the box for a mine phone. When he tugged at the jacket, a black blasting box came down with it. The click it made when he tested it told him it still worked. "My partner came back and we talked," Normandin said, and decided to replace the gear in case it was related to the blast. From the smoke and dust on it, they thought it had been there for at least two years. Normandin went to the courthouse about ten days later and told Warren's lawyers what he'd found. The lawyers, police, Normandin, and a shift boss went to investigate, entering the mine through the 1-38 portal. About 75 feet from the discovery was a small lunchroom, where police found a blasting cap sitting on the table. In a garbage bag they found a glove. All the items became exhibits in Warren's trial.

In cross-examination, Martin questioned Normandin's motives in coming forward. You came here to help Mr. Warren, your friend?

"I'm here to help find the truth," Normandin said.

After the discovery, you did not go to the police? Martin asked.

"That's right ... Under normal circumstance, I would go to the RCMP, but I had bad experience with [them]."

Mr. Normandin, let's stop playing games—you don't know if that item was there four days or four years, correct? Martin challenged.

"No I don't."

Whether or not Normandin's find had anything to do with the crime, it was within feet of the notorious boot prints on B-3 first level and a party-line phone that could be used to eavesdrop on communications within the mine. It was in an inactive area where it was easy to hide, near exits. It was impossible to tell if this was a missed clue within spitting distance of what the police believed were the very steps of the murderer, but it raised questions. How many clues could have eluded police, and how many more were disturbed after the mine reopened on September 25? It was becoming apparent that the RCMP had not known what to look for or where to find it—and to tell them, they had depended primarily on a man who was probably in shock after the blast: former mine foreman Noel O'Sullivan.

The new year in court began with Al Shearing in the witness box. Orris was severely limited in what he could ask. The judge would brook no mention of other intruders into the mine, including Tim Bettger. In a voir dire, Shearing said that he had seriously contemplated confessing to the murders himself; Orris was not allowed to ask that before the jury but Shearing said it anyway.

Shearing's lawyer, Neil Sharkey, was present in case of emergency. Shearing says that he and Bettger were advised by their lawyers not to testify in the Warren trial when they were first subpoenaed by Martin. "Neil told the Crown," Shearing says, "'My client don't have any respect for the justice system. He doesn't trust the RCMP and he's quite willing to take contempt of court. Now if you want to take chances with him, go right ahead. I'll throw in something else, for two cents. He believes Mr. Warren didn't do it.' Martin even said, 'How do I know that your client won't get up and say, I did it, and he's protected under the Canada Evidence Act?'" Sharkey's reply, Shearing says, was, "I can't tell you what my client's going to do. If you get in an argument, he's quite willing."

Shearing testified that he led two others down the Akaitcho shaft on June 29, 1992, fully equipped with mine gear. They entered the mine about midnight. "Wire cutters" were left at the base of the Akaitcho shaft, the homemade billy club was left on a pipe hangar at the bottom of the man way to 750. By 6:30 A.M., he said, the group was in a trailer at Gate 7 to change out of their wet, muddy clothes. The purpose of the trip and the graffiti they painted in the 7-12 scoop shop was "more or less to scare the replacement workers—let 'em know that people could get in, anytime they feel like it." Pictures of slogans on scooptrams and walls became exhibits.

Shearing also said that on October 14, 1993, he and Warren had discussed the route in and out of the mine for the graffiti raid. They reviewed the *Edmonton Journal* article and the idea of someone confessing so that Peggy Witte would have to negotiate. In an interview, Shearing said that he and Warren had heard about items that police had mentioned in various interrogations—including the discovery of DCD caps and the mysterious Pepsi can left underground.

Perhaps most important to Orris, Shearing left the jury with the note he and Bettger received from Warren in December, denying the confession. The undated note was entered as an exhibit, and the timing of it was later confirmed by CASAW president Rick Cassidy.

Peter Martin was also very careful and got what he wanted. Shearing denied involvement in the blast. The closest Martin came to challenging Shearing was by calling another man a union clown or fool, and suggesting that Warren's note was a fraud.

Warren's psychiatrist was Shabehram Lohrasbe, who had done forensic assessments on about 3,000 people, had testified in court hundreds of times and had assessed inmates for the national parole board. Justice de Weerdt forbade Lohrasbe from speaking of Warren's disposition to commit the murders, giving an opinion about the truth of the confession, or mentioning literature on the subject of false confessions.

Lohrasbe, contacted by Orris in early 1994 after his client had recanted his confession, didn't meet Warren until September 10, during the voir dire. For his assessment, Lohrasbe spent about ten hours with Warren in jail, an hour and a half with Helen and Ann Warren, and used tests done by psychologist Robert Ley, who would testify later. Lohrasbe had studied McMartin's interrogation and the *Edmonton Journal* article.

Warren had suffered from post-traumatic stress disorder after the 1987 blast that blinded Danny Mino and killed Vince Corcoran, Lohrasbe concluded. Warren "would not think about the possibility of another blast being done" that would recreate the symptoms. At first Warren had felt disconnected, then the incident was always in his thoughts. "He suffered from nightmares." But after Warren quit mining, he missed it "intensely."

Lohrasbe found Warren "very intelligent and extraordinarily well-read" for a man without higher education. "He takes great enjoyment in being a perfectionist," and doesn't shirk responsibility. During the strike, "he was surprised how much the lack of work affected him, how linked it was to his identity. He is very devoted to work and to his family ... It's very difficult to read him as a person, which I found unusual." It took time. "He is very much a macho fellow," who nevertheless enjoys intellectual and philosophical issues. Despite an impressive vocabulary, Warren is fairly inarticulate, Lohrasbe said. "He is somewhat ashamed of emotion and is reluctant to show it." He tended to stoically dismiss his own ailments, making him prone to depression. By the time Warren found the growth in his testes in February 1993, he was seriously depressed, Lohrasbe said. "I had no doubt."

And "he certainly felt the stress of some of the younger miners" during the labour dispute. Warren told Lohrasbe that, after September 18, "all the pressures that existed prior to the blast were dramatically escalated. [He had the] sense that people [in] the union were being singled out and frightened," causing paranoia. The situation became increasingly hopeless, and Warren's heart condition and medication contributed to that feeling. "He was becoming increasingly impotent. His sort of macho sexuality was a very important part of his life ... He had musings along the lines, 'so this is what it feels like when you reach the end of your rope.'" Lohrasbe said he couldn't say exactly when Warren's major depressive episode set in, but believed he was still somewhat depressed.

Depressed people do illogical things and suffer from distorted judgment, Lohrasbe said. People in severe depression "simply cannot see the way out ... I don't think even his family was clear what he was going through." Lohrasbe said that Warren could hide his ailments and feelings but was not accomplished in deceit.

By the time of McMartin's interrogation, Warren was "relatively sleepless and tired. He perceived the sergeant as a figure of strong authority" who made it very clear Warren was the culprit and that intent was the only issue. "That was a key feature. He believed that his guilt was a given by police." Depressed and unable to make a rational choice, Warren saw McMartin's option as attractive compared to being branded a cold-blooded killer, Lohrasbe said. "In Mr. Warren's mind, by the time Mr. McMartin was finished, he had no choice ... The payoff on the other side, confessing, was far more attractive." Remarkably, McMartin's pitch "hit just the right note" to a man who was out of work, impotent, and feeling that he's failing his wife—but he could go down in a blaze of glory by ending the labour dispute. For most of the interview, Warren was barely a participant.

Peter Martin's reply to this was that Lohrasbe had been duped by Warren, a skilled liar. The psychiatrist should have talked to jailers and police to see if Warren's behaviour was that of a depressed man. Lohrasbe insisted that was not sound psychiatric method. "I know nothing about the qualifications of those observers. I know a lot about Mr. Warren ... Please, I am not naive in these matters." Nevertheless, Lohrasbe agreed that, if Warren was conning him, the alternative but unlikely diagnosis was "malingering." Lohrasbe admitted he hadn't spoken to the jail psychologist, a man Warren described after the trial as "a moron." Neither could Lohrasbe be sure that Warren's depression was not caused by the realization that, in setting the bomb, he'd prolonged the strike. "There's no way to rule that out," Lohrasbe said. "The origins of Mr. Warren's depression can never be nailed down."

Ironically, had Lohrasbe spoken with Warren's jailers, he would have found at least two who doubted Warren's guilt. One who watched closely and thought

Warren was seriously depressed when he came to jail was Dave Talbot, the man who quit visiting the picket line after the B-shaft vent shack blew up. Talbot had been a police officer in Toronto, had worked in a psychiatric hospital, and was frequently the corrections officer on duty in Warren's cell area. "I watched Warren in the jail, and also Allan [Shearing] and Tim Bettger," Talbot says. From the start, Warren was different. "The day he came in there, I don't think he wanted to get out. He walked in there meek as a lamb ... He seems to have given up on life, and he took this cancer threat a lot more seriously than he should've ... I think he felt that he would be a hero out of this. He would be seen as the person who brought the strike to an end, who gave all these people their jobs back, and a contract. That was the overriding thing. He had very little to live for, he had very little to lose, his kids were grown up ... Even in prison he read three or four newspapers, all sorts of historical books ... He believed in the union movement a lot ... Within a year or two he will be looked upon as a hero in the labour movement ... But he has to remember that the persons who did this are still out there."

When it comes to false confessions, Dr. Robert Ley is probably Canada's leading forensic psychologist. In his own informal and admittedly unscientific research, he found that most false confessors did so to protect other people. Before this case, Ley was involved in eight cases in which false confession was an issue, but he was not called to qualify as an expert in that area. The only precedents cited were two infamous British cases, those involving "The Birmingham Six" and "The Guildford Four." With no prior Canadian case in which an expert was qualified to address false confessions, Ley's evidence was subject to a hard-fought voir dire. "Once again, we're being invited to pioneer," de Weerdt noted.

Studies show that most false confessions occur during interrogations by police and are prompted by psychological pressure, not physical violence, Ley said. In the 1970s, researchers found that people who confess falsely tend to be psychologically vulnerable. To help assess Warren's vulnerability to false confession, Ley gave him three tests developed by Gisli Gudjonsson, the uncontested world leader in the field. In scoring some of Warren's answers, Ley sought advice from Gudjonsson himself.

Based on those tests, other common psychological tests, about twenty-five hours with Warren, and a review of statements to police, "my opinion is that there's a significant number of factors in this case that raise the likelihood of a false confession," Ley said.

Under cross-examination, he agreed that research on false confessions is a relatively new field of study and Gudjonsson's tests have not yet been proven as statistically reliable as other psychological tests. Few other researchers have critiqued them, and the number working in the field is small.

Martin called his own expert in the voir dire, Calgary psychiatrist Julio Arboleda Florez. He taught a course on medicine and law, as well as psychiatry at the University of Calgary, and is a director of a regional centre of the World Health Organization.

Florez said Gudjonsson's tests were not yet widely accepted in the scientific community, and too few researchers had verified his results. There were no psychological profiles of proven false confessors against which to measure test results. Only the classifications of false confessors had been accepted, he said. Florez had only started to study Gudjonsson's work over the previous three weeks and hadn't read his book until "last night." Then, to Martin's mortification and a guffaw from the gallery, Florez revealed that he had testified in court on the subject of false confessions in 1977. He'd been called by the defense. "I said there are some things here that suggest the confession may be false," he said, and, if he had been involved in Warren's defense, he admitted that he would have used Gudjonsson's book "and possibly the tests."

Argument over Dr. Ley's qualifications was testy. He had assessed approximately 200 people charged with or convicted of murder. Martin branded the study of false confessions as "junk science" which could mislead and confuse the jury. Ley's evidence on false confessions was essential for the jury to understand Warren's statements, Orris argued.

De Weerdt knew this would be an appeal issue for both sides, and took the weekend to rule that Ley was not a qualified expert on false confessions. "It is not for Dr. Ley or any other expert to say whether the confession is or is not true ... reliable or unreliable."

Ley's work on the Warren case hadn't begun until September 29, but it was extensive. He reviewed reams of Warren's statements, notes from the police hypnotist, statements of witnesses, Warren's note to Shearing and Bettger, a handwritten statement by Warren about his thoughts and feelings, and newspaper articles. He interviewed Ann Warren as well as Roger, and gave him a battery of standard psychological tests. Ley found Warren to be "not psychologically minded at all. A very modest man. He's moderately obsessive. He was trying to be accurate—he's got a perfectionist streak. Mr. Warren is quite emotionally inhibited. He's reluctant to express his feelings. [He is] a very proud, stoic man. He was very self-critical ... He's not an assertive person," which was very significant in his dealings with police, Ley said. Warren seemed unable to understand why he kept doing more interviews with police.

Warren felt guilt and shame over his impotency, Ley said, and tests showed that emotional and psychological problems tended to influence his health. He loves mining, so he worried about his physical deterioration. His identity was strongly linked to his physical ability. "Mr. Warren was frightened of having cancer [and] anxious at his mortality. His cancer was not ruled out until February 1994," while he was in jail.

Tests confirmed that "he's an avoidant person, a procrastinator," who is well organized, industrious, and more compulsive than average. Nothing pointed to antisocial or psychopathic tendencies. In intelligence tests, Warren had a perfect score on the vocabulary section, but did poorly on the measure of cognitive and motor ability. His total IQ was 108, high average.

Ley agreed with Lohrasbe that Warren was "significantly depressed" in the summer and fall of 1993 and considered himself "a very inferior, inadequate, useless person." He had wanted to do "something bold, something courageous." While his concept of himself was being dramatically rearranged, "it's likely that Mr. Warren did not know he was depressed, in a diagnostic sense ... What he was aware of were changes in his activity level, his sleep habits. Mr. Warren's mood was less likely to be sad than irritable [and] agitated"—an evaluation consistent with his periodic invective on the picket line.

Warren was the "psychological equivalent of a terminally ill person ... He was in a conflict between cooperating [with] and defying the police." Sergeant McMartin's interview style probably fed Warren's inner turmoil and self-loathing, Ley believed. The interrogator's repetition reinforced Warren's fear of failure. Whenever Warren resisted, "he was overwhelmed by Sergeant McMartin." The fact that Warren forgot Helen's birthday dinner on the night of October 15 was very unusual behaviour for him. In Ley's opinion, the interrogation "was the most stressful experience in Mr. Warren's life, psychologically." He was self-destructive but not suicidal.

Ley said that Warren may have seen his confession as an act of hostility toward police who were bent on destruction of the union and members who supported it. Warren's words, Ley said, were: "I might not have a dick, but I can fuck you guys."

Martin began his cross-examination of Ley in a lower key than he had used before in the trial. He quickly gave up on discrediting Ley's work and zeroed in on Warren's responses to a sentence-completion test. "If I only could ..." and Warren added, "change the last couple of years, I'd be happy," and later, "If only I could ... have left here when the strike started like I was going to." And, "The thing I like best about myself ... is my ability to solve problems." Moreover, "I guess I'm ... the kind of person who will never give an inch."

To dispel the image of Warren as a man who was overwhelmed during his interrogation, Martin pointed to Warren's thirty-one-page handwritten memory of it, noting that he had called McMartin a "pismire"[9] and an "asshole."

Any possible contradictions in Warren's feelings were emphasized; Ley's belief that Warren was disturbed by the death of six former colleagues, versus his written statement of contempt for people who "need counseling because scabs got killed ... not this guy, mister." Another note referred to Warren slapping his daughter when she was 14, undermining his testimony that he'd never even slapped anyone.

But Ley's notes contained a bombshell: he had asked Warren if he'd admitted his guilt to his lawyer. Orris rose immediately to defend solicitor–client privilege, but the judge ruled that Warren had already waived it. The conversation began with Ley asking Warren, "When did you first say to someone you didn't do this?"

"I guess in that letter [to] Al and Tim."

Then Ley asked, why not earlier?

"After I fucked myself, I thought I'd go ahead ... It warmed the cockles of my heart when they started to go back to work."

According to Ley's notes, Orris was told, "I did do it. But I was getting to the point where I was really pissed off ... Then Leo McGrady, the union lawyer, came to talk to me. He wanted to know if the company paid me to do it. I told him no way. I did it on my own, no one paid me to do nothing."

"Did you tell Glen you did not do it?" Ley asked.

"No, not there ... In February, when he came for the preliminary."

The jury showed no reaction at all, but people in the gallery were stunned. Warren said after the trial that his daughter Pat felt that the revelation was a turning point. Warren says that Orris's and McGrady's visit was just days after his arrest, in maximum security at the Edmonton Institution. The room could have been bugged. "I didn't know Glen from a hole in the ground. He was really skeptical [and] I was on the verge of not telling him that, until McGrady came along. I figured if one whisper of this shit comes out, I've done all this for nothing." When he heard the strike was over after coming back to Yellowknife, "I was walking around the jail there about 10 feet off the ground. I was just exuberant." That would have been lost if either lawyer had said a word about a false confession, Warren said.

Now that Martin had culled what he wanted from Warren's essay, he successfully opposed it going to the jury. "It is so self-serving, it is almost vulgar," Martin said. "Enough damage like this has been done—more than [my friend] should have been allowed to do."

After Rick Cassidy confirmed that many people knew about Warren's first denial of his confession to Shearing and Bettger, Orris closed the defense case.

Martin had rebuttal evidence, however. Yellowknife jail psychologist Don Bossin's Mona Lisa smile never varied throughout his testimony. On October 29, 1993, he'd met Warren for under an hour to assess his mental state and see if he was suicidal. "He was handling the situation very well," with no signs of depression, Bossin said. He saw Warren again on November 9, after his return from Edmonton. In a note to prison officers, Bossin wrote, "Roger is occupying his time constructively. Things starting to change. More stress since his wife began visiting. I think Roger is only now becoming aware of the full weight of his situation." Bossin produced no other notes from his talks with Warren.

The courtroom was packed on January 13 for Peter Martin's address. Martin described Warren as a man who lied to protect himself and deflect his guilt, as a problem solver now facing the high-stakes challenge of a lifetime. His parka had vanished. Warren mistakenly believed he'd worn size 10 boots on the night of September 18 and burned the wrong ones. The stories he concocted about his boots are "the work of a guilty mind ... The one person who knows the truth is not telling it now ... The entire defense depends on his credibility. If you find he is not credible, his defense fails." The Crown's case could only have been more compelling if it had been in a movie, Martin said. "The why, the where, the when, the how—it's all there. [Warren] even provided information that the police were unaware of ... He is speaking about his emotions at the time—what he felt, what he thought ... This is not a confession of a sick or disturbed man," but of a man who prolonged the strike when he had tried to shorten it, and thus felt remorse. "This is a confession that is corroborated." Inconsistencies in the confession or between it and the evidence were simply related to matters unimportant to Warren, including the type of powder and the scooptram used.

Warren's depression was fabricated for a defense that does not exist, Martin said. "You can figure out for yourself if he is depressed or not by looking at these [video] tapes." Is our system so vulnerable that a dishonest man will escape justice by lying to two experts? Can Warren subvert the system with "a few lies and a few friends"? The note to Shearing was "silly," and Kelly Rhodes is "simply wrong" or lying when he said he saw Warren at Gate 3 at 2:00 A.M. Tom Krahn lied for a friend. As for Pamela MacQuarrie-Higden, "I didn't mean to be unkind, [but] this is just not reliable evidence." Martin requoted Warren's comment about wrecking the system and asked, "Was this another reason why he confessed? Or was this an answer to why he killed? ... He now stands before you, this problem solver, having done his best to dance through the Crown's evidence." He is wondering if he has fooled you, "and he is wondering whether he will get away with murder."

Orris's turn came after lunch. "It is difficult enough to defend a case, any case, when one is aligned against the police [and the resources of] the Crown ... We have to deal with my own client's attempts at self-destruction ... We wanted to get to the truth," and that's why Warren testified. Even in the so-called re-enactment, Warren said the trip underground had taken four and a half hours, but he hadn't been seen on the picket line for only four hours. Shearing said that his June 29 trip underground took six and a half hours. And it's unlikely that the Crown's theory is correct that only one person entered the mine, set up the explosives, and left. Why would someone who was expected to be on the picket line do this crime? It's the Crown's theory that a man with whitehand, a bad back, and heart trouble climbed down seventy-five stories of ladders, set this device, came back out in the morning, and "there's no sign about him that he's done it." In the underground video, McGowan said he was glad he didn't have to climb back out of the mine, he might not have made it. Warren says, "'Me too, I can't believe I did all that.' He didn't do all that." But the police were not interested in inconsistencies and didn't ask many questions about them. They had someone willing to take the rap and that's all they wanted. They ignored the fact that Warren's description of his route did not match the path of the bootprints.

Yes, Warren lied to the police, Orris said. But what if he had told them the truth? They would've said, "Ha, you're in the 1-38 pit—you're our man." Warren didn't want to tell the police what he had seen there because they were so focused on the union, so he tried to check things out himself. The evidence was that other people also felt they had to lie to the police, but that didn't make them guilty. And if Warren had committed the crime, why talk to police at all, and then attract their attention by telling them about two people he'd seen? The people he described fit MacQuarrie-Higden's evidence, and Brian Broda's. The Crown brushed MacQuarrie-Higden aside, but the police interviewed her thirteen times. In the summer of 1993, union members feared being framed by the police. Then, it seemed imminent that two former union executives, Shearing and Bettger, would be arrested. Warren believed, if that happened, "the union's gone, the strike's gone, everything's gone," after a year and a half of struggle and sacrifice.

Planting the bag and the boots were stupid acts that show how irrational Warren was in 1993, Orris said. And when Warren finally stepped into the abyss, "he had no intention of being dragged out. He was prepared to sacrifice himself." He told the police on the way back from Cameron Falls that he was "deeply depressed," but that went unnoticed by Bossin, the jail psychologist. It's obvious from the tapes and the testimony of Ley and Lohrasbe that Warren is a man who doesn't show his emotions. The doctors have their own methods of testing the veracity of what they're told, and applied them. Under the circumstances, Warren saw no real choice when he was branded as guilty by Sergeant McMartin, who threatened to wield the power of the attorney general until Warren was charged with first-degree murder. So Warren told the police he did it, using the same scenario he'd given them in the questionnaire eleven months earlier.

The postblast team did not produce one piece of the device Warren described, Orris stressed, and believed that the explosives were set off the ground, contrary to Warren's account. He recanted his confession just days after the strike ended, as one would expect.

The Crown's theory about the boots doesn't make much sense, Orris added. You'd have to believe Warren mistook the boots he used, then bought and defaced new Kamik boots when he could have bought some other green boots. Then, when the police took his boots and gave them back, he had them long enough to dispose of them and say he'd worn them out. Why keep them, if he had a guilty conscience? Is it likely that Roger Warren went into the mine and set a blast "wearing a light that's held together by a paper clip"? Warren set out to wreck a system that wasn't working for everybody, and "that was a very stupid thing for him to do ... It's there to protect everybody, even those who are self-destructive ... He is presumed to be innocent until the Crown has proven otherwise, beyond a reasonable doubt ... The evidence proves his innocence. If you convict Mr. Warren, the people who did this terrible crime would have gotten away with murder."

Off went the jury. Martin angrily accused Orris of mistakes in referring to the evidence, and there were minor ones. Martin then listed them inaccurately and warned that he might apply for a mistrial.

When de Weerdt charged the jury, he split his address into segments so that Martin and Orris could comment at strategic points. "Apart from the alleged confessions, there is only circumstantial evidence in the Crown's case against Roger Warren," de Weerdt said at one point. Martin was livid. "His confession is direct evidence." In saying it's not, "the effect of that is, you have told them, sir, to acquit." De Weerdt called for a break, but appeared unfazed by this slur or attempt to influence the remainder of the charge. When he returned, he stressed that the confession was circumstantial evidence and politely asked Martin to recant. He declined.

De Weerdt's summary of the evidence was perhaps one of the weakest in his distinguished career, formidable task that it was. It was less than a thumbnail sketch of evidence that had taken three months to present, to jurors who had taken very few notes of testimony but had binders full of confessional transcripts. De Weerdt urged jurors to consider if witnesses had a greater loyalty to some cause other than the truth. This was perhaps his most sage advice; one can only assume he intended it to apply equally to all witnesses. Neither Crown nor defense lawyers were happy with the summary, and the next day Martin tried to get additions to it. As Martin gave examples, Warren rolled his eyes skyward. De Weerdt decided that changes might make matters worse, and make it appear that the court was involved in the jury's deliberations.

The summary wasn't the only problem. De Weerdt's outline of the differences between first- and second-degree murder was so confusing that the jury asked for a clarification, which was still somewhat hard to follow. They also requested and were given transcripts of Alex Mikus's and Roger Warren's testimony.

While the jury was out, Warren waited nervously in a little room downstairs in the courthouse. Late in the day, the jury asked for a transcript of the section of de Weerdt's charge on culpable homicide and the possible verdicts. It was a blow to Warren; his eyes welled with tears and his RCMP guard whisked him away as court adjourned. De Weerdt answered the jury's request on Friday morning, January 20. The jury reached a verdict just before 4:00 P.M. The news spread quickly. The gallery was full, but only one member of the union was present; Warren's family was not. Warren came in, dressed conservatively in a blue and gray suit but looking tense and drawn. The jury was polled.

"How say you?" the clerk asked.

"We find the defendant not guilty of first-degree murder. We find the defendant guilty of second-degree murder," forewoman Marg Halifax said, meaning the act was not planned and deliberate. There was no audible reaction in the room. Warren's gaze remained fixed, as if he'd braced himself for whatever might happen. The sentence was life in prison with a minimum of ten years without parole. It was now the jury's duty to recommend a period from ten to twenty-five years, although the advice is not binding on the judge.

"I still think he's innocent," said Amos Simon, a union loyalist, while the jury met.

The jury returned after fifteen minutes. "We recommend that the defendant not be eligible for parole for twenty years," Halifax said. Warren stood, flanked by his lawyers. "You are convicted accordingly," de Weerdt said.

Reporters made their way to the victims' families. Judit Pandev smiled sadly and said she was happy with the outcome. On the front of her shirt was a picture of herself and Joe, hugging. "Forever loved, forever remembered," the caption said. Carol Riggs wore an image of her son Shane.

The verdict "makes me feel like there's a law," said Rick Titterton, who'd crossed the picket line in the summer of 1992. "There's some justice. Some."

The court sat again briefly as de Weerdt announced that he would sentence Warren on January 25. Martin said he'd probably support the jury's recommendation about parole. "If my friend is going to submit that Mr. Warren is a danger and a continuing danger after ten years, that's ludicrous," Orris replied.

Dave Grundy was back on TV for the RCMP, outside the courthouse in the cold, being asked about winners and losers. "I think everybody's a loser in cases such as this," he said. "It puts a close on the investigation. It allows people to get on with their lives. The community can now start to get back to the way it was before." It seemed like a trite notion, after three years of calamity, deaths, bombings, fights, subterfuge, mistrust, paranoia, and daily hardship.

Trammer Milan Tuma, who said he respected Warren and felt he was basically an honest man, nevertheless thought "he was the murderer or he knew the murderer and it should be first-degree." He was thankful the verdict wasn't manslaughter.

Inspector Al Macintyre was mobbed when he emerged from the building. "Did you feel any special pressure to get a suspect, make an arrest in this case, given all that went on with this strike?" a reporter asked.

"Not so much pressure to get a suspect, but simply that we had to get on with this investigation and—yeah, there was pressure, you bet there was pressure. It was a very difficult investigation, it was a very high-profile matter, and we dealt with it appropriately," Macintyre said.

Peter Martin was modest. "It was a thoughtful and well-considered verdict ... It was a difficult case for everyone. I ask that you not lose sight of the fact that nine men were killed. Nine families are grieving. And a tenth man now is in jail, and will be sentenced to imprisonment for life."

The defense team did not comment; neither did the Warrens.

That night, some of the victims' families held a press conference at the Salvation Army's office. Judit Pandev, Carol and Peter Riggs, and Doreen Hourie sat under the television lights as camera motor drives whirred. A brief statement was read: "The last two years has been a long and trying time. Grief from a murder is unlike any other pain. Someone makes a decision to take a husband, a father, a brother, an uncle, a grandfather, a friend, a son. From that time on your life is changed. While our grief is not over, we feel we can return to our homes and families believing that now, the nine men can rest in peace. And we can look to the future with God's blessing."

The families present felt they had been a symbol for the jury of all the nine bereaved families. "We had lots of time," Judit Pandev said. "The rest of the ladies all have little kids. So the three of us represented the nine." Hearing Warren's confession was "like someone ripped the heart out of you. The worst part was, he doesn't care ... even today. What was the purpose? Nothing ... But out of all this, what I think, just because somebody tells you, do something, you don't have to follow it, blindly. This is what the union wanted. The decision you make [on crossing the picket line], it should be your own. And you don't have to die for this decision."

Peter Riggs said that he didn't think the verdict would change the belief of some mine workers that Warren "didn't do it. Whatever they were told they still, to this day, don't believe he did it all by himself." That opinion is widely held in mining circles.

CHAPTER NINE

EXTENDING THE DRIFTS

Life can only be understood backward, but it must be lived forward.

—Søren Kierkegaard (1813–55)

Like the underground, Stony Mountain Penitentiary is a hidden world, but it is perched like a gigantic feudal castle upon a lone hill surrounded by prairie. Behind massive stone blocks, sliding doors, barbed wire, and guard towers, inmates make alcoholic brew and peddle prison currency. It is more difficult to visit the jail than many foreign countries, but Roger Warren's newspapers get through. He has a cell among other "lifers," where guards turn a large metal wheel to allow the cell doors to open. On the way into their section is a large painting of the Four Horsemen of the Apocalypse. Warren works in the machine shop, dressed in drab green prison garb. He is reserved and unassuming, but commands the respect of other inmates because he is "in" for murder. As ever, he reads voraciously, including Chaucer, English history of the eleventh and twelfth centuries, and James Joyce's *Ulysses*. Warren has family in nearby Winnipeg, but his wife and daughters still live in Yellowknife and Peace River. They visit when they can, standing in line outside the large visiting room with twenty-year-old women in short skirts and high heels, and others with babies and toddlers waiting to see their fathers. Visitors become familiar faces to each other, strangers linked by a peculiar bond. For a couple of hours they huddle with their men around small, round tables similar to those in the Gold Range bar. They speak in hushed tones. One feels like a voyeur in a strangely intimate setting. Guards watch continuously from behind one-way windows.

Removed as Warren is from Giant mine, events of 1992–95 were still foremost in his thoughts in mid-1995. In the only interview he has granted since his arrest, he spoke candidly about Giant, his trial, and his past. He appeared to have no memory of parts of his confession and seemed astounded at some of the things he had said—such as asking Corporal White if there was a cage in the Akaitcho shaft. He had heard tapes of his confession at least twice in court, and had read the transcripts, but some details had escaped him. He chuckled to hear that, during an adjournment in court while the jury was still out, a senior manager from Royal Oak and a police officer talked about potential new charges against him, based on his testimony, if he was found not guilty. The company was worried that Warren might want to come back to work at Giant.

Warren appealed his conviction immediately after the trial, and the Crown later appealed the second-degree murder verdict. Warren's lawyers cited eighteen reasons for the appeal, challenging the very core of the Crown's case against him. First, they said that Justice Mark de Weerdt should not have ruled that Warren's confessions were voluntary, and therefore admissible in court. They argued that Warren's Kamik boots were twice seized illegally, in violation of the Charter of Rights and Freedoms. The lawyers claim that they were wrongly prevented from leading evidence the RCMP had against other suspects, including Rob Wells's testimony that he had found explosives in a tent trailer that had been on the picket line the day of the fatal blast.

Similarly, the defense was not permitted to cross-examine RCMP officers about numerous statements Warren made to police. The defense also objected to Justice de Weerdt's refusal to hear evidence on false confessions from Dr. Ley and Dr. Lohrasbe. In passing sentence, de Weerdt also rejected their opinions that Warren suffered from clinical depression at the time of his confession. Lawyers Glen Orris and Gillian Boothroyd said that de Weerdt made errors in his instructions to the jury. His summary of evidence did not "fairly relate the evidence to the issues the jury had to determine," and he "unfairly emphasized the cross-examination of [Warren] as it related to [his] credibility," states the application for appeal.

It still seemed to Warren that the system was stacked against him. While he sat in jail, court battles resumed to determine if the federal government would continue to pay Glen Orris through the appeal, or if Warren would have to hire a local lawyer through NWT legal aid. Warren's lawyers won that fight in June 1995. His appeal is scheduled to be heard May 20–22, 1997.

Controversy was brewing behind the scenes even before the verdict in Warren's trial. Word leaked out that the NWT Workers' Compensation Board (WCB) had filed a civil suit on September 12 against three unnamed culprits in murder, pending the outcome of the trial. The suit also named every other party involved in the labour dispute except the RCMP—including CASAW, Harry Seeton, Peggy Witte, lawyer Bill Sheridan, Royal Oak, Pinkerton's of Canada, Mine Safety chief Dave Turner, and the NWT government. The suit alleges that their actions or negligence led to the deaths on September 18. Jury forewoman Marg Halifax, a senior official with the WCB, knew about a potential lawsuit and that, if it proceeded, her employer would have a significant financial interest in any murder conviction. The $33-million lawsuit was filed on behalf of the victims' families, but also to recover the WCB's huge payouts. The court file, however, was kept secret by a judge's order, and the full story did not break until January 30, 1995, ten days after the jury's verdict.

Later, the WCB added a host of defendants to the lawsuit: Warren, Al Shearing, Tim Bettger, Terry Legge, Conrad and Blaine Lisoway, Dale Johnston, Bob Kosta, James Mager, Harold David, Jim Evoy, the Canadian Auto Workers, and several other union members. Evoy told the court that his inclusion, made not long before he ran for election as MLA, was "scandalous, frivolous [and] vexatious." He lost the election and returned to the presidency of the NWT Federation of Labour. He was eventually severed from the lawsuit due to lack of evidence against him. At the same time, the judge severed Dave Turner and the NWT government, ruling that "there is nothing in the [Mine Safety Act] to impose an obligation on the part of government to take some step to prevent crime on the [mine] site ... It is plain and obvious that the claim against these defendants cannot succeed." The WCB appealed all the severances and won.

Meanwhile, Mine Safety had been transferred to the WCB, putting Turner in the position of being sued by his employer. He quit in December 1996 to take a management job at Quinsam Coal, on Vancouver Island.

Proceedings in the WCB's suit will probably continue well into the next century. Warren denies involvement in the blast or any prior knowledge of it, and insists he will hold the plaintiffs to strict proof of their allegations against him.

Warren's trial wasn't over for the remaining jurors either. In July 1995 they were questioned by the RCMP, in the very interrogation suite in which Warren had confessed, by officers who had been on the Giant task force. One woman was shocked by the RCMP's actions, didn't know what she could tell them as a juror, and sought legal help. "I was petrified," she says. "You're being taped, you feel like a suspect or a criminal ... That room had memories. I remember the kind of interrogation that was in there." The officer asked her why she'd called a lawyer. "They assume that if you talk to anybody, you're guilty. I felt that he was rude." Questioning jurors was a very unusual tactic, and it wasn't clear what the RCMP were investigating. Juror Roy Desjarlais says that the police asked if he'd been hassled by anyone or if he'd violated his oath of secrecy (a criminal offense). The officer said he was investigating allegations that the jury had been "infiltrated." According to Inspector Al Macintyre, no official complaint had been made about the jury; Sergeant Dave Grundy said the opposite.

Bill Schram, who had run for MP in 1993 as a New Democrat and lost to Liberal Ethel Blondin-Andrew, had tried earlier to cast a shadow over the jury in some comments printed in *yellowknifer*. The articles were related to his efforts to raise money to help the Warrens with legal costs they'd had to pay on their own.

Al Shearing and Tim Bettger pleaded guilty to breaking and entering Giant mine for the graffiti run, and to setting the explosion at the B-shaft vent shack. Bettger pleaded guilty to blowing a hole in the satellite dish. He got three years in a federal prison, while Shearing was sentenced to two and a half years. Their request to be incarcerated together was not granted. Bettger served his time in Prince Albert, Saskatchewan, near his family, while Shearing was sent to a medium-security prison in Innisfail, Alberta.

Shearing was released on probation in January 1996, and lived in an Edmonton apartment block for former inmates. He wanted to return to Yellowknife and had a job lined up, but his plan was opposed by the RCMP and a Salvation Army captain who had counseled the blast victims' families. The "automatic parole report" written by Sergeant Bill Code and Constable Ken Morrison (heavily edited before it was finally given to him) states that "Shearing, along with his associates, continued their terrorist activity, even when the police in Yellowknife were investigating one of the most horrific crimes in Canadian history." Most of these claims were founded in material provided by Marvin Ferriss. "Shearing throughout the investigation considered it a game to outsmart the police," the writers added. "[He] was for the most part always polite, however provided very little assistance, and hinder[ed] the investigation with his constant antagonistic approach to the police ... We will never know the actual effect of his crimes [on unseen victims in Yellowknife], however we do know that it was the support of actions such as these which led to the death of nine men on September 18, 1992 ... He created fear and distrust within the community. Many [people] would be outraged at an early release, as they see this sentence as an end to the fear they have had to live with for a long time." At his parole hearing, Shearing says, he pointed out that "the writers are very biased against me."

A psychologist who saw Shearing in prison didn't help his case either. The psychologist found that Shearing has "impaired empathy" and is not introspective or psychologically minded. "This type of individual functions best under circumstances where rules are clearly spelled out and a fair degree of structure exists in their life space," he wrote. On the other hand, "his aggressive behaviour was the result of pressures from the labour dispute in which he was so intensely involved. It is doubtful that once this phase of his life is over, he would be seen in correctional circles again."

Shearing took the temporary move to Edmonton in stride. His shared apartment was basic but tidy; he quickly found a good job as a transport-truck mechanic, and his freedom was limited by a curfew. He didn't think he was free of police surveillance. "I got a shadow every once in a while uptown," he said. "They're still seeing who I'm in contact with." Shearing was convinced that the murder investigation quietly continued, even after his return to Yellowknife in September 1996. He arrived without any apparent reaction in the community and works for a mechanical contractor.

Tim Bettger served his time in Prince Albert, Saskatchewan, working at the penitentiary's farm annex. He says it reminded him of working at Giant. By the time of his full parole in 1996, Bettger had lost more than 100 pounds, most of it put on during the labour dispute. "Imagine my surprise, the first time I saw him," his wife, Izzie, says cheerfully. The Bettgers left Yellowknife in August 1996 to be closer to Prince Albert, due to Tim's parole restrictions. They prevent his return to Yellowknife before his sentence expires.

The other vent-shack bombers fared better than Shearing and Bettger; they were never charged. Terry Legge built a new house, but he and his wife soon separated. He still works at Giant. Conrad Lisoway returned to his farm in Saskatchewan during the labour dispute and took severance rather than return to Giant. Several others made similar choices, including Dale Johnston, who still operates Wolverine Sports.

Art St. Amand, the veteran miner who took part in the graffiti raid, is back at Giant doing development mining. His boss says that what St. Amand brings to his job, you couldn't get from ten young guys.

Marvin Ferriss and his wife left town, and only rumours of their whereabouts remain. Gordie Kendall is reportedly in the Vancouver area.

After being interviewed for this book, Bob Robertson decided to tell his story to the CAW executive. He said the union leaders took it well but weren't convinced of the error of their ways or of Shearing's guilt.

Big Mark Eveson and shaft hand Bob Kosta were teamed up and reassigned as trammers at Giant. Kosta is still the local's treasurer. His common-law wife, Ursula Daniels, died of an aneurism in the fall of 1996.

Luc Normandin, Blaine Lisoway, and Jim Fournier also returned to work. James Mager, the only man fired as a result of June 14's melee, maintains a local office and apartment tower.

In the spring of 1995, former CASAW president Harry Seeton, who led the local through most of the strike/lockout, got a motion passed in a union meeting to remove the gigantic "Scab on the Run" sign from the hall. Though Seeton has retired from union politics in what is now a Canadian Auto Workers local, he knows that integrating ex-strikebreakers into the union is the only way to keep the local strong. It was a bitter pill to swallow for some staunch unionists, including Seeton. He confines his communication with "scabs" to the workplace. Seeton was assigned to the carpentry shop, but was laid off in 1996. Ironically, he bumped back into a job in the shaft, where he was when the labour dispute began.

The CAW union local seems stronger than ever, despite the national's refusal to defend any members named in the WCB's civil lawsuit, including Seeton and Kosta. Attendance at meetings is very high, surpassing even some of the meetings during the negotiations of 1992. Rick Cassidy was reelected as president for another term. Contract talks began again on October 8, 1996. The collective agreement expired on November 16 without a new settlement, so the union called in industrial inquiry commissioners Ready and Munroe. "Royal Oak has once again demand[ed] massive concessions, jeopardizing job security, despite productivity improvements," Cassidy said. "Royal Oak was not prepared to make any decent proposal." Royal Oak apparently lived up to a pledge in its annual report, released in June, to return to its "tough management style" of the early 1990s. By March 1997, no agreement had been reached.

June and Derek Roberts had to sell their trailer and move into subsidized housing. They had to sell the truck too, and struggled with their debts well into 1996. Another daughter, Hayley, was born prematurely during the strike, in the middle of the RCMP's "blitz package." She will need a glass eye, but she's an energetic little girl who gets plenty of attention from her big sisters. June was interviewed by the producers of a CBC-TV "docudrama" entitled *Giant Mine*, but accurately predicted it would not tell the true story. "I can't believe they're basing it on two scabs," she said. Ironically, the movie was filmed near Kirkland Lake, Ontario. Judit Pandev visited the set during production and met the man who portrayed her late husband, Josef.

Harold David was saddened in 1995 by the death of Barney McGuire, a spirited unionist who helped organize the Northwest Territories' first union local, under Mine–Mill back in the 1940s. David worked part-time for the CAW before starting a janitorial-services business. Amazingly, the union refused to fund his defense in the WCB's civil lawsuit.

Hemi Mitic is still Buzz Hargrove's right arm at the CAW.

Kurt Lehniger's health has prevented his return to work, and he is still deeply troubled by the treatment he received at the hands of the police, the courts, and Royal Oak during the labour dispute.

Jim O'Neil isn't working at Giant either. In 1995 he was finally diagnosed as suffering from posttraumatic stress, went on leave, received treatment, and remains on workers' compensation. He and Jane divorced, and Jim moved to Edmonton. They sold their house. Jane married Mike Magrum, whose new mansion features a spectacular view of Yellowknife and Great Slave Lake.

Keith Murray is working at a mine in Snow Lake, Manitoba. Noel O'Sullivan had a hip operation and can no longer work underground. He now reviews the miners' bonus payments.

Mike Werner became a vice president at TVX Gold. They parted company in 1996, but he still works in mining. Terry Byberg headed a major TVX mining operation in Greece before returning to Canadian operations. He has since left TVX also, and at last report was a mine manager for Exall Resources in Northern Ontario.

Major Ralph Sinke and Chris Morton no longer work for Pinkerton's of Canada. Both say they are engaged in executive security. Sinke sent his book of poems as a gift, warmly inscribed, to Inspector Dennis Massey. The three men were quite friendly during hearings of the RCMP Public Complaints Commission in February 1995.

Superintendent Brian Watt's command of the NWT division of the RCMP ended on September 1, 1995. He became assistant commissioner in Saskatchewan.

Sergeant Vern White received a commendation in the fall of 1995 from the commissioner of the RCMP for his work as primary investigator in the murder investigation. White was then in charge of media liaison, but has since been transferred to Ottawa. Dave Grundy, who had the job during the labour dispute, became a staff sergeant, his second promotion in as many years.

Sergeant Gregg McMartin, interrogator extraordinaire, retired from the RCMP and has his own consulting business in Airdrie, Alberta. He specializes in polygraph, statement analysis, and investigations.

Peter Martin resigned from the federal Justice Department, but has been retained to contest Roger Warren's appeal. He spent a year as president of the Law Society of Alberta and went into private practice in Calgary.

Justice Mark de Weerdt moved to British Columbia soon after Roger Warren's trial. He is still active as a judge.

After retiring from politics, Marcel Danis concentrated on his legal and academic career. He teaches political science at Concordia University in Montreal and took on a controversial case in Bangladesh. His client, former president Hossain Mohammed Ershad, was charged with the murder of a rebel general in 1981. Ershad was already serving twenty-three years for corruption and possession of unlicensed firearms.

The end of the Giant mine dispute boosted the already stellar stock of Vince Ready and Don Munroe, who remain much in demand on the arbitration circuit. Munroe helped avert a work stoppage at Con mine in 1994.

The Supreme Court of Canada upheld the Canada Labour Relations Board order that resulted in a collective agreement at Giant. Worry was widespread that the strike/lockout might resume if Royal Oak won the case. People who spent the night in the union hall before the 4–3 decision was announced breathed sighs of relief when it came off the fax machine. Despite a substantial dissenting argument, the ruling strongly supported the CLRB's "eminently sensible" remedy.

Peggy Witte and Royal Oak startled the financial community and mining industry in 1994 with a bid to take over Lac Minerals, a far larger company. American Barrick (now Barrick Gold) eventually edged out Royal Oak for the prize, but Witte's team emerged with new respect and a much higher profile. Witte predicts that Royal Oak will crack North America's top ten gold producers with production of a million ounces annually by the year 2000.

In late 1994, Royal Oak's headquarters was moved from Vancouver to a suburb of Seattle, Washington. Witte pointed out that personal tax rates are lower in the United States. She was also incensed with the BC government for its decision to halt plans for a mine in an environmentally sensitive northern watershed. At one stage she accused the New Democratic Party of turning the province into a "Third World country." In August 1995, the NDP government decided to pay compensation, which resulted in a profit on Royal Oak's initial investment, at taxpayers' expense. Later, the BC government agreed to subsidize infrastructure for Royal Oak's new Kemess mining project.

Royal Oak continued to lose managers and supervisors into 1995. At corporate headquarters, vice president Colin Benner and human resources manager Bill Heath left Royal Oak in late 1994. At Giant, mine managers at first lasted about six months. A new one started in mid-1995. Only one of the lower-level supervisors who were at Giant when the labour dispute started works for Royal Oak today.

Royal Oak's stock has languished, despite the company's growth. Under Witte's direction, Royal Oak planned "the acquisition of an intermediate-tier gold producer" in 1996, hoping to "increase the company's production and decrease the average cash cost" of $358 US per ounce. The goal wasn't accomplished. Despite the high cost of production, Royal Oak has steadily made modest profits. Witte herself hauled in over $520,000 US as Royal Oak's CEO in 1995. In January 1997, the company asked the city of Yellowknife to refund half its taxes, and requested a cut in electricity rates from the NWT Power Corp.

Aggressive as ever, Witte remains a controversial figure. She and her husband, Bill, have separated. "He woke up one day and said, 'Where is all this going?' I'm 38, and I'd like to have a family," Witte told *Chatelaine* magazine, which named her "woman of the year" in January 1995. "I kept saying, 'Next year, my job's going to get better ... Next year, I'll be home more. And the next thing you know, next year you're not married anymore." *Chatelaine*'s award sparked outrage in Yellowknife, where many people blame her, at least in part, for the disastrous events at Giant mine. A comment Witte made to *Chatelaine* suggests that she rejects such opinions. Before the loss of Colomac mine in 1989, the accidental death of her mother in 1991, the Giant dispute and the murder, the disintegration of her marriage, and the stress of the attempted takeover of Lac Minerals, "I think I was kind of a naive person who hadn't been touched by what life is all about."

MUCKING OUT

I'm not in business to be screwed over.

—Peggy Witte, November 1992

There are more victims than the nine men who died and their families; put that in your book.

—Sergeant Wayne Locke, May 11, 1995

There has been amazingly little political fallout from the Giant mine dispute, given the tremendous human and public costs that continue to this day. Perhaps politicians still consider these factors too trivial, or too hot to handle, or as just another sordid mess that developed during the corrupt reign of the Mulroney Tories. Perhaps because it took place "on the back of beyond" in the Northwest Territories, beyond the Canadian "mainstream," the Giant mine dispute never received the attention it warranted, from the opening salvos by two bullheaded opponents, Royal Oak Mines and CASAW. No public inquiry has been held, although there was talk in 1992 of establishing one after the murder investigation concluded.

Events at Giant had an impact on the federal task force that reviewed the Canada Labour Code, however. Three distinguished labour-relations professionals began their work in June 1995. The review led to instant public debate over the issue of banning the use of replacement workers—a debate in which Jim O'Neil, Mayor Pat McMahon, and CAW president Buzz Hargrove participated on CBC radio. The last word on the program was Jane O'Neil's, pretending to be "Mary Smith." She said that banning replacement workers after the murders at Giant would be like banning women from going to engineering school after the infamous massacre at the École Polytechnique in Montreal. As expected, business groups opposed banning the use of replacement workers, while labour organizations were heartily in favour. Much, though not all, of the public debate was more ideological than rational, unlike most submissions to the task force.

Members of the task force were themselves divided on the issue. The sole Quebec member favoured banning the use of replacement workers, but was outvoted by the chairman (the former chairman of the Alberta Labour Relations Board who wrote the Zeidler decision) and the third member, a vice-chair of Ontario's board. It was agreed that it should be an unfair labour practice to use replacement workers to undermine a union's right to represent employees. Furthermore, "we share the view that permanent replacements are inappropriate and the right to return to work at the end of a strike should receive statutory protection, as should the right to arbitrate discipline or dismissal imposed during a strike or lockout." Thus, the task force acknowledged the CLRB's decision in ending the Giant dispute, as the Supreme Court of Canada would months later.

Changes to the CLRB were recommended. The task force noted in its executive summary that the board "is torn by internal dissension," and "steps must be taken to ensure appointees with the highest calibre of labour relations expertise." The task force recommended that the CLRB "once again become a representational board, with members drawn from labour and management." And, "immediate steps must be taken to improve and speed up the board's case-handling processes."

A glaring oversight in the task force's review of the labour code was the failure to define picketing rights and limits, and their enforcement. This was a serious problem at Giant. A very restrictive court injunction rendered picketing ineffective. Reliance on remedies provided under criminal and civil law resulted in clogged courts, and justifiable accusations of systemic bias. Respect for the law waned. When the RCMP were conscripted to Royal Oak's cause, confrontation became likely, perhaps inevitable.

The Liberal government stuck close to the task force's recommendations when proposing amendments to the Canada Labour Code in the Fall of 1996. (MPs were expected to pass them in the Spring of 1997, following a debate that barely attracted public notice.) Under the terms of Bill C-66, employers will be prohibited from hiring strikebreakers "for the purpose of undermining a trade union's representational capacity," a provision whose practical effect is unclear. The bill confirmed the CLRB's decision in the Giant case that strikebreakers should not be allowed to participate in certification votes, and more clearly established the powers of the board (renamed the Canada Industrial Relations Board) to dictate terms when employers or unions bargain in bad faith. However, the main thrust of Bill C-66 was to reform the structure of the CLRB, which had compounded the problems at Giant. More fundamental reforms will apparently have to wait.

Another lesson from the Giant dispute should be on the political agenda, but probably won't be for many years: Canada's strict limits on the right to strike, which are among the most restrictive in the industrialized world. In this country, permission from the Minister of Labour is required before a strike or lockout can begin, and work stoppages can occur only when no collective agreement is in force. As the Giant case shows, this is no guarantee of industrial peace. Miserable labour relations can fester for many months and then explode when a contract finally expires.

Had Giant mine been in Britain, for example, workers might have walked out when mine manager Mike Werner announced the step system of discipline in February 1991, or when he laid off three union officials in August 1991. This could have served as a wake-up call to both sides to improve relations, and at the very least would have made it clear to the public—and to government—what the crucial issues were at Giant. Instead, tensions built up for another year. When they were finally released, it was extraordinarily difficult to determine the root issues.

The changes recommended by the task force might have resulted in a swifter resolution of the Giant dispute but probably could not have prevented it. Our system of free collective bargaining depends on responsible action by the parties themselves, who must consider the potential impacts on the surrounding community. The same principle applies to government agencies which often become involved, such as the RCMP. In the first crucial days of the Giant dispute, provocation replaced conciliatory gestures that were necessary from all parties to bring about a resolution, or even maintain peace. As the CLRB would state later, a collective agreement could have and should have been reached. Royal Oak and CASAW share the blame for this failure, in varying degrees. It is significant that Royal Oak's top management had weak links to the community of Yellowknife, the Pinkerton's guards had none at all, and RCMP reinforcements were similarly imported. They were an action force when the situation called for peacekeepers. The federal government must bear some responsibility for the situation at Giant that culminated in the death of nine miners. Ottawa ignored all warnings that the dispute was escalating out of control. The Department of Labour did not send anyone to Yellowknife to assess the situation. The RCMP and Pinkerton's men were allowed to play war games with the strikers, while Ottawa refused to appoint an industrial inquiry commission until three months after the September 18 explosion. It is also significant that the RCMP attempted to recruit informants from among the strikers long before the blast, and that this tactic was used again at Con mine during negotiations in 1993–94. Such espionage can only deepen distrust between unions, police, and governments.

To a public kept informed by corporate-owned and state-run media, "union busting" seems like a figment of trade unionists' paranoid imaginations. The reality is that recent Canadian history is rife with union busting and avoidance, on scales large and small. According to the Labour Department, strikes or lockouts involving the use of outside replacement workers last five times longer than when they are not employed. In 1992, strikebreakers were used at the Clearwater fish plant, Nationair, and Giant; in 1993 the union at Zeidler Forest Industries was finally broken; in the 1980s, Peter Pocklington took on the unions at Gainers in Edmonton, intent on never signing another collective agreement. For every one of these notorious cases, there are many routine cases of union avoidance.

These historical conflicts influence collective-bargaining relationships today, as they did at Giant. They are part of the industrial-relations climate, which is particularly important when a company or a union changes in any given workplace. More important is the internal relationship of management and labour, because it will be reflected in their collective bargaining. Where confrontation rules a relationship, there is great potential for severe social and economic disruption— meaning, people will suffer, including many who are not directly involved.

At its heart, the Giant dispute was about power: whether mine workers would retain their traditional autonomy in the workplace—autonomy dearly paid for in the form of rough working conditions and a high risk of accidents— or whether Peggy Witte would impose a top-down, military model of workplace control. Management never seriously explored options of mutually beneficial power-sharing: Witte (or Werner) always "knew best." This was in part due to inexperience, in part due to clashes of personality, and in part due to a widespread mentality in North American management. Firms that espouse buzzwords like "partnership" and "teamwork" often seem more interested in using them to weaken union solidarity than in efficiency gained through real management–labour cooperation, as seen in countries like Germany.

In Yellowknife, unlike most places, these abstract issues were manifested in drama, death, and loss of public order. One of the many reasons for this catastrophe should be drummed into the heads of politicians and mining executives: for mine workers, most aspects of their jobs are matters of life and death. The Peggy Wittes of this world risk money—frequently other people's money; the Kurt Lehnigers, Max Dillmans, and Joe Pandevs risk life and limb.

NOTES

THE VICTIMS

VERNE FULLOWKA

Verne Fullowka, 36, a miner since 1974 and a CASAW member, lived in Yellowknife with his wife, Sheila, and their two children, Karen, 8, and Steven, 5.

Fullowka, known to be a quiet man, surprised almost everyone when he crossed the picket line in early August. Until the day before he went in, he had been a diligent picketer, and was even picket captain.

"I sat on the picket line with him that night, before he went in," says striker Max Dillman. "At midnight he give me everything, he said, 'Here. I'm going home. I'm sick.' I said, 'How sick are you?' 'Well,' he said, 'just be standing on the shoulder of the road at twenty after seven tomorrow morning.'"

According to men from both sides of the line, Fullowka supplied Pinkerton's and police with information on strikers' activities and their organizational set-up, including the code-names strikers used when talking to each other on two-way radio.

It was rumoured after the fatal blast that Fullowka had been the main target because he had allegedly fingered Al Shearing and Tim Bettger for earlier explosions on mine property. The authors have seen no evidence to support that rumour.

NORMAN HOURIE

Norm Hourie, 53, a miner since age 18, came to work at Giant in 1991. He is survived by his wife, Doreen, their two teenaged children, and two children from a previous marriage.

Hourie was one of the first CASAW members to cross the picket line after the labour dispute began in May and he kept a low profile throughout the summer.

Doreen Hourie was shattered by Norm's death. The fact that the first rescuers had counted only seven bodies at the scene of the fatal explosion gave Doreen hope that her husband had not been killed and would soon emerge from the mine. She clung to that belief even when the bodies were raised from the mine, and was comforted by Peggy Witte. Doreen later suffered from memory loss.

CHRISTOPHER NEILL

Chris Neill, 29, was a miner and volunteer firefighter. Sociable and full of ambition, he played a crucial role in the early part of the dispute through his attempts, with Jim O'Neil, to circumvent the union executive and negotiate a last-minute deal with Royal Oak.

Neill was a safety-conscious miner. His father had died in a mine accident, also at age 29.

Neill's widow, Tracey, worked for the federal Department of Justice. Highly articulate, she became an unofficial spokesperson for the relatives of the blast victims. Like others widowed by the explosion, she chose to leave Yellowknife, and moved to Alberta.

JOSEF PANDEV

Joe Pandev, 55, had been working at Giant since 1963—a period spanning more than half the town's modern history—and was less than a year away from retirement when he was killed.

A Yugoslav immigrant with a generous temperament, and a Knight of Columbus, Joe Pandev was known as an extremely hard worker and a stickler for safety. "He worked there for well over twenty-five years without ever having a lost-time accident," recalls former mine manager Steve McAlpine. This exceptional safety record was quoted often in the days after the blast to attack union theories that the explosion had been an accident caused by improper handling of explosives.

Joe nevertheless had nerves of steel, as mechanic Steve Cooper remembers well. "I was helping Joe in 450 main, helping him bolt and screen. What a character he was. There was a slab let go; it had to go about 3 ton. And it just missed his feet. Me, I just went, 'I don't need to be here! I'm outta here!' And I was. He didn't even flinch."

Pandev was against going on strike from the beginning and, unlike others, did not hesitate to say so at union meetings. But he thought long and hard before deciding to cross the picket line, alone, in mid or late August. He called one of his best friends, shifter Martin Kolenko, who had been union local president years earlier.

"I couldn't say, 'Joe, go back to work,'" Kolenko recalls. "I says, 'You and your wife and your family make decision; not me.'"

Pandev was apparently afraid he would lose his pension rights if CASAW was busted or the labour dispute was never resolved. He was also grandpa to a new baby and there were five other mouths to feed.

Pandev's family took his death extremely hard. His wife, Judit, had already lost her first husband in a mine accident; she found Joe's death by bombing even harder to accept. His three children by an earlier marriage were also bitter.

After several months, Judit Pandev decided she needed to leave Yellowknife to get away from the town's poisoned atmosphere. But she returned to sit through much of Roger Warren's trial.

SHANE RIGGS

Shane Riggs, 27, was known as "Spanky" for his resemblance to Spanky of the Little Rascals. He shared a trailer with his sister, Lynda, and her boyfriend, a city by-law officer.

"Good old Spanky! Just wanted to be a miner so bad," one supervisor says. "He was a scoop operator and he wanted to be a miner ... Always joking around."

Riggs's decision to cross the picket line in August came as a shock to other CASAW members. Riggs had previously been an enthusiastic picketer and was charged with offenses in connection with the June 14 melee. But he was rapidly running out of money.

Riggs was turned back by Royal Oak when he first tried to cross; his charges were soon dropped, and he came in August 10. This episode led to widespread rumours on the union side that Riggs had cut a deal and given information on offenses by strikers. In fact, all that is known is that Riggs helped Chris Neill identify strikers who had been captured on surveillance video.

Riggs's death made his sister and his mother, Carol Riggs, extremely bitter. Things were particularly trying for Lynda, who happened to work side by side with the widow of union activist Ken Cawley, who had been killed in a car accident eight weeks earlier. "When Ken died, she was very supportive," says Linda Cawley. "When this blast happened, then I became her worst enemy."

The Riggs family soon moved to British Columbia, although Shane's brother, Peter, remained in Yellowknife, working for Royal Oak.

ROBERT (BOB) ROWSELL

Robert Rowsell, 37, had been thrown out of work when Shebandowan mine near Thunder Bay was shut down by Inco in the spring of 1992. He lived in Hawk Junction, near Wawa in Northern Ontario, with his wife, Carlene. Their eldest daughter, Rachel, was 7, and her sister, Camilla, just a year old when their father was killed.

Rowsell, who was from Quebec, had been mining for fifteen years. He was scheduled to finish his rotation at Giant about a week after the fatal blast.

His brother-in-law told *News/North* shortly after the explosion that Rowsell had turned down his first offer to hire on as a strikebreaker at Giant. When he received a second offer, he decided providing for his family was more important than anything else, and accepted.

ARNOLD RUSSELL

Arnold Russell, 41, was from Bathurst, New Brunswick; very little is known about him because his family kept a very low profile after the blast. According to a supervisor, Russell was a miner who had been out of work for about two years when he hired on as a strikebreaker at Giant. He left a wife, three daughters, and one son.

MALCOLM SAWLER

Malcolm Sawler, 38, had been mining since his early 20s. Like Robert Rowsell, he was thrown out of work when Inco closed down Shebandowan, a small nickel mine near Thunder Bay, where he lived with his wife, Bonnie, and their young son. (He also had two children by a previous marriage.) After almost five months of unemployment, he hired on as a strikebreaker at Giant, where he began work on August 1.

Sawler came from Nova Scotia, but, like many other miners, had lived in many parts of Canada, relocating when mines hired and laid off men. He and his wife had even lived in Yellowknife in 1987–88, when he worked at the city's other major gold mine, Con.

One of Sawler's best friends, Don Patterson, came to town in June 1992 as a strikebreaker. Patterson, who had been best man at Sawler's wedding, worked on the 750 level and would likely have also been one of the blast victims had he not decided to take a break to visit his family down south. Sawler was not so fortunate: he was scheduled to finish his six-week rotation at Giant and fly back to Thunder Bay four days after the blast.

About a week before the fatal explosion, Sawler had been the butt of a morbid practical joke: somebody painted a hangman's noose on his workface while he was off-shift. The crude drawing was the subject of many wild rumours after Sawler was killed; police eventually concluded that it was painted by a strike-breaker working another shift. Rivalries between different shifts, friendly or otherwise, are probably as old as mining itself.

Sawler's family coped better than many others with their loss, perhaps in part because they were far away from Yellowknife and weren't caught up in day-to-day hostilities between strikers and strikebreakers.

DAVID VODNOSKI

Dave Vodnoski was just 25 and recently married when he was killed on September 18, 1992. He and Doreen had lived together for three and a half years, but "they were forever laughing and bugging each other like they were dating," her sister says.

Vodnoski grew up in Saskatchewan and worked as a scoop operator and a trammer at Giant before the labour dispute.

"He was one of those easygoing guys you don't very often meet, and so honest and sincere," a colleague recalls. "You don't meet many honest and sincere guys underground."

Vodnoski hesitated for several months before crossing the picket line, though he kept in touch with those who had already crossed. Finally, he joined the group that went in early in August. His wife's vehicle was promptly spray-painted by vandals.

According to another line-crosser, Vodnoski encountered Peggy Witte soon after he crossed. She said she wanted to give him a break, and asked him what job he would like to do; he said he wanted to train as a miner. And so he became Chris Neill's work partner—and one of the blast victims.

Vodnoski's widow, Doreen, channelled the anger she experienced after her loss into the Giant Mine Employees' Association, Jim O'Neil's attempt to dislodge CASAW by forming a rival union. She and her children returned to Saskatchewan after GMEA failed.

CHAPTER NOTES

CHAPTER TWO

1. It might well have been expected that the law and the NWT government ministers would be on Royal Oak's side. In the summer of 1991, Mike Werner asked a

reporter about likely winners in the upcoming election and then made well-placed donations, along with Neptune Resources, owner of the then-defunct Colomac mine. The unsolicited contributions included $1,500 to future premier Nellie Cournoyea, $1,000 to Deputy Premier Steve Kakfwi, $1,000 to House Speaker Mike Ballantyne, $1,000 to Justice Minister Dennis Patterson, and a total of $3,500 to several other MLAs. Public Works Minister Don Morin got $500, plus $1,500 from Mike Magrum, a family friend and president of the NWT Chamber of Mines. Mike Werner gave $500 to Bruce McLaughlin's failed campaign, but he was then hired as a special adviser to federal Indian and Northern Affairs Minister Tom Siddon. No donations were made by other mining companies in the NWT's biggest industry. When Patterson learned about the contributions, he commented, "Maybe they had their replacement-worker scenario all hatched." The story was not broken until September 11, 1992.

2. Significantly, Lisoway was first charged with assault on a police officer, but it was amended to the lesser charge.

3. Kendall was a waiter at Winnipeg's Charles Hotel when he plotted with a loans officer at the Bank of Montreal and another man to pass phony certified checks. He pleaded guilty to three counts of conspiracy to commit theft and was sentenced to four years in prison. In court in 1978, Kendall testified that two prostitutes in Vancouver stole $800,000 of his checks while he was taking a shower, a tale that the judge did not believe. In an interview, Kendall claimed that about $300,000 in certified checks and traveler's checks "eventually were passed."

CHAPTER THREE

1. Titterton later crossed the picket line to work.

2. Riggs was lucky that day. "The new style of Def Tec stun grenades are useless. They are heavy, bulky and pack much less of a punch than the previous units that we used for years," Sergeant Al Macintyre wrote in his June 14 report. Three months later, Riggs was killed.

3. The majority of Steel's unionists got their jobs back via arbitration, but it took years.

4. Areas of the mine are identified by engineering numbers. The first corresponds to the level, i.e., 7 for 750, the second to a specific working.

CHAPTER FOUR

1. The list was never made public, but the law requires that targets be notified after the intercepts cease. The names were compiled, and there are probably many more than we obtained. Among them were lawyers Gina Fiorillo and Austin Marshall, which precipitated lengthy legal wrangling. Police claim that bugging the lawyers was inadvertent, but admit that information was given to investigators. The court's authorization allows police to listen to any communication considered private, not just telephone conversations, but criteria are very stringent for bugging lawyers.
2. The law was passed, then repealed by the Progressive Conservative government that took over from the NDP.

3. Shearing says he also told the RCMP this.

4. Kendall told the police that he had not entered the mine.

5. See Gordie Kendall's comments in Chapter Two, page 65.

CHAPTER FIVE

1. By this time, Grundy had been promoted from corporal.

2. O'Neil actually applied within weeks, asking the board to use its discretionary powers to waive the six-month waiting requirement.

3. He wasn't alone in this sentiment. The president of the Status of Women Council of the Northwest Territories wrote to a local newspaper, citing examples of sentences, including some from the same judge, Mark de Weerdt. "I guess the message is, if you were frustrated by the strike, Mr. Shearing, you should have beaten up a woman to get your anger out. You would probably have gotten a fine or probation," Rita Arey wrote.

4. Campbell was interviewed by one of the authors shortly after he talked with police. It appears that either the police lied to him or other officers lied later in court. The former is legal and was common in this investigation, but the issue of what was or wasn't found underground became significant later, in Warren's murder trial.

5. Warren denies ever saying this about Bettger.

CHAPTER SIX

1. Colleen Tremblay, the owner of the shop in Peace River, said in April 1995 that the RCMP had not contacted her or her staff. She had no idea a bag from her store had become evidence in a murder case. Names of customers making cash purchases aren't recorded, but there was a credit-card sale to Helen Warren in August 1992.

2. Another statement by O'Sullivan was about the same length in its typed form, but the interview was only eight minutes long.

CHAPTER SEVEN

1. The RCMP listed his occupation as "part-time parcel courier" at the time of his October 1992 interrogation in Vancouver.

2. See Chapter Three, pages 85-86.

3. The authors have a copy of the original note, which later became an exhibit in Warren's trial. The Crown suggested then that it was recently manufactured, but that is not the case.

4. Both initiated court action to find out what the grounds were for interception of their communications with clients, as a very stiff legal test must be met for permission. Much later they were told that they were not targets of police wire-taps, but in Fiorillo's case, one or two solicitor–client conversations were passed on to officers doing the murder investigation. In July 1995, a judge granted Marshall and Fiorillo permission to review the court's sealed documents on the matter, despite strenuous opposition from the Crown, which appealed the case. In early 1996, the appeal was dropped and special arrangements were made for the lawyers to review the material.
5. The likelihood of the authors' list being complete is extremely remote, because it had to be compiled one by one.

6. A nearby sheriff did nothing to stop the attack, and rebuffed Seeton when he asked for help. Seeton didn't even know Hourie, but she persisted in pursuing him, later calling him "Mr. Dead." Finally, he went to the RCMP and asked that she be charged with assault. The police refused, and Seeton laid charges himself for a private prosecution. A court date was set, but the Crown stayed the charges.

7. Warren's confession made no mention of passing the Muir raise, as the notorious footprints did. O'Sullivan's testimony in the preliminary hearing was that the intruder was also lost coming into the mine via Akaitcho, on 425 and 575.

8. The time Warren mentioned came from O'Sullivan's testimony, but he was incorrect. The central blast went off at 3:16. Warren's note implies that he had no idea either way, himself, and did not suspect Shearing or Bettger of the crime.

9. Gainers' CEO Peter Pocklington is notorious for his use of strikebreakers and refusal to bargain with unions during a strike in the 1980s. The strike bears some interesting similarities to Giant's.

CHAPTER EIGHT

1. There was no evidence in court that the police tried to determine how long the items had been in the pond or Cameron River.

2. This coincides with Gordie Kendall's opinion; see Chapter Five, page 193.

3. See Chapter Five, page 193.

4. In an interview after the trial, Warren conceded that he might have mistaken bolt cutters for a rifle.

5. "Why didn't you tell us this before?" McMartin asked. "Fear ...," Warren said.

6. See Chapter Four, page 152.

7. See Chapter Four, page 124.

8. Word of Crown offers surfaced twice before and once during the trial, from reliable sources, but neither Warren nor his lawyers would comment.

9. A urinating ant.

SELECT BIBLIOGRAPHY

Bandzak, Ruth A. "A Productive Systems Analysis of the 1983 Phelps Dodge Strike." *Journal of Economic Issues* 25/4 (December 1991), 1105–25.

Bélanger, Guy. "La grève de Murdochville (1957)." *Labour/Le Travailleur* 8/9 (Autumn/Spring 1981/82), 101–35.

Boychuk, Rick. *River of Grit: Six Months On the Line at Suncor*. Edmonton: Duval House, 1996.

Cameron, Stevie. *On the Take: Crime, Corruption and Greed in the Mulroney Years*. Toronto: Macfarlane, Walter & Ross, 1994.

Canada, Minister of Public Works and Services. *Seeking a Balance*. Hull, PQ, 1995.

Cornwell, Kim S. *Post-Strike Job Security of Strikers and Replacement Workers*. Research Essay No. 27. Kingston: Industrial Relations Centre, Queen's University, 1990.

Drache, Daniel, and Harry Glasbeek. *The Changing Workplace: Reshaping Canada's Industrial Relations System*. Toronto: James Lorimer, 1992.

Geoghegan, Thomas. *Which Side Are You On?* New York: Farrar, Straus & Giroux, 1991.

Jobb, Dean. *Calculated Risk: Greed, Politics and the Westray Tragedy*. Halifax: Nimbus, 1994.

Kingsolver, Barbara. *Holding the Line: Women in the Great Arizona Mine Strike of 1983*. Ithaca, NY: ILR Press, 1989.

Lens, Sidney. *The Labor Wars: From the Molly Maguires to the Sitdowns*. Garden City, NY: Doubleday, 1973.

Levitt, Martin Jay, and Terry Conrow. *Confessions of a Union Buster*. New York: Crown, 1993.

MacDowell, Laurel Sefton. *"Remember Kirkland Lake" : The History and Effects of the Kirkland Lake Gold Miners' Strike, 1941–1942*. Toronto: University of Toronto Press, 1983.

Perry, Charles R., Andrew M. Kramer, and Thomas J Schneider. *Operating During Strikes: Company Experience, NLRB Policies, and Governmental Regulations*. Philadelphia: Industrial Research Unit, The Wharton School, University of Pennsylvania, 1982.

Rosenblum, Jonathan D. *Copper Crucible*. Ithaca, NY: ILR Press, 1995.

Salutin, Rick. *Kent Rowley: The Organizer*. Toronto: James Lorimer, 1980.

Sawatsky, John. *Mulroney: The Politics of Ambition*. Toronto: McClelland & Stewart, 1992.

Scott, Jack. *A Communist Life: Jack Scott and the Canadian Workers Movement, 1927–1985*, edited and introduced by Bryan D. Palmer. St. John's, NF: Committee on Canadian Labour History, *c.* 1988.

White, Howard. *A Hard Man to Beat*. Vancouver: Pulp Press, 1983.

INDEX

INDEX

INDEX